Joachim Küpper
The Cultural Net: Early Modern Drama as a Paradigm

Joachim Küpper

The Cultural Net: Early Modern Drama as a Paradigm

DE GRUYTER

This book is published in cooperation with the DramaNet project, funded by the European Research Council

Early Modern European Drama
and the Cultural Net

European Research Council
Established by the European Commission

ISBN 978-3-11-068493-3
e-ISBN (PDF) 978-3-11-053663-8
e-ISBN (EPUB) 978-3-11-060173-2

This work is licensed under the Creative Commons Attribution-NonCommercial-NoDerivs 3.0 License. For details go to http://creativecommons.org/licenses/by-nc-nd/3.0/.

Library of Congress Control Number: 2018934498

Bibliographic information published by the Deutsche Nationalbibliothek
The Deutsche Nationalbibliothek lists this publication in the Deutsche Nationalbibliografie; detailed bibliographic data are available on the Internet at http://dnb.dnb.de.

© 2019 Joachim Küpper, published by Walter de Gruyter GmbH, Berlin/Boston
This volume is text- and page-identical with the hardback published in 2018.
Cover illustration: photodeedooo/iStock/Thinkstock
Typesetting: Meta Sytems Publishing & Printservices GmbH, Wustermark
Printing and binding: CPI books GmbH, Leck
♾ Printed on acid-free paper
Printed in Germany

www.degruyter.com

Acknowledgements

This book could not have been written without the generous support of an Advanced Grant from the European Research Council in Brussels. Over a period of five years, the grant enables the project's principal investigator to hire a team of junior researchers with whom he works on the topic for whose investigation the funding was granted. These younger scholars are obliged to independently publish the results of their investigation. The grant-holder is expected to submit a publication that systematizes the findings of the entire team, including his own ideas concerning the research question which is at the center of the team's scholarly work. The grants are meant to encourage "frontier research"—thus the term coined by the ERC—, in the sense of concepts that are novel and may or may not turn out to be convincing.

I developed the basic theoretical approach here outlined, which consists in a network theory of cultural (specifically literary) production. The main area of exemplification for the theoretical assumptions, early modern European drama, was chosen to accord with one of my primary fields of expertise. Over the years during which I was able to devote myself to this project—for which we created the name "DramaNet"—I profited enormously from working with the members of my team, who introduced me to ramifications of the questions pertaining to the field of exemplification previously unknown to me. The present book will refer to their publications wherever this is indicated according to standards of scholarly ethics; in order to provide some orientation, I will briefly characterize the thematic and methodological frames of the various more specialized studies resulting from the research team's endeavors in the last section of the chapter "Outline of the Argument".—In addition, I drew much invaluable inspiration from the papers read at the five conferences we were able to organize; the proceedings of these conferences have been published or will be published in the near future. Whenever this or that idea of "mine" might have been inspired by one of these papers, I have made this explicit.—During the tenure of the project, I was invited by prestigious universities from all over the world to present my hypotheses and provisional results. I am grateful in particular for the intense discussions I had with friends and colleagues at Princeton University, the École des Hautes Études en Sciences Sociales, Paris, the Chinese University of Hong Kong, the Hebrew University of Jerusalem, Columbia University, the National Research University – HSE, Moscow, and, finally, UCLA.

Samuel Walker took up the task of correcting my English, and de Gruyter Publishing was ready to print the manuscript.

I should like to conclude this preface with an attempt at briefly contextualizing my approach within a broader framework reaching beyond the limits of cultural studies in the strict sense.

I need not give expression to the generally accepted view (which I share) that the concept of the nation-state—as it emerged embryonically after the Treaty of Westphalia (1648) and unfolded in the course of, and after, the Napoleonic Wars—was the basis of certain major achievements, such as the equality of all citizens with respect to political and juridical rights. It would not have been possible for humankind to immediately "leap" from the level of absolutist monarchies to a global state, in which every member of the species would be guaranteed equal rights.[1] This said, the modern national wars, starting with the Franco-Prussian war of 1870/1, and continued by the massacres of World War I and World War II, show that the concept of the nation-state is no longer viable in our times. Weapons technology has reached a level that will cause future wars in technologically advanced parts of the globe to result in collective extermination. The United Nations, the European Union, and the Transatlantic Alliance were answers to the questions put on the agenda by the two world wars of the twentieth century. In present-day Europe and beyond, industrial production, finance, and, in part, politics are no longer taking place within national circuits, but rather in decentralized network structures more or less analogous to those described in this book. Cultural consciousness seems to somewhat lag behind these "real-world" trends. My polemics against a concept of culture that originated in Romanticism are also meant as a contribution to a larger reconsideration of basic configurations which extends beyond the confines of literary and artistic production.

Berlin, November 2016   Joachim Küpper

European Research Council
Established by the European Commission

---

[1] The economic problems and the refugee crisis the European Union is facing at this point in time (2016) demonstrate that egalitarian politics that go further, culminating in the idea of a welfare state, are bound to the separation of a more or less homogeneous community from the rest of the species. It is a prerequisite of the much-acclaimed virtue of solidarity that all members of the community in question share certain general attitudes of behavior, including work ethics.

Contents

Acknowledgements —— v

0. **Outline of the Argument, Basic Hypotheses, and Remarks on Methodology** —— 1

I. **The Cultural Net** —— 34
    The Basic Metaphor —— 34
    Nodes and Contact Zones —— 45
    Processes and Rationales of Assembly —— 53
    Formal Organization and Mediatedness —— 75
    Temporal Incongruences —— 84
    Accessibility —— 92
    Borderlines —— 99
    Transnational Cultural Agencies —— 115
    Control and Demand —— 134
    Basic Prerequisites —— 150
    The Economy of Cultural Transfer —— 153

II. **Mass Media, Early Modern** —— 157
    The Masses —— 157
    Mediality —— 164
    The "Orientation Toward The Message" —— 174
    The Predilection for Tragedy —— 190
    Devices of Enticement: Love, Horror, and Marvel —— 202
    Mass Media, Early Modern and Present —— 209

III. **Historical Issues, Theoretical Perspectives** —— 212
    Some Case Studies —— 212
    "Rootedness": Johann Gottfried Herder —— 232
    "National Literatures": Topoi and Languages —— 250
    "National" Styles? "Hybridity"? "Third Spaces"? —— 274

IV. **Concluding Remarks** —— 292
    Culture as Network: Subversive and Innovative Potentialities —— 292
    Limits of the Basic Metaphor —— 303

References —— 313

0. Outline of the Argument, Basic Hypotheses, and Remarks on Methodology

"Our philological home is the earth: it can no longer be the nation."
(Erich Auerbach, "Philology and *Weltliteratur*" [1952/1969])

0.—This book has two main objectives, one theoretical, the other historical. In terms of theory, it tries to explore the metaphor of culture as originating from processes of transfer and extraction evolving within a virtual network. In this respect, it is inspired by technological developments that were and go on taking place in the period of its conception. But the theoretical concept here submitted is not systematically linked to such recent trends of technological evolution.

This feature shall become evident in a second part which will investigate the productivity of this new approach to conceptualizing culture by targeting a specific field of cultural production from the pre-technological era: literary texts, specifically dramatic texts, mainly "Western", from the early modern age. The choice of the period was, at least in part, driven by the intention to keep the present-day context of inspiration to which the general theoretical concept is linked strictly separate from the theoretical claims that may be derived from the investigation of a specific section of the literary field. By way of discussing a range of concrete examples of processes of cultural transfer and exchange, the second section of this book shall also help elucidate facets and implications of the theoretical approach presented in the first section that may otherwise remain all too abstract. In addition, this part on early modern drama as mass media has the ambition to provide a portrait of the literary text corpus in question that might yield new historical insights for scholars working in that specific field. It is thus intended to demonstrate that the new approach submitted here may be valid and valuable beyond the limits of theoretical speculation.

In a third part, I will present succinct case studies which are apt to cast a light on specific problems of a network theory of cultural production and reception that require a more detailed reflection. As the claim linked to the theoretical approach suggested in this book is a more general one, there will be passages in which I shall deal with texts from other genres and periods (e.g. the nineteenth-century realist novel) in order to further develop the implications of the main theoretical ideas.—In this last major section, I will also address at some length the approach to conceptualizing cultural production and reception which is opposite to mine, namely the assumption of the existence of "national literatures", including the derivatives of this latter concept, up to postcolonial theory.—A brief concluding part will attempt to highlight some problems involved in my theorizing that might lead to further scholarly discussions.

There is a characteristic regarding methodology I should already like to formulate at this point: A book is, by necessity, a linear structure. According to the tradition of scholarship as established in this part of the world since Aristotle's *Rhetoric* at the latest, it is to follow, in addition, a hierarchical order (from more abstract to concrete, or vice versa). Against this backdrop, it would be far too ambitious to consistently try to demonstrate my main thesis—that network structures are a very useful model for conceiving of how cultural production works—in the structuring of the present study. That said, I have attempted to bring content and form closer together in this volume than was my practice in previous books. Accordingly, there will be much more cross-references to be found in the following pages than is usually the case in scholarly publications. In addition, I will repeatedly address, in simulation of "recursive structures", identical abstract topics under varying aspects and in different parts of this book. And, finally, the chapters of the more theoretical Part I, as well as the ones of Parts II and III, will be characterized by a string-like and additive structure, rather than by a structure of (supposed) causal or "logical" order, as is traditionally the case in scholarship.

There is not only an "aesthetic", but also a rhetorical element involved in my decision to present this book according to the structuring just outlined. In my discussions with the junior researchers of the DramaNet team, as well as in my readings of their books and papers, I believe to have realized that such a decentered structure might be more appropriate, at this moment of cultural and scholarly history, for presenting an argument than what would result from a routine application of the traditional principles, all the more as the practice of reading, including "serious" reading, has changed dramatically over the last decades: from integral to interruptive, from focused to dispersed. From the perspective of a book that tries to take advantage, at least by way of converting it into a useful metaphorical resource, of the "agent" of these transformations, the Internet, it would be somewhat self-contradictory to lament these processes as phenomena of decadence and to try fighting against them.

This introductory chapter seeks to give a concise overview of the book's argument in its entirety. The theoretical frame that is meant to be challenged by the attempt at conceptualizing a network theory of cultural production is, as already hinted at, the concept of "national literatures", in the sense that the concrete language in which a literary text is written is not regarded as subordinate, but as the primary characteristic of the text in question; all relevant discussion in this respect shall be relegated to a separate chapter in Part III of this book. In this introduction, I will limit my remarks as to existing theoretical framings of cultural production to some critical points with regard to approaches that are in principle close to my perspective, that is, that may qualify as "post-Romantic", in the sense that they intentionally go beyond the deeply rooted notion of cultural production as a sort of godlike creation, as being based on rationally inexplicable parameters commonly labelled "inspiration" or "ingenuity".

1.—It was a major achievement of twentieth-century structuralism to substantiate the claim that pre-existing relational configurations ("structures") of any kind—conceptual, linguistic, generic—are essential for cultural production. Accordingly, culture as a whole, starting with the first productions by the very first humans, was cast as a process whose logic is ramification, in other words, specification based on previous manifestations of cultural productivity. The metaphor of this approach was, consequently, the image of a tree. Postmodernist theorizing of larger cultural contexts replaced this metaphor with the one of the rhizome (Gilles Deleuze/Félix Guattari).[2] The main achievement of this approach was the overcoming of the concepts of strictly defined hierarchies and of unidirectional processes which were implied by the tree metaphor.— The problem inherent in the rhizome concept might perhaps be characterized as follows: it seems to suggest, even more than its classical predecessor, the image of the tree, a "naturalistic", biology-inspired model of cultural processes, which nevertheless may follow a logic that is independent from the general patterns of the evolution of life. Cultural artifacts differ from biological entities in that they do not necessarily concretize a preestablished program (as encoded in the genes), but are rather subject to relatively free decisions by humans.[3]—The weakest aspect of the rhizome concept may, however, be that it is still all too structuralist, notwithstanding its claims to being poststructuralist: a rhizome is a non-hierarchical, decentered structure; but it is an ongoing replication of one basic pattern that remains identical to itself during the processes of replication.—A last point to be raised critically is the question of the transformation of (visible) forms, that is, of entities consisting of larger quantities of elementary units. In the realm of biological life, such transformations do occur,

---

[2] *A Thousand Plateaus*, Brian Massumi (tr.), Minneapolis, MN 1987.
[3] I do not wish to engage here with the discussion of whether "free will" or "free decisions" are illusions by which we try to hide from ourselves that we are carrying out natural programs; making culture my theme, I stick to surface phenomena and consider nothing but the observable logic of their development.

but mutations of genes and the (possibly) ensuing emergence of new species are relatively rare; they happen within chronological frames which transcend the existence of human individuals. Culture, in contrast, is characterised by rapid and erratic changes of phenomena. If there is stability at all, it is to be found neither in the pheno- nor in the genotype, but rather in function. – Briefly put, if the notion of rhizome is applied to the cultural sphere, its shortcomings are the problem of agency, the overestimation of standardizing with regard to the elementary units of cultural structures, and the undervaluation of morphic change as a distinctive characteristic of cultural evolution.

The metaphor, or rather, metonymy of circulating social energy introduced by Stephen Greenblatt with regard to modeling cultural processes has the advantage of accounting for the high degree of flexibility of the relevant processes.[4] The risks implied by this concept seem to converge in two points: firstly, there is the question of whether such circulation happens freely, according to a largely non-causal logic (contingency), and by means of an immanent propulsive potential of the material concerned, or whether it is dependent on structures that enable it to a greater degree than is suggested by the assumption of an inherent "social energy". The latter alternative would stress, much more than the New Historicism approach, the discussion of items revolving around the problem of agency: such structures may be established or not; they may be enhanced or restricted; they may be extended or interrupted.[5] The relevance of these problems becomes visible as soon as one transcends the analysis of "national" circuits. There are incontestable differences to be observed, for example, between early modern English and early modern Spanish drama, which

---

4 *Shakespearean Negotiations: The Circulation of Social Energy in Renaissance England*, Berkeley and Los Angeles, CA 1988.
5 In the volume *Cultural Mobility: A Manifesto*, co-edited by Stephen Greenblatt, Ines G. Zupanov, Reinhard Meyer-Kalkus, Heike Paul, Pál Nyíri and Friederike Pannewick, Cambridge, MA 2010, especially in the Introduction (pp. 1–23) and in the short essay "A Mobility Studies Manifesto" (pp. 250–253), Greenblatt articulates some ideas that are close to my basic assumptions. As is the case here, Greenblatt's argument is directed against the traditional theorizing of cultural phenomena as characterized by "fixity", "coherence", and "rooted[ness]" (p. 3). He, too, insists on the observation that a highly mobile "global culture" (p. 6) is nothing that is completely new or modern. Greenblatt also stresses the importance of a physical substratum for cultural exchange to take place (p. 250). The main difference between our approaches consists in the way mobility and "rootedness" are conceived of. Greenblatt leaves it at drawing attention to the point that there is a tension between these two parameters, whereas I suggest in what follows a specific relation between them.–The quoted volume contains a number of case studies pertaining to the problem addressed in the title; many of them are interesting, but do not have further theoretical bearing. As to Greenblatt's own case study and to Friederike Pannewick's, which do have such implications, see below, pp. 104–106 and pp. 280–283.

solicit an answer to the question of what in particular is different in the processes of circulation and where the difference originates.—A second point in Greenblatt's approach which might be worth reconsidering is his assumption of the "separation of artistic practices from other social practices".[6] This separation is, indeed, crucial with regard to the readers' or viewers' perspective, that is, to processes of reception.[7] But the extent to which it is appropriate to consider artistic material and other cultural material as separate with regard to processes of transfer and circulation requires further deliberation. Here, too, there is certainly a separation as far as the materialized forms are concerned; paintings and pragmatic manufactured goods may travel on one ship, but as material forms they are distinct and travel as distinct items. Yet the separation seems much more difficult to establish in terms of conceptual forms. It needs to be specified what exactly is transferred when, for example, a dramatic text is "exported" into another country, or even to another part of the same country; firstly, of course, a specific literary text, but along with it, as shall be argued here, all the non-artistic cultural forms and concepts it is made up of (philosophical, theological, anthropological, juridical, political discourses, etc.). Cultural dynamics is to a large extent based on this feature: organized forms (artistic works) are not only transported themselves, but along with them the whole range of non-artistic cultural material they contain.

Is the actor-network theory a possible source of inspiration? The problem with Bruno Latour's numerous publications seems to be that they present prolegomena to a crucial question that remains without a precise answer: what is ANT,[8] according to Latour? Even in his most recent major work, Latour does not provide a consistent description of what exactly he has in mind.[9] This said,

---

6 *Shakespearean Negotiations*, p. 12f.
7 The most famous narrative text of that age, the *Quijote* (1605/1615), deals exactly with this problem, in the sense that it presents a hero who seems to be incapable of or not willing to effect this separation.
8 It belongs to Latour's manifold strategies of self-promotion to claim that his theory has acquired a resonance that would call for making use of the above acronym only.
9 *Reassembling the Social: An Introduction to Actor-Network-Theory*, Oxford 2005. The book abounds in sentences like the following, that is, propositions that stress the difficulties of defining the concept instead of trying to solve them: "It is this increased level of abstraction in social theory which makes ANT hard to grasp at first" (p. 23). A second recurrent pattern are propositions amounting to somewhat banal postmodern standard topoi ("ANT simply claims that once we are accustomed to these many shifting frames of reference a very good grasp of how the social is generated can be provided, since a relativist connection between frames of reference offers a better source of objective judgment than the absolute (that is, arbitrary) settings suggested by common sense." [p. 30]), or even to statements devoid of any reference, but, as in the example to be quoted, full of metaphorical allusions the inapt profile of which may not even be apparent to the author ("[...] ANT is simply the realization that

there are some general features of the network metaphor that both my conception and Latour's suggestion of it have in common: the accentuation of the randomness of cultural processes produced by the contingent interaction of very many actors; the relative indifference of the outcome of mediating processes to the intentionality of the mediators involved; the a-teleological and, thus, unpredictable profile of processes of cultural evolution; the importance of "assembly", that is, of putting together diverse materials and shaping them into units the formal consistency of which may be a property ascribed in retrospect; finally, the assumption that when one is dealing with culture, mediation of any kind (even mere "transportation") will affect the material that is mediated.—The most problematic part of Latour's approach may be the fashionable "post-human" features he does not get tired of propagating and which become apparent in such formulations as "objects too have agency".[10] I shall rather hold on to the view that "objects", in this case material items, do play an important role in processes of cultural, especially literary production,[11] but that they do not have an agency of their own. The role they may hold is contingent upon the fact that human agency is never a godlike *creatio ex nihilo*, but always

---

something unusual had happened in the history and sociology of scientific hard facts, something so unusual that social theory could no more go through it than a camel through the eye of a needle" [p. 106]). In many cases, Latour indulges in displaying a mimicking of what "American academic prose" might be according to the typical immigrant professor. I shall just quote one of the close to innumerable sentences one could adduce in this respect and which are, indeed, quite amusing to read: "I will start by saying that there are four things that do not work with actor-network theory, the word actor, the word network, the word theory and the hyphen!" ("On Recalling ANT", in: John Law and John Hassard [eds.], *Actor Network Theory and After*, Oxford 1999, pp. 15–25, quote: p. 15).

10 This is the title of a sub-chapter in the above-quoted book (p. 63). See also p. 71 ("[…] *any thing* that does modify a state of affairs by making a difference is an actor—or, if it has no figuration yet, an actant" [Latour's italics]). From my perspective, such sensationalist claims are hardly anything other than a relapse into archaic thought-patterns typically qualified as magic. I should mention that Latour frequently revokes the radical claims by which he believes to provoke his readers some pages later; it is one reason for my rather acerbic critique that the author then arrives at statements which are sensible, but at the same time somewhat commonplace, so that the entire discursive move seems to be not much more that rather shallow rhetoric ("ANT states that if we wish to be a bit more realistic about social ties than "reasonable" sociologists, then we have to accept that the continuity of any course of action will rarely consist of human-to-human connections […] or of object-object connections, but will probably zigzag from one to the other" [p. 75]).

11 To give just one example from the concrete field to be explored in what follows, an example I will come back to at various occasions: had the Ottomans not conquered Constantinople in 1453, had the Byzantine scholars not escaped by ship, or had they only taken with them their personal riches and not their books, the history of early modern European drama would look dramatically different from what it actually looks like.

based on, and framed by, specific material or object-related parameters the existence of which, in a given place and at a given moment, is in most cases not under the control of the human agents in question.

Following from this brief review, I define as the aims of my theoretical approach to formulate a concept that accounts for the specificity of cultural processes as distinct from natural processes; to conceive a model that enables and favours transnational perspectives; to formulate an approach that allows for an adequate consideration of the problem of agency; to establish a frame that opens up possibilities for the discussion of literary phenomena as at the same time separate from and part of a larger sphere of discourses and cultural practices; to reconsider the dichotomy of teleology vs. contingency as the two main concepts available so far for a conceptualization of cultural processes.

The main implications of this new concept shall be briefly outlined in the following passages of this introduction.[12] In conclusion, a sketch of the meta-

---

[12] My description turns out to be parallel to some points made by Jan A. G. M. van Dijk's attempt at conceptualizing the present-day world by recourse to this metaphor (*The Network Society: Social Aspects of New Media*, London 2006; for a similar study with a slightly larger temporal scope, see Armand Mattelart, *Networking the World, 1794–1900*, Liz Carey-Libbrecht and James A. Cohen [tr.], Minneapolis, MN 2000). As is evident from the subtitles, van Dijk's and Mattelart's approaches differ from my concepts by positing cultural nets and networks as resulting from the introduction of technologies which are linked to modernity in the strict sense (railways, telegraph cables, phone lines, digital media); for an even more pointed approach in this fashion, see N. Katherine Hayles, *How We Became Posthuman: Virtual Bodies in Cybernetics*. Literature and Information, Chicago, IL 1999. As I shall argue in Part I of the present study, these more recent technological achievements are not negligible with regard to the effects they have on what is produced by the cultural net, but the difference is, more or less, a phenomenon linked to the quantity and the celerity of the material floating in the net. What I shall call the cultural net emerges in principle at the point of human development where the practices of symbolic communication (language, painting) arise. The cultural net as such is nothing particularly modern, but an anthropological constant. Van Dijk does mention in passing human networks previous to modern networks, so the difference between his approach and mine is, more or less, a difference of scope.—For a highly inspiring approach drawing readers' attention to large-scale cultural exchange (without making use of the net metaphor) before the era of modernity proper, see Claude Lévi-Strauss, *L'autre face de la lune*. Ecrits sur le Japon, Paris 2011.—As to scholarship in the field done so far, I consider Wai-Chee Dimock's description of American literature to display an approach close to mine (*Through Other Continents: American Literature Across Deep Time*, Princeton, NJ 2006). The focus on the first nation in history that is consciously and intentionally hybrid as far as culture is concerned, marks, obviously, the difference between Dimock's and my investigation, which concentrates on a phase of European history that has so far been conceived of in patterns of relatively hermetic "national cultures". Another publication worth mentioning is Manuel De Landa's *A Thousand Years of Nonlinear History*, New York, NY 1997. De Landa's highly interesting though

phor's application to early modern European drama shall be given. This sketch will also contain an overview of problems discussed in more detail in the second and third parts of the book, which present general observations concerning early modern European drama as mass media (Part II) and references to more particular historical scenarios and ensuing theoretical problems (Part III).

2.—A network is a non-hierarchical structure without a center. In the cultural sphere,[13] it does not originate spontaneously or by means of an extra-human, evolution-driven process. It is, rather, produced by humans and created with deliberate aims. The initial intentions may be fulfilled or not. If they are not fulfilled, the net may be destroyed by those who constructed it. Very frequently, however, network structures which do not evolve according to initial expectations assume other, often unforeseen (and in that sense potentially "revolutionary") functions.[14]—The main purpose of networks is the enabling of processes of transfer of a material that would remain inert without the existence of such structures.—Net structures may be set up anywhere and everywhere. Apart from the will to set them up, they do not need any further specified substratum.—There is no entelechial form of a net. Nets are never complete. They are not created once and for all. Nets may thus extend and ramify to regions which are completely unknown to those who set them up.

As soon as they exist, even net structures functioning according to initial purposes frequently come to transport not only the specific material for whose circulation they were created, but other, at times completely heterogeneous material as well. This happens in many cases without being noticed, at least for some time. Cultural transfer in particular has been taking place for long periods in the species' history as a "by-product" of circulation processes within network structures whose purpose was not primarily cultural, let alone artistic. It is in many cases a parasitic phenomenon linked to processes organized in view of economic or power-related aims; for that reason, the strictures to which

---

somewhat general observations try to apply basic insights of thermodynamics to the question of what keeps human "history" moving.

13 The term is meant in its etymological sense (from Latin *colere*), that is, as referring to any activities—not only artistic ones—by which humans produce items that do not exist in the natural world.

14 One might think in particular of the network established between Europe and the Americas, starting in 1492. Its original purpose was merely economic; its establishment was motivated by the quest for an *El Dorado* in the literal sense of the term. Especially with regard to South America, it became an infrastructure for the perhaps most important and most radical transculturation in the species' history, as early as from the first decades of the sixteenth century onward.

the circulation of cultural material is submitted may be less rigid than is the case for the spheres of material goods and physical power. Even in later times, when there are conscious transfer processes of cultural material, it seems to be a specific feature of the form of floating-in-the-net unique to cultural material to be less restricted in terms of homogeneity than circulating physical items.[15] Cultural "innovation" very frequently[16] is a consequence of a transfer of heterogeneous material that in many cases remains unnoticed, and may even have been rejected had it been noticed.

The commonalities with more "common" networks notwithstanding, cultural nets are a specific variant of network structures.[17] The main difference with regard to regular networks consists in the fact that cultural networks may

---

15 One might think about attributing this reduced requirement as to homogeneity to the "complexity" of all cultural items, in contrast to the rather simple, standardized structure of all material items. To give an example: if a specific country decides to define rules for agricultural or industrial products allowed to be transferred to the territory it controls, the examination of such items according to these rules is a relatively easy task. With regard to cultural products also, many countries have defined rules for allowing concrete items to be transferred into their territories; but due to the multifaceted semantics of all cultural items, it is difficult to determine what is still within the limits—and what should be rejected as subversive. Strictly totalitarian countries try to cope with this problem by taking measures intended to completely cut off their countries from the universal cultural net. But, as history demonstrates, this is almost impossible (as to possible reasons, see below, Part I). Subversive material finds its way, sooner or later, into totalitarian countries also—which may be an important reason why rigid totalitarian systems have never been sustainable structures.

16 The above qualification is meant to refer to the huge divide that separates the mechanisms of cultural production from the era of Romanticism onward from all previous eras of Western and non-Western culture. When "innovation" and "originality" become the main parameters of valuation, the archaic concept—active in many societies up to the present—of controlling and thus restricting the movement of cultural material becomes replaced by an attitude that is shaped by the permanent attempt at enhancing such processes.—As I shall stress in a later footnote (n. 34), generalizations such as the one just formulated are always in need of a benevolent reading; the replacement of the parameter of "control" by the one of "enhancing innovation", taking place at the inception of cultural modernity proper, that is, around 1800 CE, is, of course, a *tendency* which seems to become more and more dominant; meaning: as recessive phenomena, there are instances of controlling cultural circulation processes by way of authoritarian means also in the era starting with Romanticism (see n. 283).

17 In order to avoid misunderstanding, I should like to express that the metaphor of the net as intended here has little or close to nothing in common with the primary meaning as apparent in terms like "fishing net". As is almost always the case when the same term is employed in order to designate different objects, there is, of course, some commonality between net structures as characterized above and a fishing net. The highway system of a densely populated country like Germany, viewed from a bird's perspective, and a fishing net, viewed through a magnifying glass, will look pretty much alike. But in terms of function, the two variants of net are radically different. In a road network (as in the cultural net here theorized), all motion

have a stable material substratum or not; in any case, they need a material substratum, but not necessarily a stable one.[18] In that sense, their character is in most cases virtual.[19] This virtual character may be specified in two different, but complementary ways: as mentioned, up to the age of sedentary life, cultural transfer is in almost all cases a parasitic phenomenon taking place within network structures whose purpose is not the circulation of cultural items.[20] The second dimension of the basic virtuality of cultural networks, which also applies to later periods including the present, concerns the variance of the physical substratum: in contrast to road networks or pipeline systems, cultural transfer is almost always[21] a process taking place by means of a variety of specific media.—This high degree of virtuality of cultural network structures is facilitated by the circulating items. "Culture" conceived in the broadest possible way, that is, as consisting of all activities by which humans transform their nature-given habitats, differs from elementary processes of customising

---

takes place *inside* the various strings that constitute the net. With respect to a fishing net, all motion (of water, of fish) takes place *in between* the strings. The purpose of a road network is to *enable* motion, the purpose of a fishing net is to *restrain* motion and to finally reduce it to point zero (the "catch"). A road network and all similar net structures (electric grids, railroad systems, flight routes, postal transport systems, etc.) are media, that is, indifferent at least to a certain degree to the purposes for which they are used; in the case specified, they may serve in order to circulate private cars, trucks, or tanks; the intention linked to the processes of motion may be touristic, economic, or military. Fishing nets are not media, they are instruments. They serve one purpose and one clear-cut intention. (For evident reasons, I pass over re-functionalizations such as the exhibition of fishing nets in museums.)

18 I should like to draw readers' attention to the fact that it is mainly this point which differentiates the phenomenon here theorized as "cultural net" from the phenomena apostrophized by the common use of the term. See pp. 34–45 for a more elaborate discussion of the point.

19 The modal qualification ("in most cases") refers to the trivial fact that there are obviously non-virtual structures involved whose observation is, however, bound to narrowing down the local and temporal scope. The distribution of printed books, e.g., in the era of multinational publishing companies may be described as taking place within "real", materially manifest network structures. But when it comes to the question of how the concepts contained in these books circulate within the community of readers and also beyond, the assumption of these processes taking place within network-like structures seems as plausible as the pretense seems problematic that these structures compare, as to their "material" essence, with networks such as standardized mailing services (etc.).

20 In the chapter "Borderlines", I will present some speculations concerning the question of what these early processes of cultural transfer might have looked like.

21 In very recent times of human history, there are, of course, network structures transporting cultural material which do have a stable physical substratum, the most prominent ones being TV networks or the Internet (radio waves). Their predecessors in terms of media history were publication companies, or state agencies created with a view to circulating cultural material to other countries.

natural habitats to be observed among animals in the sense that it exists in two different registers bound to each other: as material forms, and as conscious concepts which inform the respective forms or can be extrapolated from them. This "double nature" of human culture is of a high relevance with regard to processes of transfer. Cultural networks primarily contribute to transferring the conceptual forms underlying the actual artifacts. The material forms may "travel" as well (paintings, statues, books), but this does not constitute a necessary condition for cultural activity and exchange.[22]—Yet the circulation of conceptual forms also needs a material substratum in order to take place. In the periods of human history preceding the establishment of institutionalized infrastructures for circulation (the print industry; TV; the Internet), this physical substratum consists most frequently of circulating humans (merchants, warriors, courtiers or diplomats, future spouses, religious officials, academics, artists).—In many cases, such transfer processes take on the shape of "chains" of the human agents involved. A story migrating from China to Europe or vice versa will have been transported by quite a few human mediators, who may have pursued very diverse intentions when transporting the cultural material in question.

The movement of material mediated by cultural net structures is not exclusively unidirectional. It remains to be discussed in detail whether this aspect can be better accounted for by conceiving of cultural networks as being organized according to circuit structures, or whether it is more adequate to assume them to be shaped according to a pattern of roads. The advantage of the latter alternative consists in that, in such structures, inverse movement of the transferred material is possible, but not compulsory, mandatory, or necessary. Total reciprocity and the complete absence of hierarchies as a feature of culture may be as problematic an assumption as the obsolete metaphor of culture as a tree.[23]

---

[22] In that sense, the circulation of "ideas" in the Platonic sense (the "idea" of a table, or a house) would be conceived, from my perspective, as taking place within what I here try to theorize as the cultural network; there are, however, certain characteristics of cultural items in the sense of concepts informing artworks which distinguish them with regard to their way of "floating" (and also with regard to the virtuality of the floating process) from the floating of other non-material, but pragmatic items such as "ideas" or blueprints (in present-day times). I shall address this point in the subsequent paragraphs.

[23] In that sense I should like to distance myself from more politicized approaches to the question of cultural exchange as advocated, say, by Gayatri Chakravorty Spivak (see, amongst other titles by the author, *Death of a Discipline*, New York, NY 2003). As legitimate as Spivak's plea for a de-Westernization of what we presently understand by "World Literature" (or "global culture") may be, there is no way to change the past; as William Occam, following Aristotle, argued, even an omnipotent God is not able to accomplish that. The past may be unjust, it may be the result of aggression and subjugation, but it is factual. And there is no evidence that communities "subalternized" by the Western powers in the age of imperialism were morally superior; they were either technologically less developed, or less fortunate, or both.

Since they are constructed and operated by humans, networks, including cultural networks, are subject to the human will as far as their capacity for transportation is concerned. They may be extended, or, rather, parts of them may be extended. They may be restricted or interrupted temporarily, or even be destroyed completely. The transported material may be allowed to circulate freely, or it may be submitted to a more or less systematic scrutiny and then allowed to travel on or not, or partly so. In the period of interest here, these regulatory activities are performed by institutional agents.[24] These agents are not contingent upon the material circulating in the net, but obey an external logic. If agents of control are not changed from time to time, they may be affected by the material under review and thus fail to exercise their task.—The rationale of control may be motivated by ideology, authority (power), or economic considerations. It may be an illusion that movements within the cultural net are exclusively or even mainly driven by immanent quality standards.—The reasons for regulation do not exist in "pure" versions, but as specific and varying configurations of the three above-mentioned components. In almost all observable cases, there are internal frictions between the components. Much of cultural difference, in the age under consideration but in other ages and places as well, seems to result from divergent regulatory factors. In the early modern world, just as in the present, different concepts of what constitutes the "right" form that regulatory rationales should take provoked "culture clashes".

Cultural production is, from this perspective, a process that is primarily based on the withdrawal of elements already circulating in the net, in contrast to material production, which is mainly contingent upon raw material deriving from external sources.[25] In both cases, the material is submitted to a pre-con-

---

24 The Inquisition set up by the Roman Catholic Church in the thirteenth century and reshaped into a bureaucracy in the sixteenth century is the prototype of all posterior institutions of censorship. It needs to be stressed that it would be nothing but an idealization of more pristine periods of human culture to assume that such processes of controlling the material floating in the cultural net had been inexistent before. It is well known that the Egyptian pharaos as well as the Roman emperors did not only promote certain cultural productions, but also worked with the intention to repress or even eradicate items which did not comply with their ideas; what was still absent is the institutional frame, the pattern of an agency of control as a permanently existing bureaucratic structure. Besides the activities of those in power, there are in all human societies, with the relative exception of some present-day Western-European societies that value personal freedom above all else, informal mechanisms controlling cultural activities. These mechanisms are usually called norms or values; they define what may be articulated and what must not be articulated.

25 My formulation implies that "material" production is part of cultural production *lato sensu*, since the "shaping" of the raw material is done according to concepts which are in most cases not original, but are—if not pre-typified anyway—recombinations of previous concepts. This said, I believe it to be reasonable to consider the manufacturing of goods as not completely

ceived conceptual shaping; but it seems to be an important characteristic of the "material" extracted from the net with a view to cultural production in the artistic sense that it is, in many cases, conceptual only, or, if physical (paintings, statues, texts), informed by concepts that may be extrapolated from the materialized forms.—Circulating material may be withdrawn from the cultural net at any given point. At least up to the age of copyright laws, the withdrawal is free of charge.[26] As soon as withdrawn, the material is shaped into formally defined entities by humans, individuals or groups. This shaping consists in most cases in a "novel" combination of single items moving in the net.—It is of primary importance for the specificity of the movement of artworks (that is, of goods that are not immediately pragmatic)[27] that they may be conceptualized as circulating at the same time as ready-made works (texts, painting) and as components into which these might be decomposed.[28] In order to characterize the corresponding processes, I will suggest the metaphors of "assembly" and "disassembly", specifically with the intention to stress the "technical" aspect of artistic production, rather than the "creative" one (in the literal meaning of the term).—In case the material is language-based, the first step of formal shaping is the homogenization of differing symbolic codes (languages) if necessary, that is, whenever the floating elements cross linguistic borders.— The levels of formal organization typically attained differ dramatically.[29] Established hierarchies of cultural products ("low" and "high" culture, popular and

---

identical with the "creation" of art works. The differences as well as the commonalities are captured in a quite adequate fashion by a terminology (*artes liberales*; *artes mechanicae*) which has disappeared in modern times under the pressure of Romantic art theory.

26 I should like to argue that this applies to later periods as well. What is fended off by copyright regulations is flagrant (verbatim) plagiarism. But, to take a famous case, no one could have hindered Fontane from rewriting Flaubert's *Madame Bovary* (1857) as *Effi Briest* (1896). In the course of the reception, it is the aesthetic and conceptual productivity originating from such configurations which decides whether the later text is received as a great work of art or as a poor, epigonic imitation.

27 For the reasons touched upon in passing above, I will not use the current term of depragmatized goods for artworks in general. As useful as the dichotomy of pragmatic and depragmatized may be for all of specifically modernist art, it is problematic with regard to previous art production. Of course, there is a difference between a catechism and a religious drama, or between a collection of laws and a dramatic text that deals with the fate of personages transgressing these laws. But what may, indeed, be a dichotomy in modern times may have been a gradual difference in previous periods of human history. Such a statement does not imply that the difference is negligeable in theoretical terms.

28 At a later stage of my argument, I will come back to a third way in which artworks may move in the net: as abstractions (of various levels) by way of which they might be condensed.

29 We commonly differentiate between highly organized and less highly organized texts as "canonical" literature on the one hand, "popular" literature on the other.

elitist) are mainly contingent upon the level of formal shaping and its recognizability in a given work.—The formal entities (works) are then "used" with regard to different functions, mainly didactics, entertainment, and reflection.

Since they exist in a material as well as in a conceptual mode, the entities originating from the cultural net are inconsumable, at least as long as the human mind exists. After having been used, they continue to exist, in some cases both in the material and the conceptual mode (paintings, books), but in any case in the conceptual mode. They are stored in what could be summarized under the formula of "the human mind (in general)", that is, in the collective memory of the species, while this concept is not meant to refer to a common memory—which hardly exists before the epoch of thoroughgoing globalization—but, rather, to a random inventory of items of various grades of organization present in the memory of the diverse cultural communities constituting the species in its entirety.—After the accomplishment of one such novel artistic item, the previously existing material as well as its new shaping are re-absorbed by the material circulating in the net and continue their potentially endless travel.—As is true with regard to physical networks, e.g. road networks, the circulating material may assume different degrees of formal organization, from the level of elementary components up to the level of organized entities capable in certain cases of being auto-motive within the net.— Since cultural items in most cases[30] have been floating in the net rather in the conceptual mode before the inception of the technological era and its invention of standardized duplication (print) along with the establishment of generally accessible material archives (libraries, traditional or electronic), the new synthesizations may, in principle, be considered to continue floating in either a synthesized or a decomposed fashion. —The fact that the material circulating in cultural nets is not homogeneous (in the sense of not being formally standardized) is a strong plea for discarding alternative metaphors, such as a web or grid, which might in principle be considered as well.

Literary texts could, from this perspective, be characterized as a configuration of cultural material organized with a view to all three above-mentioned functional dimensions (didactics, entertainment, and reflection). The relative weight of each purpose varies from work to work and is subject to reassessment

---

30 Even in the pre-technological era, certain manuscripts or artworks, such as statues, were circulated as gifts or for cultic purposes; but these pre-technological processes of circulation of finite works cannot be compared, in terms of quantity or qualitative impact, to what happened as soon as industrial copy techniques were introduced.

from the perspective of different recipients. Pragmatic cultural texts,[31] in contrast, are mainly characterized by just one of these functions; there may, however, be traces of the non-dominant functions in pragmatic texts as well, as in the case of the pleasurable, in a way "entertaining" presentation of a philosophical text or of a religious sermon.[32]—Drama may be considered a particularly interesting phenomenon in the context of a network theory of cultural production and reception, insofar as it comprises textual and, as soon as performed, non-textual configurations of pre-existing cultural entities. It may thus allow for a more refined description of the "interaction" between strictly textual and non-textual forms of cultural practices.

3.—The following part of this introduction is dedicated to briefly characterizing the specific period and the specific texts by which I shall try to illustrate and differentiate my theoretical speculations in the more extended presentation of the theoretical approach (Part I) and in the subsequent Parts II and III, where I will focus on concrete phenomena and configurations. These texts are taken from the corpus of early modern European drama.

The early modern age bears its name because the basis of modernity proper was cast in that period. This applies to the natural sciences,[33] religion,[34] politi-

---

31 I pass over the question concerning the status of scientific texts as well as of those texts, such as political treatises, which first emerged as separate corpora in this period. The theoretical problems involved are addressed in a satisfactory fashion within Niklas Luhmann's thesis of modernity as an age of ever-growing functional specialization, that is, separation of discursive items which in former periods constituted one section of the discursive field (the latter term according to Michel Foucault, *L'Archéologie du savoir*, Paris 1969, pp. 44–101; as to Luhmann's theory of modernity, see *Social Systems*, John Bednarz and Dirk Baecker [tr.], Stanford, CA 1995).—Need I stress that I will not try including cultural items like music or painting in my tentative theorizing? This said, I believe that the theoretical speculations offered above may be useful, *mutatis mutandis*, for the non-verbal arts as well. Accordingly, there will be some occasional hints at these art forms.
32 This latter point and the aforementioned aspect that different purposes inform a literary text to different degrees may account for the affinities between certain literary and certain non-literary texts, mainly philosophical or religious. "Literature" as strictly distinct from the other discourses is not a phenomenon, it is an ideal concept, and one should even consider the hypothesis that it came into being only with the rise of philosophical aesthetics, that is, at the end of the eighteenth century (Kant, *Critique of Judgment* [1790]).
33 I am referring to the theoretical foundation of empiricism and of rationalism.
34 The main point is the establishment of (intra-Christian) religious pluralism as the result of the Thirty Years War.—As with every generalization, my remarks, particularly in this introduction, are in need of a benevolent reading. Since it is evident that I will be dealing with "Western" literature in this book, although my general theoretical approach tries to go beyond such firmly established borderlines, or, rather, tries to re-conceptualize them in a much less dichot-

cal organisation,³⁵ political theory,³⁶ the understanding of Scripture,³⁷ and the general model of world and cosmos, to name the most important points only. In all these respects, European societies crossed a threshold of global historical importance: the abandonment of cyclical conceptualizations of time and the introduction of the concept of possibly never-ending "progress".³⁸ It was this conceptual distancing from the cyclical model which laid the foundations for the effective material transformation of the world beginning in the eighteenth century, that is, industrialization.

According to the dominant view as emblematized in the term "Renaissance", changes in the cultural sphere in general and in the literary sphere in particular were much less radical. The overcoming of medieval patterns is supposed to have largely taken the path of reactivating an existing paradigm, the culture of classical antiquity, blending it with a limited set of "new" ideas. Early modern culture would thus have to be subsumed under an age that begins already in the middle of the fourteenth century.³⁹ Cultural modernity proper—understood as the emancipation from culture as cyclical recurrence—would thus set in only during the Enlightenment, or rather with the age of Romanticism and its anti-classical, anti-normative turn. Early modern literary culture would be, as it were, belated with regard to contemporary scientific progress, philosophical achievements, or even religious diversity.

The drama of the period, however, is an apt example for showing that these current views neglect important, even crucial traits of the cultural dynamics of that age. Sixteenth- and seventeenth-century European drama was, indeed, inspired by classical models (mainly Seneca and Terence) and by classical poe-

---

omous way than usual, I do not consider in the above remark the problem of the schism between Byzantine and Roman Christianity, which occurred as early as at the end of the first millenium CE. This hint is meant to apply to all other generalizing statements in this introduction as well. I leave it to my readers whether or not they find my generalizations useful. As to the point in question, I believe it to be legitimate because there is a difference between religious pluralism existing in territories otherwise, that is, politically unified, and a plurality that does not require a theoretical effort because it exists with regard to territories otherwise separate from each other.

35 I am thinking of the "invention" of the centralized and bureaucratized modern state.
36 Absolutism as well as international law were first theorized in that age.
37 A pervasively allegorical reading of Scripture, in contrast to the selectively allegorical interpretation practiced since Origen and Augustine, and the ensuing destabilization of the concept of the "one and ever identical truth" arose only in this age, within certain Protestant denominations (the quote is from Augustine, *De vera religione* III: 3 ["veritas una et eadem semper"]).
38 See my essay "The Traditional Cosmos and the New World", *MLN* vol. 118/2003, pp. 363–392.
39 I am referring to the (finally not misled) cliché of Petrarch as the "father of humanism".

tology (neo-Aristotelianism). Nevertheless, it differs fundamentally from its sources. The pragmatic context in which dramatic performances took place changed substantially. In that period, drama as performance established the basis of a new cultural practice that has become the main element of present-day culture, occidental and non-occidental: visual culture as mass media. In the terminology of the above-characterized theoretical approach, the particularly fascinating characteristic of this subgenre of literary texts consists in redefining what literature is meant to be by fusing more traditional functions of drama and theater with pre-existing functional dimensions circulating in the cultural net that had up to that period belonged to the domain of other types of cultural practices, mainly religious.[40] This rather significant "leap" in terms of cultural practices may be observed in all major Western and Central European countries, with slight differences regarding periodization: first in England, then in Spain, and some decades later in France and Germany. The prehistory of the development is to be found in early sixteenth-century Italy, where one might rightly speak of a "Renaissance", as we are dealing mainly with a revival of classical models. The new cultural patterns spread rapidly, by way of a virtual network as outlined above, to other Western and Central European countries (the Netherlands and Scandinavia, Portugal, Poland, and the non-German-speaking parts of the Habsburg Empire), where they came in contact with a partly still existing local theater culture which goes back to the shared European tradition of medieval Christian drama (morality plays, mystery plays).[41] Roughly one century later, they were transported by the infrastructure of the cultural net to a part of Europe which up to that period did not have a refined dramatic production of its own,[42] Russia. And another century later, they spread to colonial India, where they initiated a visual mass culture that might see its greatest impact only in the twenty-first century.

The primary common characteristic of early modern drama is to have been written for stage performance, thus differing from (early) Renaissance drama,

---

40 In the further course of my argument, I shall come back to the intricate question as to what, in essence, differentiates the performative practices of theater from Mass (pp. 167–171).
41 The nomenclature for the subgenres of medieval didactic drama differs from one vernacular to another, but in all the relevant "national" theater cultures there is the bi-partition designated by the above English terms, namely, dramas which are meant to be primarily moralizing, and which make use of the device of allegory—mostly in the sense of personifications of vices and virtues—and, secondly, dramas which present the miracles and mysteries from biblical history and the saints' and martyrs' lives.
42 The adjective is to refer to the fact that there were, in pre-eighteenth-century Russia, elementary performances one might compare to medieval farces, as well as liturgical plays; but there was no drama proper.

which was conceived mainly to be read, particularly when it was not intended for the court.[43] This entails a radical change of recipients. Early modern drama addressed highly diverse audiences, from the illiterate to the intellectuals and the nobility. As such, its themes and objectives underwent a fundamental transformation: the refined and elitist Renaissance culture became replaced by a mass culture, a phenomenon which would affect the other genres, mainly narrative, only in an age when literacy became ubiquitous, i.e. in the nineteenth century.

Early modern drama was performed either in institutional theaters[44] and theatrical courtyards (*corrales*), depending on climate conditions, or on carts, by itinerant companies. Performances were public in the sense that everyone who was ready to pay an (affordable) fee was admitted. It is mainly the features of common accessibility and of presentation-as-performance which may be considered as being drawn from another cultural configuration floating in the net, namely the practice of religious service, of Mass.[45] It is evident that the intensity of circulatory processes increases dramatically as soon as the (illiterate) masses become connected to the cultural network. A comparison with religious drama in the strict sense, which went on existing in certain countries—mainly Spain—allows for the determination of the difference between early modern drama and the medieval drama performances which were commonly accessible as well, but re-

---

43 I am thinking in particular of a text such as the most famous drama of that period, the *Celestina* (1499/1504). As to the intellectual depth of the play, which is from my viewpoint one of the most significant texts of European early modernity, see my "Mittelalterlich kosmische Ordnung und rinascimentales Bewußtsein von Kontingenz. Fernando de Rojas' *Celestina* als Inszenierung sinnfremder Faktizität (mit Bemerkungen zu Boccaccio, Petrarca, Machiavelli und Montaigne)", in: Gerhart v. Graevenitz and Odo Marquard (eds.), *Kontingenz*, München 1998, pp. 173–223.

44 Court theater, which emerged at the end of the fifteenth and the beginning of the sixteenth centuries, goes on existing, but becomes more and more a receding phenomenon; this said, it remains an important site of cultural floating processes and will thus be addressed in due terms in the following sections of this book.

45 In English, the relation established by me between early modern drama as the first instance of visual *mass* culture and the religious practice of the (Catholic) *Mass* may seem confusing, or to be yet another of the somewhat outdated examples of postmodernist playing with signifiers. In my own language, there is no such equivalence regarding the signifiers implied. Mass media reads "Massen-Medien" in German, while the word for Mass is "Messe". Accordingly, my above remarks are meant seriously; they refer to the signifieds of the respective terms: early modern drama applies the feature of general accessibility to a performance, which is derived from religious ritual, to a cultural practice that was characterized by restriction up to that period (literacy, and the quite extensive financial as well as cultural resources that it requires). For further differentiations, see below, pp. 167–169.

stricted in time because they were bound to the most important festivals of the Christian calendar, primarily Christmas and Easter: the theater as created in the sixteenth century CE establishes for the first time in human history the practice of a public visual culture that is not bound to ritual patterns (religious, or, as was the case in classical Athens, political) and the ensuing constraints.[46]

The research conducted so far on early modern European drama[47] has been confined to the companion-style monograph; the relevant books largely lack a discussion of extra-literary discourses and follow traditional patterns of literary history, including some general remarks regarding staging. Numerous articles in journals or in collective volumes which pursue a comparative perspective are mostly restricted to a more or less updated variant of motif history or to comparisons between single works of specific authors.[48] Highly sophisticated new approaches to great dramatic authors of that age, such as Stephen Green-

---

46 These constraints are highly diverse, but regardless of the difference, they have in common the restriction of the process of circulation of cultural material. As to religious ritual, there are content-bound (dogmatic) strictures; in addition, there are processes of automatization and the ensuing reduction of receptivity. As to the first documented theater culture in human history, it is a frequently neglected point that the term "democracy" meant something different in fifth-century-BCE Athens than it does in later times. Not only those entitled to vote, but also those admitted to theatrical performances were a relatively small minority of the population (adult "free" citizens, males and their wives); children, adolescents, slaves, and metics were not admitted.
47 Meaning: there are, of course, a lot of important, separate publications on English, French, German, and Spanish drama of the period (see my remarks below).
48 The most recent instance of these theoretically more traditional undertakings is the *Theater Without Borders* project conducted by Robert Henke et alii, which has resulted in two collective volumes so far (Robert Henke and Eric Nicholson [eds.], *Transnational Exchange in Early Modern Theater*, Burlington, VT 2008, containing an "Introduction" by Henke describing the entire project [pp. 1–18]; Robert Henke and Eric Nicholson [eds.], *Transnational Mobilities in Early Modern Theater*, Burlington, VT 2014). Although the research project comprises certain theoretical ambitions, its main focus is on the description of singular phenomena of cultural exchange within the frame of early modern European theater. The approach is comparative, but English theater is the pivotal point of the research carried out, with a secondary focus on Italian theater.—I should like to stress something that is, to a certain extent, evident from the titles published by the team: much more than is the case here, the accent is on theater in the sense of performance, while texts are of minor importance. This attitude limits to a considerable extent the theoretical bearing of the discussions. The entire question of cultural transfer, for instance, is linked to a large extent to the point of specialized human intermediaries, that is, wandering troupes, and not to the multifarious and even unintentional processes of transmission that result from many different forms of "migration" of humans and of material objects. As to the detailed description of various specific practices of cultural exchange in that period (itinerant theater troupes, "migration" of motifs and character types, or of performative practices from one country

blatt's publications on Elizabethan theatre,[49] have considered the questions raised by early modern theater from the perspective of one particular "national" culture; exogenous sources, mainly Italian and French, are taken into consideration if applicable, but the perspective as a whole is not comparative. This applies as well, *mutatis mutandis*, to Antonio Maravall's research on the Spanish Golden Age drama.[50] Maravall characterizes the *corral* theaters as part of a propaganda system, which is a hypothesis worth being considered;[51] but the focus on Iberian drama entails certain limitations with regard to a possible generalization of this thesis. Walter Benjamin's essay on German Baroque drama is still a source of inspiration,[52] as is Albrecht Schöne's monograph on emblem books and German Baroque drama,[53] which was the first publication to draw attention to the close links between drama and the visual culture of the age.—Succinctly expressed: the research done in the field is committed, in a way that remains unproblematized for the most part, to a framing which is contested by the theoretical approach here submitted, namely to the concept of "national literature", in the sense of an "organic" relationship between the conceptual and the linguistic level of a given corpus of literary texts, which entails conceiving the latter as being linked to a specific configuration of pragmatic parameters.

What might be the results of a new approach to early modern European drama according to the concepts outlined in the first part of this introduction? The

---

to another, etc.), the volumes mentioned are a highly useful source. Over the years, the team has become more and more committed to Louise George Clubb's concept of "theatergram", which I do not discuss critically here; suffice it to say that it is evident from my entire approach that the restriction of the investigation to borders established by genre seems to me as problematic as restrictions established by language or by "national" borders. Dramatic texts, to put it briefly, are very frequently based on non-dramatic (narrative) texts, and also share very many features with them; following Aristotle, I consider *opsis* to be a relevant, but not the most relevant component of texts conceived with a view to being performed on stage (Clubb, *Italian Drama in Shakespeare's Time*, New Haven, CN 1989).—The *Theater Without Borders* and the *DramaNet* research teams exchanged their views on the occasion of several conferences (see, e.g., Joachim Küpper and Leonie Pawlita [eds.], *Theatre Cultures within Globalising Empires: Looking at Early Modern England and Spain*, Berlin and Boston, MA 2018).
49 See, once again, *Shakespearean Negotiations*.
50 *Culture of the Baroque: Analysis of a Historical Structure*, Terry Cochran (tr.), Manchester 1986.
51 See also Greenblatt's similar views with regard to the situation in England ("The Elizabethan stage functions as one of the public uses of spectacle to impose normative ethical patterns on the urban masses." [*Renaissance Self-Fashioning*, Chicago, IL and London 2005 (1st print 1980), p. 253]).
52 *The Origin of the German Tragic Drama*, John Osborne (tr.), London 1998.
53 *Emblematik und Drama im Zeitalter des Barock*, München 1964.

most important point might consist in the fact that a network theory of cultural production frees the texts and the actual practices from being considered within the boundaries of national cultures. Transculturality would thus become the standard case, while "nationality" of cultural artifacts would be considered the particular case to be explained according to the logic of control outlined above (mainly: power- or belief-driven attempts to restrict the material available at a given time and place). Common traits between spatially or temporally separated works of art would no longer have to be considered an astonishing phenomenon. Reception in later times or in remote regions could be accounted for either by the varying impact of the aforementioned three basic control mechanisms, by the expansion of the net structure, or both. Fundamental formal standards that can be observed in all European "national" cultures could be explained by considering the floating of the material on differing levels of formal organization, including abstract instructions of formulation: shaping thus need not start at the basic level whenever a quantity of material is extracted from the net in view of being shaped. Relative difference with regard to form could be accounted for on the grounds of the possibility to impose any form on the material circulating in the net.

4.—In order to give a first impression of the outlined theoretical hypotheses' viability in relation to the field in question, early modern European drama, some points shall be illustrated by referring briefly to authors, texts, and cultural materials which are still well known today.

The most prominent English drama of the period is Shakespeare's *Hamlet* (ca. 1600); for Spain one would have to point to Calderón's *La vida es sueño* (ca. 1635). Both dramas rely on source material from other authors, but there seems to be no direct influence that the Shakespearean play could have exerted on Calderón's *comedia*. Nevertheless, the commonalities between the two texts are striking.[54] Their basic plots build on the oedipal triangle:[55] a young prince

---

54 For a more detailed comparative analysis of these two dramas, see my "*Hamlet*, by Shakespeare, and *La vida es sueño*, by Calderón, or the Problem of Scepticism", *Germanisch-Romanische Monatsschrift* vol. 58/2008, pp. 367–399.

55 I take the occasion to draw readers' attention to a point that needs to be addressed in my further analyses: are there anthropological constants grounded in our belonging to one species that could account for certain observable commonalities between texts of different or even separate cultural contexts? Or, to put it more precisely: on which level of formal and content-related organization should these anthropological commonalities be assumed to be located? As is well known, Sigmund Freud claimed that the oedipal triangle is in a way related to the existence of culture as such. Mid-twentieth-century structuralist anthropologists such as Claude Lévi-Strauss would have agreed, though from a different theoretical vantage point. The experience to be made in the present-day, rapidly globalizing world, however, raises questions concerning the commonality of patterns such as the one mentioned. It seems not to exist in

struggles for power and is opposed in his efforts by his father, or by a father-substitute, respectively. The mother figure (in Calderón's case a mother-imago) holds an ambivalent position between the two conflicting male characters. The main difference consists in that, in Shakespeare, the oedipal material has been assembled into a tragic pattern, whereas in Calderón the conflict is resolved by a fairytale-like ending, as is standard in comedy.—The two dramas do not only make use of the same material regarding the basic plot, but also with regard to the fundamental concept underlying the plot. In both plays, what is at stake is the problem of the reliability of sense perception. In Calderón, the question emblematized by the play's title is a sort of "direct" extraction of material floating in the net, namely, the fourth trope of Sextus Empiricus' summary of the basic theorems advocated by Pyrrhonian skepticism. In Shakespeare, the question as such, which is none other than the one raised in Calderón, becomes linked ("assembled") to a material whose provenance and profile is more popular than in Calderón, namely, the existence or non-existence of apparitions authenticated by sensory perception, of "ghosts". In both plays, the "epistemological" problem is linked to material deriving from moral-philosophical discourses, namely to the question of the conditions of certainty regarding knowledge about what has happened under which it is ethically justifiable to take another person's life.—While the oedipal triangle provides for entertainment by gratifying the spectators' more or less conscious libidinous desires, in the sense of both sex and aggression,[56] the endings refer to specific world-models related to the generic patterns mentioned.[57] The basic question

---

traditional Islamic societies or in Far Eastern contexts. It cannot be excluded that the "commonality" of the pattern in the West originates in its circulation in the occidental section of the cultural net, which may have started before Sophocles wrote his drama; Gen 3 might be a historically much older instance. This said, the decisive question would remain to be resolved: why is it that particularly this interactional pattern was "extracted" from the net so frequently in the course of Western cultural history?

56 I am referring to Freud's—in my opinion highly convincing—attempt at theorizing literature in the sense of fiction ("The Relation of the Poet to Day-Dreaming" in: *Art and Interpretation: An Anthology of Readings in Aesthetics and the Philosophy of Art*, Eric Dayton [ed.], Orchard Park, NY 1998, pp. 300–304). The sophisticated formal organization of "high canon" literary texts is, according to Freud, nothing but a structure of enticement allowing the cultured recipient to approach these works with the conscious intention of satisfying the intellect, while then (and thereby) indulging, mostly subconsciously, in libidinous configurations and fantasies the direct "consumption" of which would otherwise be contravened by a strict veto from his or her superego.

57 It is, indeed, a simplification to apostrophize Catholicism as an interpretation of the Christian dogma according to the basic pattern of comedy, but I suggest considering it as a useful one, and my view may invoke an authority as important as Dante. I shall not engage in the discussion of whether Shakespearean drama is written from a standpoint informed by Catholicism (which I would exclude from my perspective), Protestantism, agnosticism, or even athe-

underlying the plot connects the plays to contemporary philosophical and epistemological discussions (skepticism), and the aspect under which this question is integrated into the action establishes, as already said, links to moral philosophy. In both dramas, there is a host of additional cultural material to be found, deriving from religious or theological discourses (the question of hell and purgatory; *opera meritoria* as useful or not, etc.).—All these materials could be considered as items floating in the contemporary cultural net. They precede the works mentioned and are not individual "creations" on the part of the playwrights. This implies that, at other points within the net, there is a high probability of finding comparable or partly comparable discursive configurations which need not be mediated by direct influences.

Starting from these most elementary findings, there remains the task of describing in detail the formal entity ("work") to which this material is synthesized in both cases. At this point, a more elaborate version of the ideas I am presenting here would have to address the question of how to account for the incontestable differences which always exist between two different works, even in the case of far-reaching commonalities.[58] For the time being, I will leave it at saying that, within the framework suggested by me, such differences are conceptualized as being based to a much greater extent on external factors than in the common view informed by categories like "creativity" or "ingenuity". The ending Calderón constructs for his version of a conflict that is not that different from the one to be found in *Hamlet* is most likely not primarily contingent on the author's personal choice or genius, but rather on what I am calling demand and control. The concept of definitive failure does not have its place within the worldview of Counter-Reformation Catholicism. It is not without reason that the generic term for Spanish Baroque drama is *comedia*; the meaning of the term is similar to the one intended by Dante when he named his great poem the *Divine Comedy*. And I should like to add that the fact that Shakespeare, rather than Calderón, is considered a timeless genius from the nineteenth century through the present might be less due to the intrinsic qualities of his texts, hence, to his personal creativity, than to the course that, for reasons we are hardly able to discuss within the field of literary studies proper, general and intellectual history has taken from the eighteenth century onward—a course which favours the ongoing extraction of Shakespeare's dramas from the cultural net, while disadvantaging Calderón's *comedias* in this respect.

---

ism; in any case, the world-model conveyed by (serious) Skakespearean dramas has affinities to the pattern of tragedy. The oedipal configuration is thus "assembled" into a different basic template than in the case of Calderón's play.

58 —unless we are dealing with epigonic texts.

A network theory of cultural production becomes, however, intriguing once one is prepared to go beyond the frame of a two-text comparison, as is standard in the discipline. One need not transgress the generic boundaries of the phenomena scrutinized in order to integrate the works of the second author of world-literary stature of that age, Cervantes, into the scenario.[59] It would be tempting to say a few words about the *Quijote* (1605/1615). But within this context, it may even be more illuminating to stay with the genre of drama. The play in question bears the title of *Entremés del retablo de las maravillas* (1615).[60] The title is intentionally ambiguous. A "retablo" is, primarily, an altarpiece presenting religious paintings, including miracles—in Spanish: *maravillas*;[61] in Golden Age usage, "retablo" might also refer to a stage where a show is performed.[62]

The plot of the piece might be summarized as follows: a troupe of wandering actors enters a village, sets up its stage (the *retablo*), and then performs various short scenes; one is thus dealing with a play within the play. The only link between these scenes is their sensational content: the biblical Samson tearing

---

[59] For a detailed analysis, see Leonie Pawlita, *Skeptizismus im europäischen Drama der Frühen Neuzeit. Untersuchungen zu Dramentexten von Shakespeare, Calderón, Lope de Vega, Rotrou und Cervantes*, Berlin 2015.
[60] *Entremés* is a generic term. The French equivalent, *farce*, also used in English and German, may be more familiar, the literal meaning of the two terms being exactly the same: something that is put in between two other items. The original field of application of the French term is the culinary sphere; it designates a mixture of meat and spices put into a bigger piece of meat, mostly poultry, in order to enhance the taste of the entire roast. In the case of drama, these further items are acts of a serious drama, often with a didactic—in that age: religious—content. In the High Middle Ages, such didactic plays (Nativity and Passion plays, referring to biblical history, or morality plays, presenting allegories of virtues and vices fighting against each other) attained a length which made representations last for more than one or two days. In order to provide some relief from these huge quantities of doctrinal or moralizing profile, dramatists started creating short intermediate one-act plays (*entremeses* or farces) whose action was independent from the main play and whose content was meant to be entertaining, that is, at least comic, and in many cases also obscene. The reaction of the contemporary audience to these interludes seems to have been so positive that, as early as from the thirteenth century onward, they developed into independent plays typically performed by itinerant troupes on occasions such as fairs. High canon comedy, such as that of the French author Molière, owes much to this tradition of farce, which was productive up to the end of the fifteenth century. As to the function of these plays, as well as their development into independent plays, the theory of the carnivalesque by Mikhail M. Bakhtin provides all necessary details (*Rabelais and His World*, Hélène Iswolsky [tr.], Bloomington, IN 1984).
[61] Frequent subjects were for instance Christ's Ascension or the descent of the Holy Spirit on Pentecost (etc.).
[62] I shall come back to the intentional ambiguity of the term in a later passage of the present study.

down the columns of a temple dedicated to an idol; a huge number of mice appearing on the stage and scaring in particular the female contingent of the audience; wild and dangerous beasts—such as bears and lions, or a bull who is said to have killed a man in Salamanca—running around on stage (etc.). Actually, however, there is nothing to be seen on the stage. The actors behave and talk to each other as if the scenes mentioned were being performed, and the villagers enthusiastically agree, to the point of being seized by fear when the lions are allegedly prowling around the stage. The reason for their readiness to accept the actors' pretentions as true is conveyed in a scene taking place before the (non-)performances within the performance: the stage director tells the villagers that the contraption set up is named "the stage of miracles" because only people of legitimate birth (stemming from a couple who is united by the bond of sacramental marriage) and who are, in addition, so-called "old Christians" (*cristianos viejos*), that is, who are free from the suspicion of having Jewish ancestors, would be able to perceive what is presented onstage.—The striking peculiarity of the Cervantian functionalization of a well-known motif is encoded in the ending. A quartermaster of the royal army suddenly appears. He announces that there are some dozen military men to be hosted, and asks the villagers to make the necessary preparations. These, however, or the bigger part of them, believe the quartermaster to be part of the stage action. They ask the stage director to present more entertaining scenes, and start hitting the quartermaster, as the latter does not show any readiness to leave the "stage". The military man reacts accordingly: he draws his sword and stabs a great number of the villagers.[63] The play thus ends in a bloody disaster.

The skeptical tenor of the entire construction is provided by the fact that the villagers really believe to be seeing what is only recounted to them: sensory perception might be biased by ideological commitments or societal constraints. Yet quite like *La vida es sueño* and *Hamlet*, the Cervantian *entremés* is not content to reassert the basic tenets of skepticism. The breach of generic conventions practiced by Cervantes, the mix of comedy and disaster, lays bare the impasse into which skepticism leads in an even more drastic way than the plays of Calderón and Shakespeare. The general tendency of the plays, however, is analogous, and it may be characterized as follows: The assumptions of skepticism may be irrefutable. There are quite a number of various factors which may bias sensory perceptions in such a way that perceiving humans are

---

[63] In those times, hosting military men from one's own country on their demand was, indeed, a legal obligation. If there was resistance to this law, the soldiers were entitled to take by physical force what was not conceded voluntarily.

not able to decide what is "real" and what is only an illusion produced by the potentially fallacious interaction between their sensory apparatuses and their minds. But human life is full of situations in which serene *isosthenia* and *ataraxia* are not a convincing answer to the problems raised by the skeptics' hypotheses. Especially when it comes to questions of life and death, there is a difference between a sword that is merely perceived and a sword that is both perceived and real. The former one may cause fear; the latter may cause fear, but it may in addition kill.—Like the other dramatists, Cervantes does not have an epistemological answer to the problem he stages in his *entremés*. But it may be that the final unacceptability of the skeptical positions for humans who want to survive, presented by the dramatists, paved the way for the either provisional or logically problematic solutions to the question, as devised in contemporary philosophical discourses, to become acceptable.[64]

There are similar dramatic texts in other European countries of that age, in particular in France.[65] The main difference between the processes to be observed in Spain and England on the one hand and France on the other consists in the fact that, within the latter context, the skeptical material was also direct-

---

[64] With the above remark, I am referring to empiricism on the one hand (Bacon) and rationalism (Descartes) on the other. Empiricism programmatically rejects the attempts at finding out the "true nature" of the phenomena and limits the results of human conceptualization to the status of provisional framings, liable to be revised as soon as a new item pertaining to the phenomenon in question is detected. Descartes's attempt at constructing a reliable conceptualization of the world by grounding it in some basic "innate" rational concepts is contingent upon the assumption that there is a God who is not a deceiver (a *genius malignus*); at closer scrutiny, it thus turns out that Descartes's alleged establishment of autonomous reason goes on being linked to religious belief—not to concrete dogmas, but to the idea of a benevolent creator and prime mover (see my "*La vida es sueño*. 'Aufhebung' des Skeptizismus, Recusatio der Moderne", in: Friedrich Wolfzettel and Joachim Küpper [eds.], *Diskurse des Barock: Dezentrierte oder rezentrierte Welt?*, München 2000, pp. 383–428).

[65] One might think of Rotrou's *Le véritable Saint Genest* (1647), directly inspired by Lope de Vega's *Lo fingido verdadero* (1609); yet as "all-too Spanish" and all-too unoriginal, the play was only of minor importance in contemporary France.—In addition, there is a host of further plays in French, not only comedies, but also "tragi-comédies", in which the potentially fallacious character of sensory impressions constitutes an element of the intrigue. In the first place, one would have to mention Corneille's *L'Illusion comique* (1636), a play that shares, as may be said in passing, quite a few elements with similar plays by Calderón, such as *El mágico prodigioso* (1637) or *En esta vida, todo es verdad y todo mentira* (1659). My above differentiation of the situation in France from England and Spain might become more plausible if one takes into consideration the relative weight of the plays in question within their respective contexts. Amongst all of the plays written by Shakespeare as well as those by Calderón, the two mentioned are considered outstanding. As to Corneille's oeuvre in its entirety, *L'Illusion comique* is regarded as rather marginal.

ly assembled into an abstract epistemological frame, namely in Descartes's *Meditations* (ca. 1650).[66] In the text's first section, the philosopher refers almost verbatim to the famous fourth trope of Sextus Empiricus, also present in Calderón's play, which illustrates the unreliability of sensory perception by drawing attention to the fact that subjective impressions concerning the world that arise while humans are awake may be undistinguishable from those that arise during sleep. In contrast to the two playwrights, Descartes finally does present a solution to the problem: namely, to scrutinize the data collected by the senses in the light of certain basic mathematical concepts.

Whether or not Descartes's solution to the problem that is at the center of the three dramas as well is tenable or not shall not be discussed at this point. The mere fact that a question of high discursive importance was extracted from the cultural net with a view to assembling it in the frame of drama on the one hand and in an epistemological frame on the other, is quite remarkable, and one might derive from this observation a hypothesis which may seem at first glance daring: seventeenth-century France may have chosen a path that differs from England and Spain with regard to culture. Mass media phenomena are confined to the field of a highly sophisticated comedy which takes up serious problems, but always under the imperative limitation to entertainment. Thus, high culture and low culture remain separate, or rather remain much more separate than in other countries during that age. "Serious" themes are discussed in tragedies whose representations were not accessible to the common people, but only to a social elite (*la cour et la ville*[67]). But even tragedy is, within the strictly hierarchical French cultural pattern of that period, only a relatively low level of organizing cultural material. The relevant level is that of philosophical texts which do not exist *stricto sensu* in Spain and England in that age, where they either are confined to epistemology[68] or are "scholastic", that is, unoriginal in content.[69] Early modern France produces social cohesion by a means which

---

66 For the striking parallels, down to specific formulations, regarding the reliability of sensory perception in *La vida es sueño* and the *Meditations*, see the essay quoted in n. 64; as to a possible explanation within the frame of my theoretical approach, see below, pp. 115–134, esp. pp. 118 f. and pp. 126 f.
67 For a description of the social configuration apostrophized in this formula, see the famous essay by Erich Auerbach, in: E. A., *Scenes from the Drama of European Literature*, Ralph Manheim (tr.), Manchester 1984, pp. 133–182.
68 The most important example would be Francis Bacon's *Novum organum scientiarum* (1620).
69 It might seem inadequate to qualify all of scholastic philosophizing, including the texts of Francisco Sanches and Francisco Suárez, as lacking originality. But one has to put the contribution they made to the philosophical discourse of that time in perspective. Compared to the anti-scholastic revolution as theorized by Descartes, implying the rejection of authority and tradition as a source of truth, seventeenth-century scholasticism is not as yet as "exhausted"

also exists in the two other countries, but at a much lower degree of societal relevance: the imaginary identification of the people with the State symbolized by the monarch.[70] The stage of seventeenth-century France is not the stage, it is the court, which, however, is not directly accessible to the people in terms of perception.[71] In early modern French culture, there is a relatively strict separation between the discursive sphere and the sphere of the imaginary.[72] It remains to be discussed how such "national" exceptions may be accounted for within the frame of a network theory of cultural production, on the basis of which it would be in principle questionable for there to be such "national" circuits.—The configuration outlined above may suffice as a first, provisional example of what a network theory of cultural production may be able to yield.

5.—As to methodology, it needs to be emphasized that the problems discussed within this book were investigated at two different levels of generality. The research group working on the question produced a variety of books, major articles, and conference proceedings, all of which deal with specific configurations within the framework outlined above.[73] The present book tries to systematize the findings of the various investigations and to synthesize the insights

---

a paradigm as it will be in the eighteenth century; but in terms of intellectual history, it is a framework on the verge of obsolescence.

70 The distinctive feature of French absolutism in that age is stability. In England, stability was contravened by dynastic controversies, combined with religious schisms and clashes. In Spain—Europe's first absolutist state—it was drastic economic instability, caused by a premodern, essentialist theory of money and value, which made the monarchy more and more into a problematic institution, or at any rate, into a power which was in no way apt to serve as a focal point for imaginary societal identification.

71 It was roughly one hundred years later when the reverse side of this configuration produced political effects of world-historical impact. The complete and strict separation of court and populace allowed for the spreading of rumors regarding the life at court which provoked the people to scrutinize things themselves. From the moment the fishwives forced King Louis XVI to "accompany" them from Versailles to the city, the chance to preserve the traditional system and to protect it against being revolutionized vanished.

72 The long-lasting impact of this separation can still be observed today. At least up to the end of the twentieth century, and perhaps even into the twenty-first century, mass media culture, although existent, is of lesser importance in France than in countries like Britain, Spain, or Germany.

73 In cases where the monographs are published or will be published at about the same time as this book, I shall only quote these titles, although chapters of the books in question may have appeared or may appear in the proceedings of the five conferences the DramaNet research group convened, or in reviews. In cases where the book publications will need some more time before becoming accessible to possible readers, I shall add titles of articles related to the book in question which have been published or will be published at around the same time as this book.

gained there by further developing the theory of culture as a virtual network. At the same time, it provides an attempt at integrating the historically specific panorama of texts which was at the center of all specific investigations by presenting the thesis of contemporary theater as an early modern mass media culture.—The "mapping" of the field researched implies that this book will consistently refer to specific cases and configurations, but in a concentrated fashion. Readers longing for more philological substantiation are invited to take a look at the books and articles originating from the various subprojects and conference proceedings. This said, the present study and its theses are written with the intention of being self-explanatory; referring to the other publications produced by the research group is thus meant to be a possibility, but not a necessity.

In order to provide orientation regarding the entire field which was taken into consideration, I will briefly give some basic information concerning the various specific investigations that constitute the, so to speak, material basis of the theses and assumptions developed in the present book.

According to the above-mentioned fact that it is primarily the traditional concept of "national literatures" which is contested by the DramaNet research group's approach, there is a range of investigations targeting the question of a circulation of literary and cultural material beyond linguistic borders and the insights that might be gained from a careful observation of the phenomena in question.

Post-medieval drama first emerged in Italy. Italian drama and theater of the early sixteenth century "floated" to all the other major dramatic cultures of the time. The question as to why there is no or only scarce "floating back" of the transformed material to Italy has been raised in terms of historical description[74] as well as in terms of theory.[75]—English and Spanish early modern drama[76] stand in a most interesting configuration in that age with regard to the particular and the larger implications of the material investigated, as both rely on the "infrastructure" of public theater. The questions emerging from this configuration concern the point of whether there is anything reasonable to be predicated with respect to "origin", or whether one is bound to the thesis that

---

74 See specifically Katja Gvozdeva, *Compagnie d'hommes joyeux*. Performances carnavalesques (rite, jeu, théâtre) et culture académique en Italie et en France au seizième siècle.
75 See below, pp. 231 f.
76 See Pawlita, *Skeptizismus im europäischen Drama der Frühen Neuzeit*, and Jan Mosch, *Moral Agency and Heteronomy in Shakespearean and Racinian Tragedy*; see also Madeline Rüegg, *The 'Patient Griselda' Myth in Late Medieval and Early Modern Literature*.

"new" cultural forms and patterns are contingent agglomerations of heterogeneous material available in the net. Whether there was "influence" or not, it is striking that both nations developed mass media infrastructures at the same time. Both are imperial powers in the period concerned, one of them, however, on the rise, the other in rapid decline.[77]—French drama of the period is peculiarly pertinent with regard to the theoretical frame here suggested in that it did *not* adopt the formal patterns of early modern drama developed in England and Spain in order to "fill" it with its "own" contents, as, for example, German Protestant drama did with respect to Jesuit drama. The question to be discussed is that of possible reasons for this exception. Nevertheless, France partakes in the contemporary cultural net. As to material, both content as well as formal or poetological concepts, there is hardly anything original to be found in seventeenth-century French theatrical culture.[78] The overall cultural configuration, however, is different. This may lead to the hypothesis that (early modern) France may constitute an alternative model of culture and society with respect to the rest of Europe.—German drama of the period[79] is of interest for a network theory of culture in that it shares with Spanish drama of the time the denominator of being heavily informed by a logic of control based on religion. In addition, cultural transfer in both directions is intense; it is facilitated by political and dynastic configurations (the house of Habsburg). The great difference consists in that there are conflicting logics of religious control in German early modern theater (Protestant vs. Catholic), whereas Spain knows an ideological homogeneity brought about by the Inquisition as the first bureaucratic cultural control agency in human history. Notwithstanding this difference, the general intention behind the writing of dramas and their representation on stage was identical in both countries: it was to produce mental habits.—It is a remarkable phenomenon with regard to the reception of drama of the sixteenth and seventeenth centuries, at that time but also in later periods, that it operates right from the beginning beyond the boundaries of the "national" communities from which the texts originated. As to the period concerned, there is, amongst other cases, the spectacular Europe-wide reception of a drama as difficult to read as the *Celestina*;[80] as to phenomena at the same

---

[77] See also the articles in the collective volume *Theatre Cultures within Globalising Empires* (Küpper et al. [eds.]).
[78] See Mosch, *Moral Agency and Heteronomy in Shakespearean and Racinian Tragedy*.
[79] See Toni Bernhart, *Volksschauspiele. Dimensionen einer Gattung*.
[80] See Sven-Thorsten Kilian, *"Escrituras andantes": Concepts of Text and Scripture in Early Modern Drama*; by "reading" I mean in this context the reception on the conceptual level; the difficulty is not linked to the text's original language; it is thus preserved in the many translations which were produced and circulated all over Europe.

time trans-"national" and trans-temporal, there is the German reception of Shakespearean and of Spanish Golden Age drama in the age of Romanticism,[81] and the French reception of Shakespearean drama in that same age. The most intriguing point may consist in that these phenomena of cultural "importation" are to be observed particularly in an age of rising nationalism. At first sight, the configuration may be considered to be linked to the specific ingenuity of this specific author, Shakespeare. But there is a parallel to this paradoxical configuration, largely neglected by research so far, which is the reception of French and English drama, mediated by its previous reception in German-speaking principalities, at the eighteenth-century Russian court, and the ensuing emergence of dramatic production in Russian, which was one main component in the construction of a specifically Russian "identity".[82]—The corresponding phenomena in their entirety constitute a feature of cultural dynamics which impressively contests the nationalistic assumptions regarding culture that were officially prevalent in that period in all countries concerned.

There is one investigation dealing with the floating of cultural material across a border considered in traditional conceptualization as even more basic or "essential" than language, namely a border between civilizations which did not entertain relations of intense exchange for the larger part of their history. The problems for a network theory of cultural production emerging from such a configuration were dealt with by studying the "floating" of early modern European drama to colonial India, and the long-lasting effects this floating produced with regard to the emergence of "autochthonous" theater production (meaning: in Indian vernaculars), but also with regard to larger societal, even political developments observable in the second half of the nineteenth century.[83]—The intricate question of dominance and cultural imperialism, which cannot be avoided within a theory postulating a universal cultural net, has also been scrutinized with regard to the cultural activities of so-called "smaller" nations (*littératures mineures*, to use a term that has become current in recent years), namely, by analyzing the dramatic production of a small Slavic

---

81 Regarding Shakespeare, see Günther Erken, "Die Rezeption Shakespeares in Literatur und Kultur. Deutschland", in: *Shakespeare-Handbuch*, Ina Schabert (ed.), Stuttgart 2009 (5th print), pp. 627–651; the seminal publication as to the reception of Calderón's dramas in Germany is Swana L. Hardy, *Goethe, Calderón und die romantische Theorie des Dramas*, Heidelberg 1965.
82 See Kirill Ospovat, *Terror and Pity: Aleksandr Sumarokov and the Theater of Power in Elizabethan Russia*, Boston, MA 2016.
83 See Gautam Chakrabarti, *Familiarising the Exotic: Introducing European Drama in Early Modern India*, Berlin 2016.

country, one, however, that borders on the West: Slovenia.[84] There is another such *littérature mineure* study focussing on popular drama (*Volkstheater*) written in a German dialect—hardly accessible to speakers of standard German—as utilized in remote villages in the valleys of the Alps, in Tyrol.[85] It is mainly these two investigations which yield the basis for a critical discussion of what is, in terms of theory, the antagonist of the line of argument developed in this book, namely, the concept of "national literatures" as first developed in Johann Gottfried Herder's theorizing of culture as essentially *Volkskultur*—specific works being linked organically to the specific tribes amongst whom they emerged—which was widely accepted in all European countries in the age of Romanticism and seems to be the more or less unconscious basis of literary studies, including postcolonialism, up to the present era.

The above-mentioned comparative studies scrutinize the problem of how to account for the relevance of "borders" within a frame assuming that the production of culture takes place within a universal (virtual) net by taking into consideration mainly dramatic texts. In addition, there is a number of more focused studies foregrounding a particular compound of material and its circulation in the net. One of these more specific studies targets a motif tradition from which a genre originated, the pastoral,[86] which is highly interesting for the general frame at issue here, as it was "extracted" from the net with high frequency all over Europe for a certain period in early modern times, but stopped being reactivated in modernity proper.—Another such study discusses the relation between astrology and astronomy in dramatic texts of the age, and thus opens up questions concerning the multitude of discourses floating in the cultural net, including discourses of scientific profile, and their interaction.[87]— A third such focused investigation deals with the role and function of institutions or concepts of institutions enabling the circulation of the material in the net, its subsequent withdrawal, and its reassembly, in this case the concept of "academies".[88]—A fourth study scrutinizes the extent to which cultural practic-

---

[84] See Jaša Drnovšek, *"Certa Mina Dant VICtorIas"*. Die Prozessionsspiele der Gegenreformation zwischen Politik und Poetik.
[85] See Bernhart, *Volksschauspiele*.
[86] See Pauline Beaucé, *Parodies d'opéra au siècle des Lumières. Evolution d'un genre comique*, Rennes 2013.
[87] See Sabine Kalff, "Sterne auf der Bühne. Astronomie und Astrologie im Drama des 17. und 18. Jahrhunderts", *Comparatio* vol. 8/2016, pp. 35–58.
[88] See Stephanie Bung, "Playful Institutions. Social and Textual Practices in Spanish Academies", in: Toni Bernhart, Jaša Drnovšek, Sven Torsten Kilian, Joachim Küpper and Jan Mosch (eds.), *Poetics and Politics: Net Structures and Agencies in Early Modern Europe*, Berlin and Boston, MA 2018.

es received as performance and "real life" (cultural) practices might interact in order to implement behavioural patterns considered mandatory within a specific societal frame.[89]

Finally, there is a variety of investigations addressing the question of how to deal with specific configurations that may, in one way or other, cast a doubt on the basic assumptions implied by a network theory of cultural production. One such study is dedicated to what at first sight appears to be a most traditional investigation of motif or reception history; it deals with the story narrated in the last novella—the tale of Griselda—from Boccaccio's *Decameron* (1351) and its "floating" to almost all major and minor European dramatic cultures in the early modern age.[90] This study is of particular importance, as it allows for the assessment of what exactly differentiates the theoretical approach here suggested from more conventional approaches to literary history.—There is an investigation dealing with the floating of cultural material that has to be assigned to a meta-level, namely, the question of the extent to which it may be productive to theorize the transculturation of aesthetic concepts within the framework here submitted, that is, concepts assessed as being of a general, transnational profile even in traditional literary and cultural theory.[91]—Finally, there is a study which follows a line of thought that may be considered an alternative to the one here pursued. Starting from Hans Blumenberg's posthumously published deliberations on anthropology,[92] it discusses the question of whether or not the assumption of transfer is necessary when it comes to observing certain commonalities between (literary) texts from different times and places, or whether such parallel structures may more sensibly be accounted for by hypothesizing that there are universal anthropological constants.[93]

This range of concrete phenomena might allow for a substantive, though not as yet definitive specification of the theoretical assumptions which shall be expounded in Part I of this book.

---

[89] See, once again, Gvozdeva, *Compagnie d'hommes joyeux*.
[90] See Rüegg, *The 'Patient Griselda' Myth in Late Medieval and Early Modern Literature*.
[91] See Tatiana Korneeva, *The Dramaturgy of the Spectator: Theatre, Audience, and the Public Sphere in Late Seventeenth- and Eighteenth-Century Italy*.
[92] See Hans Blumenberg, *Beschreibung des Menschen*, Berlin 2014.
[93] See D. S. Mayfield, *The Vicarious: Variants in Blumenberg. Delegation in Early Modern Drama (Rojas, Machiavelli, Shakespeare)*.

I. The Cultural Net

The Basic Metaphor

0.—As to the metaphorical nature of my central concept, the cultural net, I shall skip the obligatory reference to Nietzsche[94] and leave it at saying that scholarly theory cannot do without the "transference" of terms from one semantic field to another, which is precisely the meaning of *metaphora* in Ancient Greek. The point which in fact needs to be carefully discussed when one suggests the introduction of a new metaphor is whether it is illuminating and productive for an understanding of the phenomena at issue, or whether it produces misleading lines of thought.

1.—I shall begin with some negative delimitations. As to the term "cultural net", one could think of alternatives, the "cultural web" or the "cultural grid" being those which come quite close to what I wish to convey. The reason for having discarded them lies mainly in the fact that their associative potential is all too fraught with materiality, that is, with the idea of a physically stable infrastructure. This is evident for the term "grid", but it also applies to some extent to the concept of a web, which derives from the verb "to weave" and evokes the structure of a spiderweb. The motive for choosing the metaphor of the net is its being relatively emancipated from the idea of a material basis that *necessarily* exists permanently; this associative potential of the net metaphor as I wish to understand it is a sort of spin-off of its current use within IT contexts.[95]

The affinity of this book's central metaphor to terms and concepts that emerged in the electronic age is, however, a relative one. One difference between the Internet and the cultural net as theorized here[96] is the speed of circulation and, as a consequence, the dramatically increased possibility of spreading and of accessing information, which is also linked to the fact that material circulating on the Internet is available everywhere, or at least in all places penetrable by

---

[94] "What is truth? a mobile army of metaphors, metonyms, anthropomorphisms [...] which were poetically and rhetorically heightened, transferred [...] and after long use seem solid, canonical, and binding [..]" (*On Truth and Lies in an Extra-Moral Sense* [1873]; translation according to: Friedrich Nietzsche, *On Rhetoric and Language*, Sander L. Gilman, Carole Blair and David J. Parent [eds.], New York, NY 1989, p. 250).

[95] In the next chapter, I shall address in more detail the question of what differentiates the net I have in mind from more traditional network structures.

[96] —setting aside the fact that what floats in the Internet requires an even broader conceptualization of culture than the material under scrutiny in this book.

radio waves. In the case of the cultural net as understood in this book, every process of mediation is linked to the direct or indirect, but in any case physical presence of a mediating human mind or of a (physical) cultural item produced by a human mind. At first sight, such a description seems to convey that the cultural net might be a site of restricted or limited circulation when compared to the Internet. What may counterbalance the (seemingly) restricted or limited circulation capacities of "pre-IT" network structures that make use of symbolic encoding is the possibility of what in actual IT structures is extremely rare, if only for reasons of the enormous quantity of circulating material: the pattern of fortuitous, contingent, totally un-preconceived, but nevertheless meaningful encounters. On the Internet, a recipient must consciously search for a certain material; otherwise he or she will get lost in the immense ocean of information. In the cultural net, the information actually transmitted is always linked to a "filter" constituted by the one human mind (or his products) serving as a transporting device. Since these "transporters" won't communicate with just anyone, but with a selection of other human minds, serendipity, meaning, the chance (not the necessity) that a culturally relevant result of a contingent contact between two units will emerge, may be much greater than in the case of a recipient surfing the Internet and gathering random information.

In qualitative terms, however, the similarities between IT networks and what I suggest calling the cultural net seem quite striking. They concern first of all the non-necessity of a stable and permanent material net structure and the ensuing characteristics already partially mentioned above.[97] Flexibility, the ease of rami-

---

[97] It is mainly this feature which led me to discard a number of further metaphorical constructs proposed in previous scholarship which I will not discuss here in detail. As an example, I shall briefly mention Peter Burke's "hydraulic model" for describing the way in which Renaissance culture floated to all regions of Europe (*The European Renaissance: Centers and Peripheries*, Oxford 1998; quote: p. 6). Would it be sensible to use this metaphor to describe the floating of cultural material into the remote valleys of the Alps, which one would have to assume to be an "uphill" movement (see Bernhart, *Volksschauspiele*)? And what about the idea of a hydraulic mediation device leading from Paris to Saint Petersburg (see Ospovat, *Terror and Pity*)? If one admitted that the Baltic Sea, and the rudimentary road system existing in that age, were part of the structure, the entire approach would perhaps be less counterintuitive than it actually is; but including such varying material substrates would bring the entire idea quite close to my suggestion of a virtual, rather than a physical configuration of cultural network structures, that is, to a conceptualization that contrasts with Burke's theorizing. This said, I am ready to concede that such more "materialistic" metaphors were useful insofar as they helped liberate the discussions revolving around processes of cultural exchange from the aura of the numinous and arcane that surrounds them in more traditional contexts. And I should add that Burke renders his initial terms more flexible in the course of the investigation ("[...] the channels, networks or groups through which the process of reception took place" [p. 10]).

fying into distant and remote regions, a non-hierarchical conformation, and the (relative) difficulty of exerting control over the circulating material are the main commonalities deriving from this feature. All of these characteristics may also be found in net structures that date from the pre-electronic age, for example in postal transport systems, which seem to have existed as structures consciously set up and maintained since the inception of written culture in the high civilizations of the Euphrates. But even digital encoding, be it by way of traditional script or by way of radio waves, does not seem to be an indispensable prerequisite for virtual network structures as described above. It is symbolic encoding as such, in more current terms: language, which does seem to be such a necessary prerequisite. Language enables the "saving" of cultural items of any kind in the structures of human brains. As soon as the bodies these brains are part of set themselves in motion and communicate what has been saved in their minds to other beings capable of symbolic interaction, there are instantiations of what is here called the cultural net.—This delimitation entails that such networks do not exist in the non-human world, a "fact" substantiated by the simple observation that there is no culture in the world of non-humans, no *colere*—that is, no systematic and progressive[98] alteration of the nature-given habitat.

2.—Cultural material may float in the net, as already said in passing, in the mode of entire, finite works (paintings, statues, scores, texts). "Below" this level, components of texts[99] (motifs, personages, particularly well-conceived

---

[98] It is, in the first place, this latter feature which differentiates humans from those animals who also transform their natural habitat in order to customize it according to their needs (birds, beavers, etc.). The fact that their "cultural" activities are the exact repetition of what previous generations of their species did testifies to the assumption that there is nothing in the animal world that corresponds to what I here call the cultural network, which is, in essence, a huge virtual container of all forms of interaction between humans and nature (including humans and humans), whose content is accessible in principle to all members of the species and actually accessed ("withdrawn from the net") in order to generate new forms of interaction between humans and nature. The cumulative effects characterizing human culture ("development"; "progress") are only able to take place in case individuals have access to patterns of customizing the natural habitat which transcend what they can learn by imitating their parents.

[99] —or of images, or of pieces of music. As said, books like the present one are in need of benevolent readers. My primary field of application for the theoretical frame here developed is literature, that is, cultural products sedimented as texts. For this reason, I draw illustrating remarks above all from this "field" of culture, while neglecting, for convenience's sake, to formulate analogous remarks that would refer to visual art and music. This said, I should like to stress once again that these non-linguistic cultural practices and the production of concrete works obey a logic which may, *mutatis mutandis*, not be all that dissimilar from the one described above. In a nutshell: it is my claim that the metaphor of culture as a (virtual) net applies at least to all artistic production (if not also to phenomena such as religion, science, techniques of power, etc.).

formulations [*dicta*]) may be items integrated into the floating process. "Above" this level, cultural material may float as formal concepts, partly rhetorical, partly generic, whose components—that is, specific tropes and topoi, or the range of *procédés* ascribed to the genre of tragedy in Aristotle's *Poetics*, e.g., peripety or anagnorisis—may likewise float on their own. On an even higher level of abstraction, one may identify the floating of world-modeling concepts linked to certain texts or genres, such as, in the case just mentioned, the "tragic vision" of life as doomed to (unredeemable) failure, which may be expressed by texts whose formal shaping differs from Aristotle's definition of the genre of tragedy—one may think of certain pieces by Samuel Beckett—but also from the genre as such—one might think of Baudelaire's famous poem *A une passante* (1855/1857). Finally—and this may be the most abstract level of culturally relevant material floating in the net—it may be enabling structures which float and are thus transferred from one cultural community to another. These are institutions that favor the production of concrete cultural material, but are not linked to any specific variant of such material. They serve as incubators for creative processes. As to culture *sensu lato*, one could point to schools, universities, and academies.

I would like to come back in more detail to the question of the standardization of the material floating in the net and to the related question of the actual items floating. One could argue that the circulating material—at least if one limits to texts the domain with respect to which one claims the metaphor to be valid[100]—is just as standardized as electricity. The elementary units, the "waves" or "particles", would in this case be the letters; script is indeed a variant of digitization. But such a radical use of my central metaphor would deprive it of its descriptive adequacy. Casting the "cultural net" as consisting in the fluctuation of an inventory of letters would lead to a view of cultural production as ironically displayed in Borges's *La biblioteca de Babel* (1941); texts would be a random combination of elementary digital units which make sense only in some very rare cases. In addition, emphasizing digitization to such an extent would exclude all possible discussions of the extent to which the approach here suggested might be useful for non-digitized cultural items, that is, items of visual culture; the mere fact that drama as theater comprises such non-digitized variants renders it necessary to refrain from consistently linking the metaphor here suggested to frames that are current in present-day IT structures.

---

100 That is, if we exclude paintings for a while.

If culture and text production are conceived not as a combinatory algorithm, but, rather, as a conscious and intention-driven or a sub-conscious human activity, one is led to postulate that items floating in such a net need to be identifiable or recognizable by humans. This claim is evident for ready-made texts, so-called "works". The crucial question is that of the extent to which one may proceed to more elementary units and still be reasonably entitled to say that there is something specific, namely, a unit, that is floating in the net, and not some random string of letters or digits. Provisionally, I am inclined to hold that what are called "motifs" and "characters" are the most elementary units to be considered, at least when we are discussing that specific variant of cultural production we are used to calling literature. But it is not to be excluded that even parts of motifs and specific traits constituting a character may be taken into consideration. As an illustration of the latter case, I should like to point to the personage of Hamlet. The combination of "hesitancy" (content) and "centrality" (hierarchical status) may suffice in order to constitute a unit floating in the net. In common language: a writer may draw from Shakespeare's text the inspiration to create a central personage whose character is mainly informed by hesitance, without adopting for his newly created character the full range of further traits constituting in their entirety what is said about Hamlet in Shakespeare's play. To continue this line of reasoning, one could hypothesize that even single characteristics assignable to personages may constitute units capable of floating, since it is possible to create, on the basis of material available in the net from the moment Shakespeare devised the eponymous hero of his greatest play, a non-central, secondary personage whose main trait is hesitancy and inertia; one might think, for instance, of Innstetten, Effi Briest's husband, in Theodor Fontane's most famous novel.

I should like to highlight explicitly that, starting no later than with Plato and Aristotle, it is not only literary texts and their components that constitute the material circulating in the net. It is at the same time the theoretical reflections at the basis of these texts that may be found in the virtual net: e.g., devices in a broad sense, including all sorts of generic concepts, but also formal rules and regulations, aesthetic concepts, functional ascriptions, rhetorical patterns, etc.

3.—Making cultural items apt for circulation requires in any case a sort of encoding. As already emphasized, this need not be a written encoding (texts or scores); but on the other hand, one should not underestimate the fact that written encoding and its various technological realizations—hand-written texts, printed texts, electronically recorded texts—are the most effective means to accelerate the spread of cultural material in the net, since they make its movement at least partly independent from the movements of actual humans.

If there is no such written encoding, the processes of circulation must necessarily be operated by actually moving human beings.

The point just made triggers the question of whether it is, indeed, only material shaped according to notational (non-compact) encoding,[101] specifically verbalized material, that is able to float in the net on levels of organization below the one of the integral work. It is evident that actual paintings and statues as well as musical works may be conceived of as floating in a net as here understood, but it is questionable whether they are able to do so other than at the level of the finite work. Is it conceivable that "styles", artistic or non-artistic (styles of painting, musical styles, features of body language, etc.), travel as such in the net? And is it possible that they travel—as is a potentiality for everything articulated in language—in a conceptual fashion only, or is everything cultural yet not articulated by way of the discreet arbitrary code always bound to certain material realizations in order to be able to travel? Is it conceivable that a new dress style[102] travels without the movement of actual people wearing it? Is it conceivable that the new and refined body language practiced at table at the French court and introduced on the initiative of the two Medici princesses married off to French kings or heirs to the throne would have gained terrain without the very material cutlery transported by the princesses in their baggage when they traveled from Florence to Paris? And is it possible to imagine the circulation of features of body language without traveling humans who demonstrated to people in Berlin or Saint Petersburg how a distinguished per-

---

101 I here refer to Nelson Goodman's categories (*Languages of Art: An Approach to a Theory of Symbols*, Indianapolis, IN 1968). I do not follow Goodman's highly illuminating theoretical model with regard to the relation between text and music (see in detail my "Einige Überlegungen zu Musik und Sprache", *Zeitschrift für Ästhetik und Allgemeine Kunstwissenschaft* vol. 51/2006, pp. 9–41). Music and texts share, indeed, the characteristic of non-compact encoding; but music as system lacks the intermediary level of what we call "words" with regard to texts. A musical composition is a combination of standardized sounds (notes); a text is a composition of standardized units (words) consisting of standardized sounds. These intermediate sound-combinations are defined as units by their being semanticized. As a consequence, texts may be decomposed into more elementary units which may float in the net on their own. In the case of musical works, this is not a systematically given dimension; it occurs only in very rare, isolated cases (the destiny motif of Beethoven's Fifth Symphony would be an example). Usually, musical works (like paintings) float in the net as integral items only. The "fragments" into which they may be decomposed, and which may float in addition to the integral works, are not fragments in the literal sense, but abstractions, general formal principles, which vary from the highly abstract (polyphony or homophony) to the epoch-bound (sonata form).

102 For instance, men wearing long pants, a style which arose only after the French Revolution, and which seems to vanish, at least in summer, in our present-day age, with its predilection for the "very casual".

son moves, laughs, frowns (etc.) at the Parisian court? I will leave it at raising these questions without proposing definitive answers. I am a literary scholar by training, so my views may be biased by what I have been doing for decades now. Without being an expert in the field, it is my impression that non-verbal cultural items do float in the cultural net, but in a much less flexible and rapid manner than in the case of textual material, because their floating, based as it is on analogue rather than arbitrary sign systems, is linked to a human substratum displaying or actually transporting them.

It is an implication of this hypothesis that the situation changes radically as soon as the technology of notational encoding of analogue symbolic communication[103] emerges in the electronic age. There is an important predecessor to this development in the age of "simple", analogue duplication: once the technique of shooting and displaying photographs and films was invented, there was no need for humans to travel to distant places in order to discover new styles of body language. It may even be the case that, at least for some time into the future, the species' cultural development will pay more attention to those features of culture whose more general propagation was discouraged heretofore because of their purely analogue encoding, and which have nowadays become as easy to disseminate as was the case with texts in former times.[104]

4.—But what is it that makes the material contained in the net float; what is it that keeps it moving? Thinking again and again about the point made in the introduction, namely that the circulation of cultural material is "in most cases" effected by humans, I am ready to postulate that the formulation "is in *all* cases effected by humans" would not be misconceived. To circulate conceptual forms, one must have human brains to store them, and these brains need human bodies that circulate, thereby causing the circulation of the concepts stored or recorded in them. Material forms—books, paintings, statues—most evidently need humans (sailors, riders, pilots, postmen, etc.) in order to be transported, even if those who do so are not aware of what they are transport-

---

103 The terminology is obviously, once again, Goodman's (*Languages of Art*).
104 My above remarks are meant to apply to music as well, although its reduced circulation in the past was not primarily contingent upon the mode of encoding, but, as explained above (n. 101), on its internal structuration. As to music, there is no intermediate stage of "simple" duplication, but there was likewise no need for such a stage. Since music is (already) notational, it sufficed to transfer it to an easily multipliable and transportable notationally organized medium (discs) in order to drastically increase the circulation of finite musical works in the net even before the inception of the IT era.

ing. And in the case of the present-day electronic circulation of cultural material via the Internet, it would mean falling prey to mythical concepts if one postulated that such circulation occurs "autonomously" or "automatically".[105] The infrastructure (the Internet) is created by humans; the encoding as well as the decoding devices ("computers") are man-made; electric energy on whose availability the floating processes are contingent does not originate from modern descendants of a figure like Prometheus, but needs to be produced by humans. The only difference consists in the fact that not even one of the seven billion members of the species needs to transport her or his body in order to provide access to cultural material circulated via the Internet. The "novelty" is quantitative. The speed of transfer increases dramatically, the quantity of material that is able to be conveyed increases dramatically, and the cost of transfer decreases dramatically. It remains to be seen whether this quantitative "leap" will lead to cultural phenomena whose theorization would lie beyond this book's theoretical frame.

5.—The most difficult point to be tackled in view of the proposed metaphorical field seems to consist in giving a satisfactory answer to the question of the "ontological" status of the cultural net. Is it more of a material phenomenon, or is it merely virtual? I shall leave it to my colleagues in philosophy departments to decide whether my provisional answer—that it seems to be both—is logically viable. The role of mediation device is fulfilled either by human brains (in the case of material circulating in the conceptual mode only) or by material artifacts (in the case of the circulation of items such as paintings, statues, books, or scores). In either case, one is dealing with material "phenomena". As difficult as it might be to conceptualize what we call the "human mind", if it is considered as a "container" in which certain ideas, narratives, poetological rules, etc., are stored and then transported as soon as the body sustaining a particular mind sets itself in motion, there is no reason not to consider the mind as a phenomenal entity.—The difficulty which leads me to suggest, for the point in question, the above transgression of basic logical categories emerges when one asks the question of where cultural items are to be found during times of inactivity: forgotten books in libraries; texts in languages no one is able to understand any more (Egyptian hieroglyphics up to the beginning of the nineteenth century), statues or frescoes covered by ashes (Pompeii up to the eighteenth century)—items that exist, but are not made use of, and which may be reactivated even after a long period of inactivity.

---

105 I remind readers of my above critique of Latour's mystifications (pp. 5–7).

Yet it is evident that such inactive material can be reactivated only in case there is at least some material substratum preserved, otherwise it would belong to that subset of cultural production that is definitively lost.—The quantity of lost material, however, may be less significant from the vantage point of a network theory of culture than one might at first believe against the backdrop of human history as an endless concatenation of conflict and destruction. Cultural material may never die as long as humans exist. At least in its conceptual form, it may survive even after real-world catastrophes of any kind, though not necessarily in its integrity. Survival may occur in fragments, or on the level of highly condensed imaginary narratives (myths), or on the level of abstract concepts reconverted into narrative (religions). In these forms, it continues to float in the cultural net, even if its actual material realizations on the level of single "works" are destroyed. It remains "available" in principle, that is, at hand for reutilization.

This observation may even provide a solution to the logical dilemma articulated above. The items possibly[106] floating in the net seem to have in all cases the character of material phenomena. What differs is the degree of materiality involved in the process of floating, which varies from matter proper (statues) to material substrates of concepts (books, scores), to transporting devices (bodies, brains) for containers of concepts—that is, minds, whose exact description and "ontological" classification is a task still to be accomplished by the natural sciences. Possible and actual circulation would be differentiated with respect to already existing but inactive material by the same factor as in the case of possible and actual artifacts, namely, by an act to be carried out by a human being who thereby renders the material in question ready for circulation: in the case of the "creation" of an actual artifact, writing down the idea of a text, or executing a painting according to an already existent idea, and then divulging the phenomenal items; in the case of the reactivation of a "forgotten" artifact, reading and talking about a book that has been rediscovered,[107] deciphering the hieroglyphics, or uncovering the remains of Pompeii.

6.—If one provisionally accepts the concept of the net for describing the structure of culture, an important consequential point to be discussed is whether or not the term "circulation" is adequate for the description of the processes oc-

---

106 With this adverb I want to highlight that they need not float permanently.
107 I am thinking, e.g., of the rediscovery of what was then called the "Oxford Roland", which occurred in 1835—for nearly eight centuries, the French had been totally ignorant of the text they then started to divulge via the cultural net as their "national" epic and the essence of "francité".

curring within this net structure. An alternative term that is more neutral as to its implications would be "transfer", to be understood in a strictly etymological sense, that is, as a "carrying" (Lat. *ferre*) of a specific object from one place to another, more specifically to a place which is separated from the initial site of the object by a (semantic, that is, conceptual) border, so that the "carrying" is considered not just as a movement, but as a significant change of location.—As already mentioned in passing, the problem involved with the term "circulation" primarily consists in the fact that processes of cultural transfer are not in all cases circular. Very frequently, a certain "portion" of cultural material is transposed from one place or context to another, where it becomes recontextualized. In most cases, processes of cultural contact do not, indeed, remain unilateral, even if the partners involved are clearly distinguished within a hierarchy of power or of prestige, as in the cases of England and India or France and Russia in the period at issue here. So a certain "reverse flow" of cultural material is the more or less inevitable implication even of processes of cultural subjugation. But one has to consider the possibility that what flows back is incongruous with what first flowed forth. Processes of transfer might consequently be considered the initiators of processes of circulation, with the qualification, however, that the latter encompass much larger sections of the entire cultural field than the one within which the initial transfer took place. The "exportation" of an instance of high culture may be reciprocated by an importation of a variety of instances of popular culture. The exportation of a text may lead to the importation of various performative practices. And, very frequently, the circulatory process, even if it occurs in the literal sense of the term, is stretched out over time in such a way that the material floating back has undergone substantive changes as a consequence of its having been recontextualized. A paradigm for this latter case would be the "transfer" of late nineteenth- and early twentieth-century Russian drama (Chekhov and Tolstoy) to Western Europe, which would not have been possible without the previous transfer of (a Germanized variant of) French court theater to eighteenth-century Russia. But the material flowing back had evolved into a completely new variant of the genre, making its former, imported origins almost unrecognizable. Similarly, it was not in the nineteenth, but only in the second half of the twentieth century that the much more body-oriented cultural practices of traditional Indian performance culture were imported by Western theatrical culture, bringing about a quite radical transformation of the cultural pattern of staged performances which one hundred and fifty years earlier had been "exported" to India in the context of a configuration of imperialism.

To put it in a more abstract way: all processes of circulation occur within the frame of what we call time. One may discuss the question of whether or not a merely material and lifeless object—e.g., a certain quantity of raw material—still is the same after having performed, or rather undergone, a process of circulation. Any pragmatically reasonable answer to this somewhat sophistic question would have to take into consideration the amount of time spent on the circulatory movement and the level of organization of the material under scrutiny. The fundamental elements out of which our world is made, the atoms, or rather the particles constituting them, stay stable for very long periods of time. The higher the level of organization, the more the material in question is affected by the time span involved in circulatory processes. Ore is less affected than steel, steel is less affected than a product consisting of steel (for instance, an automobile), and highly organized, but merely material objects are much less affected than cultural items, which only become "objects"—even if they exist as material forms (paintings, written texts)—by being submitted to a process we call decoding or interpretation and which is, on behalf of this feature, always dependent on specific conditions that apply only to the one respective act of reception. —For all of these reasons, it may in principle be questionable to make use of the term "circulation", since it implies that what finally gets back to where it came from is, at least in substance, still the same as when the circulatory process was initiated.

It follows from the points just made that the problem is to a certain extent liable to variations contingent upon the perspective from which the cultural scenario in question is viewed. If not systematically, one would at least from a pragmatic perspective consider the points mentioned above as almost negligible in case the scenario consists of one specific linguistic community within a rather short time span. With regard to late sixteenth- and early seventeenth-century English dramatic and theatrical culture, it certainly does make sense to consistently apply the concept of circulation when describing processes of cultural activity occurring within this frame.[108] If, however, the scenario at stake is all of Europe; if, in addition, the historical period in question is the one in which Europe extended its power and culture over the entire globe; and if, thirdly, the processes observed cannot be limited to the period primarily considered, since they triggered medium- and long-term reverse effects, it may be less adequate to indiscriminately[109] apply the concept of circulation.

---

108 The reference here is obviously to the research done by Greenblatt on Shakespearean drama and theater.

109 —which implies that (as may be extrapolated from my formulations so far) in many *specific* cases the term of circulation might reasonably be made use of.

At least provisionally, the phenomena of cultural dynamics considered within this book, as well as the questions at issue here, seem to speak for the suitability of the suggested metaphor of the net. Within networks, movements of mere transport or transfer may occur. There may also be circulatory movements. And, most importantly, there may be indirect circular movements, that is, processes which take place only because there have been previous processes of movement, while the latter do not have any "organic" or content-bound relation to the former. The main descriptive and explanatory achievement of the metaphor proposed seems to be that it does not refer to specific configurations of procedural instantiations, but rather describes a structure enabling a large variety of such processes to take place.

Nodes and Contact Zones

0.—Readers will have realized at this point that my approach implies not only a critical, but also a polemical stance vis-à-vis the traditional concept of "national literature"; in Part III, there will be a detailed discussion of the underlying assumptions.[110] If one rejects the notion of an essentially compartmentalized cultural and literary "landscape", there remains, however, the question of how to conceptualize the trans-"national" structures within which the "transculturation" of items originally related to one specific cultural framework actually does take place. There are two existing approaches to the question which require some attention, not only with respect to their differences, but also with respect to their basic commonalities, which will be the points I will be arguing against from the vantage point of my theoretical metaphor.

1.—The first one, propagated by leftist cultural theory and taking—according to its Marxist basis—a globalized stance towards the question of cultural production, differentiates between center and periphery, while inverting the traditional evaluative hierarchy linked to these terms. But does this argumentative pattern have any relevance beyond the political sphere from which it is derived? There are many examples which are contrary to the assumption—which has become a sort of standard indicator of "political correctness"—that artifacts created by the "subaltern", by people residing at the "periphery", or by people belonging to "minorities" of various profile, are by necessity "better" than artifacts created by aristocratic or middle-class people from the Western

---

110 See pp. 232–250.

metropoles who do not belong to a minority or for whom belonging to a minority is without significant importance as regards their self-description.[111]

On the other hand, from my theoretical perspective, positions diametrically opposed to leftist cultural theory, the most prominent one in recent times being Pascale Casanova's,[112] seem questionable as well, though not to the same extent. The positive characteristic of Casanova's theory which needs to be mentioned is that her criterion of quality is not explicitly ideological in the sense of an unveiled partisan profile, but, rather, descriptive. It is the good old parameter of success and impact, which, of course, is not totally free of ideological implications. It has its roots in Calvinist theology.[113] A leftist critique would object—in congruence with Marx's *dictum* "The ideas of the ruling class are [...] the ruling ideas"[114]—that it is not astonishing to see great powers promote their cultural products and try to spread them. But the limitations of Marx's famous formula become apparent when taking into consideration the at times tremendous impact of texts that do not derive from imperial centers and their cultural agents—the most prominent example being the Bible—and also of texts that originate from former centers which have lost their metropolitan status in the course of history (classical Greek texts in Roman times, *matière de Bretagne* texts after the destruction of Celtic culture and its sites, etc.).

Casanova's basically descriptive approach enables her to see what leftist theory has to relegate to the background on behalf of its own premises: "great" works

---

111 If there were a discussion between leftist cultural theoreticians and the (small) rest of scholars who work in the field—in fact, there is none—it would quickly turn out that the entire controversy is about what the term "better" might mean. From the standpoint of partisans of "revolution", every deed, work, etc. that favors the expected revolutionary process is "good", while everything that emblematizes an indifferent or even a reactionary or retrograde tendency is "bad". So, finally, there is no discussion necessary; it suffices to agree that political convictions differ and that everyone writes for his or her own audience.
112 *The World Republic of Letters*, M. B. DeBevoise (tr.), Cambridge, MA and London 2004.
113 Calvinism is a derivative of theological nominalism as described in this book on various occasions: if God's will cannot be legitimately extrapolated from Scripture, since He is free to change it, it can, however, be abstracted from what has happened, since even God is not able to change the past. The believer whose life has been successful can be sure that he has lived in accordance with God's will. The future, however, is open. For this reason, the devout Calvinist does (nearly) everything and anything to stay successful in the present as well, and he does this until the end of his life. Abstracted from its theological horizon and thus fit to be adopted by worshippers of other religions, as well as by agnostics and atheists, Calvinism is the ideological basis of US-American society, down to the minute details of everyday behavior, such as body language.
114 See *Die deutsche Ideologie* (1845), in: *Marx-Engels Werke*, 43 vols., Berlin [GDR] 1956–1990, vol. 3, p. 35.

may originate indiscriminately from "centers" as well as from "peripheries", and they may be conceived by members of an elite as well as by members of the marginalized strata of a given social community. Her insistence on the indispensable role and function of "centers" and on cultural rituals like "consecration" might be, however, informed to a problematic extent by her culture of origin—which is, to date, a secular analogue of the structural features of the Roman Catholic Church.[115]

As far as net theories are concerned, metropoles have come to be qualified by the metaphor of the "node".[116] In addition, there is the concept of "contact zones",[117] which to my knowledge has not been adapted to the vocabulary of the net as yet. What the two concepts have in common is the assumption that there are privileged sites of cultural production as well as less privileged ones. The concept of the contact zone may be conceived of as a supplement to Casanova's theory as well as to the dominant leftist theories. It provides answers to the question of how people (in this case authors) or texts from the periphery might get access to the metropole, that is, to the places where "consecration" may happen or where they might enter the radius of attention of the "revolutionary intellectuals" who typically reside in the metropoles.

2.—I shall not attempt to contest the existence of such nodes, nor challenge the idea of contact zones. In the early modern age, cities like Paris, Madrid, and London were immensely important sites of cultural production. And I have already had the occasion to stress that geographical and cultural regions of unstable and fluctuating status, such as early modern Italy—a country where Spanish, German, and French cultures literally met, a "zone" where "contacts" actually happened—held a prominent role in terms of literary, specifically dramatic production. The point in question is whether such places and regions are automatically favored and, if so, in what exactly the privilege consists.

My skeptical attitude towards the concepts of nodes and contact zones[118] starts from the observation that they are both inspired by variants of network struc-

---

115 I have to admit that my approach may be conditioned, perhaps even a bit more than useful, by my background, that is, a "cultural nation" that is basically polycentric and whose borders are not congruent with political borders, in essence a somewhat "fluid" and unstable entity. I thus consider my remarks to be just one further facet that might be added to a debate with those who are ready to engage in mutual intellectual exchange.
116 See Vilashini Cooppan, "Codes for World Literature: Network Theory and the Imaginary Field", in: Joachim Küpper (ed.), *Approaches to World Literature*, Berlin 2013, pp. 103–119.
117 First introduced by Mary Louise Pratt (*Imperial Eyes: Travel Writing and Transculturation*, London 1992).
118 As suggested above, I consider both concepts to be specific instantiations of an overarching concept of "privileged zones".

tures which have a stable physical substratum. There are, of course, such nodes in road and railroad networks, in electricity grids, and in canal systems, as well as in nets constructed for communication purposes. But as to the latter variant, the privileged status of nodes exists only in the case of the—as I shall call them—classical communication networks, such as caravanserais, postal systems, telephone systems, and broadcast systems. The metaphorical resource for my attempt at theorizing the problems at issue is, however, the present-day web, the Internet, which seems not to have attained its definitive structure as yet. As far as I understand it, certain nodal centers (servers) are necessary, at least at the present (2016) stage of technological development, in order to keep the information in the net circulating. But there seems to be one major difference with respect to the role nodes held in previous information-net structures. There is (still) the need for a physical, material basis in order to uphold the circulation processes. The "nodes", however, can quite easily be substituted by other ones, or by a connection between a few other ones, in case they are inactivated (when destroyed by an enemy force, or switched off by the power that controls the specific node). This difference dramatically affects the profile of data flow in such a net. Nodes become de-territorialized and "ephemeralized"; circulation is facilitated; control becomes difficult. This holds true for the information circulated as well as for the information extracted from the net. I do not want to endorse the somewhat naïve picture of a world of unrestricted communication propounded by some IT proponents. But there is no denying that the present day electronic web has changed things with respect to an era in which it sufficed to control or destroy one central point of a road or railroad network, of a post system or of a telephone or broadcast network, in order to regulate, inhibit, or even interrupt the flow of items for a considerable time. What is taking place today is certainly not a complete "de-materialization" of the web; it might just be a huge and very rapidly taken step within a long process of de-materialization of man-made nets, which is so significant that we sense its consequences more immediately than in former times characterized by a very slow decrease of network physicality.[119]

---

[119] I hope that what I wish to convey is not all too cryptic. In the case of traditional networks, too, it was possible to replace nodes that were destroyed or came under enemy control. It is possible to replace the pumping device which regulates the flow of a canal system; but to do that takes time. It is possible to replace a central railroad station, or the crossing of several different motorways, or a central post office, or the operators' headquarters of an old-fashioned telephone system. But in all these cases, the material, physical work to be done is significant, and the time it takes to make the replacement effectual is considerable. This said, there is a decreasing line with respect to both parameters according to technological progress and the concrete inventions linked to it; it takes much more effort to repair a centrally damaged canal system than to repair the headquarters of a telephone system. But the truly important

3.—This recent technological development might provide a more adequate metaphor for describing the processes of cultural transfer and exchange under discussion here. The commonalities seem to consist in two points of distinct order: firstly, cultural nets as here theorized differ from traditional information networks in that they do not rely on one specific material mediation device, but rather on a wide range of highly diverse vehicles; as to physicality in the strict sense, this feature also distinguishes them from present-day IT networks, since the latter make use of one specific physical medium only, namely, radio waves or electricity. In terms of structure, it is this feature that endows cultural networks with exactly that extremely high flexibility which is characteristic of electronic networks in contrast to previous matter-bound network systems— which derives, in the case of electronic nets, not from the multiplicity of mediation devices, but from their reduced physicality. The second feature cultural networks share with electronic networks, and which differentiates them from classical information networks, is the erratic and unpredictable proportion of the information transferred on the one hand to the effect of this information on the other. As in the case of the first commonality mentioned, the "reasons" behind this shared quality differ. With respect to IT, it is mainly based on a consequential feature of the reduced physicality of the mediating devices, namely, the possibility of a very high number of potential recipients gaining access to the information in question; in the case of the cultural net, it is, once again, not primarily the convenience of access, but rather the potential for rapid diffusion, based on the variety of mediating devices, which explains the astonishing disproportion between cause and effect (the quantity of information actually transferred and the quantity of acts of "extraction").

These two features come close to invalidating the dichotomies of "center" and "periphery" and of "nodes" and "strings", the critical components of all classical information systems. Or, to put this argument in the terminology used by the approaches criticized in this chapter: culturally relevant "contacts" may occur anywhere where one mediating device (typically a human mind) comes into contact with another. There are certainly privileged places where such contacts may occur more frequently; but as to the actual result, it seems to be of no importance whether a contact occurs in a "contact zone" or at a random place. As to the worldwide dissemination of Christianity's holy book, it seems to have been Paul's reconsideration of the "Gentile" tradition, which occurred at Ephesus, rather than his subsequent missions to Athens and Rome, the relevant contact zones of that age, which marks the decisive step. And as to the

---

leap seems to have been taken only in present times, when it suffices to change the computer directories, if one server is damaged, in order to reset the entire system.

dichotomy of periphery and center, it is not the differentiation as such which seems to be questionable; it is, rather, the assumed difference it entails with regard to the impact factor which evidences the extent to which both Casanova and standard leftist cultural theory fall prey, on behalf of their own premises, to what one may call "the hierarchical fallacy". Places, concepts, and artistic forms at the top of the cultural hierarchy remain in this position for (very) short periods of human cultural history only. The constant and finally uncontrollable circulation of all cultural material in a limitless and decentered network is at the origin of a permanent shifting of "hierarchical" structures pertaining to culture in general, but even more so to de-pragmatized cultural products (artistic works)—which enjoy, on behalf of this characteristic, a control on the part of the "hierarchs" that is in many cases somewhat more benign than in the case of cultural products of a more serious, pragmatically relevant profile.

4.—I should like to illustrate my view by referring to an example given on various occasions in this book because it is so telling with regard to cultural exchange in its specificity. In order to "transfer" early modern French, English, and German culture to Russia,[120] there was no need to build an infrastructure for the transfer, to construct nodes, to rely on the specific capacities, in terms of activities of exchange, of contact zones, or to provide for points of access, let alone to have the transported material "consecrated" by an academy, etc. It sufficed to organize one (unhappy) imperial marriage, and the entire development began almost automatically. The female partner involved was a German princess from a small principality whose education was French and who became known in later times as Catherine the Great. The consequences of this single and random example of exchange were enormous.[121] I leave it to the competency of specialists to assess the quality of Russian plays of the eighteenth century written in emulation of the "imported" plays in terms of aesthetic quality and sophistication. But no one will contest that the quality of the works written by the heirs of the tradition initiated by the event referred to above match the highest standards of world literature. And would it be sensible

---

120 I should stress that drama and theater as a specific item of culture had already been introduced to Russia some decades before (I will elaborate on that point in Part III). But the pervasive "Europeanization" of Russia commenced only in the above-characterized period.
121 Must I stress that they by far transcend the sphere of the fine arts? The all-encompassing Westernization of the country—basically, its reorganization according to the ideals of the French and German Enlightenment—also paved the way for leftist political theories to make their way into Russia. Assuming that Leninism and Stalinism would hardly have been able to emerge without the cultural process described above, a point I shall discuss in detail in a later chapter becomes evident: cultural exchange is by no means a "good" thing as such. As everything human, it is ambivalent. What counts is that it is a reality informing humans' existence.

to say that the quality of the plays written in the nineteenth century metropoles, in Paris and London, is higher than that of those written by Chekhov?

Significant urban centers of cultural production do not last forever. They are even more ephemeral than their political counterparts. For a given city to become such a cultural center, it is requisite for a number of acclaimed works to be produced there during a specific time period. To take, for example, the case of Germany, it sufficed that two great minds settled in the only mentionable town of a tiny principality (i.e. Weimar) with negligible economic and military power, and then attuned themselves to the European cultural network of the period, while producing works that circulated in and were acclaimed by that network, for that principality to become a cultural center of world-literary prominence. Since cultural items, and specifically digitized and multipliable ones, such as books, are almost universally available, it is not economic and military power or population size that establishes a given area as a cultural center, but rather the productivity of those of its residents linked to the net.[122]

5.—The purpose of my examples has been to demonstrate the sense in which Casanova's theories are biased by the specific situation of the most centralized (nation-)state in human history—France.[123] But it should be noted that my argument likewise applies to the above-mentioned conceptions prominent in cultural studies. As unnecessary as it is to reside in a center in order to contribute to the cultural net, it is just as possible to do so if one does reside in a metropole as if one does not. Peripheral status does not inhibit, but it also does not favor successful contribution to the net. Works considered "great" in later times might have been assembled in Paris, Madrid, or London, in culturally "underdeveloped" places such as eighteenth-century Moscow, in marginal places such as

---

[122] I should like to add that the same line of argument seems to apply to a non-artistic variant of cultural activity we typically call research or scholarship. In order to write an outstanding book, one need not reside in a metropole, not even in a scientific or scholarly metropole (which are in many cases, not least for the reasons mentioned above, *not* located in the "real" metropoles). Very many eminent scholars of world renown began their careers at small and rather unknown universities. Erich Auerbach wrote *Mimesis*, in my view the most important work of literary history published in the twentieth century, while living as a refugee in Istanbul. The connectivity to the cultural net he had at his disposal was almost exclusively based on what was stored in his own memory.

[123] There was a (fortunately ephemeral) radicalization of the French model of centralization in twentieth-century totalitarian states, namely, the Soviet Union and Nazi Germany; during the period of the regimes in question, there were, indeed, no other places of relevant cultural production in the respective states than Moscow or Berlin. As may be gathered from the scenario of a totalitarianism in reluctant transition, namely that of mainland China, cultural production becomes cautiously decentralized at the very moment of a general relaxation of the system.

nineteenth-century Copenhagen or Oslo, in early modern provincial towns (in times when the province was truly "provincial") such as Bordeaux, or in very small places—not much more than a market-place or a castle and some individual houses—such as Stratford-upon-Avon. The only thing needed to produce literary texts, even outstanding ones, is a mind capable of doing the job[124] and the possibility to connect to what I call the cultural net, which in the era I am talking about is typically based on the actual availability of a number of books, or on the fact that such books were read by the great mind in question in the past. In the age before script and print,[125] the connectivity might have been based on items such as a conversation with a traveler who had listened to a minstrel's presentation in a nearby castle, or it may have been established by way of a

---

124 This formulation might appear at first sight to be a relapse into a Romantic theory of ingenuity; it is meant, however, as an abbreviation of what I shall expound in detail in the chapter on "Control and Demand"; it refers to someone who—for whatever reason—succeeds in assembling an artwork that meets the demands of its time.

125 This might be the appropriate moment to explain why I do not make use of the concepts of "archive" and of "accessing archives" in order to metaphorically convey how processes of cultural production may be conceptualized. In its literal acceptation, the term "archive" is bound to a relatively recent phase of the species' history, whereas my concept of cultural production is meant to be characteristic of the species right from the beginning (as to details, see below, pp. 82 f.); one might, however, think of liberating the term from this implication by using it in a metaphorical way. But what can hardly be discarded, even if one suggests taking the term metaphorically, are the basic structural characteristics of archives, which are at odds with my conceptualization of cultural processes. It is not primarily the fact that an archive is a "real" (physically existent) rather than a virtual structure which prevents me from integrating the concept into my design; in very recent times, virtual archives have indeed emerged. It is rather the role of systematic ordering principles and of clear-cut intentionality that have led me to avoid the concept of archive. Cultural networks are only in very recent times based on the concrete intentions of those who establish them; in most cases, even in the present, they are by-products of the deployment of power techniques (conquest or dynastic alliances), of economic processes (trade and exchange), of migration triggered by external factors (climate change, overpopulation), or of cultural imperialism that is not based on concrete "archival" material, but rather on ideological convictions (general world-interpreting schemata, in former times mainly in the form of religions or philosophical schools, in more recent times in the form of normative anthropological and evolutionary conceptualizations such as "human rights" or "progress"). What may be even more important: in almost all cases, cultural networks are based on quite a few of these transfer structures; they are a fortuitous and erratic combination of various instrumentalizations of a parasitic kind. As such, they almost totally lack the primary characteristic of archives: systematic organization.—Need I make explicit that (actual) archives may play a role, at times an important one, in cultural production, specifically over the last 2,500 years? But if they do so, it is as *part* of the network structures I am trying to theorize here. Archives are one of many components of cultural networks, and, as said, not a necessary one.

ship-wrecked warrior who narrated his past endeavors to his loyal wife and adult son after having returned home at the end of a journey of no less than twenty years.[126]—The question of whether or not artifacts first emerging in places considered peripheral to the world of their time benefit from a wider diffusion via the cultural net is certainly contingent to a certain extent upon the cultural activities of the politically and economically ruling elite.[127] Additionally, however, it depends on a factor that I will call "demand", which is difficult to stimulate or direct, since it relies on a multiplicity of conditions which become systematically describable only in retrospect.[128]

Processes and Rationales of Assembly

0.—Setting aside for the present a further and more detailed discussion of the conditions of access to the cultural net, I should like to engage in some hypothesizing concerning the question of how "working with the net" actually functions.

1.—Were I to describe the processes that lead to the emergence of a work of art in the metaphorical terms suggested in this book, this might result in formulations such as the following: Driven by a momentary inspiration gathered from a conversation, something read, or something viewed—that is, in my terminology, by connecting to the material floating in the virtual net of culture—the author or artist conceives a project for a work of his own. He then consciously but tentatively extracts a variety of content-related and formal material from the net, meaning: everything he has read or heard of that might be pertinent

---

126 —by which I do not wish to convey that the actual person behind the name "Homer" is in fact Penelope or Telemachus; but if we assume that the *Iliad* and the *Odyssey* are based on an authentic substratum consisting of wars fought in territories far away from the small islands surrounding mainland Greece, it would not be unreasonable to consider a survivor, such as the one known by the name of Odysseus, to have been the agent of an enormous cultural transfer from the highly developed Asia Minor to the remote provinces of northwestern Greece.
127 This is the assumption that leftist cultural theory and Casanova's more "conservative" approach have in common.
128 Neglect of this latter factor—that success in the past by no means guarantees success in the future—, or, to put it in different terms, the underestimation of the erratic course of cultural history, indicates that, notwithstanding the basic criterion described by me above as "Calvinist", Cassanova's entire approach is informed not by nominalistic theology, but rather by the traditional (Catholic) approach of attempting to "match" God's intentions by imitating the order of the universe created by Him. Theological nominalism would object that an omnipotent God is free to change His will, including the order of His creation, at any point in time, so that any project intended to secure lasting success by way of imitating what He has done in the past is illusory.

to his initial idea. Next, he starts provisionally assembling this diverse material with the goal of creating something that is at the same time "novel" and constitutes a compelling unity (a "work") on the level of content as well as on the level of form. He reworks the assembled material again and again, while adding to the mix further components drawn from the items floating in the net, and possibly rejecting some of the material he withdrew previously; when he arrives at the impression that the result may be made public, he terminates his work.

2.—In order to explain this idea in greater detail, I shall propose to differentiate between three steps in the net-bound "creation" of a work of art. The first step is based on the state of being connected to the cultural net,[129] which results in the possibility of a "withdrawal" of circulating material. Since human minds are, from my perspective, components of the cultural net, the object of the withdrawal can be, apart from "external" material, items stored in the author's own memory. This step may be subdivided into what is traditionally called the "inspiration"[130] (a "first idea") and the subsequent more detailed conceptualization of the work to be created. The main feature differentiating the "artistic" variant of net-connectivity from the regular and quasi-permanent state of being connected to the cultural net is the conscious intention of extracting not random, but specific material with the aim of reassembling it, that is to say, the attitude of approaching the circulating material with a view to selecting and reusing it in order to produce "new" items.

In both cases ("inspiration"; conceptualization), the choices actually made seem to obey a logic of need or demand. In view of my entire approach, I have

---

[129] It would necessitate detailed discussions to decide whether, as beings endowed with what we call consciousness or mind, there are any situations at all in which a specific person is *not* connected to the cultural net. As we were taught by Freud, even in moments of sleep we go on conceptualizing—meaning: drawing on previous material—though disassembling and then reassembling it in a fashion not allowed in the daytime. And even when we have the impression of simply letting the phenomena we perceive "directly" interact with our psyche (when contemplating a beautiful landscape, for instance), we are inevitably bound to certain pre-existing parameters of perception and association. It may be that, in situations of hard physical labor, namely in situations of modern, fragmented, industrial labor as theorized by Marx with the formula of *entfremdete Arbeit* ("alienated labor"), there is conscious human activity which could arguably be said to take place without being connected to the material floating in the cultural net. The repetitive labor routine would deactivate the "working" of the mind. But, for all other real-life situations thinkable, I would posit that humans are indeed consistently and permanently connected to the cultural net (even before they became hybrids of regular bodies and smartphones, as I allow myself to add in an ironic mode).
[130] —not by the Muses, of course, but by something that is floating in the cultural net.

to insist on this point: the primary factor that "shapes" artistic works is demand; control—the active influencing of cultural items by external agents of political, religious, or economic power—is, indeed, a very important factor, but it is nevertheless a secondary one.

To give two examples from the period investigated: the "extraction", on the part of famous Baroque operas,[131] of mythical fables, e.g. the story of Orpheus and Eurydice, or of "historical" plots, e.g. the story of a love affair between Caesar and the Egyptian Queen Cleopatra, is primarily motivated by the creators' desire to elevate the genre introduced by them, which arose from previous courtly multimedia performances, to an artistic dignity comparable to "serious" drama, and to endow it with the prestige of humanistic culture. The choice of Shakespeare's *Hamlet* as a "source" for one of the first two dramas ever written in the Russian language,[132] Sumarokov's *Gamlet* (1748),[133] is primarily motivated by its author's prestige, which Sumarokov exploits in order to promote himself in his role as a not-yet-established playwright; secondly, by the fact that relying on an English play was apt to impede the danger against which the "founding" of serious drama in the Russian language was meant to react, namely of French cultural hegemony; and, thirdly, by the fact that the wild plot of bloody dynastic struggle taking place in a Northern European kingdom resonated with the real-world experience of the intended audience, the Russian court society of a century that saw several tsars or tsarinas overthrown, imprisoned, or even violently put to death.

---

131 I am referring to Jacopo Peri's and Ottavio Rinuccini's *Orfeo e Euridice* (1600), commonly held to be the first (or, after their *Dafne*, which is no longer extant as a whole, the second) opera ever in the occidental tradition, and to Händel's *Giulio Cesare in Egitto* (1723/4).

132 The term (early modern) "drama" is meant, here as elsewhere—if not specified otherwise—to refer to the genre (re-)emerging in the Renaissance. In Russia, as in many premodern societies, there were, before the times in consideration above, pantomimic street performances with a farcical profile. In addition, in the course of the seventeenth century, there were religious plays in the vein I call in this book "dramatized catechism" or "dramatized biblical history", plays dealing, for example, with the biblical account of King Nebuchadnezzar, or of Artaxerxes, or with the New Testament Parable of the Prodigal Son. I do not comment on these plays, since it is evident that they perfectly conform to what I otherwise say about the material floating in the cultural net.

133 See in particular Kirill Ospovat, "The Catharsis of Prosecution: Royal Violence, Poetic Justice, and Public Emotion in the Russian *Hamlet* (1748)", in: Katja Gvozdeva, Tatiana Korneeva, and Kirill Ospovat (eds.), *Dramatic Experience: The Poetics of Drama and the Early Modern Public Sphere(s)*, Leiden and Boston, MA 2017, pp. 189–219.

3.–The next step, and the one on which I would like to focus in the present chapter, I shall refer to as the stage of "assembly",[134] meaning: of synthesizing the material available in order to produce a new work—as opposed to merely reproducing or receiving an existing work, which is the "standard" use made of the material floating in the cultural net and which, for reasons of the relative simplicity of the processes involved,[135] shall not be considered here in detail. The two examples just given are apt to illustrate a thesis that is crucial from the perspective of my approach: in the creation of new works, one is not dealing with "organic" processes—processes that constitute a prolongation, or an "unfolding", of something that was already there—but with the putting together of elements which seem at times, considered individually, not to fit together at all. In the opera by Jacopo Peri and Ottavio Rinuccini alluded to above, the tragic outcome of the story as transmitted by Virgil and Ovid is replaced by a happy ending, that is, an element taken from available material usually labeled "comedy" or "fairy tale"; after Orpheus' descent into Hades, the mythical couple returns to the world above and goes on living together in love and hap-

---

134 I have a preference for the term "assembly", since it seems apt to stress what I am foregrounding here: the production of art as *techne*, not as based on an ecstatic state—*mania*—, and, consequently, not as an instance of truth (*aletheia*), but rather of didactics, entertainment, and reflection at the same time (the order of these functional dimensions is intentionally alphabetical; in terms of hierarchy, it is liable to change with periods, genres, and the audiences targeted).—One might think of further, somewhat "technical" metaphors in order to adequately conceptualize what I wish to convey (fusing; melding; smelting; alloying; blending; amalgamating). The main reason I suggest the term "assembly" is the fact that texts, quite like industrial products produced by assembly lines, allow the recipient who wishes to do so to identify the different components out of which they have been assembled. The more "chemical" metaphors enumerated above may suggest a homogeneity of the final product which affects the "substance" as such, whereas, according to my view, the homogeneity of an artwork is always, in the final analysis, a composite one.

135 The qualification of reception processes given above is, of course, a simplification. As is known from the discussions initiated by the theoretical paradigm of reader-response theory (*Rezeptionsästhetik*), every reception is an interpretation of its own, the "originality" of which might be no less great than in case of the creation of a "new" work. This problem is of particular importance for all genres that necessarily call for an interpretation *before* being committed to regular reception, as in the case of theater. This said, I should like to insist on the position that the creation of a novel work is something qualitatively different from the interpretation of a work already existing, albeit not as different as it was conceived within traditional (Romantic, pre-*Rezeptionsästhetik*) art theory. If every act of "authentic" creation is, indeed, no less based on pre-existing material floating in the cultural net than "mere" reception, the main difference would consist in that between the attitude of (only) wishing to understand what is already existing on the one hand, and the ambition to transform what already exists and to give the result of the transformation an explicit articulation on the other.

piness.¹³⁶ Something similar occurs in Sumarokov's *Gamlet*: the usurper is put to death; the disloyal mother and queen repents her past actions; the eponymous figure does not die in the final imbroglio; instead, with Ophelia at his side, he assumes his role as the legitimate heir to the throne.

As to the logic of such at first sight somewhat astonishing combinations of preexistent material, the question of need and demand seems to call for further elaboration. In the case of the first opera ever written, the pragmatic configuration of its premiere was a royal wedding, namely, the courtly feast on the occasion of Maria de Medici's ascension to the rank of Queen of France. The context of Sumarokov's *Gamlet* was the end of the dynastic turmoil that had been shaking Russia for decades, with the accession of the "legal" heir, Elizabeth, to the throne.¹³⁷ In both cases, it is the festive context with a view to which the "new" works were assembled that likely accounts for the disassembly of the "tragic" endings and their substitution by a more joyful resolution of the plot. It should be added that in the case of cultured recipients, such erratic processes of assembling very heterogeneous elements—tragedy and fairy tale—permit the introduction of unarticulated subtexts which may be essential to the message as a whole. In the case of the royal wedding, the audience's consciousness of the original plot may have served as a reminder of the transiency of fortune and marital happiness.¹³⁸ The subtext works in the direction of a stabilization of

---

136 As to this opera, see also Déborah Blocker, "The Accademia degli Alterati and the Invention of a New Form of Dramatic Experience: Myth, Allegory, and Theory in Jacopo Peri's and Ottavio Rinuccini's *Euridice* (1600)", in: Gvozdeva et al. (eds.), *Dramatic Experience*, pp. 77–117.
137 Elizabeth was Peter the Great's daughter. The problem that caused the turmoil mentioned was Peter's own stipulation that succession should no longer be based on blood; the ruling tsar should rather be free to choose his own successor. Elizabeth was finally successful in reasserting the traditional genealogical succession.
138 A reworking of the Ovidian material which is both parallel in structure and partly analogous as to intent is the Christian allegorization of the story of Orpheus and Eurydice as documented from the twelfth-century *Ovide moralisé* onward. Eurydice, representing the human soul, is freed by her husband, Jesus Christ, from the bonds of death by his "song"—the divine *logos*. She is allowed to return to life with him, with the qualification that she does not look "back" upon hell. ("¿Qué importa que ellos la lleven, / si siempre que ella inconstante / pequé y tú el rostro la vuelvas / ha de volver a mí cárcel?"/ "What does it matter if they [Orpheus-Christ and his companions] lead her [Eurydice] out of hell, if she, inconstant as ever, relapses into sin and you make her turn her head backwards, so that she has to return to my prison?") The quote is from Calderón's "divinization" of the pagan myth, but the idea is not his own. It can be traced back to the above-mentioned medieval allegorizations of pagan myth (*El divino Orfeo* [the 1663 version], in: *Obras completas*, Ángel Valbuena Prat [ed.], Madrid 1952–1959, vol. 3, pp. 1835–1855; quote: p. 1854 b). The personage speaking is the Devil; the one whom

the context of power within which the opera's first representation took place. In a feudal society, political power is bound to the institution of marriage; legitimacy is based on birth. Even in moments of festive happiness, a monarch should never forget that human life might end abruptly. He should always keep in mind that, in order to guarantee the kingdom's stability, he has to provide for situations of reversals of fortune such as sudden, accidental death, since he and his spouse are living in a world where (earthly) resurrection may only occur in fictional plots.—The same might apply to Sumarokov's play: having the Shakespearean original in mind, the spectators would not have forgotten that a small portion of poison, administered at the right moment and at the right place, may completely overturn a configuration of serene stability and lead to situations of civil war and conquest by enemies.

4.—It should be emphasized that in the case of cultural artifacts, the metaphor of "assembly" differs from what is suggested by the proper meaning of the term for the simple reason that the (relative, historically varying, but always given) autonomy of artworks allows for the synthesis of items whose diversity by far transcends the dimension typically attained within regular processes of assembly, as in industrial production.[139] If the products of construction are in any case subject to the imperative that there must be people who are ready to "buy" them, the margins for what is acceptable are incommensurably higher for de-pragmatized than for pragmatic goods. This configuration implies that (artistic) cultures may be at the same time thoroughly intertwined, on behalf of their connection to the universal cultural net, and extremely diverse as to the actual cultural items produced.

---

he addresses ("tú") and who is said to be able to make Eurydice act so as to be obliged to return to hell is, most probably, his companion, the allegory of "envidia"/envy, whose power is countered by the "nave de la Iglesia", which the bride of Orpheus-Christ boards at the end of the trip. The oblique allusion to the original story serves as a reminder of the fact that a "sad" outcome continues to be a potentiality. For a detailed presentation of Calderón's text, including the previous reception history of the pagan myth at its basis, see my *Discursive Renovatio in Lope de Vega and Calderón. Studies on Spanish Baroque Drama. With an Excursus on the Evolution of Discourse in the Middle Ages, the Renaissance, and Mannerism*, Berlin and Boston, MA 2017, chap. 3.

139 —which is the sphere from which the term "assembly" originates. Industrial production is, however, nothing but a highly efficient stage of a cultural practice existing since the inception of the species' cultural activities: putting objects together which do *not* co-occur in the natural world (e.g. a wooden rod, a stone, and some sinew taken from an animal to fix the contraption) in order to create a new object which is meant to better fulfill certain desirable purposes.

I should like to illustrate this feature by reference to a striking example: as I shall stress on various occasions, we do not know exactly to what extent there was a circulation of cultural material between premodern Europe and premodern China; but given the fact that there have always been mediated trade relations, it is highly probable that certain similarities between early modern European drama and Chinese performing arts of the same age are based on transfer rather than polygenesis. The (late sixteenth- or early seventeenth-century) Chinese opera entitled in translation *The Peony Pavilion*, a work still performed today on stage,[140] displays a plethora of motifs which are very familiar to a reader of Calderón, in particular of *La vida es sueño* and, perhaps even more significantly, of *El mágico prodigioso*. While the difficulty or inability to distinguish between dream and reality might be less pertinent in this respect, since the idea is widespread, the motifs of "death", "resurrection" (or reappearing as a ghost), and sexual encounters without the loss of virginity, all to be found in the Chinese play, are close to what is perhaps Calderón's most extravagant *comedia*. This said, the resulting pieces are highly dissimilar. Calderón's play is, as is always the case with this author, a Christian didactic drama, propagating the ethical imperative of *obrar bien* and demonstrating that God is ultimately "stronger" than the Devil and his many human agents. The Chinese opera, by contrast, is a highly sophisticated amusing play that likewise ends in a happy fashion, but without any didactic tenor linked to this ending.

The reason I should like to highlight this complicated mix of similarity and dissimilarity is the simple fact that the parallel motifs, which may owe their commonalities to processes of cultural transfer, are assembled against different philosophical and religious backgrounds. In the Christian tradition, life is considered to be finite and unique; once a person dies, her or his fate is sealed in eternity, and this fate is contingent upon the person's actions during her or his lifetime.[141] For this very reason, it is a matter of the highest relevance whether one is dreaming or awake, or whether the "persons" with whom one interacts are real human beings or nothing but "ghosts" produced by the powers of evil. "Real" deeds within a "real" setting do matter. Consequently, the distinction between reality and illusion is of primary importance for Western thinking in general, not only within the world of Calderón's dramas. Within Buddhism,

---

140 For a more detailed discussion of the play, see Kilian, *"Escrituras andantes"*.
141 Up to this point, there is no difference between the Protestant and the Catholic world-models; the differences concern the question of the extent to which the individual is free to choose what she or he does; from a Protestant standpoint, a person who does not act in the "right" way is doomed to hell, even if she or he was not granted by God the grace of being capable of willingly opting for the "right" way.

Daoism, and Confucianism, by contrast, the concept of "beginning" and (definitive) "end" does not exist. Particularly within Buddhism, death is a step within a nearly endless chain of reincarnations. There is, of course, the threat of being reincarnated as a particularly base animal in the case of grave moral transgression, and the promise of nirvana in the case of morally exemplary behavior. But, as the prospect of gaining access to this state is linked to the prerequisite of a process of maturation mediated by a close to infinite number of metempsychoses, and as the close to endless character of this migration implies by necessity that one is incarnated quite a few times as a "base" being, the imperative of acting in "the right way" is much less strict than within Western culture. For that reason, the question of whether one is acting in a "real" situation or within an illusory framework is less important than within a cultural framework without the concept of metempsychosis. Within Chinese dramatic art, everything is playful comedy, while in the West this merely constitutes one variant—considered of minor value—of a dramatic system whose pillars are tragedy and serious didactic drama.

5.—The last step within the process of artistic creation which I would like to posit is a decisive one if the bits and pieces combined have the ambition to be more than a satire in the etymological sense,[142] that is, to become accepted as a serious work of art: there must be a level on which the disparate material is homogenized in a convincing way, so as to establish what we call the "unity" of the work in question. So far, I have only mentioned the use of a specific linguistic code as a device for implementing homogeneity.

Language, in the sense of the vernacular in which a text is written, is, indeed, the standard device for homogenizing the diverse parts assembled. Arbitrary symbolic codes have a striking capacity—which may be linked to their arbitrary character—to produce within their recipients the impression of "unity" of a material which is, phenomenally and in terms of provenance, extremely composite; the importance of this homogenizing device must certainly not be underestimated, all the more as it has produced highly influential theories of culture claiming an "essential" relationship between specific vernaculars and specific artistic works. Before engaging in a more detailed discussion of such theories,[143] I should like to restrict myself, for the time being, to some short critical remarks in this respect: In the field of human creation, and in contrast to the natural world, there is no rule without exceptions; they are rare, but

---

[142] The word is said to derive from Latin *satura*, meaning: a platter with a huge variety of different things to eat.
[143] See, above all, my discussion of Herder's cultural theory, pp. 232–250.

instructive. In the age I am dealing with, there are so-called "macaronic" texts, that is, texts containing passages in Latin as well as passages in vernacular languages. In later times there are decidedly multilingual texts such as Diderot's *Les bijoux indiscrets* (1748). Prominent texts from the period of high modernism, such as T. S. Eliot's *The Waste Land* (1922), even make systematic use of the device.

These exceptions to the rule of language as the most explicit device for bestowing the impression of unity on the assembled material, resulting in what we are used to calling a "text" or a literary "work", show that the decisive level of homogenizing is rather the one of conceptual unity. If a text succeeds in communicating the basic concept by which it is informed to the intended recipients, the elements it is made up of may be as diverse as one can imagine—the text will be accepted as a work of art. Macaronism was not an irritating feature at a time when the educated switched from Latin to a vernacular, and from one vernacular to another, as part of their daily routine. Diderot's multilingualism is a sort of playful esotericism; by occasionally employing languages allegedly not understood by the majority of the recipients, it was possible to give explicit expression to obscenities which it would not have been permissible to articulate in French at that time. Eliot's text belongs to an important strand of high modernist art in general—including literary texts, but also paintings and music—which is perhaps best characterized by a term typically applied to works of visual art: conceptual art. The unity of such works does not primarily reside in their internal structuring. It is to be found in a concept that is in most cases external to the work in question, but known to, or, at least, accessible to those familiar with the history and evolutionary logic of (Western) art. Eliot's text, while referring to typically Romantic elements, is a rejection of Romantic aesthetics, and it attacks the Romantic ideal, amongst others, on its most basic level, by undermining in an ostentatious way the link between the artistic text and the specific language in which it is written, a link that is essential to the idea of a literary text as a "spontaneous" expression of an "inspiration". Artificiality laid bare is the rationale behind Eliot's multilingualism. It may be added that such an "externalization" and "conceptualization" of the principle of homogeneity makes a work of art esoteric; this is the dilemma of high modernism. The ensuing restriction of the recipients to relatively small circles of connoisseurs was the main reason for the emergence of postmodernism, which is at least partly a return to more "concrete" devices of homogenizing diverse material.

6.—In the case of (literary) texts, the most elementary of the devices for establishing unity—secondary to homogenizing on the linguistic level—consists in what Aristotle calls in his *Poetics* the creation of a story (*mythos*), saying that a story needs to have "a beginning, a middle, and an end";[144] lyrics—not discussed by Aristotle—, if they do not narrate a story as well,[145] but rather present a thought, an "atmosphere", or a feeling, likewise follow a content-bound internal logic in their actual structuring. As banal as this description seems to appear at first sight, it is in fact crucial. In the case of texts prior to high modernism, readers expect a certain logic to be followed by the events we are told to have taken place, or, in the case of lyrical texts, by the feelings ascribed to the speaker. The order we expect from literary texts is certainly more flexible than the one we suppose to regulate the "real" material world as conceptualized by the laws of physics, but the impression of erratic contingency—as in certain dramatic texts of the twentieth century, the most radical case perhaps being Federico García Lorca's *Don Perlimplín* (1933)—would undermine, if not destroy, the acceptability of a text.[146] The logic readers expect is in very many cases grounded in an idea (one could say: an ideologeme) that is commonly accepted at a given time in a given place, which means that recipients typically do not assess the plausibility of the action presented according to "mimesis" strictly understood, but most frequently by referring to a level of abstraction, that is, by allegorizing what they read or see. I would speculate that the fusion of tragedy and fairy tale in Peri/Rinuccini attained (and still attains) the level of acceptability on the grounds of the somewhat lofty idea of the "power of love", which becomes associated in Christian times with the concept of love's ability to defeat death, a concept transposed to the field of secular love (*eros*) as early as in the Middle Ages. And Sumarokov's at first sight somewhat strange rewriting of *Hamlet* as a fairy tale gains unity only on the grounds of the idea that there is something like a divine investiture of kings and emperors and a transcendental guarantee of the concept of legitimacy as based on inheritance.—We call the age of artistic creation during which it was the authors' or painters' (or even composers'[147]) ambition to base the internal unity of their works no longer on ideologemes, but on an immanent causal concatenation of

---

144 *Poetics*, chap. 7.
145 The dominant tradition of lyrical poetry in Western vernaculars is based on the paradigm first established by Petrarch's *Canzoniere* (ca. 1370). Not only the collection as a whole, but almost all of the poems have a narrative substrate.
146 As to the uncontested unity of Lorca's text, it is to be found—as in the case of *The Waste Land*—not on the primary level of text-immanent structure, but rather on a conceptual meta-level which is external to the actual text. In this respect, Lorca's text is even more representative of high modernist art than Eliot's, since it does not target the poetic principles of one specific epoch, but rather—according to the concept of art as unrestricted "revolution"—the principles of order and coherence which are basic to the Western conception of what art is, starting with chap. 9 of Aristotle's *Poetics*.
147 I am here thinking of nineteenth-century program music.

the elements themselves, the age of "realism", whose basic device is, as stated by Roman Jakobson, *motivirovka*, the consistent motivation of all the events recounted in the text.[148]

7.—The homogenizing devices mentioned so far[149] are related to what we typically call semantics, to signs referring to (specific) meanings.[150] Is there also the possibility to confer unity upon a diverse ensemble of assembled elements by making use of non-semantic, formal structures, or even: only such formal structures? The question is in particular need of discussion with regard to textual genres that are linked to a high and visible degree of formal organization, namely poetry. Since I do not wish to deal here with literary texts in the most general way, I shall leave this question open; suffice it to say that in the case of traditional drama also, there is such a device, and a highly important one, of formally homogenizing the textual material, namely versification. But I would call into question the capacity even of very strict patterns such as the French alexandrine to bestow unity upon a fund of material that has not undergone previous processes of semantically relevant homogenizing, and I would doubt this possibility with regard to poetry proper as well.[151]

I shall limit the discussion of this point to a subgenre of drama or theater otherwise neglected in this book, but which has just been thematized, namely opera, where the level of external formal organization is a particularly obvious one, since it can be completely detached from the text as such and even en-

---

148 "O chudožestvennom realizme" (1921), English version in: Roman Jakobson, *Language in Literature*, Krystyna Pomorska and Stephen Rudy (eds.), Cambridge, MA and London 1987, pp. 19–27, quote: p. 27.
149 Meaning: the secondary homogenizing devices, the first one being the linguistic homogenization.
150 From my not mentioning explicitly the question of assembling a "homogeneous" central personage, readers may infer that I am basically an Aristotelian (in general, but also with regard to this specific point, namely, the assumption of the primacy of plot/*mythos*).
151 In the cultural sphere, in contrast to the natural sphere, there is no rule without an exception. In addition, artistic cultural items are defined by being liberated from a number of constraints to which all pragmatic cultural items have to bow in the final analysis. This "freedom" has been taken advantage of in the period we typically call modernism. As to poetry in particular, there are experiments trying to base the unity of poems no longer on semantic, but only on euphonic consistency (Mallarmé). But as is demonstrated by the genre's further history, this was, finally, a dead end; and one could legitimately raise the question of the extent to which Mallarmé's texts can reasonably be assigned the label of poetry or whether it is more sensible to classify them as (vocal) music. They are, in any case, a phenomenon of transgression; they intentionally blur pre-existing categorial divides and are thus representative of the concept of "art as revolution" that first emerged in Romanticism.

joyed without it, which is not the case with respect to the "musical" dimension of poetry. Is the music and its coherence, that is, its organization according to certain patterns familiar to the audience, a means of conferring unity upon a disparate fund of personages, events, and actions which are not homogenized on the level of text, that is, in terms of semantics? One could very well imagine that compositional techniques current in Baroque music, which call for a grandiose, triumphant *finale*, may have repressed, in the case of Peri's opera, concerns with regard to the plausibility of the narrated story which might come up when reading Rinuccini's *libretto* alone. Thinking of posterior stages of operatic production, I would speculate that many scenes from Verdi's or Wagner's operas would appear incoherent, strange, or even ridiculous if we only had access to the *libretti*. And in the case of a highly sophisticated work like Benjamin Britten's *Curlew River* (1964), which is a wild mix of Noh-inspired elements, Christian liturgical drama, and a more or less veiled layer of homoeroticism,[152] I would doubt that it could have gained convincing unity without the homogenizing power of the text-external formal element, the music. But in the end, I am inclined to say that no artistic work (even not the most avant-garde) consisting, amongst other levels, of language, can completely do without a certain homogeneity located on the level of the text. The margins for admitting textual disparity, however, are (much) greater in genres that have recourse to visual or auditive channels of non-textual formal organization than in works consisting of text alone.

When it comes to discussing my specific field of investigation, early modern drama, there are, indeed, also textual devices independent from semantics which are apt to palliate a certain amount of semantic disparity. The presence of a system of instructions for formulating texts, classical rhetoric, provides a sort of second-level language facilitating the homogenization of the assembled material;[153] in addition, the nearly omnipresent device of versification allows the process of semantic homogenization to be kept at a level which is below what we typically require from texts written in prose. But the difference seems not to be a drastic one.

---

[152] See Carrie J. Preston, "Trouble with Titles and Directors: Benjamin Britten and William Plomer's *Curlew River* and Samuel Beckett's *Footfalls/Pas*", in: C. J. P., *Learning to Kneel: Noh, Modernism, and Journeys in Teaching*, New York, NY 2016, pp. 203–242.
[153] See the proceedings of the DramaNet conference *Rhetoric and Drama* (ed. D. S. Mayfield, Berlin and Boston, MA 2017); see in particular the article by Jan Bloemendal which addresses the entire question from a concrete, but also a theoretical vantage point ("Rhetoric and Early Modern Latin Drama: The Two Tragedies by the "Polish Pindar" Simon Simonides [1558–1629]: *Castus Ioseph* and *Pentesilea*", pp. 115–134).

8.—Things may differ to a more considerable degree when one proceeds to take into account a feature that is specific to the text corpus under scrutiny in the present study, namely, the fact that the texts were written with the intention of having them received as performance. If the recipient does not read and study the text, but rather receives the drama in question by attending a performance, the external formal structure of the performance (the theater as *lieu autre* [Michel Foucault], that is, the separation of stage and audience), as well as the specific formal structure of the actual performance which she or he attends—the costumes of the actors, their specific body language, the coherence of the entire visual level as conceived by the stage director of that specific performance—might create an impression of sufficient homogeneity in cases where a reader would be left startled by the numerous discrepancies he is confronted with. The most popular drama in world literature might be an instructive example of the specific requirements regarding homogenization for theater on the one hand, drama as text on the other. Shakespeare's *Hamlet* has fascinated and goes on fascinating diverse audiences from various cultural backgrounds when performed on stage; however, readers of the play—professionals, academics as well as authors—frequently articulate the impression that the drama is somewhat strange or obscure, not really worked through;[154] given the success of Shakespeare's creation, such a critique is audacious. In other words: it would probably be even sharper if it did not target one of the best-known dramas of all of literary history so far.

9.—The general processes described above are preceded in the act of creation, in almost all cases, by a step which is of primary importance with regard to cultural production. This step might be called the decomposition of pre-existent cultural material and its subsequent refunctionalization. It is, indeed, one of the peculiar features of shaped material we tend to call "cultural", in contrast to "material" material in the sense of manufactured goods,[155] that it may either be extracted from the net and then used as it is or partially extracted and made a component of "new" cultural units whose functions may differ from the work it was initially part of. This fundamental difference even applies to the sphere of art itself, where it differentiates artifacts constituted by "dense" signs from those based on "notational" signs (Goodman). In the case of the former, there is hardly the possibility to make productive use of them once they have been disassembled. If one cuts a painting into pieces, it is de-

---

154 See, for example, T. S. Eliot, "Hamlet and His Problems", in: T. S. E., *The Sacred Wood: Essays on Poetry and Criticism*, London 1921, pp. 47–50.
155 —which may comprise cultural items as well; one may think of paintings.

stroyed, and the only ambition of those who have the pieces at their disposal would be to reconstitute the former unit;[156] the same holds true for most kinds of manufactured, "practical" goods. As for texts (as well, to a certain extent, as musical works[157]), matters are different, and this difference: the possible productivity of "fragments", even small fragments, of what was formerly a coherent unit, may weigh a lot when it comes to discussing the reasons why cultural evolution follows a much more flexible scheme than, say, industrial evolution[158] (and why literary history is different from art history). Succinctly put, cultural products that make use of notational encoding or that have been transposed into notational encoding[159] float in the net in two different registers: as finite works, that is, entities intentionally conceived by their creator (or creators, if the creation process is collective), but also as a multitude of identifiable units, concrete or abstract, into which they might be decomposed on behalf of their notational encoding. The process of decomposing may take place as a conscious one (in the case of a commentator—a humanist, a critic—who "analyzes" a work, or a number of works, or a genre, and then commits

---

156 In order to avoid misunderstandings, I stress, once again, that most of the generalizing claims in this book do not pretend to systematically apply to high modernist art, unless otherwise said. High modernism is a period based on the attempt to radically problematize all principles governing previous art production. From this perspective, it is an era in which art focuses on the reflection of its own (traditional) principles. In the case above, the technique of *collage* would be a device which problematizes—or was even designed in order to problematize—the general assumption given expression to by my formulations. But at least to my knowledge, the cultural revolutions in the West gained their acceptance by always keeping their practices within the limits of—an at times provocative—playfulness. Cutting paintings by Michelangelo, Dürer, and Rembrandt into pieces in order to reassemble them by way of a *collage* was never undertaken or suggested, not even in the most radical modernist manifestos.
157 —keeping in mind the differentiations detailed above (n. 101).
158 One could object with respect to industrial production that there is the practice called "recycling"; but, as a systematically implemented practice, it is a very recent one. It is, more or less, linked to the technology of so-called module-based production, which was introduced only in the course of the last three decades. In addition, it remains to be discussed if there aren't profound differences between industrial and cultural "recycling" with respect to re-functionalization. In industrial processes, the "original" function of the module gained from the disassembly of an object is typically preserved when the module in question is being assigned to use in a newly assembled object. Authentic re-functionalization is bound to the breaking-down of the module into its elements (steel, aluminum, plastics, etc.), that is to say, to the destruction of the initial structure. Within culture, specifically within literary culture, things seem to be different. Re-functionalization may operate both ways: by bestowing an entirely new function on a pre-existing, highly organized structure, or by decomposing this highly organized structure and making use of its elements or of some of them only.
159 Meaning: comments on or analyses of works of graphic art.

the results of his "dissection" to the cultural net); it may take place as a more or less unconscious process of amateur abstraction or compression (in the case of a recipient who tells a friend or a business partner about some features of a book he read or a performance he watched); or it may take place as an intentional act on the part of a posterior artist who makes use of selected semantic and formal features of a specific work originating from the activities of a previous creative mind.

10.—I would like to illustrate this peculiarity by providing a prominent example from early modern poetological discussions revolving around the concept of tragedy. We commonly subsume these discussions under the heading of "neo-Aristotelianism". Much ink has been spilt over the last decades in order to demonstrate that (Italian, Spanish, French) neo-Aristotelianism is a gross distortion of Aristotle's concept of tragedy as exposed in the *Poetics*. Such attempts to "prove" that the European early modern age "misread" Aristotle follow a logic based on the dynamics of scholarly discourses rather than that of a reasonable attitude towards the actual problem. It is trivial to say that the reception of a text two and a half millenia after its composition is not loyal to the original.[160] But these somewhat questionable controversies and discussions do not matter here. I should just like to propose that seventeenth-century neo-Aristotelianism follows in its basic arguments Aristotle's central positions: the function of tragedy is the arousal of affects, mainly "fear" and "pity", with the intention of purifying these affects or of relieving the spectators of them.[161] In order to provoke these emotions in the spectators, Aristotle argues, the plot of the play must be such that it can be regarded as possible; it has to respect the limits of what is called verisimilitude. If the action is chiefly or even entirely fantasmatic, the spectators do not consider the situations performed to be possible configurations[162] of their own lives and consequently are not seized by fear (*phobos*). The claim regarding the *mythos* is supplemented by a claim

---

[160] I shall set aside the question of the grounds on which twentieth- and twenty-first-century mainstream classicists believe to be able to say what Aristotle's original intentions were, or, rather, to assume that they are better suited to resolve this question than the theoreticians of the seventeenth century.

[161] This latter point is, as is well known, not at all clear in Aristotle's text either.

[162] It is the structural analogy, which I try to highlight by choosing this term, that counts; of course, a situation in which one kills a person who later turns out to be one's own father and marries one's mother without being conscious of the previous biological relationship is beyond any similarity to the recipients' lifeworld; but it may occur to humans that in emotionally charged situations they perform actions they believe to be ethically justified or at least tenable and which later turn out to have been actions they would never have performed had they known what they were "really" doing.

concerning the central character: he or she must be *homoion* (equal in the sense of similar)¹⁶³ to what the spectators conceive as real.

At the beginning of the seventeenth century, this structure, which inextricably links mimesis and emotionalization, is decomposed into two units which then become, each separately, the poetological bases of the further two prominent subgenres of narrative in the West.¹⁶⁴ As far as we are able to reconstruct, it was Jean-Baptiste Du Bos who—for whatever reason¹⁶⁵—was the first to actually put into practice this decomposition of the original Aristotelian unit.¹⁶⁶ In his *Réflexions critiques sur la poésie et sur la peinture* (1719), he privileges the aspect of emotionalization ("les poemes et les tableaux ne sont de bons ouvrages qu'à proportion qu'ils nous émeuvent et qu'ils nous attachent.").¹⁶⁷ The decisive step I here call "decomposing" occurs a few lines later, where Du Bos proceeds not only to qualify the mimetic dimension as negligible, but to advise the construction of a plot against the rules of verisimilitude if it thereby gains in emotionalizing potential ("un ouvrage peut etre mauvais sans qu'il y ait des fautes contre les règles, comme un ouvrage plein de fautes contre les règles peut etre un ouvrage excellent.").¹⁶⁸

---

163 In Aristotle, this similarity seems to be primarily meant in terms of psychic mechanisms, that is, in terms of patterns of situations and reactions; on a secondary level, it is thus linked to social similarity (only an "honorable" man, that is, a full citizen—meaning: an aristocrat—behaves in the way Oedipus does when he is provoked by Laios; if a metic or a slave behaved this way, it would be beyond verisimilitude, at least from the perspective of fifth-century Athenian spectators). In the early modern age, these criteria establishing the similarity of the character with respect to the spectators are inverted in a way; similarity is conceived primarily in terms of social stratification, interactional mechanisms being conceived of as immediately linked to social class (*honnête homme*). The reasons for this shift may be found in the more rigid regulation of interactional patterns in courtly societies as compared to the aristocratic ("democratic") Athenian society of classical times.
164 By "narrative" I refer to all literary genres that are based on a story, namely the novel and the drama, as well as to related genres of various profile (short stories, films, performances, etc.).—I shall address the possible origins of the third modern subgenre of narrative, the self-reflexive mode, in a chapter below (pp. 298–303).
165 I will offer some speculation on this point below (p. 70).
166 For details, see Tatiana Korneeva, "Entertainment for Melancholics: The Public and the Public Stage in Carlo Gozzi's *L'amore delle tre melarance*", in: Gvozdeva et al. (eds.), *Dramatic Experience*, pp. 140–171. See also Logan J. Connors, "Pierre Nicole, Jean-Baptiste Dubos, and the Psychological Experience of Theatrical Performance in Early Modern France", in: *Dramatic Experience*, pp. 172–188.
167 *Réflexions critiques*, Paris 1770 (17th print), reprint Geneva 1967, vol. 2, pp. 339 f.
168 Pp. 339 f. The "règles" in the quote refer primarily to the famous "trois unités" (of place, time, and action), which served as formal guidelines in order to guarantee the verisimilitude of the action as a whole.—Du Bos's argument is still linked, in a certain way, to Aristotle's text. The Stagirite allows breaches of the rule of verisimilitude in case the overall effect is thus

It is not astonishing at all that shortly after Du Bos's provocative decomposition of the unity of mimesis and emotion, there emerge concepts which give privilege to the other part of the former unit. The theory of the *drame bourgeois*, mainly developed by Diderot, continues to dedicate some attention to the aim of emotionalizing spectators; but Diderot argues that in order to achieve this aim, playwrights must first of all convert to a radical mimeticism. It is no longer a broadly understood concept of verisimilitude, but the analogy of dramatic scenes to the daily experience and specific feelings of the audience—middle-class Parisians belonging to the Third Estate—which guarantees the spectators' identification with what they see on stage. According to Diderot, it is only such an identification which is apt to provoke emotional involvement.

Diderot's theory of the *drame bourgeois* forms, as has been frequently argued, the basis for the broad strand of literary realism which becomes dominant in the nineteenth century.[169] The privileging of mimesis over emotionalization marks the end of "heroes", knights, princesses, gods, and mythical beings as personages of literary texts. The drama as well as the novel convert to the ideal of the reproduction of what the audience is ready to accept as "their" world (and not, as was formerly the case, a "possible world"). Emotionalization, which is still present in Diderot, even on the theoretical level, becomes more and more a recessive phenomenon; the criterion of the well-conceived narrative work is its mimetic capacity. Are readers seized by fear and pity as they read *Madame Bovary* (1857)?

Spectators do weep, however, as one may see in any present-day movie theater, when they expose themselves to those variants of fictional narrative which follow the precepts first theorized by Du Bos. With a slightly condescending attitude, we usually call these artifacts "trivial". Fictions like *Titanic* (1997) do not thematize what is completely out of reach of the real, but they deal with configurations whose exceptional status is evident. Dying from an accident while traveling is a rare, but possible incident to be taken into account when making a journey; dying in such an accident while simultaneously experiencing a bittersweet love story is certainly beyond the limits of verisimilitude. Such a story seems, however, to appeal to deeply rooted emotional needs that our actual daily lives do not satisfy.

---

better achieved; but he emphasizes that such devices must remain an exception (*Poetics*, chap. 18, 1456 a 25; 25, 1461 b 15). Du Bos claims general relevance for what was exceptional in Aristotle and thus subverts Aristotle's most basic definition of drama as *mimesis*.

169 Regarding this point (including the extensive research done in the second half of the twentieth century), see my *Ästhetik der Wirklichkeitsdarstellung und Evolution des Romans von der französischen Spätaufklärung bis zu Robbe-Grillet*, Stuttgart 1987.

As a result of this process, the decomposition of Aristotle's theory of the tragic, there are no longer tragedies in modern Western literature. On the one hand, there is the literary staging of somewhat banal mishaps and disappointments of everyday life, which are all too common to provoke deep emotions, even if the ending is the premature death of the central personage. On the other hand, there are highly charged stories which satisfy the recipients' affective needs, but which they would never take for real in the sense that they might become involved in similar situations. From the above-specified moment in literary history onward, narratives are split into two functionally very different categories: *representations* we mainly read or view in order to reflect upon what (our) reality is like, and *compensations* we read or view in order to obtain, at least fantasmatically, what we most probably will never obtain in reality.

The question of the reasons for Du Bos's decomposition of the link firmly established in the Aristotelian theory of tragedy is a very intriguing one, although it is of much less relevance than the question of the actual effects generated by this decomposition. Du Bos was not only a theoretician of literature, but also a theologian; he was specifically influenced by the basically pessimistic variant of Christian anthropology to be found in Pascal. In the final account, it is the mighty strand of Pauline and Augustinian theology floating in the net upon which he drew, while completely overturning its original anti-theatrical implications. If humans have a hardly controllable propensity to commit sinful acts, the situation of idleness (in the terms of moral theology: *acedia*[170]) is a particularly dangerous one. When the mind is not preoccupied with a specific goal it is pursuing, it will almost inevitably fall prey to the temptations of sin. For this reason, it might be a highly useful preventive to engage the mind in activities for which it has a predilection, namely: emotional arousal, but to do so in a way that does not have any real-life consequences. Thus, involving humans in fantasizing by exposing them to emotionalizing performances is the best way to prevent them from actually sinning.[171] The extent to which the situations represented on stage entertain at least some analogy with what the recipients would be ready to classify as "real" is of minor relevance within such a functionalization.

11.—It is a theoretically stimulating problem of another logical order, relevant to the context of disassembly and refunctionalization, to scrutinize the movement, or rather the conscious transposition, of cultural material extracted from

---

170 I shall give a more detailed comment on this sin below (pp. 84–87).
171 For an extensive account of Du Bos's argumentative steps, see Korneeva, "Entertainment for Melancholics".

the net from one "level" of cultural production to another, including the consequences this entails. Katja Gvozdeva's study[172] elucidates a process which not only occurred in the period under consideration, but may have taken place, *mutatis mutandis*, quite a few times under different circumstances. The theater pieces written and performed by companies of "merrymen" like the *Accademia degli Intronati* were based on models from classical antiquity (Plautus, Terence); in this regard, the theatrical work of the *Intronati* is typical of what academies and learned societies in Italy did at that time. They actively worked to revitalize the cultural patrimony from the pre-Christian age. At the time of their original production, classical comedies were popular pieces conceived for reception by a socially non-stratified audience including the uneducated,[173] as is evidenced by a variety of quite condescending remarks to be found in Aristotle's *Poetics*.[174] But when the pieces were "reborn" in early modern Europe, the course of time and the new context had rendered them specimens of highbrow, elitist culture. Common people were not able to directly understand the text of a performance, because social practices, codes of conduct, and allusions to political life which were accessible to everyone in the Roman audience of Plautus' times had turned into hermetic features by the time the "Renaissance" took place. In order to grasp what the pieces wished to convey, a spectator had to be a very cultured, learned person. The work done by the *Intronati*, their rewriting of classical comedies, consisted mainly in the attempt at re-popularizing a genre which, though popular in its origins, had become elitist. The process consisted in hybridizing the classical models with features of contemporary oral popular drama. By so doing, for example by rewriting the *Menaechmi* (ca. 200 BCE) as the *Ingannati* (1532 CE),[175] the *Intronati* succeeded in creating an entirely new variant of comic theater, a mixture of refined or learned and of vulgar if not obscene traits—a variant which then became the embryo of what we are accustomed to regard as the apogee of early modern comedy, the comedic works of Shakespeare and Molière.[176]

---

172 *Compagnie d'hommes joyeux*.
173 In the Athens of classical times, citizenship was linked to extraction, but the elite constituted by this criterion was not at all homogeneous in terms of levels of education and cultivation; the latter also applies to the status of *civis romanus* (not only after, but also before its emancipation from the criterion of extraction), which guaranteed access to the performances in the arenas and amphitheaters.
174 *Poetics*, chap. 5.
175 As to this play in particular, see Katja Gvozdeva, "Why Do Men Go Blind in the Theatre? Gender Riddles and Fools' Play in the Italian Renaissance Comedy *Gl'Ingannati* (1532)", in: Gvozdeva et al. (eds.), *Dramatic Experience*, pp. 35–76.
176 The implication of my above characterization is that I see classical Greek ("old") comedy as mainly dedicated to vulgar and obscene registers.

12.—The question of the modern reception of the classical genre of tragedy allows for the consideration of a particularly intricate point involved in a theory of cultural dynamics based on the assumption that creation functions by means of extraction of material floating in a universal cultural net—a point that is veiled, in the case of the comic genre(s), by the comparatively high standardization of its elements. It is a commonplace to hold that early modern European tragedies were much more influenced by Seneca's plays than by the Greek plays European culture from the late eighteenth century through today has valued as the apogee of the "tragic". Seneca's plays, however, are based on these Greek plays; the existence of many of the Greek originals is known to us only because these served as the bases of still extant plays written in Latin. With respect to early modern European plays, the crucial question would thus be whether we should consider them to be products of an extraction of Senecan tragedy from the net, or whether what is extracted is only superficially Senecan, but in essence Sophoclean, Euripidean, or Aeschylean. Just posing the question makes clear, however, that we are at risk of falling prey to a *regressus ad infinitum*. It is well known, and clearly expressed already by Aristotle, that very many of the plots of the famous Greek tragedies were not created by the respective authors of these tragedies. Myth, however, is a cultural repertoire which is characterized not least by basic plot instability, which raises the question of identifiability. If one considers mythical stories to be the "real" originals underlying the supposed originals currently connected with the names of the three famous Greek tragedians, one is rapidly approaching a level of generality or of anthropological commonality which makes it difficult to decide whether or not a concrete story should be considered the result of cultural contact and exchange or whether it is in its origins autochthonous in the literal sense of the term.

Keeping these elementary difficulties in mind, it may be useful to differentiate between direct and mediated transfer if the specific questions at issue are of a more historical profile, that is, if they pertain to the description of concrete processes of net-bound production. Early modern European tragedy first emerged in Italy, but the relevant works never made it to the level of world literature. On behalf of dynastic and territorial configurations, sixteenth-century Italy maintained close relations with France and Spain, as well as with those German-language territories which were part of the Habsburg empire. The exchange of people from all social classes, in the one direction as well as in the other, the exchange of material goods, and the exchange of cultural practices and artifacts was intense. The affinities between the vernaculars concerned, particularly in the case of Spain, facilitated these processes. As part of this scenario, groups of Italian actors travelled to Spain and France and performed their pieces in these countries. Young literary authors from Spain, Portugal, and France frequently traveled to Italy, not only as soldiers, or to visit the remains of the Roman Empire, or to worship the Christian God in Rome, where his vicar resides, but also to find inspiration for their work. The commonalities originating from this "migration" of sixteenth-century Italian theatrical and dramatic culture to the west and to the north notwithstanding, the results were very different. Lope de Vega and Corneille, Calderón and Racine have many things in common; the neo-Aristotelian treatises on drama in both countries evidently share a great many "norms" and "rules"; but it is not least the properly modern reception history of the twentieth century which testifies to the fact that the two Italy-based dramatic cultures are very dissimilar. Racine and even Corneille are still represented on stage and attract a considerable audience, whereas it would be difficult to find a staging of pieces by Calderón or Lope, even of their most famous works.

It may be the late eighteenth-century Russian drama that is apt to demonstrate that the importance of an exact description of the processes of mediation may, however, finally be a quite relative one. The commonalities between Russian eighteenth-century drama and early modern Italian drama are rather small, but they are not smaller than the commonalities between Italian drama and French drama of the early modern age. However, in the former case, there is one more step of mediation involved than in the latter. To put it abstractly: mediated "import" (as in the case of Russia with respect to Italian drama) should in principle be differentiated from direct import (as in the case of France and Spain with respect to Italian drama); but, finally, it seems not to be the degree of "mediatedness" which determines the degree to which an artifact based on material extracted from the net is considered by recipients to be imitative or "original". One could even venture the hypothesis that multilayered mediation is in this case—against what intuition would suggest—a positive factor, since in the domain of culture the distortive effects typically brought about by several subsequent acts of mediated transmission are not necessarily "damaging", but may rather have a "creative" function; for artistic units, in contrast to both the pragmatic and the ideological sphere, there is no preestablished ideal type. Without the mediation of French court theater, early modern Italian-style, that is Renaissance tragedy would most probably have never made its way to Russia, since direct contacts between Italian and Russian literary culture were rare at the time. The "distortions" the initial pieces underwent on their way—from Italy to France, and then to Russia (mediated by the German reception)—were enormous; this said, the final results were of world-literary dimension. Would, for instance, Chekhov have been able to conceive his modern reshapings of the tragic had he not been able to rely on a thoroughly established practice of Russian tragedy-writing—initiating in the above-outlined multilayered processes of transfer and distortion—when he started out as a dramatist?

13.—There is, finally, one further crucial point thematized in passing above which still needs to be discussed in more detail, namely, the question of historically specific rationales behind the assembly of material extracted from the net. The logic or logics discussed in this respect so far have mainly been ahistorical, that is anthropological. For reasons of the limits of my areas of competence, this point can only be thematized with regards to Western (literary) history.

With this qualification, it is evident that it is appropriate to differentiate between two predominant historical rationales of assembly, in addition, perhaps, to a few minor ones. The large-scale parameters I am referring to are known in current terminology as the era of imitation and the era of innovation, in other words of traditional and of modernist art.[177] The epochs we typically refer to when dealing with cultural history (Renaissance, Enlightenment, Romanticism, Modernism, etc.) are minor entities which shall not be considered here, since their heuristic, quasi-auxiliary status has frequently been pointed out in recent scholarship. From the theoretical perspective devised in this study, there is no need to reject these categories, neither the major nor the minor ones. Their difference is, however, of a much more gradual character than assumed in traditional scholarship. "Imitation" and "innovation" translate in this book's approach to a restricted versus a more and more unrestricted liberty to assemble random material floating in the net. And it would certainly not be unreasonable to see this gradual shift as corresponding to a shift occurring in the same age in the spheres of the political and of material production. The "democratic" revolutions and the mechanization of commodity production are factors relevant in this respect. I do not believe to have anything pertinent to say with regard to the question of where the "real" driving force is to be found.[178] Literary scholars have an unreflecting tendency to highlight the "liberating" role of modern, Romantic, and post-Romantic art with respect to society at large. Traditional historians focusing on the political sphere and "materialist" historians focusing on the evolution of technology would present different scenarios. I am not sure that there will ever be a satisfactory answer. The point to be

---

[177] The most important theoretical work on this point was produced by Yuri M. Lotman, *The Structure of the Artistic Text*, Ladislav Matejka and Mark E. Suino (eds.), Gail Lenhoff and Ronald Vroon (tr.), Ann Arbor, MI 1977.
[178] Regarding this point, see my more detailed speculations below (pp. 284 f.).

stressed is linked to one of the present book's basic theses: art production never takes place for its own sake. Particularly in modern times, art producers have to "sell" their products in order to do what they wish to do, namely, produce further artifacts (rather than become librarians, teachers, or professors). For this reason, they have to address their possible audiences or readers and their needs and preferences. These needs and preferences are diverse. The demands of the highly educated have another profile than those of "normal" people. But, as stressed previously, one should not forget that theoreticians as lucid as Freud never ceased to remind us of the commonalities linked to our physical nature, implying that the cultural differences we believe to exist between high and popular culture may be self-deceptions in the first place.[179] Leaving these differentiations aside, it seems to be a constant that there are strong links between the rationales of art production in a given period and the "production" of other societal spheres (politics, material production, dominant world views, ideologies, religions). The question of what or who the "prime mover" could be in this entire scenario of culture at large may remain irresolvable. But for the simple reason that art, and literature in particular, is created for people living under certain configurations,[180] it is not at all astonishing that the logics of extraction and assembly observable in this sub-field are structurally homologous to the parameters at work in culture at large.

Formal Organization and Mediatedness

0.–There is a point touched upon in passing on various occasions, amongst others in the above chapter, which might require some further elaboration. If one assumes with Vladimir Propp that literary texts, including dramatic texts, are comprised of elementary motifs whose referential bases are anthropological constants ("real" configurations, wishes, fears, fantasies), the mere presence of comparable items in different literary cultures need not be mediated

---

179 See the reference above, n. 56.
180 If a newly written text is not received at the time of its production, it may be that it does not acquire access to the net, and is therefore forgotten; but if the text is materially preserved, there is some prospect of it becoming "resurrected" in later times. For reasons that shall be briefly addressed below, the specific semiotic structure of fictional texts in general allows for their reception and reactivation under configurations totally different from those obtaining at the time of production (pp. 256 f.; see also my "Das Denken, das Unterscheiden und die Literatur", *Poetica* vol. 45/2013, pp. 249–269).

by processes of transfer as theorized here.[181] It only makes sense to postulate that a given text owes its origin to another, pre-existing text, or to fragments of texts which have been received and reworked, if the texts under scrutiny are also comparable, in some way, in terms of formal organization. Formal organization may thus be considered as an indicator which allows for the assessment of the profile of an item floating in the cultural net with regard to its mediatedness. The truly difficult question, however, consists in defining the level of similarity of formal organization that would entitle an observer to speak of cultural transfer (instead of "emergence" or "creation") as being at the origin of the historically posterior item.

1.—With respect to many concrete cases the question seems relatively easy to answer; if there is a variety of formal parameters characterizing "new" works which may be obviously assigned to works already floating in the net, there is good reason to make the claim of transfer rather than genuine "originality". In the case of the Russian court theater of the eighteenth century, for instance, there is no doubt that the first texts in Russian owe their formal characteristics to imported French and English dramas (Shakespeare, Racine, Corneille). There is documentary evidence that there had been a previous transfer of actual plays from France and England to the Russian court; in addition, there is textual evidence that this transfer was made use of in the creation of the "autochthonous" plays, since these share their formal organization with the French plays on all levels which are not directly affected by the difference of language.—As to the Griselda story and its many dramatizations in early modern European literatures,[182] it is not primarily the formal organization in the strict sense which enables one to reasonably postulate that the post-Boccaccian versions are drawn from the *Decameron*. It is mainly the configuration of personages, perhaps even of proper names, which allows for the exclusion of the possibility that we are facing different and independent modelings of a moral-philosophical problem which bears a certain universality, at least among cultures where strict female monogamy is the rule.[183]—Things become more

---

181 As said, such an alternative approach to the problems here discussed forms the basis of Mayfield's study (*The Vicarious*).
182 See Rüegg, *The 'Patient Griselda' Myth in Late Medieval and Early Modern Literature*.
183 The *Decameron*'s last story deals with a high-ranking nobleman who marries a virtuous girl of humble origin. After she has given birth to two children, the husband begins to put her unconditional marital loyalty and her readiness to accept strict subordination to the test. First, he humiliates her in public. Then he has the two children taken away, saying that he has decided to have them killed. Finally, he divorces her and obliges her to wait upon her successor on the occasion of his second marriage. Griselda patiently suffers all the cruelties inflicted upon her without protesting or revolting. During the wedding ceremony, the marquis reveals that his past actions were nothing but a test. The children are still alive, and the second mar-

difficult the more abstract the common features of two given texts are. It is, of course, striking to observe that the two most famous dramas of early modern England and Spain, *Hamlet* and *La vida es sueño*, are characterized by their combination of a basic oedipal configuration with a specific epistemological question, that of the reliability of sense perception. Given the fact that we are dealing with the two leading European powers of that age, and that their political and military enmity notwithstanding, economic, dynastic, and even cultural exchange between the two nations did take place, one cannot systematically exclude the possibility that the English play, or a précis of its action, came to the attention of Spanish authors of the next generation, that one amongst them, namely Calderón, received the *Hamlet* material and then decided to rework it, with the intention of delivering a polemical answer, inspired by Counter-Reformation Catholicism, to the questions raised in Shakespeare's play from a more or less agnostic standpoint. The lack of exhaustive documentation of cultural contacts between England and Spain at that time will, however, make it improbable that there will ever be evidence for such a configuration. In very many cases one has to limit oneself to expounding the alternatives and leave to further discussion the question of which is the most probable. In the case just mentioned, one could also assume that commonalities with regard to the oedipal basis of the two plots might be mediated by the authors' knowledge of Sophocles' play or—this would be a Freudian interpretation of the striking parallel—that they just emerged, independent from each other, on behalf of the universality of the problem which is associated since Freud with the name of the eponymous hero of Sophocles' play. And the discussions revolving around fundamental epistemological questions need not owe their incontestable comparability to a direct transfer of Shakespeare's play to the Iberian Peninsula. As is known not least from the works of Descartes, the basic assumption of skepticism, that is, the unreliability of sensory perception, was a problem which intrigued academics and intellectuals from all over Europe at that time; and there are evident external reasons why this question in particular was so important in that age.[184]—For the time being, there is perhaps nothing more to be reasonably predicated with respect to the theoretical question outlined at the beginning of this chapter than to point to the fact that whether one should

---

riage was a fake; Griselda is restored to her former position as wife and looks forward to a bright future.

184 For a more detailed explanation of the link between the discoveries of new lands and the reemergence of skepticism in early modern Europe, see my essay "The Traditional Cosmos and the New World"; in an abridged fashion, I will come back to the entire configuration in the further course of this part of the present study.

speak of transfer and subsequent remodeling, of a parallel "drawing" upon a fund of material floating in the net, or of emergence (in the sense of "originality") is contingent upon our own judgment, a faculty Immanuel Kant called *Urteilskraft*. The philosopher intended to designate by this term that, notwithstanding the irreducible subjectivity of such acts of judgment, they need to be "universally acceptable", while acceptability need not be identical to consent.

2.—There are substantial reasons for considering the criterion of comprehensive formal organization as a convenient indicator of mediatedness to be of a less consistent expediency than one would expect against the backdrop of some of the above examples. Formal organization seems to be culture-bound. The basic mode of narrative is most probably universal. But as for (secular) poetry and drama, there is strong evidence that there have been highly developed cultures without these formal registers. Even more so, this holds true for more specified formal configurations, for instance tragedy, which originated in ancient Greece, but for which there is no equivalent in the geographically not so distant culture of early Israel—for evident reasons, as may be extrapolated from Old Testament narratives which contain all the prerequisites of tragedy, the story of Abraham and Isaac and the story of Job being the most prominent ones. The biblical stories do not end in disaster but, rather, in a complete restitution that one could assign, in terms of (classical) genres, to comedy, if not fairytale. A Mono-Theos cannot be conceived as a cynic or as someone who does not care any longer about what he once created. Or, to give it a different accent: when a monotheistic culture develops such concepts—as was the case in parts of early modern Europe[185]—it seems to be a concomitant phenomenon that it rapidly loses its faith. The entire problem—the conceptual incongruence of the genre of tragedy and monotheism—thus evaporates.

If one adds to this observation the fact that not only traditional Jewish, but also Islamic cultures did not receive the pattern of tragedy,[186] one would be tempted to conclude that incongruences between comprehensive ideological features and cultural material floating in the net might be obstacles for an extraction of the material in question; this would lead to the postulate—if not

---

[185] I am referring to the concept of *deus absconditus* which emerged in the late Middle Ages and had its most dramatic impact on European thinking in seventeenth-century France (see Lucien Goldmann, *Le Dieu caché*. Etude sur la vision tragique dans les *Pensées* de Pascal et dans le théâtre de Racine, Paris 1955).

[186] There are tragic patterns, however, to be found in Yiddish literature; the Yiddish language as well as Yiddish culture are hybrid phenomena whose structures could well be conceptualized, I might say in passing, within the theoretical framework developed here.

of "national" cultures—of a variety of larger cultural communities, integrated by a shared world-model,[187] which, on behalf of the strictures produced by the respective model, are separated from one another in terms of cultural production of any more refined nature.[188]

An aspect which should, however, not be neglected in this context is the possibility of disassembly, partial extraction, and subsequent re-functionalization. Worldviews and even religions are much more flexible complexes of stories and beliefs than is commonly assumed; for that reason alone, there is the possibility (but certainly not the necessity) of transfer of "heterodox" material under certain conditions which obey a logic not directly linked to the cultural material in question. The Christian West, while integrating the Hebrew Bible, including the Akedah and the Book of Job, into its canon, also received the pattern of tragedy. What remains to be discussed are the changes Christian belief underwent before classical Roman and Greek tragedies were extracted from the net after having not been extracted for centuries; at least as far as the plays existing in Latin are concerned, the reason for this lack of extraction was not a lack of linguistic competency. In addition, one would have to carefully scrutinize to what extent the basic features of the classical (that is, Aristotelian) tragedy were preserved.

3.—It might be useful in this context to consider in more detail the concept of re-functionalization. Within processes of cultural transfer, contents and even most aspects of formal organization may be preserved to the extent that one is tempted to speak of "imitation"; nevertheless, the message might be altered and integrated into ideological configurations alien to the original material. Tragedy may thus be converted to a form of (Christian and/or absolutist) didacticism, as is the case with many French tragedies of the age. The complexity of the issue here discussed reaches an even higher level if one proceeds to ponder the problem of why the ideologically heterogeneous material is extracted at all if it is acceptable only after its assimilation to the basic schemata of the receiving cultural context. Why rewrite a pagan tragedy as a play of Christian didacticism? Why not, if this is the final aim, just invent "new plays"

---

187 The term is Lotman's ("*model' mira*"); the semiotician posits that every narrative text implicitly contains a "world-model", that is, an interpretation of the world and an explication of its state (*The Structure of the Artistic Text*, p. 210 [the English translation employs the formulation "model of the universe"]).

188 —by which I wish to convey that religious belief certainly does not preclude the adoption from other religious communities of basic technologies of everyday life, e.g., the manufacturing of knives.

which are anti-tragic and Christian right from the start? This is indeed what Spain did in that age; and the Spanish authors of the time rightly named their plays, including those with a bloody ending, *comedias*, or *comedias nuevas* to put it precisely.[189] Spain was, in terms of ideology, the most rigid community of the age. In many ways, its literary production "lays bare" what in other countries of the time was hidden behind a façade of *imitatio auctorum*. The still extant paradigms of the classical genre were, indeed, received; no early modern European drama can reasonably be conceptualized in terms of "creation" without taking the dependency on the classical tradition into account. The mediated profile of the humanistic dramas notwithstanding, they are to be considered at the same time as transformations—more or less complete—of the classical material on whose extraction from the net they are obviously based.

As to the differences observable between the specific transformations the classical material underwent in different countries, one might consider, once again, the possible divergence of the respective national scenarios with regard to demand and control. As to the "demand" side, there is an almost unrestricted commonality: extracting classical material was about elevating the "modern" European literary cultures to a rank that could rival with that of the *antiqui* by emulating their most dignified genres, tragedy and epic. But during this period, characterized by the establishment of the first systematically bureaucratized states in European history, the criterion of demand was in any case outweighed by the one of control, at least where these two criteria were in conflict.[190] In a literary culture such as that of France or England, where mechanisms of control were much more driven by power than belief, there was no obstacle to satisfying the demand of cultural self-elevation by adopting at least the label of "tragedy". In Spain, the situation was different; the primary impetus of control was belief. Thus, Spain did not adopt the classical mode of

---

[189] I try to provide an answer to the question of why seventeenth-century France extracted the classical tragic plots in my "Das Tragische der Racineschen Phèdre", in: Niklas Bender, Max Grosse, and Stephan Schneider (eds.), *Ethos und Form der Tragödie. Für Maria Moog-Grünewald zum 65. Geburtstag*, Heidelberg 2014, pp. 295–313. The possible explanation given there only covers the one piece by Racine mentioned in the title. It would require further efforts to explore the more general reasons for early modern France's remarkably "imitative" reception of Greek and Latin tragedy.—As for an archeological reading of the Spanish *comedia nueva*, that is, a reading directed against the widely spread modernizing interpretation of the plays as tragedy, see my book *Discursive* Renovatio *in Lope de Vega and Calderón*, passim.

[190] In order to avoid misunderstandings: the primacy of demand claimed further above (pp. 54 f.) referred to the impulses directing the "creation" (the assembly) of a new work; the point I am talking about here concerns reception, or, rather, the frameworks governing the reception of artworks as established by diverse cultural communities of different ages.

tragedy; if it extracted its plots, it remodeled them according to the in tendency optimistic template of Christian salvation history.[191]

4.–Taking into account the entirety of aspects discussed in this chapter, the problem as such may be conceptually condensed by putting forth the following question: is there a means of distinguishing between works of art (or cultural artifacts in a more general sense) which are produced in the manner conceived in this book, that is, in a way that is contingent upon a quantity of pre-existing cultural material, and works which are "real" originals? It should be stressed that the state of being based on previous works need not take the shape of imitation; it may as well—as is frequently the case with works from the high modernist period—take the form of a polemical distancing from previous works, on the level of content as well as of form. Insofar as the distancing is not only part of the message, but rather its essence, there is no sensible approach to such works without considering them to be based on material extracted from the net.

Yet, even in the case of artworks which do not exhibit their "intertextuality", it is problematic in principle to assume that they were created *ex nihilo*. If we exclude the possibility of the origins of culture being laid down by a transcendent power (by the gods or a God), we are led to assume that there was, in the history of humankind, at least one "first" narrative, one first tune, one first statue or painting. For all subsequent works of culture, however, I am tempted to hold that there is none that is not at least partially based on previous works. After the "first" start of what we call culture, originality is thus not an absolute, but a relative category. We attribute the term to works and ideas whose overall structures—comprising form as well as content—seem so different from previous structures that we *call* them "original", although they are, to varying extents, results of a recombination of existing material. It seems to be the originality of the combination and the "convincing" character of its result which make us say about a work of art or an idea that it is "original" or an "original creation"—which means that in most cases we mean to say that it is "new". Novelty is the characteristic of works and ideas to which we ascribe the feature of being something more than just a repetition of pre-existing works. The act of withdrawing a unit from the net (mere repetition) is supplemented by the

---

[191] The above-mentioned remodeling of the in tendency tragic story of Orpheus and Eurydice is paradigmatic for the rationale that governed Spain's dealings with the material circulating in the net which stemmed from classical pagan times. I shall return to the discursive strategies mobilized in order to justify this process of disassembly and reassembly in a later chapter (pp. 179 f.).

more or less thoroughgoing reworking, primarily in terms of formal organization, of the extracted unit.

The differentiation between "convincing" and "strange" or "aberrant" recombinations of existing material is to a large extent contingent upon the general historical dynamics of which culture proper is a part. The radical abstractionism of high modernist art would hardly have been received and accepted as "original" rather than "strange" without the context of industrialization, which is based on fragmentation, standardization, and the assembly of "new" items as a process of combination of such standardized material. I would speculate that without the existence of this horizon, works of art such as Picasso's paintings of the cubist period, Marinetti's poems, or the postwar *nouveau roman* would not have been considered "new" and fascinating, but, rather, "bizarre" products of strange or lunatic minds. Recombinations of existing materials whose formal organization appears audacious or even aberrant at first sight—that is, considered from the standpoint of the traditional modes—are accepted as new and original in case these artifacts suggest "answers" to questions pertinent to problems at issue during a given period within a given cultural community. Regardless of the fact of a complete breech of conventional modes, they may even attain the rank of "great" works of art.[192]

5.—If one assumes that, specifically in the case of culture, there is hardly ever anything genuinely "new under the sun", there remains the question of how to theorize the status of the above-characterized "first" narrative or painting or statue—that is, of the not only nominally, but factually original items—whose existence one has to postulate if pursuing the idea of culture as produced within net-like structures, and without appealing to the mythical pattern of a "first conveyance" by way of divine revelation.[193] In this respect, I would tend to

---

[192] As a highly illuminating example for the general problem presented above, see Michael Fried's analysis of Caspar David Friedrich's *Rückenfiguren* as engaging with a problem of self-orientation which was discussed by Kant in his essay "What Does it Mean to Orient Oneself in Thinking?" ("Was heisst: sich im Denken orientiren?" [1786]). Fried does not suggest that Friedrich read Kant and then developed his paintings with *Rückenfiguren* as a sort of illustration of Kant's philosophy. He rather conveys that Friedrich's paintings provide an answer to a problem at issue in that period, an answer articulated by way of presenting paintings whose status as reactions to an open question indeed becomes more accessible when one takes Kant's discursive treatment of the problem into account ("Orientation in Painting: Caspar David Friedrich", in: M. F., *Another Light: Jacques-Louis David to Thomas Demand*, New Haven, CN and London 2014, pp. 111–149).
[193] This difficulty might apply to the exact characterization of the first *homo sapiens sapiens* as well. So far, modern science has simply given her a proper name, Lucy, thus circumventing the necessary question as to what made this living organism, in contrast to her biological parents, into the first human being.

rely upon the concept of "emergence", that is, on the idea that certain objects or concepts are not suddenly "there", but rather come gradually to the "surface", and that, consequently, their being recognized as coherent structures occurs in retrospect only. The "first" narrative, albeit a very short or elementary one, the first, even rudimentary pictorial representation of an animal, might not have been the results of a conscious *creatio ex nihilo*, but rather of gradual augmentations of very elementary units: a singular sound produced by an early human, or a bar drawn in the sand with a rod while pointing at an object, for instance an animal which was either a predator or possible prey. The spontaneous products of acts which initially were not driven by the intention of representation might have been recognized *a posteriori* to have such a representational potential. From this moment of awareness onward, they might have been intentionally used as "signs", that is, as iterable instruments apt to convey meanings and messages to other humans. Starting in times when this potential became conscious to the human mind, the first traces of what is here called the cultural net emerge: the semiotically re-functionalized material items (sounds, lines) are able to operate as semes only in case this re-functionalization is—not even necessarily in an explicit way—agreed upon by a certain quantity of humans, the minimum being two. As soon as this tacit consensus is put into practice, the first and most rudimentary instantiation of the cultural net is already there. The "rest" of the species' cultural history would then be a never-ending process of making use of the existing material by way of replication, imitation, disassembly, and recombination, along with partial re-functionalization. The postulate of acts of concrete extraction from this messy fund of material relies in any case on the possibility to refer to a certain recognizable profile of formal organization, while keeping in mind that "formal organization" may include content-related items, as demonstrated previously with reference to the classical and the biblical variants of a story of loss.

6.—The pitfalls of the net metaphor and of subsidiary constructs such as the metaphor of circulation, which become apparent when discussing the intricate relation between dependency on pre-existing material and "new" configuration, might perhaps be described in the following manner: it is useful to theorize cultural processes by hypothetically positing analogies to processes occurring in the material world or in the biological sphere (as in the case of the rhizome metaphor), if only to overcome all too idealistic views of culture as something merely spiritual. Nevertheless, to whatever or whomever humans owe this characteristic, it *is* a characteristic of humans that they have the ability to act in much more diverse ways than non-human agents (portions of matter, plants, animals). Non-human agents follow in their actions specific laws which are strictly defined. Human agents are certainly not free in the sense postulated by certain strands of Renaissance philosophy, of Enlightenment philosophy, and of Marxism;[194] they are not reasonably describable by the concept of *alter Deus*. But their freedom to choose amongst different options, the possibility to mentally repeat experiences actually made in places remote in space or time or even both, the ability to synthesize items which are far more different from one another than fire and water, etc.—all this makes cultural processes so much more differentiated than their possible analogues in the material and biological worlds that the status of the metaphors designated above should not be anything other than that of a foil, that is, an optic device which renders the specificity of the object in front of it easier to define.

Temporal Incongruences

0.—One major difference between networks in the literal sense and networks in the metaphorical understanding (i.e., culture as a virtual network) may consist in the fact that what floats in the former is always bound to a specific period, whereas, in the case of the latter, there is in principle an everlasting co-presence of floating material dating from very different periods of human history. The temporal incongruences which emerge from this situation may constitute one of the most productive factors of cultural dynamics. At certain moments of cultural history, items floating in the net may contingently (or on behalf of external causes—this point remains to be discussed[195]) hit upon material whose "origin", in the sense of first observable emergence, lies in completely different times and thus within completely different cultural frames and backgrounds.

1.—To illustrate this thesis I should like to refer, once again, to the best-known drama of world literature.[196] The figure of Hamlet is mainly constructed around

---

194 It is quite telling that the anthropological optimism these three schools of modern secular thinking share in principle is on a constantly decreasing line. Marxism posits total freedom as an attainable level only for the stage of communism, and it holds that it will be only at this stage that the species will be able to fully live up to its inherent potential.
195 I shall not further discuss the question of whether it is more appropriate to speak in cases such as the one treated above of a contingent or of an intentional process as the origin of the "encounter" of cultural material dating from different times ("hit upon" versus "are combined with"). The simple reason is that I believe, after some amount of reflection, that there is no satisfactory answer to the point in question. Intentions in this case may well be (but need not be) *a posteriori* constructs.
196 My frequent references to this text are, to some extent at least, contingent upon the fact that I share the common view of considering Shakespeare's play as fascinating; but they are no less conditioned by the fact that this specific drama is well-known to any potential reader

one semantic feature: his hesitancy. Secondary literature has the tendency to consider this characteristic to be a feature that renders Hamlet a particularly "modern", that is, unheroic hero; this, however, is an assumption whose basis is the neglect of two historically distinct strands of cultural material informing the play. Hesitancy as such is the passive variant of the rift between willing and acting, intention and actual performance, the active one being transgression, in the literal sense of the term. This abstract pattern was introduced into the net as far as we know today[197] by way of the story of the Fall in Gen 3. Adam and Eve know what they are allowed to do and what they are prohibited from doing, and are in principle ready to respect God's imperatives. Notwithstanding their intention to comply with the commandment not to eat the apple, they give in to the impulse to act against their conscious will, which is thus proven to be weak, or at least not as strong as it would have to be in order to resist temptation.—In Christian times, for reasons pertaining to the immanent constraints of the rising Christian dogma,[198] Paul generalizes the Old Testament constellation in chap. VII of his Letter to the Romans, making it the basis of his description of the human being under the condition of original sin. The entire passage is built on a rhetorically most impressive dichotomy of knowing and willing on the one hand, acting on the other.[199] Human beings do not do what they intend to do, but act more or less consistently against their own will, giving in to their spontaneous impulses, which are conceived as originating from their material part, the body. Paul's argument is continued by Augustine,[200] the first to extensively elaborate on what was later-on captured by Petrarch with the formula "volui nec potui" (I willed [the good], but was not able to do it), a phrasing which has the virtue of comprising the two variants characterized above, the active as well as the passive. In his *Secretum* (ca. 1350), Petrarch presents this configuration as the reason behind "Franciscus" being a person willing to act according to God's commandments, but who is too weak to definitively abandon his predilections for *luxuria* (physical love) and the attainment of *gloria* (that is, the longing for earthly immortality as an

---

of this study. For whatever reason, *Hamlet* seems to have "survived" the fragmentation of the canon much better than many other dramas mentioned in the course of my argumentation.
197 Meaning: most probably it was introduced long before the text of Genesis that has come down to us was fixed.
198 Regarding this point, see my "Perception, Cognition, and Volition in the *Arcipreste de Talavera*", in: Stephen G. Nichols, Andreas Kablitz, and Alison Calhoun (eds.), *Rethinking the Medieval Senses: Heritage, Fascinations, Frames*, Baltimore, MD 2008, pp. 119–153.
199 Rom 7: 15 ff.
200 See *Confessiones* VIII: 20.

author).²⁰¹ While the Middle Ages developed a relatively benign view of the passive variant of the rupture between consciousness and action, known as *acedia*,²⁰² the age of the Reformation sharpened Paul's and Augustine's description of the nature of the will under the conditions of original sin. It was Luther who formulated in his drastic language this early modern variant of the concept of "weakness" of rational intentions in the most impressive way—by stating that it is not reason that commands the will, but the will that subjugates reason, transforming the latter into a mere "whore" of sin,²⁰³ that is, a force justifying sinful behavior by devising pseudo-rational motives.

Shakespeare's dramas are free of such Teutonic extremism. The portrait of Hamlet in particular²⁰⁴ draws largely on the descriptions of *acedia* circulating in the net before Luther made his somewhat radical contribution to the discussions revolving around the relationship between willing and acting. What Hamlet says about himself is structurally very close to what Petrarch conveys concerning the personage of the *Secretum* who bears the name of Franciscus and who is, at least to a certain extent, an *alter ego* of the author.—It is important to stress that when Shakespeare dramatized the question of the will, he did not draw upon classical sources that had been brought to circulation in the contemporary cultural net once again by humanism, but rather upon material from the Petrarchan tradition, that is, from a secularized Christian fund. Classical antiquity, and Plato in particular, considered *akrasia* to be a problem linked primarily to class and education: Those souls too dull to clearly perceive the ideas during their stay in the cave become the minds of the common people, who are inevitably subject to their bodies' desires, including concupiscence and idleness, and to aggression. Those, however, who are given the privilege of an "enlightened" soul have no difficulties using this "rider"—that is, their reason—to tame these two "horses", and thus to will and to do what is right.²⁰⁵ As opposed as he may have been in many respects to the lessons con-

---

201 For a detailed analysis of Petrarch's text as well as of its Augustinian foil, see my "Das Schweigen der Veritas. Zur Kontingenz von Pluralisierungsprozessen in der Frührenaissance (Überlegungen zum *Secretum*)", in: J. K., *Petrarca. Das Schweigen der Veritas und die Worte des Dichters*, Berlin and New York, NY 2002, pp. 1–53.
202 — which means something like "idleness", "sadness", "lack of initiative", "giving in to the 'natural' weakness of the flesh".
203 Luther, *Werke* (Erlangen edition), vol. 29, p. 241 (in *WA* [=Weimarer Ausgabe]: vol. 18, p. 164).
204 See Jan Mosch, "Heteronomy and Weakness of Will in Shakespeare and Racine", in: Bernhart et al. (eds.), *Poetics and Politics*.
205 Plato, *Phaedrus* 246a–257d.

veyed by his teacher, Aristotle remains largely in agreement with this view. To stay within the limits of *mesotes*—the reasonably conceived middle way between potential extremes—presents, in his thinking, no major problem for the educated man, while the uneducated do not even draw the Stagirite's attention.

What allows us to read *Hamlet*—notwithstanding its debt to Christian moral theology—as more than a morality play in the medieval sense is the fact that the problem of agency is stripped of its overtly religious ties to the Christian tradition, including Petrarch.[206] When Hamlet reflects on his shortcomings, it is not his failure to heed the imperatives of Christian morality[207] that concerns him, but rather his inability to comply with the demands imposed by the norms of masculinity, patriarchy, and his status as a prince.[208]—From the theoretical perspective of this book, this observation corroborates a point treated in a previous chapter, namely, that it is the decomposition of units circulating in the net and the combination of formerly separate parts which produce innovative effects.

But the main point I would like to discuss is the nature of the prerequisites for the modern reception of Hamlet not as a highly problematic person (a "sinner" or an "incompetent aristocrat"), but rather as someone who embodies "modern man". The Hamlet we confront in Shakespeare's play is a problematic character insofar as he ultimately commits himself to blind fate rather than continuing to exist with his—as he sees it—split identity. Contrary to this traditional perspective, the modern reception transforms Hamlet's negative self-evaluation into a positive one: hesitancy is no longer seen as a problem; to the contrary, it is considered to be the "right" attitude in a world where there are no longer any moral certainties. The evaporation of religious belief and the subsequent destabilization of secular moral norms in Western modernity have led to another breakdown of material circulating in the net, namely of the mandatory link between the recognition of the "good" and actual "action". If the notion of the good becomes first relative and then, as a consequence, problem-

---

[206] —who makes use of this tradition in order to subvert it (see my "Das Schweigen der Veritas").

[207] Concrete patterns of problematic behavior, such as the longing for *luxuria* and *gloria* in Petrarch, are not even mentioned.

[208] The most provocative scene of the play, laying bare the above-described decomposition, is certainly the one in which Hamlet decides not to kill Claudius—although the circumstances are propitious—because the latter is praying and would, therefore, *not* go to hell after having been slaughtered.

atic, there is no longer ground on which one would be able to construe hesitancy as negative. The congruence of self-description and positive self-evaluation we commonly call "identity" thus becomes able to integrate weakness of the will. Modern—and even more so postmodern—male intellectuals no longer suffer from refraining from killing their fathers or their fathers' substitutes; they have the tendency to cast themselves as "happy Hamlets" rather than committing suicide.

2.—The complete dissolution of the dichotomy of "good" and "evil" is preceded by the historicization of moral values. Construing reality as something in permanent flux first destabilizes, then problematizes the notion of the "good", as may be illustrated with reference to another great play by Shakespeare, *Julius Caesar* (1599). Although the text seems to convey a position that is close to traditional morality by casting Marc Anthony as a "good" person, the spectators' knowledge of what happened after Caesar's murder informs the play's message. The successor, Augustus, reestablished public order after centuries of civil war; in addition, he laid the grounds for the *pax romana*. It was his work that led to the spread of Roman culture to the north, including the British Isles. If it was an act of disloyalty to kill Caesar, was it for that reason a "bad" action? Or was it rather Caesar who had been the "bad" person? What was a crime at the moment it was perpetrated becomes an act of tyrannicide from the perspective of later ages. Hegelianism is the logical consequence of this process of relativization: if the *telos* of history is happiness in the shape of freedom, everything that has led to this end, that is, everything past, must in the final account be evaluated positively.

3.—One may legitimately raise the question of whether or not there are any generalizable reasons which could explain why cultural items circulating in the net are withdrawn as they are, that is, as units, and why it happens that they are decomposed and extracted from the net only in parts which are "used" in order to assemble "new" cultural material. In an age fond of the idea of "contingency" as the only principle predicable of "reality", it would be easiest to say, within this book's framework, that such decomposition occurs from time to time—accidentally, so to speak—and that by no means every assembly preceded by such a "decomposition" proves to be productive, while at least some do. Considering the examples given above, I have a slight tendency, however, not to conceive of cultural dynamics as completely "autopoietic" (in Luhmann's sense), but as susceptible to "external" impulses. By "external" I do not mean "generated by another (historical or social) net", but rather by means of constellations that first arise within the cultural net, but which would nevertheless be problematically categorized if considered to be merely cultural.

I should like to briefly provide an example: the move towards historicization—in the sense of an attitude that considers everything real to be subject to change over time rather than as instantiations of atemporal basic patterns—is evident in Western history from the Age of Discovery onward. While, up to that age, the Christian West had largely considered permanently evolving realities to be, in essence, "prefigured" in the narratives of Scripture, that is, in God's revelation,[209] the discovery of the New World problematized this "typologizing" view of the phenomenal world. From that time onward, there are no more pre-established guidelines as to what "reality" is.[210] If, however, there is no firm, trans-temporal ground of what one may consider "real", there is no trans-temporality in the case of ethical norms either; what is "good" and what is "bad" become liable to reassessment under varying conditions.

As to the mere fact of the discoveries, there is nothing more to say than that it was contingent in the sense of accidental, if one wants to avoid the invocation of "higher powers"—in this case, of the Christian God deciding that the continents thus far unaware of the gospel be freed from the obscurity of ignorance in matters of faith precisely at that moment in time. Columbus was one of the innumerable megalomaniacal narcissists in human history. His good fortune and subsequent fame was caused by favorable (in this case: meteorological) circumstances which assured that he did not fail—as do most megalomaniacs, whom we never read about in history precisely because of their failure. And one may gather from the reports of subsequent *conquistadores*, particularly from the many "miracles" worked by God they invoke to explain why they prevailed under most unfavorable conditions, to what extent it was due to mere chance (*prospera fortuna*) that the discoveries did not remain an episode of European history, to be forgotten after one or two centuries—as may indeed have happened after the very first "real" contact of Europeans with the soil of what was later named America.[211]

But the fact that people from fifteenth-century Europe began to consider the idea that the world described in Scripture might not be the "entire" world, along with the fact that such ideas were not rejected as idiocy or heresy, is, perhaps, not contingent at all, but, rather motivated by the extraction and re-

---

[209] See Erich Auerbach's seminal essay "Figura", in: Auerbach, *Scenes from the Drama of European Literature*, pp. 11–76.

[210] Regarding this point, see my "The Traditional Cosmos and the New World"; see also chap. 5 of my *Discursive* Renovatio *in Lope de Vega and Calderón*, which deals with the antecedent to the discoveries, the Portuguese expansion into North Africa.

[211] I am referring to the—as it seems—nowadays uncontested assumption that the first discoverer was Leif Ericson.

combination of material circulating in the cultural net. I am referring to concepts first identifiable in a decree by the Parisian bishop Étienne Tempier, issued in the year 1277. As astonishing as this may seem from a present-day perspective, one of the bishop's main tasks was the supervision of all instruction taking place in the different departments of the Sorbonne.[212] The problem Tempier—an otherwise unimportant figure in medieval intellectual history—sought to settle was the presence of an Islamic variant of Aristotelianism which had made its way into the net under the label of "Averroism". Without going into details, it will suffice here to say that in Islam, there is no divine "savior" who is said to have sacrificed himself in order to redeem humankind; accordingly, there is no need to conceive of all human beings as corrupted by something like original sin. For this reason, there is the possibility[213] of a radical rationalism. It seems that Averroes, for whatever reason, was one of the (not very numerous) thinkers in the Muslim tradition who took advantage of this possibility. Since his translations and commentaries were the main source at the Christian West's disposal for gaining access to the works of the one who continued to be considered *the "philosophus"* after the end of paganism, Averroes' own ideas also penetrated the parts of the cultural net accessible to the West. There is no documentary evidence which would settle the question of whether it was Tempier's own insight that the assumption of human reason's capacity to fully understand the world might be dangerous to Christian dogma.[214] In any case, in the aforementioned year, the bishop made use of his authority in order to anathematize 219 theses which were taught at the Sorbonne and which gave expression to the basic positions of a radical, Averroist Aristotelianism.[215] The line of argument to be found in the document is ex-

---

212 To put it explicitly: I am not talking about the divinity school only. In medieval Europe, the ecclesiastical authorities controlled the teaching in all schools (law school, medical school, the liberal arts college).
213 I should like to stress, specifically with present-day problems in view, this word. There is no cogent rationalism *inherent* in Islam.
214 There are hints that he promulgated his anathematization of Averroism—which, by implication, targeted Thomism as well—at the initiative of the Pope, Petrus Lusitanus (John XXI), who is said to have been an Augustinist.
215 The first modern edition of the document was printed by Henri Denifle, OP ("Opiniones ducentae undeviginti Sigeri de Brabantia, Boetii de Dacia aliorumque, a Stephano espiscopo Parisiensi de consilio doctorum sacrae scripturae condemnatae", in: *Chartularium universitatis parisiensis*, Paris 1891–1899, vol. 1, pp. 543–588; the above quotes are from the anathematized sentences 34 and 48). As to the document's importance for the intellectual history of the West, see Hans Blumenberg's *The Legitimacy of the Modern Age*, Robert M. Wallace (tr.), Cambridge, MA 1983; see also, with an interpretation partly differing from Blumenberg's, my *Discursive Renovatio in Lope de Vega and Calderón*, chap. 4.

tremely consistent. Tempier relies on the dogma of God's unrestricted omnipotence in order to fend off humans' pretense to fully penetrate the mysteries of the world by means of reason. Divine omnipotence, Tempier argues, includes the ability to change the course of the world, to add "more worlds" ("plures mundos"), and to add something new ("aliquid de novo") to Creation.—The most probably unintentional consequence of this attempt at reasserting Christian dogma in the face of the assaults of rationalism was nothing less than the debilitation of biblical revelation. For the argument implies that, as true as the world-model implied by Scripture may have been with regard to the time when it was revealed by God, it may be just as insufficient for a subsequent period in which God may have changed his views and intentions and may have acted upon these "new" ideas on behalf of his omnipotence.—It took more than a century, and the endeavors of William Occam, one of the greatest minds of that age, to substantiate and spread the ideas first written down by Tempier. Resistance from the ecclesiastical dignitaries was fierce, and the final outcome of the internal ideological conflicts triggered by the controversy was nothing less than the Reformation. The Roman Catholic Church continued to assert that God had restricted his omnipotence when he decided to produce the Creation, submitting himself to the laws of a *potentia Dei ordinata*, whereas Lutherans and Calvinists were ready to accept that God is omnipotent in the most fundamental sense of the term.—The intra-religious controversies being a separate phenomenon, Tempier's notion of a world or of worlds which may not be fully taken into account by what one reads in Scripture became, in its popularized variant, a focal point for many adventurous minds of early modern times, for early scientists as well as for adventurers in the more literal sense.

4.—Might it be possible to disentangle the complicated panorama just presented, which is only a somewhat gross rendering of the "real" intricacies to be encountered when dealing with the point in question? I have a slight preference to consider the cultural net and the effects produced by it as an enabling structure for events which themselves cannot be reasonably categorized as "only cultural". If a meteorite hits our planet, there is no man-made (cultural) logic involved; perhaps there is some cosmic or even "divine" logic behind it, but these are questions which are not of interest here. If, however, a man named Columbus reaches the shores of an island he then names "La Española" (present-day Haiti/the Dominican Republic), there is certainly more than just human logic involved, but, to a certain extent, the event is partly attributable to the workings of human logic; it is different from a win in a lottery. Above all: the event as such is real; it is not merely conceptual, imagined, textual, fantasmatic. And it is the event as a whole, not only its culturally conditioned aspects, which then produces "new" cultural effects such as the decomposition of the unit (existing, I suppose, from the beginnings of human culture) which consists of the firm link between the "real", conceived as eternal in its shape and essence, and the "good", which is, consequently, likewise conceived as immutable. If the real reveals itself as liable to change over time, the good becomes, so to speak, de-autochthonized; it loses the firm ground on which it was able to grow in the past, becoming autonomous in the sense that it has to permanently redefine itself without any external vantage point from the perspective of which it could be consistently defined. One of the many highly mediated results of the processes outlined above is the creation of the figure of Hamlet—weakness of the will, but no longer considered sinful—and the positive evaluation of a "Hamletic" attitude towards life, as observable in twentieth-century modernity, but including a literary tradition that already begins with Flaubert's *L'Éducation sentimentale* (1869).

Accessibility

0.—Up to this point, I have been discussing problems revolving around the question of how cultural "producers" might actually work with the material circulating in the net. I have thus postponed an aspect I shall now treat in more detail, namely, the possibility of gaining access to and then extracting material floating in the net. As mentioned in the introductory chapter, it seems to be appropriate to first of all take the problem of accessibility into account, and only then the activities of controlling agencies of any kind, a point I shall treat separately in a subsequent chapter.

1.—As to accessibility in general, I should like to nuance to a certain extent[216] my earlier rejection of linguistic competence as a factor of importance. Language does indeed count when it comes to accessing material circulating in the net. It was the previous diffusion of French as the language of the educated which enabled the smooth importation of French theater to the Tsarist court—a phenomenon accompanied and accentuated by a very literal migration, that is, of Princess Sophie from the house of Anhalt-Zerbst[217] to Moscow, where she took the name of Catherine and acceded to the Russian throne under somewhat questionable or, at least, obscure circumstances. One has to add that this "im-

---

216 —by which I wish to imply that it might be outweighed by other factors. I will come back to this point on various occasions, most prominently in the chapter on Herder (pp. 232–250), but also in the chapter "Borderlines" (pp. 99–115).
217 I should perhaps add, once again, that the language spoken at eighteenth-century German courts was not German, but French.

port" was supported, that is, mediated at least to some extent, by the German reception of French classical drama's main aesthetic features (Johann Christoph Gottsched), and, in addition, by the activities in Eastern Europe of itinerant German theater troupes.[218] It might be a futile but nonetheless instructive exercise to speculate about what would have happened within Russian theatrical culture, and within culture at large,[219] had the heir to the throne married a princess not from an enlightened French-style Central European court, but, for instance, from Serbia. Once again, the example evidences the centrality of material agents of processes of cultural exchange. "Concepts" as such are not able to travel.

2.–The language problem involved in the example just outlined is of even greater importance for a phase of Western culture highly relevant for the period under scrutiny in this book. It was only the readiness of Western academics to study Ancient Greek, a process initiated once again by a migration in the literal sense—the flight of Constantinople's Christian community to the West immediately before the conquest of the city by the Ottomans—which revived the "dead" material of classical Greek culture floating in the net, rendering it available for actual cultural production.

I shall dedicate some more detailed remarks to the "circulation" of Boccaccio's last *Decameron* novella, the story of Griselda, in a subsequent chapter;[220] in this context, suffice it to say that the enormous resonance of the narrative throughout early modern Europe was certainly conditioned by the fact that its translation into Latin by the author's friend Petrarch brought it to a level of accessibility which transcended the Italian original.

---

218 The aforementioned book by Ospovat and related articles of his referred to in the book contain all the details and necessary differentiations of the above, cursory remarks (*Terror and Pity*).

219 As mentioned previously, (early) modern Russian drama and theater already originated, in a way, under the reign of Catherine's predecessor Elizabeth, who was "autochthonous". But it needs to be stressed that Elizabeth's grandfather, Tsar Aleksei, had the first Russian court theater opened in 1672 with the performance of a play about Artaxerxes written by a German theologian, and that the first public theater, established in Moscow by Peter the Great, was mainly run by German itinerant troupes. Into the nineteenth century, Russian plays were mainly *peredelki*, that is, adaptations of Western and Central European plays (German, French, English) in Russian and making use of Russian names and places for setting the action. And the important role of Peter and Elizabeth notwithstanding, the systematic importation of Central and Western European Enlightenment culture into Russia (Voltaire, Diderot, the Brothers Grimm, etc.) was the work of Catherine the Great.

220 Pp. 141–143.

The reception history of the *Celestina*, as thematized by Sven Thorsten Kilian,[221] gives occasion to another remark pertinent to the question of the importance or unimportance of linguistic borders for the smoothness with which a given text circulates in the net. The *Celestina* was the most widespread literary text in Europe during the sixteenth century. It was translated into Latin; but there is indisputable evidence that the overwhelming majority of the translations into a wide range of vernaculars were based neither on the Spanish original nor on the Latin version, but on a translation into Italian that was completed as early as in 1506.

To formulate it briefly on a rather abstract level: apart from an all-encompassing *lingua franca*, there may be in certain contexts and in certain periods "partial" *linguae francae*, that is, languages read by huge portions of the educated. As my examples show, the reasons for such a status may differ. With respect to Italian in the early modern age, it is most probably the politically fragmented landscape of the country which helps to explain the phenomenon. Parts of the Apennine peninsula were ruled by the French, parts by the Spaniards, and still other parts by the Germans (the "Holy Roman Empire of the German Nation"). Educated people from these countries interacted in Italy, with the natural result that they exchanged views, communicating with one another in Italian. One should add that Rome was at that time the uncontested center of Christianity, and that almost all (male) Europeans who later on in their lives became "consumers" of culture took a "grand tour" of the country in their youth, for reasons at the same time religious and more generally cultural; the conviction that Rome was the cradle of the West was firmly rooted in all Western and Central European minds.

In other periods of cultural history, and for different reasons, it was French that assumed the role of such a partial *lingua franca*. Later on, and only with respect to certain territories, particularly Central and Eastern Europe, German played this role. Today, the fact is that if a literary work is not translated from its original language into English, it has almost no chance of circulating in the net beyond the borders of its own country.

3.—It may prove instructive to focus briefly on the cultural situation in India during the period under consideration, since it may help to throw light on a more intricate facet of accessibility than the more or less self-evident aspect of linguistic codes. It is not only in the age of colonialism that there has been an

---

221 *"Escrituras andantes"*; see also Sven Thorsten Kilian, "Opening Spaces for the Reading Audience: Fernando de Roja's *Celestina* (1499/1502) and Niccolò Machiavelli's *Mandragola* (1518)", in: Gvozdeva et al. (eds.), *Dramatic Experience*, pp. 13–34.

at times very vivid cultural exchange between the Indian subcontinent and Europe. As far as philosophy and belief systems are concerned, the lack of extant written material allows only for speculation—such as the thesis that Stoicism was influenced by Indian forms of quietism.[222] But as to the basic "tool" of all culture, language, there is incontestable evidence: the majority of modern European languages derives from the same roots as Sanskrit. Consequently, the distinction between "Eastern" and "Western" cultures has to be considered a merely conceptual one, a construction which emerged most probably with the establishment of monotheism in the West.[223] The idea that there is no more than one god seems to have first emerged in Egypt and Israel, that is among tribes whose languages do not share a (relatively recent) ancestor with Sanskrit, which adds a further facet to the point just made.

If we thus assume that there is no "real" cultural gap between the "East" and the "West", one has to raise the question of why what we call "civilization"[224] was invented twice in human history, once in the Mediterranean world and once again, or even beforehand, in China.[225] Direct exchange between the West and China remained very low-level up to the seventeenth century, and India as a possible transit zone entertaining close cultural links to both the Mediterranean and the Far East does not seem to have actually fulfilled this role, or only to an extent that was so minimal that no thoroughgoing transculturation between the West and the Far East was able to take place. The only viable

---

222 If one follows this quite probable hypothesis, one is able to conceive a possible explanation for a phenomenon that frequently accompanies processes of cultural transfer: the reduced general impact of the imported material, compared to the place of its first emergence. Stoicism has been of great importance within Western intellectual history, but its impact cannot compare with the influence of quietist attitudes towards life's contingencies within Indian cultural history. Stoicism severed Indian quietism, so to speak, from its larger religious horizon. It is much easier to accept misfortune on the basis of a belief in metempsychosis than on the basis of the highly intellectualized Stoic notion that matter and all material things are ultimately irrelevant.
223 It is an implication of the above argument that there is also no insurmountable cultural "gap" between the Indian subcontinent and China. As to language, the distance is enormous, but as to general worldviews, Buddhism constitutes a factor of highly integrative capacity. I shall come back to this point in more detail in a later chapter (pp. 121–123).
224 In view of the focus of this book, I refer primarily to what historians typically call "high civilizations" (*Hochkulturen*), meaning, those stages of human cultural development that include (be it rudimentary) writing systems. Previous stages are considered only occasionally; according to the findings available so far, it seems that the civilizations of the Eastern Mediterranean and of East Asia had a common root located in East Africa.
225 The question of whether the high civilizations of pre-Columbian America were in some way dependent on cultural patterns brought to these continents from East Asia or whether there is only a genetic (pre-civilizational) link cannot be discussed here in detail.

explanation—which would be applicable, too, in the case of further non-European high civilizations, e.g. pre-Columbian America—is to re-accentuate the very material, that is, non-linguistic aspects of accessibility. Geological factors—in the case of China, the Central Asian desert as well as the Himalayan mountain range; in the case of the Americas, the two oceans—which favor or hinder instances of exchange of any kind should not be underestimated, at least as far as the pre-technological era is concerned. As may be deduced from the spread of Buddhism from India to China, such geological factors do not necessarily make cultures into monadic entities; and it was not only the Himalayan mountain range, but also the Pacific Ocean that our ancestors from prehistorical times succeeded in crossing, as incredible as that may appear to us. But, on the other hand, one should not ignore the fact that such geological factors constituted a serious impediment to a smooth, rapid, and quantitatively significant circulation of cultural material. Accustomed as we are to global communication's ability to overcome distance, it is difficult for us to appreciate the limitations of intercultural exchange between "different" and "distant" cultures in the periods of human history before the early modern age.

4.—But what is in my view the most important point to be discussed under the heading of accessibility is yet another one. One could provisionally identify the point in question as the receptivity of a given cultural structure to phenomena from outside. There is a huge variety of sub-structures to be pondered under this category. Because they are so important, I propose to discuss some of them—e.g., religious beliefs[226]—separately.

As to further points to be considered, the primary item might be basic social structures. Cultural artifacts are transferred more easily from one hierarchical and centralized courtly society to another than from a courtly society to a loosely structured one organized around federated kinship clans. One may infer from this and comparable considerations that after a considerable period of activity, cultural configurations will become obsolete[227] in the sense that they no longer stimulate new configurations of the material they contain.[228] "Nostalgia" for the past and identity discourses (the latter being based on the construction of "traditions", that is, on historical narratives) are very recent phenomena in the species' history. One of their main implications for cultural production is that they render the aforementioned obsolescence-principle itself

---

226 See pp. 121–123 and pp. 281–284.
227 See, however, my qualifications of this statement at the end of the present chapter.
228 As shall be illustrated below with reference to the pastoral (a configuration of material that seems to have become obsolete), things are, in fact, somewhat more complicated than expressed above (pp. 226–230).

obsolete; under the label of the "interesting" or the "fascinating", or under the label of "our" prehistory, cultural material manifesting completely outdated social structures and behavioural norms may thus be extracted from the net.

5.—One factor of cultural configurations in the sense of actual "works" which is of lesser importance than generally assumed but must nevertheless be taken into account when it comes to the question of life cycles (and thus to the conditions of accessibility) is the physical substratum of the configurations in question along with its resistance to time. Configurations transmitted only in oral settings have a relatively short life cycle as far as their ability to generate new material is concerned. Material circulating in the net orally is liable to rapid change, even to decomposition. It is only on a very abstract level (i.e., that level expounded by scholars such as Vladimir Propp and Claude Lévi-Strauss in their analyses of folk tales and myths)—that is, in a form identifiable only with difficulty—that they may be preserved for longer periods of cultural history. Paintings and statues, as is well known from the history of the artifacts of classical antiquity, may literally perish in case their physical substratum is destroyed by natural catastrophes, acts of violence, or simply the corrosive effects of time. On the other hand, thanks to modern technology and its capacity for reproduction, oral material preserved textually (in manuscripts, as printed text, or in electronic formats), paintings or sculptures replicated by various processes of a "compact" or "notational" kind, as well as musical scores may have life cycles of infinite duration. This dramatically enhanced accessibility may help "resurrect" cultural material fallen into obsolescence on behalf of its outdated contexts. In societies oriented around writing systems, such artifacts may be rediscovered by disciplines like historiography or philology, brought to the renewed attention of a broader public, and re-functionalized in a manner Schiller called "sentimental". They may thus be re-actualized and become highly active once again.

6.—To continue this metonymical chain of characteristics, the latter remark leads immediately to the question of cultural institutions, that is, of agencies whose main or even sole task is to provide accessibility to material from the net such that it is continually re-circulated once its use—including its "re-profiling" by way of decomposition and synthesis into novel works—in the new context has been established. In societies that have created specialized institutions whose purpose is to keep material circulating in the net—schools and universities, for example—there is evidently a very high receptivity to cultural material of any kind, along with a strong tendency to subvert the efforts of ideologically-oriented control agencies to limit access to net-based material. The implementation of such institutional structures in societies where they did not exist previously or where they existed, but in very different configurations, triggers in a spectacular way all sorts of processes of exchange, as may be observed, under differing circumstances, in the age of colonialism and in the age of globalization.

7.—Finally, there is a factor relevant to the question of accessibility which is worth considering, but difficult to characterize terminologically. In order to illustrate it, I should like to refer, once again, to the "merry men companies" investigated by Katja Gvozdeva.[229] As already mentioned, these companies were amateur groups belonging to the middle or upper classes in sixteenth-century Italy who dedicated some of their free time to acting in drastically comic, even obscene performances, closely linked to their real lifeworld. Some inspiration was drawn from the classical tradition, but significant parts of the performances were "invented" by members of the group. The cultural practice underlying the phenomenon as a whole is the carnival qua instrument of the temporary suspension of social norms in view of the preservation of their overall sustainability.[230] This practice may have had its antecedents in classical Greece (the festivals in honor of Dionysus), but its identifiable origins lie in aspects of pagan Roman culture appropriated by the Christian West. It is beyond my competence to answer the question of whether or not there are similar patterns of coping with aggressions triggered by the pressure of rigid social and religious norms in other societies.[231] Ridiculing the norms of civic behavior, including the persons in charge of guaranteeing their application, or rather the license to do that within certain institutionalized limits, seems, however, to be a rather specific cultural pattern. This may imply that performative practices belonging to this basic pattern can migrate smoothly within the space where the pattern is present, but are unlikely to be extracted from the net in places where the pattern does not exist.[232]

---

229 *Compagnie d'hommes joyeux.*
230 Bakhtin's theory of the carnival continues to be one of the most valuable findings of twentieth-century cultural studies (*Rabelais and His World*).
231 Within traditional Jewish culture, there is a comparable social practice legitimized by the religious authorities (Purim). I continue to believe that modern occidental culture is a mix of Jewish, (pagan) Greek, (pagan) Roman, and Christian patterns. As all these cultures build on previous ones (Egyptian, Mesopotamian), this qualification is much less exclusivist than it might appear to "politically correct" readers of this study.
232 The violent reactions, in large parts of the present-day Muslim world, to the publications of some caricatures of Mohammed, the Prophet, in a newspaper issued in a provincial Danish town may be a good example of what I try to convey above: in cases where the general framework within which such cultural material has to be assessed in order to be understood appropriately is unknown, there is either no accessibility to such material or one leading to incomprehension only. If the material in question concerns features of minor importance, the reaction in the latter case will be an attitude of indifference; if more sensitive points, e.g., those pertaining to religious belief, are involved, the constellation might lead to acts of violence.

8.—These latter restrictions, along with many others, do not apply systematically in an age which is beyond this book's reach but which must at least be evoked from time to time, since it is almost impossible to abstract from the parameters of one's own age when discussing questions of cultural history or theory. In the era of modernity proper, beginning with the age of Romanticism, the West has developed—theoretically as well as practically—an approach to exogenous cultural material that one may call "exoticist", "sentimental", or "aestheticizing". This approach abstracts artifacts or cultural material in a broader sense from its original contexts, from the motivations that brought it into being, from its former meaning, etc., in order to receive it playfully, or to re-functionalize it with a view to a serious intention which might be far removed from the original one. Against this backdrop, one could legitimately posit that nineteenth- and twentieth-century Western culture has developed conceptual and technical tools to enable an almost unrestricted access to the material circulating in the universal cultural net. This period has thus become one of a level of cultural activity unprecedented in human history, and, even more so, of a configuration which seems to be evolving towards a relatively homogeneous "global culture".[233]

Borderlines

0.—In general terms, and the above-discussed partial restrictions notwithstanding, the circulation of material taking place in what is here called the cultural net is to be conceived of as limitless with regard to both time and space. The "day" of its creation is the moment when one of our very first ancestors as *homo sapiens sapiens* exchanged some information with another member of the emerging species, who then communicated it to a third member of the tribe; and its final "day" will be doomsday, the moment when the existence of the only culture-producing species on this planet will come to an end. If this day occurs before our progeny have colonized space, the territory belonging to the cultural net is limitless only as far as this planet is concerned.

1.—Conceiving of cultural processes in such a way, that is, as emancipated from humans' conscious actions, as taking place in an anonymous and erratic fashion, seems at first sight to destabilize all the ordering parameters by which we try to systematize what happens in the world. There are two fundamental patterns of such systematization. Firstly and most importantly, when dealing with

---

[233] Relapses into a narrowly defined communitarianism, as, e.g., in certain present-day Islamic countries, may of course occur at any time; cultural history is never streamlined; it seems always to consist of dominant and recessive tendencies.

"events", there is the parameter of the "period", that is, of certain identifiable units of historical time; the notion is based on the assumption that the unit under scrutiny is distinct from other such units. Secondly, there is the parameter linked to space and its "natural" divisions, such as continents and parts of continents delimitated by large rivers, lakes, or mountain chains, etc. What becomes of the current concepts of, say, classical Greek culture as distinct from present-day Chinese culture if all of culture is conceived as the reshaping of a huge fund of material circulating permanently in a limitless virtual net? Isn't there even some self-contradiction implied in talking of the "early modern period (in Europe, that is, within a specific space) and the cultural net"?

It may constitute one major benefit of the approach I am proposing that it liberates scholarly discussions from the remnants of essentialist conceptions of ages and periods which continue to flourish, consciously or not, notwithstanding that there seems to have emerged a consensus that such categories are not "real" givens, but rather concepts specialists agree upon because they are able to account for many factors that are doubtlessly "real".[234] It would be problematic to deny these differences in favor of a concept of time without periodization. The technological capacities to submit nature to human goals and purposes attained in the twentieth century differ significantly from the level attained in the tenth century. In addition, there are evident "leaps" in human cultural development, that is, certain periods during which more "real" innovation takes place than in other periods of a comparable length of time. Between the fifth and the eighth centuries CE, there was not very much going on in Europe which would be worth reporting.[235] Things are different one mil-

---

234 In this sense, even current dichotomous concepts like the Middle Ages / modernity, the early modern age / modernity proper, or classical modernity / the postmodern age do not at all seem to be devoid of sense from my perspective.

235 All such evaluations are relative, not absolute. There was some cultural transfer going on in the "Dark Ages", too. As is well known, this transfer was mainly mediated by the Norsemen (Vikings), whose violent raids into territories as far as Sicily brought items of Germanic culture to the Mediterranean south and items of classical Roman culture back to Northern Europe. But it is very difficult to assess the long-term impact of these processes of transfer. It may be the case that the military expeditions of the Norsemen and their unintentional collateral effects in the realm of culture paved the way for the rather smooth penetration of Christianity and, along with it, Roman culture into the whole of Scandinavia starting in the tenth century. There are even (in my view daring) hypotheses that courtly love lyrics, the first vestiges of which are to be found in the so-called "school of Sicily" based at the court of the Norman kings governing the island in the Middle Ages, originate from Germanic patterns of interaction between the sexes, as distinct from Mediterranean ones. The fact that one is dealing here with ages that were not without reason termed "dark", that is, which can no longer be rendered transparent, since there is not sufficient extant written material, makes it impossible to pronounce a definitive assessment of the intensity of transfer processes. From the beginning of Charlemagne's

lennium later, that is, in the period between the fifteenth and the eighteenth centuries.—To put it succinctly: periodization is not invalidated by the concept of a (temporally) limitless net. It is revealed, however, for what it is: a heuristic tool by means of which we try to mentally represent the endless flow of time, considered according to certain value-related premises, or, in other words, ideological choices we agree upon within a given community to the point of not even problematizing them. In the case above, it is the parameter of human history as progress, that is, the occidental mindset that makes such periodization seem reasonable. From a vantage point inspired by other value-related choices, such an approach would lose its justification.

2.—I should like to illustrate this point by briefly referring to my own recent experience. My contact with Chinese culture has taught me a lot about cultural differences in temporal conceptualization. On various occasions, I have had the privilege to visit the finest museums in mainland China as well as in Taiwan under the expert guidance of colleagues, Chinese professors trained in China who specialize in the history of Chinese art. Over the course of time, I came to realize that my questions regarding the differences between the paintings of this or that period (periods are, as is well known, labeled in Chinese terminology not by conceptual, but rather by proper names referring to ruling dynasties) somehow irritated my guides, and that my subsequent, very speculative hypotheses regarding the "evolution" of this or that stylistic feature I took myself to have detected in certain paintings with respect to previously dominant styles irritated them even more. From this experience, and after reflecting upon these encounters with the "other", I came to realize that a concept like the Western idea of history as progress or "evolution" does not exist in traditional Chinese thinking. It is evident that this conceptual "lack" is not contingent. Within the cyclical conceptions of time shared by Buddhism, Confucianism, and Daoism, there is no basis for such an idea. For the same reason, there is nothing that would correspond to the European concept of historical consciousness; it is not without reason that Chinese people tear down buildings when they are run-down, that is, approximately thirty years after their construction, and that they approach the carefully preserved remains of former times they visit on a trip to Europe with exactly the same "exoticizing" attitude with which they approach the imitations to be seen in places like Las Vegas on their next "grand tour".

---

restitution of the Empire onwards, things are different. On this basis, I believe the above comparison to be justifiable.

3.—But if temporal borderlines may be highly ideological, that is, arbitrary, what about the certainly more critical conceptual borderlines linked to spatial delimitations interpreted as causing cultural differences? This point concerns the concept of "national cultures" criticized on many occasions within this book.[236] Does the net metaphor, applied to the domain of culture, imply that there is no such thing as an "English", or a "Chinese", or a "native Australian" culture? In the case of space and culture, the difference between the still dominant conceptualization of Romantic provenance and my approach is not primarily linked to the difference between supposed realities and the awareness that these "realities" are based on ideological constructions; it is, rather, a question of degree that is at stake here, and, related to it, the question of how to give expression to different quantities (degrees) if one translates the differences to the level of qualities.

As to "national" cultures, it shall remain uncontested that there are different natural languages and that differences in language affect the facility with which a given cultural material circulates in the net. Works written in a *lingua franca* circulate much more easily than works written in a vernacular that no one other than its native speakers is able to understand. However, this does not mean that every single item formulated in a *lingua franca* (Latin in the period in question, English in present-day times) attains a degree of recognition comparable to the scope of the language in which it is written. There are a number of further factors, best summarized in this book's terminology as "control" on the one hand, "demand" on the other[237] (and perhaps, to add a third aspect that will call for theorization, "appeal"[238]), which heavily influence the degree of propagation of a material that, given its linguistic profile, could be expected to attain the level of universal presence.

Even in the case of material first formulated in minor languages, there is, in principle, no obstacle to gaining universal recognition. One cultural intermediary able to communicate the item in question in a less minor language suffices to turn stories "invented", or, rather, synthesized within very secluded language communities into material that is generally accessible and even made use of; the cultural net is, indeed, extremely flexible. In this case, I am thinking in particular of the work done by Western anthropologists—professionals or amateurs in the literal sense, mainly missionaries—starting in the sixteenth century in the Americas and continuing worldwide into the twentieth century,

---

236 See below, pp. 232–274, the chapter dedicated to this question.
237 See the chapter below (pp. 134–150).
238 See the corresponding chapter below (pp. 202–209).

who brought to general knowledge and to universal recognition the stories of people that had not been connected to the larger cultural net for several thousand years on behalf of the facticity of spatial borders.

4.–To give just one example: the myths or narratives concerning man and cosmos created by the Mayas and existing since time immemorial were first codified in a collection named *Popol Vuh*; this may even have happened prior to the Spanish conquest. After the conquest, the collection is said to have been written down in Latin script, but in the Mayan language. This version was translated into Spanish by Francisco Ximénez, a Dominican, in 1702; the manuscript is still extant and belongs nowadays to a rare book collection housed in the library of the University of Chicago. In the second half of the nineteenth century, the Spanish version was translated first into French, then into almost all major Western languages. Its content finally formed the basis for the mythological horizon of a novel—nevertheless at least partially nonfictional—dealing with the brutal exploitation of the twentieth-century indigenous population of Guatemala by the US-American agricultural industry, a novel entitled *Hombres de maíz* (1949), for which its author, Miguel Ángel Asturias, received the Nobel Prize in 1967. From this moment onwards, cultured people worldwide have known about the stories originally composed by the Mayas, which means that the material has been (re-)absorbed by the universal cultural net. As a result, it is not only used for the assembly of "new" literary texts, but has also become one of the many components out of which present-day social discourses as powerful as the ecological narrative of a "sustainable" interaction between humans and the other parts of the biosphere have emerged.[239]

To summarize this point: in our traditional, Herderian thinking about culture, the consequences of spatial differences and the linguistic differences linked to them—which are, as such, uncontestable facts—are grossly overestimated. And if we consider without any prejudice the astonishing number of processes of transculturation that have taken place over the centuries, we should perhaps become skeptical of the widespread idea that structural differences between different languages condition incompatible worldviews.—It was not without reason that I just referred to the most influential "father" of the concept of diverse "national cultures". The discrepancies between Herder's ideas and my approach are connected to the former's main contribution to the discussion, namely, to link linguistic difference to biological difference ("race") and to spa-

---

[239] Regarding this point, see my "'Doscientas mil jóvenes ceibas de mil años'. Autochthoner Mythos und okzidentaler Logos in Miguel Ángel Asturias' *Hombres de maíz*", *Romanistisches Jahrbuch* vol. 42 / 1991, pp. 303–327.

tial difference (autochthony in the literal sense of being "rooted" or "grounded" in one specific place and of deriving one's cultural impulses from that ground only, thus becoming "self-grounded"). It is this substantialist concept of national culture, together with its consequent features of mutual exclusiveness and of the appropriateness of cultural material only for its "own" people, that is contested by my approach.[240]

5.—This said, the concept of culture as originating from a decentered virtual net does not preclude conceiving of constellations of cultural material as characteristic of particular places and periods. These specific features mainly derive from ideological choices dominant within certain periods and in particular places; with regard to this book's historical framework, i.e. early modernity, the importance of religious denomination—Catholic, Protestant (Lutheran or Calvinist), or Anglican—certainly cannot be neglected when it comes to discussing differences linked to linguistic diversity. As a result of ideological choices operationalized by what I shall call "control agencies",[241] the Spanish language, for instance, is linked in the period in question to the basic patterns of Tridentine Catholicism; the (early modern) use of the English language is linked to a tendency to blur differences between or to avoid saying anything precise regarding religious denomination; the French language is linked in the early modern period to a surface structure of Catholic ideologemes along with a hidden strand of Augustinism, that is, of proto- or crypto-Protestantism.—Specific "national" features may also derive from political choices or contingencies; a centralized absolutist state tends to utilize material drawn from the net that differs at least partially from that drawn from the same network by smaller communities. Finally, such "national" features may be linked to the rank of the linguistic community in question in the hierarchy of powers: a dominant community such as France or England has different demands than a community in the state of emergence, as was Russia at the time in question. There is a multitude of further questions to be taken into consideration; for the time being, it shall suffice to say that there are links between language and the profile of cultural productions which justify continuing to speak heuristically of an "English", a "French", or a "Spanish" early modern drama or culture.

Nevertheless, there is one very important aspect with respect to which the traditional conceptualization and my approach differ not only in terms of theory but also as to concrete systematizations of the cultural field. If there is no "autochthony", but rather specific shapings of material extracted from a common cultur-

---

[240] See my more extensive polemics below, pp. 232–274.
[241] See pp. 134–150.

al net, specificity is nothing but a statistically relevant parameter; it is not a substantive designation, meaning: there are exceptions, and these exceptions may be of great importance. Allowing myself to tie this point in with a previous remark concerning religious denomination, I should like to briefly mention two cases I consider striking in this respect. In the case of Spanish literature from the period in question, there is a strong tendency—which I share in principle— to consider the works of authors such as Lope de Vega, Calderón, Tirso de Molina, and Quevedo as specifically Spanish in the sense of the term outlined above. But what about Cervantes? Translated into another language, and after assimilating proper names and places (by taking into account the associative dimension of these names; every country has a "la Mancha", that is, a region which is considered remote and at the same time ridiculously retrograde), wouldn't it be possible to imagine the *Quijote* as a novel from the British Isles, from France (the hero would then be a *chevalier provenant du Gers*), or even from Germany?

My second example is taken from the one European culture which in that age and even today insists more than others on its exceptional status, France. I am ready to concede that it is difficult to imagine pieces by Racine and Corneille as having been produced in other European communities of the period, since no other country developed such a sophisticated variant of courtly society as France; Molière, whose plays refer to a much less specific middle-class bourgeois world, would already be a borderline case. But my example bears the name of Montaigne. As long as one were to change certain references to the specific places where the ideas expounded in the *Essais* were first developed, I do not see any major difficulty in imagining the text as having been written in Dutch, English, German, or Spanish.—One may add a multitude of examples even if one limits oneself to the upper echelons of the canon; Shakespeare's adoption as a "German" author and his status as the most popular playwright in my country up to the present day is another case worth mentioning.

6.—I would perhaps formulate the problem as a whole like this: our traditional views on cultural difference are biased by the unconscious tendency to take the fact that the primary "tool" of all culture, language, exists only as a multitude of very different vernaculars, as a legitimate basis for a reverse conclusion. Parameters informing a given artifact (a "work"), such as plot, genre, ideological frames (explicit or implied), message, style, etc., are, however, items that are conceptually separate from, and in most cases indeed independent of specific vernaculars. Within certain periods, and linked to particular vernaculars, one may observe systematic configurations of these parameters, configurations which then induce readers (or else recipients) to form the impression that there is, indeed, something like "national cultures". These configurations are, however, never exclusive. The exceptions that evade the constellations they would have to take part in were the traditional view of autochthony appropriate do not consist only of marginal works; on the contrary, they are quite frequently classics of world literature. The concept of "national culture" is nothing but a heuristic concept. It is an "auxiliary construction" (*Hilfskonstruktion*), to use a term coined by Theodor Fontane in *Effi Briest* (1896) and later adopted and made famous by Sigmund Freud (*Das Unbehagen in der Kultur* (1930) / *Civilization and its Discontents*). But in contrast to the "auxiliary constructions" referred to in the concluding passages of the former's most famous novel, and also in Freud, conceptions of national cultures may not be necessary at all in order to deal with finally unresolvable problems;[242] they might even prevent us from gaining a view of culture adequate for our present age.

Slightly differing from the approach developed by Stephen Greenblatt in a manifesto entitled *Cultural Mobility*, I have the tendency to conceive of the "open" processes of circulation in the cultural net on the one hand and parameters like "fixity", "identity", and "rootedness" on the other not in terms of an unspecified tension between two poles,[243] but rather as a phenomenon of unintentional "taking place" on the one hand and intentional processes on the other. The floating of cultural material in the net is a given. It is a fact as soon as the human species emerges. Delimitations of specific cultures are in all cases instruments consciously devised by humans in order to fulfill certain goals which may be reduced to two causal factors, which I would perhaps label internal control on the one hand and external dominance on the other.

7.—We do not know anything about the process by which the "original" human family, whose mother has been named Lucy by modern scientists, split up into

---

[242] See the long speech of Wüllersdorf, the superior of Effi's former husband, trying to persuade the latter to adopt a more flexible attitude in order to make life easier, specifically by recourse to *Hilfskonstruktionen* (going to view popular theater performances, drinking a beer from time to time, taking delight in watching beautiful young girls playing in the public parks, etc. [*Effi Briest*, chap. 35]). As to Freud's adoption of the term "auxiliary constructions", see "Civilisation and its Discontents", in: S. F., *Complete Psychological Works*, James Strachey (ed.), vol. 21, London 1961, p. 75; interpreting the advice given by the character from Fontane on a more general level, Freud posits that it is impossible for humans to endure the multifaceted and permanent frustrations, libidinous as well as aggressive, originating from the inevitable constraints of civilized life without recourse to such auxiliary constructions, which comprise, in addition to banal entertainments of all sorts, the fabrication of an embellished self-image.

[243] See the reference already given above (n. 5).

two and subsequently into a very large number of tribes.[244] We only have access to mythical accounts of the process—the most prominent for Westerners being the one provided in the Hebrew Bible—which do not resolve the problem, but rather attempt to compensate for the nonexistence of a logical answer by creating a narrative. The murder committed by Cain, and the subsequent division of the first couple's progeny into different, mutually hostile tribes, is "explained" in Genesis by referring to envy, that is, the same emotion which drove Adam and Eve to commit the first sin, a feeling inspired in them by the "serpent" or Satan, that is, by someone who does not have his logical place in a world created *ex nihilo* by a Mono-Theos.

When it comes to historical, that is postlapsarian times, the emotion in question is in a way motivated. Its ground is scarcity: Abel is prosperous, Cain is not. Whether this is a "real", or merely a "felt" material scarcity is a point of minor importance; in essence, the mythical explanation of tribal fragmentation and the one suggested by way of speculation in the following are compatible. And I am not very optimistic that the natural sciences will one day be able to provide more satisfactory answers to the question. On this basis, I would be inclined to see the emergence of cultural borders, that is, borders of language, custom, religion, etc., as arbitrary instruments intended to provide internal homogenization and external delimitation, with the goal of better equipping a given community in the competition for scarce resources.

The first step of cultural differentiation is most probably linked to the level of symbolic interaction, to communication. Once the primordial tribe developed embryonic stages of communication patterns—linking certain standardized gestures or sounds to specific meanings ("the potential prey is approaching" / "there is a danger hidden there") or referring to more abstract levels of meaning ("the prey seems to consistently move in this direction at dusk")—resources became scarce, for the simple reason that the predators (the first humans) had thus developed techniques favoring their multiplication in a way that exceeded the corresponding processes amongst their species of prey. In this situation, a particularly intelligent member of the tribe might have developed the idea to introduce different standardized signs for signaling the elementary messages necessary for successful hunting; he then may have instructed only parts of the primordial tribe regarding this "new" language, thus excluding the other parts from successfully partaking in the hunt. As soon as this device for excluding "others" and homogenizing those included proved to work, the strategy

---

244 Monogenesis of the species seems, however, to be the generally accepted hypothesis amongst present-day scientists.

might have become generalized. The fact that the intention and the result of these early processes of cultural differentiation was nothing other than the acquisition of a relative advantage in the competition for scarce resources[245] explains the immediate emergence of hostility amongst the fractions of the primordial tribe, along with its far-reaching consequence: the readiness of the disadvantaged fraction(s) to migrate to territories unknown.—All additional features of "identity" (linking certain cultural patterns to parameters like "soil" and "blood"), including the most important one: the pretense to superiority ("we" are better than "them"), are mainly[246] superimpositions upon the initial operation of delimitation and homogenization.

From a long-term perspective, one must also take into account constellations of cultural development already addressed by me in connection with the consideration that "human civilization was invented twice", that is, of tribes or peoples who do not have direct contact over long periods of time, as in the case of the emerging Mediterranean civilizations and China. In this case as well as in similar ones, there is no competition directed at the same supply of scarce resources. But there is much cultural difference.

Given the fact that we are discussing periods of human history of which we do not have any documentary evidence, and based on the—by now, as I understand it, genetically proven—assumption of the species' monogenesis (or: mono-emergence), one could perhaps consider the following hypothesis to be tenable: in principle, the further differentiation of cultures occurs according to the initial processes and functions just described. After one second-generation tribe has secured a territory of its own, that is, a territory isolated from other second-generation tribes' territories on behalf of natural conditions (very broad

---

245 From the perspective of sedentary, that is, agricultural, and even more so of industrial societies, it might be difficult to imagine what "scarcity" meant in an age when humans did not have any techniques at their disposal for enlarging their resources. One should not forget that astonishing phenomena such as the migration of people from East Africa to regions as alien to them as the northern tundra, or even to the regions of eternal ice, were certainly not caused by our ancestors' "touristic" curiosity; when they made these efforts of readaptation to extremely different habitats, sheer necessity was the motive. In the regions familiar to them, they would have starved, or died in endless tribal wars over scarce resources.
246 The above reservation is meant to refer to the special status of "blood" (family) bonds. For very small and secluded communities, such bonds are something real, not just ideological constructs. But as soon as one transcends the confines of what is called in our times the "nuclear family", the assumption of blood bonds becomes questionable, as modern genetic science has found. The genetic commonalities between (first) cousins do not reach a higher level than the commonalities between random human beings from the same region; in the case of third cousins, there is no difference from the general average degree of genetic commonalities.

rivers, oceans, hardly surmountable mountain ranges, massive deserts), the processes described above occur once again—that is, as soon as the territory becomes overpopulated and natural resources become scarce. But the differentiation then takes place without taking the rest of the species, residing far away from the isolated territory in question, into consideration. Since there is no direct contact, it is simply not necessary for a premodern community living on the territory of what is later called "China" to develop cultural patterns that would help make it distinct from, say, a Phoenician community from the same period. But it might be very useful for the community in question to distinguish itself from other groups residing in the same region, who later became known as "Koreans" or "Japanese". And as culture and cultural practices (even language alone) are fields with an extremely wide range of possibilities, it is not very astonishing to observe that, over the millennia, the differences between cultures remote from each other have augmented continuously—until the moment when new technologies brought the period of isolated existence to an end, that is, roughly from 1492 onward. Up to this date, the processes of internal differentiation within the four great isolated territories (Europe including the Middle East and North Africa; sub-Saharan Africa; America; the Far East) can be sufficiently described by recourse to the rationales explained above.

8.—As soon as the first period of globalization, starting in the middle of the sixteenth century, was completed—that is, at the beginning of World War I— there was no longer a community of relevant size that was not in contact with other communities and thus connected to the cultural net. What happens to the processes of differentiation under these historically unprecedented conditions? It seems that homogenization—taking our origins into account, one could perhaps even say: re-homogenization—becomes the dominant trend. Hundreds or even thousands of vernaculars disappeared in the course of the modern age; cultural differences became leveled by the establishment of huge territorial entities (nation states) and even more so by the establishment of (colonial) empires. In more recent times, the vogue of industrial globalization and of electronic information technology has led and is still leading at an ever-accelerating pace to a thoroughgoing cultural homogenization. With respect to the elite and the upper strata of the middle class, including intellectuals, national provenance has become a minor component of self-description as well as of perception by others.

This seems to imply that the insistence on cultural difference ("identity") might have become a distinctive feature of the "subaltern" of any kind: the impoverished lower class in the old industrial centers; non-integrated racial minorities; worshippers of religions stuck in premodern patterns; underdeveloped nations; and failed states. As blunt as such an utterance may appear at first sight, this seems exactly to be the case. Romantic patterns of thinking which were, two hundred years ago, the ideology of an avant-garde have become indices of a disfavored position from the middle of the twentieth century onward. The constellation is perhaps most evident with respect to the Third World—a term which has become somewhat obsolete in the course of the economic rise of countries like China, India, and Brazil. It would be an exaggeration to hold that these countries have evolved into parts of a homogeneous global culture. But from a Western perspective, they certainly appear less strange or foreign or "other" than they did thirty years ago. And it is an illusion produced by the impossibility of objectively judging one's own standpoint (this term is meant in a very literal sense) that the reduction of difference and distance is a unilateral process of "ever coming closer to the West". The West, too, has changed dramatically over the last decades. The dichotomy of body and soul, along with its normative implications, which forms the most abstract basis of the traditional occidental worldview, has almost completely disappeared from the discursive stage with vertiginous celerity. It is not magic that has caused corpses (in this case: Plato's) which were able to remain intact for more than two and a half millennia to decay within two or three decades; it is cultural dynamics.

9.—In conclusion, I would like to come back to a few parameters already thematized to a certain extent, but now by way of highlighting single cases of extreme profile and at the same time of great importance, which might help to relativize—in the one direction as well as in the other—my above remarks based on attention to more general tendencies.

I should stress once again that the decontextualizing, romanticizing attitude towards the "other" which became dominant in the modern West has in a way leveled all inhibiting parameters mentioned above. But things may have been different with respect to the period at issue here.

As for language, I have already cited two examples of quite different degrees of importance (Latin in medieval and early modern Europe, French in the eighteenth century) which might illustrate that its significance is not at all negligible. Yet it may be that the mastery of the language to which a text is bound simply makes reception processes occur more smoothly, while a lack of language skills may be outweighed by factors of a different order which make an extraction of the material concerned desirable. The most striking example in global cultural history of a relatively reduced importance of language as cultural border might be the reception history of Christianity's Holy Scripture. The fact that its first section, the Hebrew Bible, was conceived in languages alien to Greeks, Romans, and Europeans did not prevent its wide reception. *Mutatis mutandis*, this also applies to the New Testament. It would seem that difference of language becomes a minor problem as soon as there is a strong motivation to appropriate an "alien" text. It remains to be discussed, however, whether such strong motivations exist at all within the sphere of artistic culture considered separately, or whether they are always linked to domains whose importance is typically considered to be higher than that of art—as is the case with religion, and as might be the case with economics or money-making, including money-making by way of industrial production.[247]

In periods after the astonishing reception of this linguistically as well as conceptually exotic holy text all over the Mediterranean world, religion seems indeed to become a marker of cultural borders inhibiting the reception of cultural material from the net, including in the present. One must, however, take into consideration the numerous cases in cultural history which seem to demonstrate that difference of religion is no less surmountable a border than linguistic difference. My disciplinary competence does not suffice to give a satisfactory answer to the corresponding problem with regard to the well-known phenomenon of Islam's reception of classical Greek philosophy, namely of Aristotle's works. As to Christianity, every scholar working in the field of European intellectual history is familiar with the two main tools—which are finally one—developed in Late Antiquity in order to make possible the almost unrestricted reception of "gentile" knowledge in the Christianized West. The first argument seems to emerge in the writings of a Hellenized Jew of the early first century CE, Philo of Alexandria,[248] and was further developed by Justinus Martyr. It is known under the name of the "priority thesis". According to Philo and Justinus, Moses and the Old Testament prophets were (historically) much older than the pagan philosophers, who "stole" all of their knowledge from the one and only source of truth, that is, Yahweh's revelation. Hence, the appropriation of the gentiles' knowledge is, in essence, a re-appropriation, an act which is not only "just" in terms of morals, but also unproblematic in terms of basic cultural parameters. The second argument is contained in Augustine's

---

247 I am thinking here of the readiness of members of today's foremost emerging world power, China, to acquire the competency to communicate in English instead of trying to impose their own language as *lingua franca*. Modern science, theoretical as well as applied, and all present-day international juridical documents express themselves in English. This is, indeed, a strong motivation for a huge nation like China to adopt this frame of communication instead of trying to change the situation.

248 The seminal publication on this topic is still Ernst Robert Curtius, *European Literature and the Middle Ages*, Princeton, NJ 2013, chap. 22.

famous allegorical reading of *Exodus*:[249] just as the (future) Israelites were encouraged by Yahweh himself to take the Egyptian temple gold, Christians are encouraged to appropriate all the conceptual treasures of classical pagan civilization and to use them in the interest of spreading and systematizing the one and only Truth.—One may reduce these two rhetorical stratagems to one common origin, namely monotheism. If there is indeed only one God governing this world from its creation to its end, there is no substantive cultural difference between people of different times, different continents, or different belief systems. The only problem is distortion on the part of the nonbelievers, a feature which can be repaired by re-contextualization, that is, by "correct" interpretation.

The enormous absorptive capacities of Western culture, which later became the basis for the West's global cultural dominance, are certainly linked to monotheism, or rather to the Western variant of monotheism. As said, I am not able to contribute anything substantive to the question of how Islam deals with cultural material that is, at least on the surface, exogenous. Christianity's specific propensity to appropriate and reinterpret material is, however, not an indicator of the fact that it is a specifically "intelligent" variant of monotheism; it is obviously linked to the fact that Christianity began as a sectarian movement within an older tradition. All of its discursive features are essentially based on the pattern of reception and recoding with a view to integration. Consequently, from the standpoint of Christian culture, difference of belief is not a serious obstacle to the appropriation of foreign cultural material from the net. For other religions, things may be different.—Within Judaism, the situation seems similar to Christianity, but for very different reasons. It was the diasporic life which made it pragmatically necessary for Jewish people to receive all sorts of foreign cultural items. But it is only within communities of modern, secularized Jews (or, as one should rather put it, people of Jewish origin) that one no longer finds what one may observe within more tradition-bound Jewish communities, present or historic: the strict consciousness of the difference between one's own (Jewish) cultural patrimony and the culture of those amongst whom one must spend one's life.

10.—And what about the delimiting qualities of basic cultural patterns which are even more elementary than religions? With my standard reservation regarding modernity proper, I believe that they are of a certain importance when it comes to deciding whether or not to extract certain material from the net. But

---

249 *De doctrina christiana* II: 40 (60).

it would seem that their tendency to exclude is not absolute (as is the case with some items briefly mentioned above, e.g., certain geographical boundaries). On the other hand, the relevance of these conceptual gaps should not be minimized because they have lost their importance in our times. "Eastern" wisdom (quietism) has become an object of interest to the "activist" West only in the age of exoticism, sentimentalism, and aestheticism, and Western activism has become attractive in the East (India, Japan, China) only after a long period of enforced Westernization, and after the implementation of occidental activism's material results: industrialization and commodification. Gautam Chakrabarti's study on modern Indian drama shows that the reception of Western discourses of egalitarianism in the hierarchical caste-based society of India occurred only as a mostly unintentional consequence of colonization, as a reaction to the thoroughly materialist mode of colonization practiced by the British. And Eastern or "pagan" circular conceptions of time, as well as the texts linked to such concepts, only became interesting to the West as the significance of Christian teleological thinking began to wane, along with the influence of its secularized variant, the belief in infinite material progress.—All these changes with regard to the reception of material floating in the net constitute a strong plea, once again, for not neglecting the question of receptivity when it comes to pondering why certain material floating in the net is actually extracted or why it is "deflected" from possible recipients by cultural borderlines.

11.—I should like to conclude my deliberations regarding the importance of religions and worldviews for the receptivity of different cultures to the material floating in the cultural net by referring to a fascinating constellation dating from the inception of early modernity, an episode from Chinese history—widely unknown amongst nonspecialists—occurring roughly sixty years before the world-historical development beginning with Columbus's voyage of 1492. At that time, an empire that had been no less ignorant of the world outside than contemporary Europe initiated expansionist activities that were in many respects comparable to those of the early modern Portuguese and Spaniards. Under Emperor Yongle (1402–1424) of the Ming dynasty, an admiral named Zheng He undertook seven voyages to territories completely unknown in fifteenth-century China.[250] In terms of quantity, these expeditions were much bigger than the voyages of Columbus. The most significant expedition corps com-

---

[250] See Wang Gungwu, *China and the Chinese Overseas*, Singapore 1992; see also Edward L. Dreyer, *Zheng He: China and the Oceans in the Early Ming Dynasty, 1405–1433*, New York, NY 2007.—I am indebted to my colleague Lee Cheuk Yin from the National University of Singapore for having drawn my attention to this episode of Chinese history.

prised over 300 ships equipped with some 27,000 sailors and trade men, including 62 huge ships carrying trade goods. As was the case with Columbus, the primary intention of the Chinese expeditions was economic: the goods carried by the cargo ships consisted mainly of silk and porcelain. Zheng He's expeditions were initially aimed at opening up rather nearby ports and countries for Chinese luxury goods: Cambodia, Siam, Brunei, Sumatra, Malacca, Ceylon, Kerala, etc. But the following expeditions reached places like Hormuz, Aden, Jeddah, Mecca, Mogadishu, and even Malindi on the coast of East Africa, that is, places with regard to which the initial motivation to sell Chinese luxury products can hardly be considered primary.

The most intriguing feature linked to these expeditions in the context here discussed is the fact that the early modern Chinese expansion stopped at this point. There were neither attempts at penetrating into regions north of Mecca, nor were there attempts at circumnavigating Africa in order to reach horizons totally unknown. This is all the more striking as it was exactly this that Columbus's emulators undertook when they made a similar trip, albeit in the other direction: when Vasco da Gama reached Malindi in 1498, he did not hesitate to explore further eastward, thus finding what Columbus had only believed to have found, a maritime route to India. By contrast, the early modern Chinese expansion, considered by some scholars to be proto-colonial,[251] was stopped soon after Emperor Yongle died, and *Zhongguo* (the Middle Kingdom) resumed its attitude of strict Sinocentrism and isolationism, which ended only with the Opium Wars (1839–1860) and the subsequent enforced integration of the country into a more and more globalized world.

All explanations of this constellation must of necessity remain speculative, since there are no documents that would instruct us about the reasons behind this double paradigm shift in China's attitude towards the rest of the world, whose result was the confirmation of the traditional parochialism.—One element to be taken into consideration, as I should like to suggest, is the biographical background of the central figure of this episode: As a boy of thirteen years of age, Zheng He had been captured by imperial troops in the course of a turmoil between the Han and Muslim Chinese, a minority he and his family were part of, and had been castrated. Later on, he made a remarkable career, leading him to the position of Grand Eunuch at the imperial court. The ambition to reach Mecca in order to sell Chinese silk to the Arabians of the peninsu-

---

[251] See Geoff Wade, "The Zheng He Voyages: A Reassessment", *Asia Research Institute, National University of Singapore, Working Papers Series* vol. 31 / 2004, pp. 1–33.

la might thus have involved the covert intention to redress the coerced abandonment of his original belief.

But there was no religious necessity to go to places like Kerala, and even less to Malindi. I would suggest that it was the universalism inherent in Islam, no less than in Christianity, that facilitated Zheng He's attitude to boldly transcend the limits of what most Chinese considered to be the center of the world. And the decision of his imperial protector's successors not to carry on with this expansionism may testify, once again, to the fact that Zheng He's activities were contingent upon world-modeling parameters alien to traditional Chinese culture.—If one is ready to consider the entire "Chinese" scenario in comparison with what happened in Europe some decades later, the constellation is a very strong plea for the type of assessment suggested here: The fact that Columbus succeeded in arriving at a coast instead of losing his life is contingent; "new" technological devices like the quadrant may have facilitated the trip to territories unknown. But the attitude of not considering one's own country or civilization to constitute the world as such, along with the quest for the "novel", calls for an explanation that goes beyond such materialist parameters. Ideological universalism seems to be one of the mightiest factors when it comes to discussing the question of why and how the "partial" cultural nets resulting from the primordial tribal fragmentation became reunited in an age that we call early modern[252] because it anticipates characteristics which developed more fully in the nineteenth and twentieth centuries.

Transnational Cultural Agencies

0.—In the introduction, I gave expression to the assumption that the floating of cultural material is in most cases, at least in the age under scrutiny here, mediated by humans—by merchants, warriors, spouses, missionaries, diplomats, artists, actors, etc., that is, by people who level the borderlines discussed in the previous chapter, at least those of a spatial or merely conceptual (ideological) order. The enumeration is evidently heterogeneous, as it comprises both active, conscious agents of cultural transfer (missionaries, actors, artists) and people without the conscious intention of transferring cultural material (merchants and warriors). But since these latter individuals, too, are humans,

---

[252] I do not repeat in the above paragraph my answer to the question of why the theoretical universalism inherent in Christianity did not have such practical implications until this point in time (see pp. 89–91).

i.e., beings with a cultural background, it is inevitable that they transport not only goods or arms, but the complete range of cultural material they carry in their minds: concepts, norms, patterns of behavior, body language, and the memories of works of art that made a strong impression on them. One is tempted to say that for most of human history, cultural transmission was such an affair. It simply happened, with no conscious intent to promote *cultural* circulation.

1.—The entire historical process which laid the basis for what later became Europe was initiated by such an unintentional "export" of culture. When the Romans first conquered present-day France, then parts of what would later become England and Germany, their intention was not to propagate Greco-Roman culture. They wanted to put a halt to the barbarian incursions into Roman territories, which were motivated by material greed. But in order to sustain the *Pax Romana*, it was ultimately necessary to definitively subjugate these limitrophic tribes, that is, to install Roman garrisons on foreign territory. Roman troops lived in these *coloniae* on a permanent basis. Consequently, a need arose for Roman culture in these places—for everyday culture in the first place, but also for the more sophisticated facets of it, e.g., arenas, places suited for public performances. As time went by, the subjugated locals began to take an interest in these instances of Mediterranean culture transplanted to Western and Northern Europe. And some centuries later, when the Empire collapsed under the military pressure of tribes from parts of present-day Europe which had not been conquered, mainly from Scandinavia, the native people of present-day France, England, and Southern and Western Germany had become so familiar with the culture brought to them by way of violent military conquest that they considered it to be their "own", even succeeding in convincing the newly arrived barbarian tribes to adopt these patterns as well, whose origins lie in Mesopotamia, Egypt, Israel, and Greece.

2.—Cultural exportation as a conscious pattern of behavior seems so natural to present-day Westerners that it might be difficult to conceptualize the extent to which it is a specific way of dealing with culture. I would hypothesize that there is one indispensable prerequisite for consciously propagating one's own culture outside of its original territory, namely, universalism, understood as the conviction that all human beings are equal and thus apt to live within comparable, if not identical cultural frames. This idea—revolutionary in the history of humankind—first originates with the emergence of Christianity; it is reinforced by the emergence of the second universalistic religion, Islam, and becomes a pattern of world-historical impact in the age of its secularization. "Human rights" is a concept based on the assumption not of the corporeal sameness of human beings, but of their "essential" sameness. Whatever this essence may be, the postulate of essential equality translates to the level of observable phenomena as the assumption of equal rights, equal wishes and aspirations, and equal norms of good and evil. In regions of the planet where there is no "autochthonous" ideological universalism, for example India and China, there is much less conscious cultural exportation to be observed than in the case of the West.[253]

Since we are considering here not only 2,000 years, but a period beginning with the emergence of the very first humans (150,000 years), it is important to state that the majority of cultural transfer is a parasitic phenomenon. As conscious activity, it is bound to specific ideological constellations. And it is not without reason that present-day global culture is mainly Western. Islam, which is in principle as able as the West to become the hub of a universalistic global culture, is caught in the shackles of its own tradition and the subsequent incapacity to develop modern technologies, including culturally relevant ones, of its own.[254]

3.—If one limits the scope to the age of universalism, it becomes requisite to add to the panorama of features favoring the floating of material in the virtual network of culture a phenomenon not considered as yet: the existence of agencies of transculturation.—I shall start by hinting at a striking textual example which is apt to elucidate the enormous impact of these agencies on cultural evolution in particular in early modern times. Drnovšek's study on the *Škofjeloški pasijon* (1725),[255] the first text written in the Slovene language still extant today, opens up a particularly illuminating perspective on a more general constellation that is frequently overlooked in a period whose basic parameters continue to be heavily influenced by the concept of "national cultures". As the

---

253 I will formulate some remarks concerning Buddhism in the course of this chapter.
254 As to possible reasons for this difference between cultures with a Christian and cultures with an Islamic background, see my "Christentum, Judentum, Islam – Säkulare Welt und Geschichtlichkeit", in: Andreas Kablitz and Christoph Markschies (eds.), *Heilige Texte*. Religion und Rationalität, Berlin and Boston, MA 2013, pp. 141–166.—My above remarks concerning Islam may at first sight seem naïve, given the virtuosic usage of technological patterns developed in the West for a cultural-religious expansionism on the part of jihadists, starting with Khomeini. But as I shall argue in the chapter "Control and Demand", I doubt that totalitarian systems of any kind are sustainable. The main obstacle that present-day political Islam will have more and more to face becomes evident when considering post-Khomeini Iran: the instrumentalization of Western technologies for purposes of parochial cultural-political propagation "establishes", as it were, the presence of these technological devices on the territory controlled by the totalitarian system in question. Once established, these devices may be used to gain access to cultural (ideological, political, artistic) material ostracized by the regime.
255 "Certa Mina Dant VICtorIas". See also Jaša Drnovšek, "Early Modern Religious Processions: The Rise and Fall of a Political Genre", in: Bernhart et al. (eds.), *Poetics and Politics*.

title states, the text is a Passion play; in this specific case, it was performed as a processional play. It displays various characteristics which make it a useful source to be studied within a project on early modern European drama. But what counts from a more theoretical perspective is the fact that the play's plot has nothing "Slovene" about it, as well as the fact that the performative practice of the processional play, which levels the distance between stage and spectators and thus enhances the emotional involvement of the recipients, is not a feature that belongs to a specifically Slovene culture. From the Middle Ages onward, plays presenting Christ's Passion are documented in many European countries, and the practice of the processional play, which may have been ubiquitous in the West, is particularly well documented in the case of Spain.[256]

None of these details would surprise a scholar of the historical and literary scenario in question. But the enabling structure of these and similar phenomena is frequently neglected when we talk about (European) cultures: from the early Middle Ages onward, there were not only itinerant individuals (merchants, warriors) transporting, more or less unintentionally, cultural items, but also cultural agencies with the conscious aim of surmounting national and linguistic borders. The most important of these agencies, and perhaps the only one amongst those to be mentioned which conceived of cultural transfer as its primary task—and not, as in the case of the other agencies, as a concomitant feature of several diverse activities—was the Roman Catholic Church. Its dogma is universalistic; the Church considers as its mission to proselytize all humans, regardless of their language or ethnicity. On behalf of this radically "global" attitude, Catholicism was right from its establishment as the official cult of the Roman Empire onward, that is, starting in the fourth century CE, a most powerful agent of encouraging the circulation of material in the cultural net and even more so of expanding the net. The more it became institutionalized, the more the Church systematically exported its cultural material from its main seat, Rome, not only to all European countries, but also, after the European conquest of other parts of the world, to almost any kind of "national culture". No one will be surprised to hear that Christian didactic drama was exported to Latin America after 1492. But it might be at first sight astonishing to register that such plays were performed in somewhat exotic parts of the world as well, for instance, in Indian Goa and in Japan.—It is worth noting in passing that

---

[256] It might be known even outside the country that there is one such procession play that continues to flourish in present-day Germany, the *Oberammergauer Passionsspiel*. It is performed only every tenth year and, in terms of function, has at least partially become an element of present-day "event culture", where the religious and ritual background has only, if at all, a secondary importance.

in the above-mentioned Slovene Passion play, allegories of the non-European continents America, Asia, and Africa appear on stage in order to express their gratitude for the "mercy" that Catholicism showed in bringing salvation to their people. This clear-cut universalistic profession is all the more remarkable as Slovenia was not at all involved in the process of spreading Christian-European culture around the globe.—The human agents of the Church's net-bound activities were mainly the members of monastic orders (the Capuchins and, in later periods, the Jesuits), but also such dignitaries as bishops and archbishops, people whose self-description was not primarily focused on national or ethnic belonging, but rather on the self-chosen role of minister (that is, servant) of a God who, according to their belief, had created all of humankind and then redeemed it by way of an act of self-sacrifice. Those who had been permitted on behalf of divine grace to gain access to the revealed truth had to earn (*mereri*) this grace retrospectively and make it thereby efficient (*gratia efficax*), not least by propagating the truth amongst those who did not have the privilege of first access.

There is one additional point to be made with regard to this most powerful transnational cultural agency of the period in question. The institution of the Church is linked to a specific ideology. It thus has a strong tendency to function not only as a propagator of cultural material, but at the same time as a control agency in the sense that will be detailed below. What was actively circulated by the Roman Church was a carefully chosen and determinate set of cultural features. However, since the circulation was mainly carried out by humans and not only by exporting books—that is, by monks or ecclesiastical dignitaries from countries like Spain, Italy, and France migrating to countries like Slovenia, Goa, Brazil, and Japan—it was more or less inevitable that these humans also carried in their mental luggage all sorts of cultural material which might have been considered problematic from the strictly defined standpoint of religious orthodoxy. While the primary focus of their conscious cultural activities was certainly the propagation of a specific message and the control of all possible heterodoxy, it might be the case that there was an unintentional dialectic at work here: since even a highly orthodox person can be orthodox only by constantly repressing anything that is not systematically orthodox within his or her own thinking, he or she inevitably becomes a means of unintentionally transporting cultural material that exceeds the limits of religious orthodoxy.— The impetus for cultural propagation of a material that transgresses the limits of the strictly defined dogmatic core is reinforced by a central characteristic of the Christian religion already mentioned above, namely its absorptive attitude with regard to previous traditions, in particular with regard to aspects of the Jewish and the pagan Mediterranean discursive spheres. The dogma, the ritualistic practices, and the religious arts (architecture, paintings, catechizing texts and performances) are assembled from pre-existing material and a very limited set of "novel" concepts which are novel only with respect to the new context into which they are integrated.[257] Since Christianity emerged on the terrain of a firmly established written culture, which was moreover developing techniques of storage of cultural material such as libraries, the elements out of which the Christian discourse was assembled also remained present in the cultural net in their unassimilated versions. This presence "*sub utraque specie*" was, as may be extrapolated from European cultural history, a permanent invitation to all users of the cultural net to disassemble the conceptual configurations that constitute what we call Christianity and to make use of the elements for secular purposes.[258]

4.—Considering the immense contribution made by members of the religious orders, in the first place the Jesuits, to the transportation of cultural material of all kinds—that is, not only religious—and in both directions (from the West to the colonies and vice versa), one might think that Catholicism was and perhaps is a much more important human "device" enabling the floating of material in the cultural net than Protestantism. And, indeed, the Protestant accentuation of the believers' direct access to divine revelation as mediated by Scripture has meant that all Reformed denominations are ultimately linked to specific linguistic communities. Their pretense to the universality that is in principle a feature of Christianity in general is restricted by the abolishment of the mediating role of the clergy and by the ensuing relative parochialism. In that sense, Protestantism was one of the most powerful agents of the emergence of nationalism. In addition, the Reformation allowed the clergy to marry

---

[257] To give just one example: the ethical component of Christianity may be described as a continuation and partial radicalization of the set of norms contained in the Decalogue, that is, in the Jewish tradition. The emerging religion detaches this ethical fund from the entire complex of ritualistic practices. It then adds to this remaining ethical component elements deriving from Eastern Mediterranean mystical religions, mainly of Egyptian provenance (the incarnation of gods by way of "regular" birth; resurrection; eternal life). In order to principally distance itself from the Jewish religion, it attaches to this compound the vaguely elaborated universalistic tendencies implied in other cults that were widespread at the time (Isis; Mithras), while fusing them with monotheism and thereby radically accentuating them.

[258] A prime example already touched upon in this book (and described in detail in chap. 3 of my *Discursive* Renovatio *in Lope de Vega and Calderón*) is the "subjugation" of the stories of Greek myth by way of allegorizing, occurring in the Middle Ages, and the "liberation" of the mythical fund from this superstructure, occurring in the era we are used to calling the "Renaissance"; as to the possible reasons behind this and comparable evolutions, see above, pp. 89–91.

and to raise families; consequently, Protestant ministers were in less of a position to dedicate their energies to interaction with believers—actual as well as potential—than Catholic priests, monks, or nuns.

This constellation notwithstanding, there were considerable Protestant missionary activities in non-Western countries. The processes of cultural transfer that accompanied these activities had, at least in part, a slightly different profile from those accompanying Catholic proselytizing. The marital status of Protestant missionaries allowed them to have children. The latter typically grew up in parts of the world whose cultural parameters differed from those of the West. Almost all of them were educated people. Some of them became ministers, but most chose to exercise secular professions; as is the case in the homelands of Protestantism, quite a few became scholars or scientists. In a considerable number of cases, they remained as adults in the countries where they had been born and raised. As a consequence of this chain of conditioning factors, many of them became professional agents of cultural transfer. They taught the locals what Western science and humanities were, and they made the local flora and fauna, as well as the local culture, into objects of Western-style scientific or scholarly scrutiny. A significant structural difference between the mediating activities of this group and those of the Catholic missionaries consists in the fact that the former were "professionals" in what they did, whereas the latter were dilettantes in the very literal meaning of the term. Particularly in an age when research in the sciences and the humanities became a disciplinary phenomenon, that is, from the early nineteenth century onward, the circulation of cultural material characterized by a professional or disciplinary formation may have had a greater impact than its "dilettantish" variant, in particular because it was at that point not only content that was to be transported, but also methodological, that is, more readily transferable parameters.

5.—*Mutatis mutandis*, many of the above points also apply to a religious tradition (specifically to the question of its dissemination) which lies outside the temporal and topographical frame of this study, but which should be addressed at least in passing: Buddhism originated in India around the fifth century BCE. For whatever reason, it started proselytizing beyond the borders of its region of origin only in the first century CE; there were efforts to make Buddhist teachings known in regions located westward of India, but the only transculturation with a significant, long-lasting impact took place between India and East Asia (China, Korea, and Japan).[259] As their Christian analogues would do in early

---

[259] It would seem that the most important publication on the topic is still Erik Zürcher's book (now nearly fifty years old) *The Buddhist Conquest of China: The Spread and Adaptation of Buddhism in Early Medieval China*, Leiden 2007 (3rd print); for the reasons mentioned above, I have slight reservations concerning the term "conquest" in this context.

modern times, Buddhist monks of the period mentioned made use of a network infrastructure which had been established for economic reasons: the Silk Road.

It is a question that shall not be discussed here why a highly developed culture with a sophisticated philosophical and ethical tradition of its own, namely China, was receptive to the penetration of an "alien" cult; but it should be mentioned that this fact marks a difference from the spread of the Christian religion to foreign regions, at least in the period under consideration in this book. The Christian missionaries travelling west- or eastward starting at the end of the fifteenth century followed the paths established previously by the conquests of military men. Consequently, it is not astonishing that the indigenous cultural communities received the material the missionaries transferred to these territories. In the state of having been (physically) conquered, they did not have the alternative of rejecting it. The penetration of Buddhism into China was, by contrast, mainly peaceful; this aspect notwithstanding, it was highly successful. One possible explanation of this difference might be the fact that China was in a period of internal difficulties, if not turmoil at that time. It may be that a cultural community is more receptive to "imported" cultural patterns in cases where the "autochthonous" ones seem no longer to be effective.

As is the case with Christianity, the original cult underwent some changes in the course of the process of transculturation; but the more important point from this book's perspective is the fact that the eastward migration of Buddhism was accompanied by cultural patterns it had adopted previously and which were related only metonymically to the cult proper. These patterns thus were able to acquire a status of their own, that is, as cultural forms that were fit for use outside of cultic practices in the strict sense. Art historians hold that the drapery patterns typical of Buddha statues were inspired by Greek cultural material, namely, the representation of female goddesses, which might have been brought to India and China by Buddhist monks who had tried to proselytize westward. Later on, when Chinese emperors began to legitimize their power emblematically by stylizing their visual representations in a Buddha-like fashion, these "Greek" drapery patterns, applied to statues of the emperors, became a feature of the Far Eastern language of symbolic secular power.— Moreover, it is striking that many Buddhist *stupas* exhibit structures which seem to be inspired by the post-basilica architecture of the Christian Churches, or vice versa.

It would be possible to multiply the examples, but, as already mentioned, this is not the ambition of the present study. In addition to this brief demonstration of the fact that it is not only the Christian denominations which assumed the role of conscious agencies of transculturation, I should like to stress a major difference between the Buddhist and the Christian deployments of their basic parameters beyond their respective regions of origin. This difference—the absence, in the case of Buddhism, of an attempt at reorganizing entire societies (political systems; social norms; education systems; economic systems) according to parameters initially inspired by doctrinal positions—would seem to be contingent on the different doctrinal cores of the two belief systems in question. On behalf of its central doctrine, the incarnation of the Godhead, Christianity is a religion focusing at the same time on the beyond and on the material, physical world. From the perspective of Buddhism, the material world has to be overcome. The ethical norm taught by the priests and monks does not consist in the imperative to reorganize the world so as to acquire the dignity to be saved, but rather in the imperative to endure the world as it is while preserving certain ethical norms, thus "earning" a future incarnation on a higher level of spirituality.

6.—At this point, it seems appropriate to highlight an important agency of transculturation which is constituted by religious identification, but which finally differs in structure from the universalistic communities already addressed. I am referring to the Jewish population of the period.[260] It was the fate of this community to live under diasporic conditions. Seen from an exterior perspective, the combination of a strongly particularistic self-description, that is, cohesion, and enforced de-autochthonization led to a situation which rendered European Jewry a very powerful instrument of transnational cultural exchange. Such dire events as prosecution and expulsion (English Jewry after 1290, French Jewry after 1306, the Rhineland Jews in the course of the crusades, and Spanish Jewry after 1492) may have had the remarkable long-term effect of a continuous cultural circulation unconstrained by national borders. It was only the emancipation of Jewish people from their status as second-class citizens and their ensuing assimilation into the various national cultures of Europe which may have reduced—though not annihilated—their role as active, if unintentional agents of transnational cultural transmission.[261]

---

260 Relevant information may be gathered from David B. Ruderman, *Early Modern Jewry: A New Cultural History*, Princeton, NJ 2010.

261 —a process that was in a way inverted by the rejection of people of Jewish origin by Nazi Germany, which forced them into a kind of renewed tribalism. The survivors of the Holocaust are much less committed to the "national" cultures of their (European) countries of residence than, say, French or German Jewish people before 1933, who in many cases conceived of themselves as "patriots", that is, as citizens not only legally, but also emotionally committed to their countries. For reasons differing from the situation in the era before the emancipation, in the present-day post-Shoah world, Jewish people continue to be active human agents of cultural exchange. Their commitment to the cultures of their respective countries of citizenship is less "deeply rooted" than it was in the period extending from the emancipation through the

The above paragraph provides an opportunity to open a parenthesis in order to briefly discuss the intricate question of "negative" variants of mobility (in the sense of migration), including cultural mobility. As problematic or sad as such mobility may have been for the humans involved, from the perspective of cultural history one must say that in very many cases even forced displacement has far-reaching and highly productive repercussions on cultural history. One very important further example from European history is the transmission of classical Greek philosophy, namely Aristotle's work, from the Eastern Mediterranean to the Christian West, which occurred concomitantly to the Muslim conquest of North Africa and the Iberian Peninsula, events which were certainly no less bellicose than the activities of present-day jihadists. The pattern of cultural transmission originating from violent expulsion is represented by the events which occurred at the end of this chapter of Mediterranean religious history. The year of the definitive Christian *reconquista* of the peninsula (1492) was also the year in which internal religious homogenization was achieved by forcing Spanish Jews to leave the country. In their flight to places like Antwerp, Amsterdam, Bordeaux, Salonica, and Hamburg, they took with them the entire cultural material available in peninsular Spain, including the material brought there by the Muslim conquerors several centuries before.

Is cultural circulation always a "good thing"? Our spontaneous narcissism as permanently travelling intellectuals of the twenty-first century might lead to such a rather naïve assumption. Subjugated or colonized communities might consider such processes differently. But it may be that the descendants of the colonized consider—after many generations—the process of cultural transfer accompanying events as violent as war and subjugation to be something ultimately positive, an evolution that has brought the achievements of modernity to their communities. Basically, the question raised above cannot be answered, at least not within a scholarly framework. It may be that a world populated by small, self-sufficient, isolated communities (a Rousseauian structure), a world without a comprehensive cultural net is an idyll; but it may also be the case that such a world would be considered a prison or even an earthly variant of hell were it to exist. Was the circulation of Greco-Roman and Christian culture from the Mediterranean to Northern Europe—a circulation mediated by war and conquest—a good thing? Or would present-day Europeans have a more

---

first decades of the twentieth century. At the same time, their commitment to their ancestors' faith has become—as is the case for Christian Westerners as well—somewhat less intense. These two parameters yield an intellectual mobility which might be higher than in the case of people with other cultural backgrounds.

felicitous life if they went on praying to Odin and Woden and living in the woods?[262] The net is a fact, as is progress. The ambition of this book is descriptive; evaluation of the process is left to readers.

7.—In addition to certain religious communities,[263] there are a number of further transnational cultural agencies to be mentioned. These agencies display a much larger ideological flexibility than the Church(es), a fact which may, at first sight, seem to entail that they are more important producers of transnational dissemination than the latter; however, their actual impact is limited by the fact that they are, in contrast to the Christian Church(es) and to the other universalistic religious communities mentioned (Islamic, Buddhist), elitist in their self-description and as regards their interactions with societies at large.

One such agency that has been referred to above on various occasions is the upper strata of the ruling class, the European higher nobility, for whom nationality did not count as a feature of self-description. If it was politically opportune, members of this social caste were ready to migrate to any part of the "civilized" world[264] as spouses of kings or queens, or as heirs to thrones for which there was no legitimate or acceptable succession to be found within the kingdom in question. I should like to adduce some particularly important cases besides the ones already mentioned (the two Italian Medici ladies who became

---

[262] For a more detailed discussion of this intricate question, see my "Some Remarks on World Literature", in: Küpper (ed.), *Approaches to World Literature*, pp. 167–175.
[263] I shall not reproduce at this point the story of the cultural by-products of the expansion of Islam, consisting first of all in the transfer of Aristotelianism to the Iberian peninsula, that is, to a Christian Europe that at that time was in partial ignorance of its own intellectual origins; the story is referred to on various occasions above and below; but, above all, in an age of a renewed Western politics of appeasement with respect to a militant opponent, it has become—in an idealized variant abstracting from the bellicose context—one of the centerpieces, propagated again and again by the media, of present-day *doxa*.
[264] Need I mention that this indifference towards "national" belonging was counterbalanced to a significant extent by the aforesaid *specific* universalistic (that is, Christian) frame within which these migration processes took place? That is the reason why I qualify the "ready-to-migrate" higher nobility as European.—There is not much information available about the marriage practices of non-European dynasties. One reason might be that monogamy, if it existed at all beyond Europe, was not practiced with the same rigor as under the rule of Christian morals. I do not know of any Chinese emperors who proposed to Japanese or Indian princesses, or vice versa; and if such exogamy occurred, it was an exception (as in the case of Alexander the Great's marriage to a "barbarian" princess, Roxane, which was a scandal for his Greek compatriots). Even if such constellations might have arisen, what I am dealing with above is something else: transnational migration was a regular pattern of behavior among the ruling class of Europe which we can trace back to around the year 1000 CE and which disappeared only, step by step, with the shift of power from the aristocracy to the bourgeoisie.

queens of France, the German princess who became tsarina). In the period concerned, Spain was governed by a German dynasty, the Habsburgs, whose members became "romanized" and then created a "Latin" variant of Teutonic culture, still existing today, and still differing from standard German culture, namely, the culture of Austria. The last queen of pre-revolutionary France, Marie Antoinette, was a Habsburg princess, as well as King Louis XIV's mother, Anne. At the end of the period in question, the British invited a German prince from the House of Hanover to become their king. Henry VIII's first wife, Catherine, was of Spanish origin (etc., etc.). The ruling class in the age of feudalism and absolutism was "transnational" to a high degree, a feature that stands in almost diametrical opposition to the period starting with the French Revolution.

Regardless of their non-tribal self-description, all these "migrating" princesses and princes were of course deeply marked by the specific cultures of the countries where they had been born. Without even problematizing this fact—without thinking or talking about "hybridity" or "internationalization"—they took their cultures of origin with them, as part of their mental baggage, when leaving their homelands, and "unpacked" them in the places where they then settled down. Much cultural exchange in the early modern period was brought about by this transnational ruling class. One has to take into account, however, that this form of circulation primarily involved those features and artifacts appealing to the social elite. On the other hand, a ruling class is able to maintain its position only if it develops effective techniques for controlling the common people. One should therefore refrain from excluding the possibility that techniques for exercising power which made use of culture at large—that is, cultural artifacts targeting a non-elite audience—circulated as well by means of migrating members of this ruling class.

8.—A further agent of transculturation which needs to be mentioned is the community of scholars. In the age under scrutiny, their language was not the vernaculars, but Latin. The institutions of higher education—mainly universities, but colleges as well—displayed a homogeneity of organization that far surpasses what we have attained today in our age of globalization. The biographies of famous humanists, scientists, and artists of the period in question display a transnationality which is at times striking. Being a student in Bologna, then accepting a position in Paris or Oxford only to end one's life as a professor in Prague or Heidelberg was not at all unusual. The main reason for this and comparable constellations is, of course, the fact that science is universal in its self-understanding; but the humanistic disciplines also conceived of themselves in such a way in that age. The *studia humanitatis* were not concerned with contemporary phenomena; the study of literary texts written in the various vernaculars attained the status of university discipline(s) only in the first half of the nineteenth century. Early modern humanities studies were directed at the patrimony shared by all European nations: the two classical languages, Christian theology, and Greek philosophy. There was no reason in that age to think about the creation of a British or a French style of studying the humanities. There was no difference, neither with regard to the material studied nor with regard to the devices by means of which it was studied. As mentioned, this homogeneity was facilitated by the existence of an academic *lingua franca*.—The vehicular effects produced by the migrating academics were more limited than those produced by the Roman Church, for the same reasons as in the case of the nobility. This limitation was counterbalanced by the fact that those living in the ivory tower were the educators of the younger generation—that is, not of the entire younger generation, but of all those who later on in their lives would have an influence on cultural production. So, even though the recipients of what they transported in their "mental valise" were restricted in terms of numbers, the role of academics as active instruments of the circulation of cultural material should not be underestimated.—*Mutatis mutandis*, this quantitative remark holds true for the nobility as well.[265]

9.—As to literary culture in particular, one further agency dedicated to the task of "making material circulate in the net" which is of particular importance in the early modern age is the academy. These institutions first arose in *cinquecento* Italy as imitations of the classical Greek academies run by Plato and Aristotle—of which contemporary learned Italians had a rather vague idea. In Renaissance Italy, the academies' primary task was to encourage their members to produce literary texts by way of drawing on the material floating in the cultural net, to discuss the drafts, and then to improve the texts before they were committed to general circulation, that is, to print. The academies provided an institutionalized infrastructure for cultural production.—It is interesting to note that it was not only the output of these institutions which circulated, but also the abstract idea underlying them. Roughly seven decades later than in Italy, one may observe the sudden flourishing of a number of academies in Spain—a country closely linked to Italy, or to parts of Italy, in the way illustrated above—followed by the establishment of the most famous academy of all

---

[265] As previously mentioned, a single princess from abroad who succeeds at ascending the throne, as in the case of Catherine the Great, has the power to change the cultural map of her host country in a most dramatic and lasting manner.

times to date, the *Académie française* (1635).²⁶⁶ It will not be necessary to demonstrate the influence the French academy had on the country's cultural production.—Looking at the French case, it becomes immediately evident that these academies served both as sites of a particularly intense and systematic circulation and re-synthesis of cultural material, and as instances of control with regard to various aspects of their output—aspects which are, however, intimately intertwined: the aesthetic, the moral, and the political.

Academies are differentiated from the other agencies mentioned in that their role as institutionalized sites of intense production based on exchange, transfer, and re-circulation can hardly be overestimated. From the age of the academies onward, cultural production—at least in Europe—transitions from a pattern of patronage-driven artistic output to a more and more market-based system of production.²⁶⁷ In terms of both the quantity and the quality of the output of the net, the invention of these institutionalized systems marks a threshold, at least with regard to the era under consideration.—In the ages of Romanticism and post-Romanticism, the traditional academies lost their influence, since they were seen as conservative bastions defending the authority of outmoded traditions, rather than as places encouraging ingenuity. But the abstract concept of institutionalized infrastructures for cultural circulation and production subsists. Such institutions have taken on a more flexible shape, which at times may veil the fact that they are institutions, that is, restricted circles of humans collaborating according to rather well-defined rules, and with clear-cut goals and purposes. I am thinking of literary or cultural festivals and of the elaborate system of attribution of prizes and awards.

It remains a separate question (which shall not be discussed here in detail) what the consequences of the remodeling of the "original" Italian version of the institution under Spanish and French auspices may have been.²⁶⁸ To illus-

---

266 See the studies by Gvozdeva (*Compagnie d'hommes joyeux*) and Bung ("Playful Institutions").
267 From the perspective of the French case only, this assessment might at first sight seem astonishing; most evidently, the monarch was the ideological "head" of the *Académie française* and, as such, its patron. In the cases of Italy, France, England, and Germany, things were different. But the main point I am making above concerns the quantity of cultural production, an aspect which applies in all countries mentioned: the establishment of institutions dedicated to cultural production created a sort of cultural "industry". Combined with the generalization of print and the continuous growth of literacy, this quantitative expansion led to the emergence of what became the new literary "market", by the latest in the second half of the eighteenth century.
268 These and many other relevant questions are discussed in the two studies just mentioned (n. 266).

trate the point in question with one sentence: it may be that the highly centralized French variant—one academy only, controlled by the king and his powerful prime minister—which differs dramatically from the polycentric Italian pattern as well as from the even more "fluid" shape the concept assumed in Spain, is one important reason for the fact that there is a rather clear-cut idea of what early modern French literary culture is, whereas in the case of Italy, and even more so of Spain (as well as Germany),[269] there is no such emblematic concept which would make it conceivable to encapsulate the entire cultural production of the country in question.

10.—Finally, one has to mention agencies of transmission that systematically help circulate cultural material, but in a completely unintentional way. For the period under scrutiny, the British East India Company is perhaps the best-known example. Its activities consisted in economic exploitation based on previous physical conquest and political subjugation. Without any conscious intention to do so, the Company helped ramify the Western, in particular the British sub-net into South Asia, thus initiating massive processes of bidirectional circulation of cultural material which completely changed traditional South Asian societies, and partly transformed Western societies as well in the process.

One example of such an agency of parasitic cultural transmission which was, in contrast to the East India Company, mainly if not totally free from attempts at spreading political power was the *Deutsche Hanse* or Hanseatic League. The organization known under this name was an alliance of for the most part German cities (the biggest one was Hamburg, which styles itself even today as *Freie und Hanse-Stadt Hamburg*) whose economic activities were focused on trade. Almost all of the towns were harbor cities: Bremen, Lübeck, Greifswald, and Rostock, to name the most important ones after Hamburg. The net they constructed starting in the twelfth century is relevant to the problems here discussed insofar as it was intended to transcend the pattern of periodic short-term contact that typically accompanied commercial exchanges. The Hanseatic

---

269 Germany has many prestigious "regional" academies which have a long-standing tradition (The Bavarian Academy; The Heidelberg Academy; The Göttingen Academy). But it was only in the year 2008 that the oldest and, as to its members, most international of these regional academies, the Leopoldina, was elevated to the rank of German national academy. Much more than in the Latin countries, the German academies focus in their activities on scholarship, scientific as well as humanistic; for the fine arts, there are separate institutions (*Akademie[n] der schönen Künste*). From the perspective of a comprehensive understanding of culture, however, the role of the German academies is comparable to the function of their analogues in other Western countries.

League established small colonies of German traders all over Northern and Eastern Europe, as far north as Novgorod. These traders sought out manufactured goods which might be needed in their host cities. They notified their Hanseatic partners of their findings, welcomed the incoming ships sent out by the merchants of these cities, entertained their crews, and sold the goods the ships had transported to the locals, with whose language and habits they had familiarized themselves. Economically, the Hanseatic League was so successful that it created the basis for the fact that Hamburg remains to this day the wealthiest community in continental Europe.

The culturally relevant specificity of the "colonies" mentioned consists in the fact that they were governed by a legal status which has become obsolete in Europe since the era of the democratic revolutions, but which can be traced back to the times of ancient Greece. It was common in the European Middle Ages and in early modern times.[270] This status might be best known under the term of "metic", in its original spelling, *metoikos*: a person who has moved (*met-*) his household (*oikos*). The implication underlying the term is the archaic idea that one's home should be located in one's place of birth. Metics were the exception to this rule. They were permitted to reside in cities where they had not been born, as, for example, in the case of Spartans living in Athens. They were allowed to trade and to become trained craftsmen. But they were not granted citizenship, not even as second- or third-generation residents. They did not have "rights", but only "privileges", that is, unilaterally conceded guarantees that could be revoked at any time. They had to pay a heavy surtax. If they committed crimes against full citizens, they were severely punished; if full citizens perpetrated crimes against them, the consequences were not very grave. To put the matter in a nutshell: their situation was far from being idyllic. But it seems that they accepted it, whether by necessity—as the diasporic Jews had in Europe before the era of emancipation, when they lived under exactly this legal status; as Christians and Jews residing in territories conquered by Islamic powers did and in certain cases still do—or in view of an economic advantage to be gained. The important point in this context is that the status of metic implied that there was no pressure, nor even an invitation or an expectation, to assimilate to the autochthonous culture. In terms of cultural patterns, Spartan *metoikoi* stayed Spartan, German *Hanse* tradesmen stayed German,

---

[270] It continues to exist in many Islamic countries even today, under the name of *dhimma*, and it regulates many uneducated Muslim immigrants' minds in Europe—thus causing, together with the ignorance regarding this status on the part of Western mainstream public opinion, a totally misconceived debate on integration and assimilation.

pre-emancipation Jews stayed Jewish, etc. The necessity to interact with the locals, however, led these communities to develop the skills necessary for doing so. As a consequence, they were able to communicate in two different cultural frames, thus unintentionally becoming classical "cultural brokers", or, in this book's terminology, agents of cultural transmission.

The men of the *Hanse* in particular paved the way for a highly marked phenomenon: the strong affinity of Eastern Europe for all sorts of cultural items of German origin.[271] This still applies today. The atrocities committed by Germans during the Nazi era notwithstanding, German culture and language, as well as manufactured goods, have a greater importance and standing in post-Soviet Eastern Europe than in any other territory in the world, including Germany's Western partners within the European Union.

11.—There is still a question as yet unanswered which transcends the geographical as well as the historical boundaries of this study: namely, whether or not there are comparable transnational agencies in other parts of the world at other times. In addition to what I have argued concerning Buddhism, I have only a few scattered remarks to make.—As already mentioned, universalistic ideologies, whether religious or secular, seem to be powerful agents promoting the transmission of cultural material. In addition to the Roman Church, one should consider under this heading the role of the *umma*, the community of those who pray to Allah. One may observe its activities as an agency of cultural transfer in countries far removed from its territory of emergence, such as Indonesia or the nations of (sub-Saharan) West Africa. For reasons of disciplinary competence, however, I shall leave it at the above speculations pertaining to the cultural impact of the Christian and the Muslim religions from a comparative perspective. One relevant point that shall be discussed later on and in a different context is the nearly complete rejection of theatrical performances within traditional Islam. The kind of mass media that emerged in Europe in the age under consideration does not exist in traditional Islamic societies. In that sense, one may hypothesize that Islam as an agency of cultural transfer is primarily dedicated to faith and related religious practices, but that its contribution to the spread of more secular cultural practices and items is limited in comparison.[272]

---

[271] Regarding the impact of diasporic Jewry on processes of cultural transfer, see above, pp. 123 f.

[272] I shall take the liberty to remind nonspecialist readers of the fact that the Roman Church exported the Spanish religious drama (*auto sacramental*), or its analogues created by the Jesuits, to the "exotic" places mentioned above; as, in terms of form and structure, these post-Renaissance didactic plays were heavily influenced by humanistic, that is Aristotelian principles, this process paved the way for the subsequent reception of secular European drama and visual culture in those regions.

On the other hand, one cannot ignore the fact that the philosophical basis of post-classical antiquity was determined by the reception of an oeuvre which most probably would have remained unknown in the Occident at least until the Fall of Constantinople had the Muslim conquerors of North Africa and the Iberian Peninsula not transported it along with their weapons, implementing it in the conquered territories along with their faith, their mosques, etc. Military conquest that is driven by nothing but material greed[273] might involve some cultural transmission as well, but typically is not associated with a systematic *translatio studii*[274] as observable in cases of military conquest fueled by universalistic ideologies. Having said this, the fact must be stressed that, with respect to the question of Islam as an agency of secular cultural transmission, the Aristotelian corpus might be a singular case.[275]

As to secular universalism as a catalyst for cultural transmission, one would have to take into consideration the concept of "human rights" and the pretense of the political model of democracy to being a template of universal suitability. It might be superfluous to comment on the cultural side effects of modern ideologies committed to universalism, since we are able to take note of them every day when watching the news. There is no military endeavor of the West that is not followed by attempts at implementing in the conquered or "liberated" territories structures, rules, and narratives whose main or even sole task is to facilitate in future times the unrestricted circulation of cultural material from the Western metropoles to the regions (re-)integrated into the "universal" net.

12.—What about the present-day situation? The role of the Christian Churches in the transmission of cultural material has diminished dramatically, in proportion to their general loss of influence. The high aristocracy as a transnational

---

[273] —as in the case of the Mongol tribes, starting in the thirteenth century under their leader Genghis Khan, who extended his power from Central Asia to the entire region subsequently known as the Ottoman Empire.

[274] I invite readers to take, in this respect, a look at my description of the cultural scenario in colonial India, which might be a particularly intricate "intermediate" case (pp. 212–215).

[275] —a point which raises many questions, indeed, but questions difficult to answer in a non-speculative way; even if it is true that the leading Arab Aristotelians were converted Jews, there is the question of why the religious authorities tolerated their activities. What is in my view the only tenable observation in this respect was already given expression to above: Islam does not need a concept analogous to original sin; on behalf of this feature, an unrestrictedly positive evaluation of abstract reason is, in principle, possible; things might become different the more the level of abstraction is lowered.—Although this will provoke an uproar of indignation amongst politically correct readers, I allow myself to express that I consider the many further items of Arab/Islamic culture transferred to Europe in the process of conquest which occurred in medieval times, mainly consisting of items of everyday culture, as being of minor importance.

ruling class has vanished.[276] For the reasons mentioned above, the importance of Jewish people (or of people of Jewish origin) as agents of transmission may have decreased;[277] but on the other hand, their reduced mobility as individuals might be compensated by the fact that the re-established Jewish nation state has become, on behalf of the prehistory of its members, a sort of laboratory of high-intensity cultural exchange, a universal cultural net *in parvo*. As to the transnational community of scholars and artists, it continues to be of great importance. But it shall remain an open question whether or not the age of "national cultures" inflicted a blow to this community's transnationality from which it has not yet recovered.—In addition, there are agencies of transculturation emerging only in technological modernity proper. The most important one is the visual media industry (film, TV, nowadays the Internet), whose revolutionary activities began in the twentieth century. It may very well be the case that the shared rhetorical ideal which withered in the age of nationalism and national cultures has been superseded today by a transnational and trans-Western "rhetorical" system whose main mediatic basis is no longer language, but visually encoded patterns.[278]—Global capitalism is said to have reached its state of maturity in the last decades. But the capitalist model of economy has been a relevant factor, including in the sphere of culture and cultural goods or commodities, not only since the age of imperialism, that is the second half of the nineteenth century; its early stages may be traced back to antiquity. If, however, we take the epithet of "global" literally, it is, indeed, a phenomenon that does not emerge until the beginning of the twentieth century.

---

276 The concept of "dynastic bonds" beyond borders as an instrument of politics has evaporated concomitantly to the complete loss of effective power on the part of the "royals". Present-day heirs to the throne typically marry women or men from their own country; in order to avoid frictions with their peers, they steer clear of the members of their country's aristocracy. The status of these royals is that of common "celebrities". In order to preserve it, they have to comply with the expectations and fantasies of the readers of the yellow press. For a girl or a young man working as a hairdresser, it is easier to fantasize about being a journalist or a fitness instructor from their own country than to fantasize about being some highbrow aristocrat from abroad.
277 But see also my deliberations concerning this point in n. 261.
278 This observation is not meant in a strictly dichotomous way; the actual performance of the speech on the rhetorician's part, that is, visual encoding, has always been a component of rhetoric; and present-day global mass media do not rely on visual codes alone, but also make use of language, albeit in a way that is rather reduced from the standpoint of a person who has been educated before the "iconic turn". The relative weight of linguistic and visual mediation seems to have been inverted. This said, the formal standardization ("rhetoricization") of visual encoding in present-day globally distributed motion pictures seems to be, indeed, no less strict than the standardization of verbal patterns was in the age of rhetoric.

It is not only for reasons of remaining within the temporal frame of this book that I do not discuss these latter agencies in detail. I think that their activities, as far as cultural transfer is concerned, do not differ qualitatively from the activities of their predecessors (printing companies, medieval *scriptoria*, traders, associations of traders, trading companies). The difference is one of quantity, and we will have to look to the future to determine whether or not the exponential increase of cultural material distributed by a globalized economic system and via the Internet as its primary medium will bring about qualitative change as well, in the sense of transformations which can no longer be captured by the concepts regarding the past developed in this book.

Control and Demand

0.—As emphasized on various occasions, the processes of circulation taking place in the cultural net may in principle be conceived of as unrestricted. But when it comes to connecting the circulating material to "consumers", whether individual or collective recipients, there are regulatory mechanisms which can be subdivided into more authoritarian and more "market-driven" variants. From a historical perspective, there is an asymmetry between these two parameters that needs to be pointed out. I believe, albeit somewhat speculatively, that "demand" is a regulatory mechanism which applies from the very first stages of the species' existence up to the present: humans want to satisfy their "needs" and "desires"; these needs are to be understood, I may add parenthetically, to comprise both the "real" and the fantasized. In the domain of symbolic encoding, too, humans show a preference for making use of that symbolically encoded material that satisfies their needs better than other available material.[279] Mechanisms of control, by contrast, might be a more historically specific phenomenon; they seem to be bound to the emergence of hierarchical struc-

---

[279] As to underlying "real" needs, I refer once again to my above speculation concerning primordial hunting practices. As to the fulfillment of fantastic needs, one might wish to first discuss the question of when fantasizing emerged in the history of the species. I should like to hypothesize that this happened quite early on. The only difference between these primordial daydreamers and their modern descendants may be the fact that in those times happiness was understood in a way that we would characterize as naïve in our common narcissistic self-centeredness. In the early periods of humankind, it might have consisted in the state of having successfully slain a particularly big bull (which is, by the way, not all that different from happiness understood as the state of being a powerful knight or a rich man). As soon as humans succeeded in symbolizing (imagining) an animal of prey which was not actually present, there was already a basic structure enabling what was in later times called "fantasizing".

tures, to the evolution leading from informally organized tribes to "societies" or even states. Only in case there are certain individuals within a community who are able to deploy physical power sufficient to coerce their fellows into doing what they do not want to do, or into not doing what they wish to do, is there the possibility of exerting control of any kind; this includes control over access to and use of cultural material floating in the net. If we are inclined to believe the Rousseauian narrative, this condition became fulfilled when sedentary life and the concept of private property set in. But I would speculate that hierarchical structures are much older. As soon as there were people who were responsible for making decisions, or for negotiating with "higher beings" (spirits, gods), it is more than probable that these individuals or small groups of individuals tried to stabilize and preserve their position by controlling the "thinking" of the other members of the tribe. This is most effectively done by controlling symbolically encoded fantasizing.

1.—Although there are significant indicators of a systematic control of cultural material circulating in the net during quite early phases of human history—possibly the most prominent being the eradication of all symbols of the first monotheism after Akhenaten's (Amenophis IV's) death[280]—it should be stressed that the institutionalized variant of control is ultimately an invention of early modern times and has not evolved very much since then. It is indeed remarkable, and should soothe some of the hysteria prevailing in the Western public sphere at the time when this chapter was written (2014), to observe that the control mechanisms to which the information floating in the present-day Internet is subjected seem to be largely identical to the devices developed by the Inquisition in the period under scrutiny in this book. There is nothing novel about them, and nightmares of an emerging Orwellian society seem much more based on media-

---

[280] Without being a Hegelian in the strict sense, the episode mentioned above gives me the occasion to express, once again, an idea already developed above: if a specific cultural material has a certain appeal for reasonable beings (as, in this example, the concept that there is only one god instead of the wild circus of hybrid beings to whom Egyptians prayed until that time), it is difficult to eradicate it once and for all. In this case, it was adopted by a frustrated prince building on Akhenaten's religious heritage in order to ideologically homogenize a number of slaves who were tired of building pyramids, to promise them a bright future, and to make them endure hardships close to unimaginable from a modern perspective. As a highly mediated result of what was achieved by Moses by overriding the traditional priests' activities of controlling access to the concept of the one and only God already floating in the net, there emerges, according to Hegel, the stage of what we call modernity in human history. It would be highly futile, but nevertheless interesting, to speculate on whether or not there may have been a more direct path towards modernity had Akhenaten's ideas remained dominant in the most powerful empire of that age after his death.

induced sensationalism[281] than on facts. When, in the year 2013, the "whistleblower" Edward Snowden revealed that agencies like the NSA were overseeing all communication taking place on the Internet, the (continental) public was not informed that this control was exercised by first searching for certain terms ("terror", "Islam", "jihad", etc.), then for concatenations of these terms, and finally by asking for the frequency of concatenations of such terms within a given message, in order to identify the very few messages which were then submitted to a qualified human agent for the purposes of a more penetrating scrutiny of the underlying intentions. The main difference between this practice and the work once done by the Inquisition is the fact that the initial search processes were performed by humans rather than machines in former times, and that the items targeted were different ones (references to Lady Fortune; all terms related to sexual activities conceived of as a source of pleasure; free will or rather its denial, etc.).[282] The structure itself continues to be identical to what it has been from the late Middle Ages onward.

With regard to the early modern period and also to modern totalitarian societies, one would have to add that such control—by the Inquisition or by secular offices of censorship—works in two different directions. In terms of the mere quantity of interventions, the mechanisms of control mostly exert pressure on what is extracted from the net. They prohibit certain pieces from being performed and certain books from being distributed. But they also try to prevent problematic material from entering the net. The main device employed to this end is the necessity imposed on authors to obtain an *imprimatur*, an official license to publish the text in question before the printing process can start. Historical evidence, however, demonstrates that neither measure is able to totally prevent cultural material from going viral, thanks to the circulatory processes in which all such material is involved. The inferior approach, in terms of effectiveness, seems to be the measures taken in order to prevent texts from entering the net.

---

281 It is not my intention to criticize the media with the above formulation. News has to sell, otherwise the companies broadcasting it could not survive. Readers or viewers would stop paying for news if these companies admitted on nine out of ten days that nothing worth reporting had happened on the previous day. As a consequence of this situation, the press, as well as electronic media, have recourse to the devices of scandalization and emotionalization in order to attract readers and viewers, that is, people who are in principle supposed to be ready to pay for their products. But media recipients should be able to differentiate between facts on the one hand and devices serving to make facts interesting to them on the other.
282 As to the processes of censorship executed by the Inquisition, see Waltraud Summer-Schindler, *Zensur und Involution. Aspekte gegenreformatorischer Überformung der italienischen Renaissance-Novelle*, Maastricht and Herzogenrath 1996.

Over the centuries, authors have produced a wide range of methods to evade attempts to control input to the net. The most elementary device is to "smuggle" a manuscript to a region out of the reach of the control agency in question. In the age of the Counter-Reformation, it was common practice to send manuscripts assumed by their authors to be problematic from Spain to the Netherlands, have them printed there, and smuggle copies back into Spain. At times, it was even sufficient to have the manuscript clandestinely printed in the country itself and to give a fake place of print (e.g., Anveres/Antwerp in the case of one of the first print editions of the *Lazarillo de Tormes* [1554]). Similar techniques were frequently made use of in later times, for example during the period of the Iron Curtain, and especially in countries located at the Western frontier of the Eastern Bloc, such as East Germany and Czechoslovakia. In the Soviet Union, where contacts between locals and foreigners were more scarce, clandestine techniques of reduplication—typewriting, mimeographing, etc.—were used to evade the censors via underground networks (*samizdat*).

Even when the harshest conceivable measures were taken—e.g., the burning of prohibited books or of their authors—the cultural material in question could rarely be entirely suppressed. Acts of cultural repression are almost always public, or are rather staged by the authorities as public events, with the intention of intimidating the public in order to discourage the reception of banned material. But it is precisely this constellation which makes such *autos da fé* into material for narration and re-narration, and which inspires curiosity about the proscribed publications, thereby providing the basis for a revival or reception of the works in question in later, more tolerant times. Even if—as may have happened in periods before the age of print—a given text existing only in the form of a unique manuscript is irrevocably destroyed, it is probable that its conceptual substrate, at whatever level of abstraction, survives and becomes part of the material circulating in the net.

Mechanisms of control also include variants that are less authoritarian than the ones thematized in the last paragraph. In many cases, they take the shape of a negotiation between control agencies and producers of culture. In the period under scrutiny, the Inquisition frequently granted the necessary *imprimatur* under the condition that the submitted first version be reworked and "purged" of all controversial content. Analogous mechanisms were developed by contemporary secular control agencies such as the *Académie française*, which supervised the political orthodoxy even of texts by renowned authors like Corneille and requested revisions in case they were considered necessary. The trials that Baudelaire and Flaubert had to stand for having published, respectively, *Les Fleurs du mal* (1857) and *Madame Bovary* (1857) may have been the last great cases of authoritarian control of the material admitted to the net to have taken place in modern Western European societies; the "crime" both authors were accused of was to have intentionally weakened "good morals".[283] Still, there are traces left of such mechanisms in present-day Western societies; they do not affect the strands of cultural production targeted in this book.[284] In comparison to previous periods of cultural history, present-day Western cultural production seems to be free to extract any material from the net and to commit it, after reworking it into a new artifact, to further circulation, to an extent that is at times shocking for people from a different background. My country is a particularly extreme case, even within the liberal culture of present-day Europe. As is well known, obscenities of the most radical kind have been admitted on German stages, in particular in Berlin, since the 1970s without any restrictions; in reaction to the massive control of the cultural net during the Nazi era, and also in the communist GDR, German culture today profits from a close to unrestricted freedom of access to and use of the material circulating in the cultural net.

Viewed from the perspective outlined above, one may feel tempted to hypothesize that pervasive authoritarian control of the material that enters and is withdrawn from the net is an exception in the long history of human culture. Indeed, it calls for effective bureaucratic control agencies on the one hand and the general acceptance of authoritarian control on the other. So it may be that its historical incidence is linked to the (early modern) sovereign state and its degenerate totalitarian variants.

2.—I will now proceed to suggest what a demand-driven cultural production might look like; these remarks will help to balance the impression that regulatory mechanisms which have an impact on the material floating in the net have simply evolved from "evil" to "good"; on the other hand, I would not deny that I prefer a regulation based on informal mechanisms to one based on bureaucratized control.

This second regulatory mechanism to be considered takes on a shape familiar from market dynamics. But—if one temporarily brackets the question of fiction

---

283 In the case of *Madame Bovary*, it was Emma's adultery, not criticized by the (absent) narrator, that was targeted by the public prosecutor. Flaubert was acquitted, but it seems that he had to make use of his close relations to the imperial court in order to evade being sentenced. Baudelaire was less fortunate. He had to produce a "purged" version of his collection of poems; the "pièces condamnées" are characterized by references to sexual practices which fell under the heading of *contra naturam* in former times.

284 I am in particular thinking of the very intense debate, conducted in recent years mainly in Germany, Ireland, and Britain, revolving around the abuse of children and the electronic circulation of recordings of such practices.

in the very strict sense, for whose demand-side profile Freud's essay on fiction and daydreaming, frequently quoted by me, yields a satisfactory answer—what is demand in this context? I should like to come back to a historical constellation already briefly addressed above, in order to scrutinize more closely the motives of a given cultural community to extract specific material circulating in the net although the material which is concomitantly neglected might be philosophically and aesthetically just as interesting as, or even more interesting than this material.

As explained to some extent in the context of my brief comparative remarks concerning *Hamlet* and *La vida es sueño*, skepticism was the dominant epistemological and philosophical school in early modern Europe. It had attained this status within a few decades following upon its "rediscovery" in the middle of the sixteenth century. What was it that led preeminent contemporary philosophers to consign traditional Aristotelian, that is, sense-based scholastic epistemology to further travel in the net and to extract, by way of translating Sextus Empiricus' *Pyrrhoneion hypothyposeon libri tres* (second century CE), skepticism from the net, where it had been floating as mostly inactive cultural material for some 1,500 years? According to my findings, there are two main determining factors which motivated contemporary human agents to make use of their freedom of choice in the way they did. Firstly, the geographical discoveries of the age—a mental shock for early modern Europeans whose impact we are hardly able to imagine—had completely destabilized the current assumption that humans may distill from their sensory perception a "true" picture of the world.[285] Our senses convey to us that the earth is a kind of disc; at the latest from Magellan's voyage onward, it was evident that this assumption is untenable. Even today, our senses convey to us that the sun rotates around the earth; but since the time of Galileo's observations, it is clear that this is not true. In this situation, early modern European epistemology took recourse to a cultural configuration at hand in the net by way of which it was possible to theorize the findings for which there was no explanation within the old paradigm, namely, skepticism.—It should be added that the process of appropriation and reactivation which thus occurred is quite typical of such "demand-induced" extractions. In cases where the demand is urgent, there is a tendency to have recourse to a cultural configuration which provides a fundamental, even a radical answer to the question irresolvable under the old paradigm. Radicalness, however, always goes along with exaggeration. This, in consequence, leads to the fact that the material enthusiastically extracted from the net is

---

[285] See my "The Traditional Cosmos and the New World".

recommitted at least to a large extent to its further travel after a relatively short period. In the case under consideration, this indeed happened with Descartes's rationalistic rejection of skepticism and with Bacon's integration of some of skepticism's assumptions into a new and revolutionary synthesis of sense-based and sense-skeptical epistemology known under the name of empiricism.

The example thematized above seems to contain a second point to be considered in similar cases. Pyrrhonian skepticism was literally resurrected in the year 1562, when the first translation into Latin appeared in print. Contrary to other classical texts re-extracted from the net in the course of the Renaissance, the radical skeptics' theses had been truly unknown in the Middle Ages, because the only language in which they had been transmitted—Greek—was not studied in that period. Nevertheless, the aforementioned sudden reactivation took place on a discursive territory which was in a way prepared for it, and thus ready to receive a theory whose conceptual profile was only vaguely known until then. Occamism, in particular theological nominalism, had postulated as early as at the beginning of the fourteenth century that an Almighty God is not obliged to manifest Himself eternally in a manner consistent with what He had revealed in Scripture. He is free to change His will. He does not owe humankind anything ("[Deus] ad nihil faciendum obligatur. [Deus] autem nulli tenetur nec obligatur tanquam debitor." / "There is nothing that God is obliged to do. He is bound to no one nor obliged to anyone as a debtor.").[286] He is even, as was held by Occam's aforementioned thirteenth-century precursor in Paris, free to create "several different worlds" ("plures mundos facere").[287] This nominalistic theology, which was for two centuries the antagonist of Thomist, Aristotelian thinking, and which later became the basis for Protestantism, is certainly not identical with skepticism. But the epistemologies deriving from the respective edifices of thought are compatible to a very high degree. If God is indeed the sole master of His volition, He is free to manipulate humans' sensory perception, whether totally or merely occasionally; and (this may be even more important) He is free to add new components to his Creation so that all knowledge based on former sense perception is instantaneously devalued. These were most propitious conditions for the rapid spread of the thoughts contained in Sextus' book, whose extraction from the net might have remained a negligible episode of cultural history had the conditions been less favorable. But the pri-

---

[286] William Occam, *Opera Philosophica et Theologica. Quaestiones in librum secundum sententiarum*, Gedeon Gál and Rega Wood (eds.), New York, NY 1981, qu. 3–4 and qu. 15.
[287] See n. 34 of the 219 propositions condemned as "Averroist" in the famous decree of 1277 by the Parisian bishop Etienne Tempier (*Chartularium universitatis parisiensis*, vol. 1, pp. 543–558).

mary factor was that there was, indeed, a strong "demand". There was an epistemological "void" waiting to be filled, and the theories summarized by Sextus exactly fit to fill that void, or rather to temporarily veil its existence and thus to palliate the *horror vacui* that accompanies inexplicability.

It remains to be discussed how this demand should be further defined when it comes to cultural artifacts in the modern sense as theorized by Kant, that is, autonomous, de-pragmatized works of art, while relegating to the background for the time being Freud's questioning of such an approach to artworks, or, rather, while assuming that there may be a sort of multilayered demand, a conscious, "Kantian" one and a subconscious, repressed, "Freudian" one. The "Kantian" demand to which these works constitute an answer is certainly not, as was the case above, pragmatic. What, however, could the profile of a merely aesthetic "demand" be? In the sphere of the pleasing but superfluous it would seem at first sight hard to imagine something like "need" and ensuing "demand". As emphasized on several occasions, the period in which this question becomes pertinent lies beyond the scope of this book. For the time being, I should like to limit myself to the remark that the theories of Russian formalism seem to provide a largely sufficient answer to the question as far as the age of "Kantian" art is concerned: the demand satisfied by modern art proper is the longing for the "novel", for new stimuli of our sensibility, which has been anaesthetized by automatization.

The absolute centrality of the ideologically understood criterion of demand for works of art from the period under scrutiny may perhaps be best observed with regard to the reception of Boccaccio's Griselda story.[288] The novella had a huge resonance all over Europe up to the end of the seventeenth century. It yielded the basis for a great variety of dramas in all major European languages, as well as in a number of minor ones, in particular in the sixteenth and seventeenth centuries. It continued to be popular, albeit to a lesser degree, up to the end of the nineteenth century. From that time onward, it seems to have become of merely historical interest in the sense that no more rewritings of the story emerged. The apogee of its reception was the first half of the seventeenth century; let me recall that it dates from the fourteenth. If one takes into consideration that the story revolves around the issue of marriage, primarily around the question of how to define the obligations that male and female partners have and of how they should treat each other, it is obvious that the demand motivat-

---

288 See above, n. 183, for a précis of the action narrated, and see Rüegg, *The 'Patient Griselda' Myth in Late Medieval and Early Modern Literature*, for the reception history summarized above.

ing the extraction of this story from the net was the renewed or perhaps even entirely new interest in the definition of marriage provoked by the theological discussions starting with the Reformation. The Protestant denominations agreed to deny marriage the status of a sacrament and instead cast it as a worldly institution, albeit one conceived by God in order to palliate humans' carnal desires by providing a frame within which they may be lived out in an "orderly" fashion. The interest in topics revolving around marriage was fueled by the Catholic Church's reaction, that is, by the dogmatization of marriage's sacramental character within the Council of Trent and the ensuing strict supervision of believers' sexual lives and of the way they performed as married couples.

3.—The Griselda story and its reception provides the opportunity to address a specific point, not discussed as yet, pertaining to the issue of demand as a driving force of cultural circulation processes. I have already mentioned the relevance of the existence of a *lingua franca* version for the smoothness of processes of circulation within the net. There is no way to conduct experiments in the field of history, but it appears at first sight to be a not at all negligible factor behind the immense propagation of the text that Petrarch, for whatever reason, translated the story created by his friend Boccaccio into Latin; on the other hand, I remain skeptical with regard to the systematic relevance of language when it comes to the integration of specific works into the floating processes taking place within the cultural net. In the case of the translation in question, however, one may observe a specific feature that may be of more general theoretical import. If one compares Petrarch's version to the original, it becomes evident that it displays a reduction of the original's semantic complexity. With regard to Boccaccio's version, one may rightly say that it is a totally enigmatic story. There is no question that the central personage, the *marchese*, is not presented as an exemplary token of what a husband is or should be. But Griselda's "patience", too, is difficult to accept as an instance of exemplarity. One should not forget that she truly believes that her children were killed by her husband and that she accepts these "facts" without revolting against the *marchese*'s (as the narrator puts it) "matta bestialità". In the times of pagan Rome, her behavior might have been acceptable, since a *pater familias* was allowed to kill his offspring. But within a Christian framework, the killing of innocent children without reason jars with the dogma that every human being is endowed with a soul created by God. The story thus highlights the question—illustrated by the female protagonist—of whether or not marital duties should precede parental duties, as well as the question of what female human beings essentially are to be: is it their main task to care for their offspring, or rather to be the unrestrictedly loyal companions of males? The only plausible interpretation of Boccaccio's version I see is to understand it as a final crystallization—it is, indeed, the last novella of the

Decameron—of the quasi-epistemological essence of the collection as a whole. While there is an implicit problematization of the novellas' didactic character in the previous ninety-nine stories, or rather in their relation to one another, the last novella renders this central message explicit: namely, that the *strani casi* (the strange, singular cases) of which the "world" presented in the stories is comprised do not allow for the extraction of any lesson regarding the essence of reality—that is, with the exception of the (nominalistic) meta-essence that there is no such (primary) essence.[289]

It is as early as in Petrarch's translation that this inextricable complexity becomes reduced with a view to creating a didactic story about the duties of a "good" wife. This semantic "primitivization" remains in place for the story's entire reception history. However, the result is not always a simplistic didacticism, in the sense of conveying a maxim by narrating a story. In very many cases, the attitude displayed by Griselda is made use of in order to trigger an intra-fictional discussion or even debate about the right way to behave within the institution of marriage. But nowhere in the later reception history is the "uncanny" character of Boccaccio's first (written) version preserved.—To put the point in more abstract terms: we have the tendency to consider processes of cultural transmission to be accompanied by an accumulation of complexity. This may, indeed, be a vector along which Western culture, considered in general terms, evolves, from its medieval beginnings up to the present day. But it may not apply to singular cultural phenomena or even to "works". One should keep in mind that the reduction of semantic complexity (or, to put it in other terms, the popularization) of a given material floating in the net is a very important feature of cultural dynamics. The reduction may even lead, as is the case here with the transformation of an uncanny enigma into a tale of exemplarity, to a complete re-functionalization.

4.—Cultural history is a part of general history, not an idyllic realm sectioned off from what is otherwise mostly bloody, cruel, and inhumane. This insight encourages me to thematize, as a second illustrative example for my postulate of demand as a causal factor of extraction from the net, the darkest period of my own country's history, Nazism. One of the striking, even bizarre features of Nazi culture was the reactivation of pagan Germanic myth and of related ritualistic practices. If one considers the success of the Christian religion as an effect

---

[289] For a more detailed account of this reading, see my "Affichierte Exemplarität, tatsächliche A-Systematik. Boccaccios *Decameron* und die Episteme der Renaissance", in: Klaus W. Hempfer (ed.), *Renaissance. Diskursstrukturen und epistemologische Voraussetzungen. Literatur – Philosophie – Bildende Kunst*, Stuttgart 1993, pp. 47–93.

of its overriding of the many highly naïve features of former polytheisms, it seems difficult to understand why a majority of people from one of the most educated nations of the globe was ready, from a certain period onward, to almost avidly extract all this, intellectually considered, obsolete cultural material revolving around Odin and Woden, places like Valhalla, runes, and the swastika from the cultural net, where it had been hovering, mostly inactive, since the times of the Germanic territories' Christianization.

The demand, in this case, was according to my view located in a sphere nowadays called identity politics. During World War I, and starting already in the two previous decades,[290] Germany had tried to obtain by military force what William II, the last emperor, called a *Platz an der Sonne*—it had attempted to become an equal player among the leading nations of Western Europe, whose political modernization and technological industrialization had taken place much earlier than in Germany. These attempts at becoming one of the world powers within the occidental system, indeed perhaps the dominant power in Europe, failed. As part of the Occident, Germany could have conceived of itself only as a minor, humiliated, defeated entity. This was the path forward suggested by the *Realpolitiker* of the Weimar Republic. The latter, however, did not take into consideration what Freud called humans' inextricable narcissism. The majority of German people then filled, so to speak, the gap with respect to a positive self-description by having recourse to the material, completely obsolete in terms of cultural history, characterized above. As was the case with skepticism, the material extracted from the net was of a very radical profile. Perhaps another parallel consists in the fact that its radicalness made the community that adopted it end up in an impasse after a relatively short period of time. And here, too, the cultural terrain was in a way prepared to receive the extracted material by previous cultural processes, namely, Romanticism and the second Romanticism commonly known as *décadence*, in this case: Wagnerism.

5.—The evolution of Russian drama and theater in the eighteenth century yields an example of a circulatory process induced by a strong demand which is, as in the previous case, political, but not immediately related to identity politics. The entire period of the country's history is characterized by political turmoil, by Tsars, Tsarinas, and heirs to the throne who are overthrown, reinstated only to be overthrown once again, and at times even killed. As demonstrated in detail in Kirill Ospovat's book,[291] this scenario created nearly ideal conditions for the reception of French and Shakespearean tragedy in a country

---

290 I here refer to Germany's belated politics of colonization.
291 *Terror and Pity*.

which up to that period did not have an autochthonous tradition of tragic plays. The pieces by Shakespeare, Corneille, and Racine adapted to the Russian language and stage by Aleksandr P. Sumarokov served two very different purposes within the logic of a culture bound to absolutism. Firstly—and this trait may represent a coincidental link between the French and the Tsarist courts, or it may be another instance of importation—the stage was a very suitable means for reflecting on the theatricality of absolutist power, that is, its reliance on the courtiers' belief, conditioned by myriad performative elements on the part of the monarchy, that the monarch in power effectively controls the country, including nature.[292] Secondly, the *topos* of a reversal of fortune as is characteristic of all variants of tragedy (*peripeteia*) and particularly of the French classicist drama is a feature which re-enacts what "reality" was for the spectators (early Russian theater is intended almost exclusively for an aristocratic audience); presenting it on stage helped to create a frame for distanciation and subsequent reflection. In this context, it is quite telling that French classical comedy (Molière) was not received in Russia. The plots of certain well-known French tragedies, for example Racine's *Esther* (1689) and Corneille's *Nicomède* (1651), by contrast, were so close to what happened at the eighteenth-century Tsarist court[293] that the reception of these pieces was conditioned by a sort of vacuum effect by which the exotic material was "drawn" to the East without any attempt by Western nations to exert an influence on the literary and cultural production of cities as remote as Moscow and St. Petersburg.

6.—I should like to conclude this chapter by referring to a particularly interesting section of Sven Kilian's contribution to the research which forms the basis of this book.[294] While discussing Théodore de Bèze's *Abraham sacrifiant* (1550), a play which is important because it is considered to be the first drama written in French according to neo-Aristotelian formal rules, Kilian notes that there are two questions that immediately emerge. One of these questions is: on what

---

292 One might thus consider the innumerable courtly festivities in Versailles or similar places, which displayed "miracles" of various kinds, as a sort of "staging" of the monarch's power over the elements; the park of Versailles may be a particularly instructive landscape variant of such a demonstration of royal power. It shows that even "nature" has to surrender to the monarch's aesthetic preferences.
293 The above qualification of some Racinian tragedies is to be understood with respect to the abstract pattern of the action. There is, of course, no "Jewish component" in Russian dynastic history, as there is in *Esther*; but there is the pattern of a ruler's wife who comes from a country that is foreign as to culture (language, religious denomination) and who is successful in preventing or countering several coups plotted against her.
294 *"Escrituras andantes"*.

grounds does the author claim his dramatization of the Akedah to be a tragedy (the subtitle is, indeed, "Tragédie Françoise")? The second question pertains to the perplexing fact that there is a rich fund of mystery plays in the French tradition, but no play which deals particularly with this story,[295] whose importance for the Jewish religion, for the unorthodox sect originating from it (Christianity), and for the history of religions in general is so obvious: the story marks the threshold between the ages during which the sacrifice of humans was an accepted practice and the more advanced periods of ritual history during which humans came to be replaced by animals in this respect.—I will start my observations by addressing this latter point, that is, the question of why the author may have extracted this story in particular from the material floating in the net. Bèze was a Protestant. He had to leave France when the persecution of the reformists began. He fled to Geneva, where he played a prominent role in the history of Swiss Calvinism, becoming the head of the Geneva Protestants after Calvin's death. From a Protestant viewpoint, the story which occurred on the slopes of Mount Moriah is the first element in a chain of substitutions regarding sacrificial practices which culminates in the Calvinist understanding of the Eucharist. The second important element implied in this chain consists in the replacement of the sacrificial object, the ram or sheep, by the one to whom the sacrifice is offered, God-Christ, thus eliminating the "bargain" underlying the archaic pattern.[296] As is evidenced by the paradoxical character informing this structure, the practice of sacrifice as such is abolished with the incarnated God's self-sacrifice. For all future times, it is substituted by the act of remembering this last sacrifice, instituted by Jesus himself during the Last Supper.[297] Catholicism, with its dogma of transubstantiation, that is, the claim that God's self-sacrifice is repeated each time Mass is celebrated, is considered by Calvinism to be a relapse into patterns from pre-Christian times, when sacrifice was still necessary. By staging the first "step" of the entire story, and by stressing that it occurred on Yahweh's own instructions (as is the case with the second step, according to the Christian narrative), Bèze is able to implicitly convey the

---

[295] As we are dealing here with the Middle Ages, it cannot be systematically ruled out that there was one such (or even several such) play(s) in the period concerned; but since the documentation of cultural history is quite extensive in the case of France, there is a high probability that such plays, had there been any, would be mentioned in other texts even if themselves no longer extant.

[296] One gives something of one's own "voluntarily" while expecting something to be given back (good weather, rich crops, numerous progeny, long-lasting health).

[297] "And he took bread, and gave thanks, and broke it, and gave unto them, saying, This is my body which is given for you: this do in my remembrance" (Luke 22: 19).

claim that Calvinism and its symbolic understanding of the Eucharist is the most cogent interpretation of Christian dogma as revealed in Scripture.

There may have been a second and more general motive for selecting this story instead of other dramatically attractive narratives (Judith, Saul and David, Absalom) when it came to considering biblical sequences suitable for shaping according to neo-Aristotelian rules.[298] I have already mentioned the importance of the Akedah for the link between European self-conceptualization (as "civilized", as "progressing") and religious history. Bèze wrote his play at a time when the first chronicles on European contact with the tribal religions of the New World began to penetrate the consciousness of the West. Most of these reports were in Spanish, but some outstanding works existed in Latin translation,[299] and it was actually a Frenchman, Montaigne, who disseminated an account of the Spanish conquest of the New World in his *Essais*.[300] The mental shock of the encounter was no less massive on this side of the Atlantic than on the other. The huge problem it confronted Europeans with was the question of why there is not a single word to be found concerning these continents in Scripture, which at the time continued to be thought of as providing, by means of revelation, a literally true and definitive account of reality. I will not go into detail concerning the consequences the question provoked.[301] But it may be obvious that one primary reflex when it came to dealing with an "other" that was difficult to categorize within existing parameters was to deprecate the autochthonous tribes as less than human, as beast-like, and, for that reason, as not having merited mention in Scripture. In order to "prove" the barbaric, primitive character of the conquered peoples and tribes, nothing was more apt than the possibility of ascribing to them cultural practices which were, indeed, obsolete in the West. The most important point was the charge of human sacrifice and of cannibalism.—To put my speculation in a nutshell: the strong demand for extracting this particular element from the net and for disseminating it by means of the stage sprang from its demonstration of the fact that, thanks to Yahweh's intervention, the West had abandoned human sacrifice, a practice still current amongst the tribes and nations of the New World. Bèze's drama is

---

298 The standard stories at the basis of medieval mystery plays (the Creation and the Fall; Christmas; the Crucifixion and the Resurrection) were, indeed, less apt for such a formal shaping because they inevitably pertain not only to the specific time actually narrated, but ultimately to all of salvation history, at least according to the standard Christian (figural) interpretation.
299 E.g., José de Acosta, *Historia natural y moral de las Indias* (1590).
300 Comparing the texts, it appears to be most probable that Montaigne made use of Francisco López de Gomara's *Primera y segunda parte de la historia general de las Indias* (1552).
301 See, once again, my "The Traditional Cosmos and the New World".

one amongst many works intended to satisfy the European demand for indicators of the superiority of their culture in the Age of Discovery.

There is a third feature of the drama worth considering in this chapter: one of the most striking sentences of the author's preface ("Theodore de Besze aux lecteurs") is the passage in which he states that while his play contains elements of both tragedy and comedy, the former predominates, which is why he has chosen to name it as he has done ("Et pource qu'il tient plus de l'un que de l'autre, j'ay mieux aimé l'appeler Tragedie.").[302] The author does not comment further on the reasons for this judgment, and so we are permitted, or indeed invited, to make up for the missing information by means of our own interpretations or speculations. There is, indeed, not much material in the story to provoke the core element of comedy, laughter. I should like to suggest that the comic element the author ascribes to his dramatized version of the story consists mainly in the social stratum of the characters involved. Abraham was to become the father of kings, and also the father of a people who would subsequently spread out over the entire globe and defeat all its enemies,[303] but as an individual he was a shepherd; he was certainly not a poor man, but his social status made it more or less impossible to consider him to be on the level of tragic characters as described in Aristotle's tract, and even more so according to the early modern standard readings of Aristotle's description of the tragic hero as *epieikes*.—At first sight, however, what is even more astonishing is Bèze's completely unproblematized description of the play as "more of a tragedy", to the extent that he feels entitled to assign his drama as a whole to this genre. The harmonious and almost fairytale-like conclusion of the biblical story seems to be in flagrant contradiction of what we are accustomed to characterizing as tragedy. A father torn between his love for his belated and only legitimate offspring and his obedience to his only god, finally doing what this god has ordered him to do and then blinding himself or cutting off the hand with which he has perpetrated the sacrifice—this could be, considered from our standard viewpoint, a tragedy; but we would be hesitant to classify as tragedy a drama ending in complete harmony.

There is indeed, as I have argued elsewhere,[304] a basic tension between the world-model of tragedy and the Christian dogma. If this world has been saved

---

[302] Théodore de Bèze, *Abraham sacrifiant*. Tragédie françoise, Marguérite Soulié and Jean-Dominique Beaudin (eds.), Paris 2006, p. 35.
[303] See lines 952–972 for these prophecies or promises, which are already included (with the exception of the reference to Christ's salvific deed) in the Hebrew Bible.
[304] See *Discursive* Renovatio *in Lope de Vega and Calderón*, esp. chaps. 2 and 6.

by God's self-sacrifice, and if every human being is able to enjoy the benefits of this redemptive act by adhering to the Christian God and obeying his commandments—that is, if every human being is able to attain to constant and limitless happiness ("paradise"), albeit after death—there seems to be little room left for the tragic vision.[305] This view, however, is contingent on the fact that, from the beginning of the nineteenth century onward, that is, starting with Hegel, we are accustomed to extracting one variant of the tragic from Aristotle's theory of the genre as available in the net, while neglecting the other. It is true that *Oedipus Rex* is the ultimate paradigm of the tragic not only in the modern understanding. When illustrating the principal characteristics of what he calls the "best" or "most beautiful variant of tragedy" (*kalliste tragoedia*),[306] Aristotle refers in most cases to the Sophoclean play. However, there is another passage of his somewhat erratic tract in which he cites *Iphigeneia* as the best tragedy. It may be that a third passage in which he says that plays conforming to this latter pattern are to be considered "*deutera tragoedia*", that is, belonging to the second-best kind of tragedy, expresses his opinion on the matter in the most consistent way, the more so as this classification is based on Aristotle's (aesthetic, social, moral) elitism: the model of *deutera tragoedia* is the more popular one because it appeals to the irenic illusions about the world cultivated amongst the common people.[307]

Be that as it may, one has to bear in mind that Aristotle does admit a model of tragedy—meaning, actions involving *pathos* (suffering) and thus causing *phobos* and *eleos* (pity and fear) amongst the spectators—which contains a happy resolution. The modern reception of Aristotle has relegated this variant to the background, for reasons which shall not be discussed at this point. When conceiving a play whose plot shows many striking similarities to *Iphigeneia he en Aulidi*,[308] Bèze extracted the secondary definition from Aristotle's tract. He was thus able to satisfy a demand contingent upon the unique situation of his time: on the one hand, there was a wish to see the classical genre renewed by the

---

305 I should like to add to this brief characterization of the traditional Catholic dogma the Reformers' renewal of Augustine's dogma of predestination, at least with respect to the question at issue here. Going to hell as a member of the *massa damnata* is not tragic because it is not an exceptional, but a rather common fate; it is as much or as little tragic as physical death. The term "tragic" only makes sense if applied to exceptional and for this reason deeply shocking constellations.
306 See chap. 13.
307 See *Poetics* 1453 a 30 ff.
308 The play explicitly referred to in the Aristotelian tract is rather the *Iphigeneia he en Taurois* (fifth century BCE; see, e.g., 1452 b 5 ff.). But with respect to the questions here discussed,

creation of tragedies in the vernacular languages; but in an age when most intellectual discourse revolved around questions of faith, there was also the demand to orchestrate this renewal in such a way as not to jar with the basic elements of the Christian worldview.

The constellation just described renders evident, once again, that cultural material floating in the net is, indeed, "material" in the literal sense. It may be disassembled and then partially reused without there being a chance for anyone to "protest" that such a reutilization may in fact constitute an abuse, a disfigurement, or a distortion with respect to the original synthesis that was submitted to the net.

Basic Prerequisites

0.—Are there, finally, specific prerequisites for a community to take part in cultural exchange mediated by a virtual network as described above, that is, an in principle universal net? Or, to put it differently: is it conceivable for communities of humans to exist and even flourish without exogenous cultural impulses? The supposedly secluded cultural territories our ancestors called "national cultures" were in the first place a politically motivated construct of the age of nationalism, in cultural terms: of Romanticism. But what about former times, that is, those periods of human history in which technological devices facilitating the circulation of cultural items in the net did not yet exist?

1.—It seems that the question is primarily one of degree, as one may extrapolate from the present, in which such recent technologies as the Internet have dramatically augmented and accelerated the circulatory processes. Today, there are almost no territorial boundaries to the extension of the cultural net, as the infrastructure required consists of such seemingly dematerialized objects as radio waves and electricity. And since access to the circulating material has become easy and cheap, the power of control agencies seems to be waning dramatically. This outline of the present situation may be all too optimistic. Be that as it may, it shows that the relevance of the cultural (in the sense of technological) level reached by a given community is not negligible when it

---

there is not much difference between the two *Iphigeneia* plays. They both have a happy ending, and in both plays there is a risk of human sacrifice, which is, however, finally not consummated. The "first" *Iphigeneia* is closer to the biblical plot insofar as the sacrifice is explicitly commanded by a god and the sacrificial object is a child of the one who is called upon to obey the god's will.

comes to the question of the extent to which this community is able to make use of the material floating in the net. As is evident from their eminent contributions to the world culture of later times, the somewhat modest cultural activities of Northern and Eastern European communities in the age under consideration and before are most probably not determined by their cultural or intellectual "inferiority", but by the fact that their net-enabling infrastructures (roads, banks, monasteries, universities) were insufficient at the time.

2.—One even more basic determining factor is certainly—in an age before devices like the Internet were invented—mere density of population. Since the net, though virtual if considered as a whole, is basically a material thing if considered with regard to its actual components, there is no cultural exchange without physical contact. The relative lack of exchange between China and the West is an example already mentioned above; another one would be that between Europe and pre-Columbian America. This applies as well to communities which are not separated by geographic obstacles but live in isolation due to the fact that there is very much space in proportion to the numbers of humans occupying it.—Further factors to be taken into consideration are tools such as money and writing systems, both of which facilitate exchanges of all kinds.—The invention of print, that is, the ability to spread a huge number of low-cost copies of a given cultural item throughout the cultural net, certainly marks a third major step in the intensification of activities of exchange.—The technique of electronic encoding (telephone, television, Internet), that is, the almost complete dematerialization of the media of transmission, is obviously the fourth and, at this point in time, the last step. Observing the provisional results of this latest step, and its consequences for the shape of what we call culture and art, one may perhaps imagine what the consequences of a possible fifth or sixth step will be.

Since we are dealing with material processes, the development just outlined is in the first place quantitative. It will remain an unresolved question within this book whether the basic assumption of dialectical materialism is tenable—i.e., that qualitative (conceptual, spiritual) developments are the more or less automatic consequences of quantitative developments ratified from time to time by way of revolutions—or whether one should rather believe that qualitative leaps occur because they have been prepared by qualitative developments of a different order. Was it print technology which—by accelerating all sorts of cultural exchange processes—led to the "enlightenment" of huge portions of the European population, to the Age of Revolution, to technological modernity? Or was it the dissolution, briefly referred to above, of the firm belief in the Bible as the one and only, definitive source of Truth which was the determining factor in early modern Europe's quest for new, undetected truths? Within this latter line of thinking, inventions such as print technology—which is not that difficult to imagine as soon as writing systems based on standardized letters begin to be used—would be conceived as based on ideas which remained latent for a certain period and presented themselves in new ways when conditions were propitious for the introduction of new or even revolutionary concepts.

3.—Floating processes of any kind do not only call for a physical medium, but also need energy to keep the material moving. If the processes are not natural (as in the case of a leaf floating in a stream), the energy must be both produced and invested in this specific floating process by humans, which implies that the quantity of material available in the cultural net is contingent upon the quantity of available energy that is not necessary for securing the physical subsistence of a given community. This somewhat tortuous statement signifies, in common language, nothing other than that the cultural net is all the more significant the wealthier a society is. Since wealth is contingent upon time, one might conclude that the quantitative dimensions of the cultural net evolve and grow with the passage from one age to the next. They do not grow continuously and smoothly, however, or it is not this kind of growth that is of primary significance. It seems that they evolve above all by means of "leaps" linked to technological evolutions whose main achievement is the reduction of the amount of energy necessary to keep material circulating in the net. Human bodies on the move require a good deal of energy. Writing technology reduces the amount of energy necessary to physically circulate cultural material; one human scribe suffices to put written cultural material (manuscripts) containing a huge quantity of information into circulation; the same quantity of information to be circulated using only the human mind and voice would necessitate sending thousands of humans out into the world. I have already mentioned the next such leap, namely the introduction of print technology, and the leap following that, the introduction of electronic information technology. The latter step, taken in the last two decades of the twentieth century, has reduced the energy necessary to keep cultural material circulating in a way inconceivable in the past. It has led to an intensity, celerity, and quantitative growth in the circulation of cultural material whose consequences are still incalculable. We may see the (from a historical perspective) quick, even abrupt rise and establishment of a largely homogenized global culture; we may face in the future attempts at violently interrupting, subverting, or destroying the infrastructure of this low-energy net.

If one keeps in mind what has been said so far regarding this point, the inevitable impression will be that this book basically endorses yet again the story of "progress" which seems to have been relegated to obsolescence during the age we call postmodern. And indeed, it is a story of nearly continuous, albeit not always smooth evolution which is presented here. But it differs from the traditional narratives of progress as conceived in the Age of Enlightenment in that it does not equate quantitative growth with a growth in quality. Whether it is "happiness" or "freedom" which evolves in the process of continuous growth of cultural material floating in the net and of continuous growth of acts of extraction, or whether the process is one of growth and nothing more, shall remain an open question here. We do not know where this entire story called "human history" will lead us. Present-day natural science, however, seems to confirm what was already expressed in the more archaic, pre-Enlightenment version of the teleological story: namely, that this world, including the world of humans, had a beginning, and that it will also have an end; moreover, that the end of the human world will occur before the end of the natural world, understood as the mode of organization of matter familiar roughly for the past fourteen billion years. One may add to this reminder of biblical cosmology a reference to Augustine's theory of the structures of the *civitas terrena*, and there are no more obstacles to telling a story of progress in terms of quantity which may be mainly static with regard to quality.

The Economy of Cultural Transfer

0.—When it comes to discussing processes of transfer of objects between humans, it is not only the case in our highly materialistic age, but has been since the beginnings of human civilization, that one is faced with the question of the extent to which the preponderance of our material necessities and of our greed, the need or the wish to appropriate material goods (food, clothing, tools facilitating our dominance over the rest of the natural world), governs the entirety of our dealings with other humans. Is the economic the hidden foundational structure of all our actions and interactions? There is no doubt that the economic principle governs, at least to a large extent, spheres of our lives that we would prefer to be ruled by more idyllic features such as emotion or love. Legal love (marriage) is to this day, and even in Western countries with their sentimentalist tradition developed in the age of Romanticism, in many respects an economic arrangement, i.e. a "deal". What differentiates the modern Western economics of marriage from more traditional variants is mainly the fact that there is no longer a separation between the goods exchanged and the contractors. But the logic is still one of exchange: one gives something away and receives something in return. The basis is reciprocity, and the "deal" is about the adequacy of what is given and what is reciprocated.

1. —Is it an idealization of a secluded sphere of culture when I postulate that cultural exchange eludes the logic of reciprocation elsewhere observable or even omnipresent, including in social spheres we have a tendency to conceive of in more romanticized terms?[309] There are, indeed, areas of cultural transfer which adhere to an economic logic. When a painting is sold, when a fee is charged for admission to a performance, when a manuscript is dedicated to a patron, or when the copyright to a book is sold to a publishing company, these transfers of cultural items evidently occur as processes of economic exchange. A work, or temporary access to a work, is exchanged for a certain amount of money (or for a service to be provided by the buyer, or for a favor expected from the patron, etc.). But interactions of this kind are not what I intend to designate when I speak of circulation of material in the cultural net. They constitute additional techniques for regulating access to the net, or rather access to materialized extractions from the net at a certain time and in a certain place.

What is characteristic of the processes taking place within the cultural net is the fact that there is no mandatory reciprocity; this seems to be a particularly decisive point when it comes to the question of whether or not the economy of cultural transfer is determined by the same laws as those of economics in the literal sense. There is in most cases no direct exchange, no *quid pro quo*. When a businessman transporting goods on the Silk Road narrates, during his stay in a caravanserai in Bagdad, a story he heard on the occasion of a dinner given for him in China, he does not do so under the condition that his business partners on the banks of the Euphrates present him with a "Mesopotamian" story that he can bring back to China and put into circulation there. Such processes may take place, and quite frequently they do, but *immediate* reciprocity is not a prerequisite for the transfer of cultural material. Cultural material is as free as air, at least as long as it has not reached the level of organization of individually attributable works of art. In cases where we are not its "creators", but rather media of transmission, we typically give it away without expecting anything in return. Of course, we narrate a story to a business partner in order to entertain him and thus to create an atmosphere propitious to further business; that is, we expect something in return, but not necessarily on the same level, and not measurable as "equal" in terms of monetary value. As to the recipients involved in such transfer processes, this implies that they may ex-

---

[309] For a view which conceives of this elusion as more than a mere idealization, but for different reasons than suggested here, see Stephen Greenblatt's short essay "Culture", in: Frank Lentricchia and Thomas McLaughlin (eds.), *Critical Terms for Literary Study*, Chicago, IL and London 1995 (2nd edition), pp. 225–229.

tract the material from the net without paying or reciprocating in some other way. If we listen to a story, we are free to remodel it and then narrate it to others. If we have writing skills, we are even free to use it as an inspiration for a story of our own which we might sell to a publishing company.

2.—This freedom of access and this emancipation from the principle of reciprocity seem to cast the cultural sphere as a space where quasi-paradisiacal structures have survived in our fallen world. To a certain extent, this is true; the uncontested esteem for, or even widespread love of cultural items may have their roots here. But it is necessary that I differentiate my argument from the nineteenth-century metaphysics of art, still current today, by drawing attention to the fact that the suspension of the reciprocity principle implies certain features that are not as popular amongst the enthusiasts of art as is freedom. Non-reciprocity implies the possibility of unidirectional cultural transfer. Unidirectional transfer leads to structures of dominance and, in the long run, to the establishment of cultural hierarchies. At least for the time being, there is much more cultural transfer from the West to the rest of the world than vice versa. Within the West, much more transfer occurs from the anglophone world to the rest than vice versa. Amongst the non-anglophone Western countries, there is much more transfer from bigger countries to smaller ones than vice versa. This tendency towards unidirectional movement in the net is not exclusive; it describes statistical preponderances only. And at least in the case of modern Western culture, it is partially compensated by what I have called "exoticism" above, the hunger of post-Romantic Western cultures, fixated on the ideal of innovation, to absorb everything that might appear as novel or "other".

Thus, regarding the cultural sphere as emancipated from the reciprocity principle does not entail that a net structure as theorized in this book would lead to a universal egalitarianism among the world's innumerable cultural communities. What it entails is rather a constant transfer, the permanent "re-culturation" of all "national" cultures on behalf of their connectedness to the one and only cultural net. It is this very fact which in turn destabilizes all sorts of statistical cultural dominance linked to the above-mentioned situation. If we accept for the moment the hypothesis that, under such conditions, the leading power of the present-day West, the United States, changes large parts of its cultural profile every fifty to one hundred years, "identity" becomes a mere ideologeme. This, however, problematizes the entire endeavor of the "legitimate fight against the dominant culture(s)" which is the centerpiece of all of present-day cultural theory.

3.—The concrete lines according to which these processes take place lie, of course, beyond the realm of culture in the strict sense. They are political and economic. Strong and great powers put many more humans—the main agents of cultural transfer—in motion than weaker and smaller communities. On the other hand, I should like to stress that the relations described here are quantitative only. It is by no means to be excluded that a "genius" may emerge within a very small community and nevertheless attain worldwide resonance; but this is not a necessity either. Ingenuity should, according to my approach, be defined as a particularly marked capacity to meet the cultural demand(s) of many people for whom the author or artist in question may not even have intentionally conceived his work. It thus may be a constellation emerging by means of contingency as theorized by Aristotle in *De Interpretatione*: that is, as the result of two totally distinct causal chains which happen by chance to touch each other (*con-tangere*) and then generate something new and unheard of—which might explain the fact that such things are extremely rare. In all cases of "ingenuity", there must be a "match" between the author in question's specific way of writing and the needs and wants of a greater audience he did not have in mind; but there must also be a quite literal encounter between a cultural broker from outside and the work in question.

I should like to conclude this entire part by reminding readers once again that the most powerful textual unit in the history of the most powerful culture of all of world history thus far is the account of the life of a carpenter's son from a tiny Roman colony on the eastern shores of the Mediterranean, first written down by people of humble background in a vernacular accessible to less than one percent of the Empire's population; its immense impact was by no means caused by the activities of "revolutionary" metropolitan intellectuals pursuing the intention of promoting the "subaltern" of that age. This story thus calls for nothing less than a "metaphysical" explanation if one holds on to the theorem of the dominant culture as the culture of the dominant—an involuntary irony which is for this reason ignored or silenced by leftist cultural theory.

II. Mass Media, Early Modern

The Masses

0.—From a present-day perspective, it might at first sight appear to be a flagrant anachronism to apply the term "mass medium" to early modern drama, not least because the texts of this tradition, as well as the practice of performing them for an audience, became instances of a sophisticated and socially exclusive "high culture" from the beginning of the nineteenth century onward.

1.—In this respect, however, it is crucial to be aware of the historical distance between the reception of these texts and performances in modernity proper, especially in our times, and the reception during the period of origin. These drastically divergent modes of reception are conditioned by a great distance in terms of technological evolution. In the early modern period, what we consider nowadays to be quasi-natural elements of our cultural habitat were not present: TV and movies. The absence of a ubiquitous and easily accessible visual culture prior to the beginning of the twentieth century is the main reason why theatrical performances—it is of no import to distinguish in this respect between street theater and performances in playhouses or theatrical courtyards *(corrales)*—once held a societal role that was incommensurably more significant than it is today and that can hardly be imagined from a present-day perspective. When the objective was to influence or guide a nearly illiterate public, the theater represented the only alternative to an authoritarian imposition of norms and patterns of thought. This is the reason why it was, in the age in question, employed for a purpose which has more recently become a symptom of triviality: didactics. And very frequently, this didactic dimension was not separate from, but rather went along with highly sophisticated artistic standards, comprising features such as reflection and self-reflection.

The hesitance to make use of the term "mass media" with regard to the performative practices of previous epochs does, however, seem to be justified to a certain extent when it comes to two other phases of occidental cultural history, which, once again, constitutes a strong plea for considering the configuration of cultural material observable in early modern drama and theater as a "novel" assembly. Considering the events which took place in the arenas of the Roman Empire, such as fights against wild beasts and fights amongst humans (gladiators), one would be ready to concede that the "masses" indeed had easy access, since entrance was free and such arenas existed not only in Rome, but in all the cities *(oppida, coloniae)* of the Empire. Yet is it sensible to consider these fights to be "mediated" events? What was taking place was, it is true, staged rather than evolving in an entirely contingent manner; but it was real nonetheless. The spectators witnessed authentic killings rather than actors pretending to dispatch an opponent, and the blood spilled before their eyes was equally real; it was physically perceived rather than imagined.[310] In order to consider these events to be a mediation of something "else", that is, something which was not really present, one would be obliged to interpret the fights as representations whose reference would be, for example, the notion of life as a constant struggle, of death as an inevitability, or of cruelties as legitimate. I will not deny that such or comparable implications were, indeed, present. But the sheer event taking place seems to have been much more important than any other "thing" which might have been additionally mediated. The proof for this view is the fact that the performances ended with the most solid and uncontestable reality there is: death.

As for pre-Roman (classical Greek) and post-Roman (medieval) times, there were, indeed, theatrical performances in the modern sense, that is, performances which were received by their spectators not as "real" events, but as representations of real or at least possible events (*dynata*, as Aristotle puts it[311]), in other words, mediations. What seems questionable in these cases is rather the application of the term "masses". We have the tendency to apply it primarily to democratic or totalitarian societies, that is, to societies which make a strong claim to be committed to generalized equality. From this perspective, one might perhaps be inclined to see the theatrical performances of fifth-century (BCE) Athens as early instances of mass media. But what finally marks such an application of the category as at least slightly inadequate is the fact that Athenian "democracy" was a quite restricted or exclusive affair: females, minors, slaves, and resident aliens (metics) were not allowed to partake in political decisions; as to the ritualistic participation in theatrical performances, this stricture was suspended only with regard to the wives of the admitted males. Citizenship was the condition of belonging to the *demos*, and this status was reserved for those who had the right to bear arms. In sheer numbers, it was approximately 10% of the resident population who were admitted. From a posterior perspective, one would therefore be inclined to call the Athenian society of that age an "aristocracy"—members were defined according to descent—rather than a "mass" society. The procedural rules according to which this aristocracy or oligarchy organized the deployment of power was, however, based

---

[310] —in the theater of that age, it was common practice to represent blood with the aid of cherry juice mixed with oil.
[311] *Poetics*, esp. chap. 9.

on voting rather than hierarchy. This mixture, somewhat exceptional in human history, of a homogeneity of norms, based on internal equality, and a strict distancing from all "others" (*barbaroi*) or foreigners living on the same territory, generated a theater and drama culture that has remained fascinating to this day. From a historicizing perspective, the high degree to which these texts meet an essential criterion of canonical literature prevalent in modernity proper—the absence of didacticism and moralizing—is obviously contingent upon the social, and, by implication, ethical homogeneity of the implied recipients.[312]

Things might be different in the case of the Roman Empire. It was not only gladiator fights and similar popular performances for which the arenas were built; they were also the site of theatrical performances, tragic (Seneca) as well as comedic (Plautus, Terence). Entrance was free, and the politics of admission were not based on rules of social exclusiveness. But not enough information has survived about these events to allow for establishing well-founded hypotheses as to their function in society. Suffice it to say that Roman theater, at least from the imperial period onward, may bear significant similarities to what we know from early modern times; I should like to add that the corresponding political systems—a frame to which I would link, as will be explained in the following, the emergence of early modern mass culture—are characterized by a number of similarities as well. On the other hand, one should not overlook the fact that plays in Latin were—like the Roman culture of classical times in general—for the most part imitations of Greek models; the plots were not altered in order to adapt them to the specific societal situation of Rome. One might thus hypothesize that Roman culture created the enabling conditions for the emergence of a visual mass culture, but, for whatever reason, did not actually make use of this infrastructure in a way that would be comparable to early modern European societies.

2.—Although European states of the early modern age were in a way aristocratic—in any case, they were certainly not democratic—they display important characteristics of the mass societies of later times. For this reason, it is less astonishing than one might assume that they developed instruments for organizing and directing such societies which became fully developed only in the twentieth century. The commonality is, finally, a product of what we are used to calling "absolutism". The societies of the sixteenth and seventeenth centuries still had a feudal class, and the legal and political differences between the first two estates and the third estate were considerable. But these differences

---

[312] In the sense of Wolfgang Iser's concept of "implied reader" (*The Implied Reader: Patterns of Communication in Prose Fiction from Bunyan to Beckett*, Baltimore, MD 1974).

were rendered insignificant by the absolute power of the monarch. The transformative process which dramatically changed the structure of European societies began in Spain. After the expulsion (1492) of those contingents of the peninsula's Muslim and Jewish populations who were not willing to comply with the politics of ideological homogenization imposed by the "Catholic Monarchs", the process was completed in a relatively smooth manner.[313] Things were more difficult in France and in England. In France, it was only with the defeat of the *fronde* (1648–1653)—the active and violent resistance of parts of the higher nobility to becoming "subjects" or courtiers—that the Versailles absolutism of Louis XIV could later be established for the rest of the Ancien Régime. It may even be that the French "exceptionalism" briefly expounded in the hypotheses-chapter is contingent on the fact that absolutism's triumph was, in France, the result of a fierce civil war conducted among factions of the higher nobility. The intimidating effects of the feudal lords' devastating defeat may have been so strong that the monarchs did not see a need for a further politics of ideological homogenization, or, to put it more precisely, for more ideological homogeneity than that established by events such as the revocation of the Edict of Nantes (1685), that is, by the abolishment of religious pluralism. Would it be overly speculative to regard the bloody revolution which occurred only seventy-four years after Louis XIV's death as a consequence of the fact that the French monarchs did not perceive the necessity for a more pervasive ideological homogenization once their absolute power seemed to have been secured?

In England, the establishment of absolutism went along with a bold step, namely, that of rendering the monarch "absolute" in a very literal sense, that of no longer being dependent upon a figure as important as Christ's vicar on earth, the Roman Pope. As is the case with almost every form of extremism in history, this was, perhaps, one step too far. The bloody consequences of the religious schism mark England's political history in the entire period under scrutiny. There is no need to provide a definitive answer to the question as to whether this struggle was "really" about faith and denomination. From what is known about the ruling class of that age, dissent regarding belief may have been a very appropriate device for emotionally affecting and thus mobilizing conflicting contingents of the population. The ideological work done by the different monarchs in order to counteract this factionalism seems to follow a very conspicuous rationale, namely, that of bracketing questions of faith and

---

[313] I would like to stress the adverb; in Spain, too, there was serious physical constraint involved in carrying the process of ideological homogenization to the intended goal; but there was no open civil war.

of addressing other questions of general worldview at issue in those times. One could consider most of Elizabethan, in particular Shakespearean theater as a device for establishing a certain ideological homogeneity which, however, did *not* encompass the highly controversial field of religious conviction; hence, perhaps, its remarkable ideological openness, which is not an openness of random profile, but an openness that seems to be modern because it leaves the question of right belief out of consideration.

Things are much more difficult to systematize when it comes to cultural "nations" which did not attain the level of political unity in that age. Amongst the bigger European countries, it is mainly Italy and Germany which are encompassed by this description. If my guiding hypothesis is correct, this political "belatedness" would provide an explanation for the obvious fact that these two nations did not make a contribution to the corpus of early modern European drama comparable to those discussed in the previous paragraphs. But it should be stressed that such an evaluation is based on an *a posteriori* perspective. There are notable Italian and German dramas from the centuries concerned. It may even be the case that these dramas could no less reasonably be described as instances of early mass culture than corresponding texts from Spain or England. But it is problematic to argue in this manner in an age when we spontaneously associate the term "Italian drama" with the nation "Italy" as it has been understood for roughly 150 years now. The same applies in the case of the fragmented territories of the German-speaking lands of those times. If the "mass" to be homogenized is the population of a small principality, perhaps with no more than 100,000 inhabitants, one would not feel a very strong inclination to speak of plays written by famous authors from such principalities, e.g. Gryphius or Lohenstein, as instruments of a *German* mass culture existing as early as in the seventeenth century. From a scholarly standpoint, however, one would have to consider the possibility that German or Italian plays from that age were written with exactly the same intention—namely, the ideological homogenization of a public of roughly equal subjects—as their Spanish or English counterparts. To put it abstractly: the "portion" of people to be homogenized does not correspond to the linguistic borders of the cultural community in question; at least intuitively, this would seem to be the main problem with the hypothesis here expounded with regard to Italy and Germany.

But it may well be that these are problems linked to a specifically modern, nineteenth- and twentieth-century view of the relationship between linguistic and political borders. As has been shown by the previously mentioned studies dealing with dramatic performances even in such small and secluded places as remote valleys of the Alps or villages in Slovenia,[314] it is very probable that the phenomena observable in those places were in principle comparable to what has been stated here with respect to Spain, England, and France: dramatic performances were instrumentalized as a means of bringing about ideological homogeneity. The inhabitants of the Alpine valleys were "taught" the basic tenets of Christian belief in its Catholic, Counter-Reformation variant by means of such performances; at the same time, they were reassured that their traditional norms, namely those of patriarchy, were "good" norms which apply in all places and at all times. And the Slovenes were given the impression that their homeland was not something separate from the Austrian mainland and its capital; notwithstanding their vernacular, which differed considerably from the one used in the metropole, their beliefs and convictions were, or, rather, were supposed to be the same as in Vienna, Salzburg, or Innsbruck.

3.—It is above all the case of Russia that would seem not to fit into this general view of early modern drama as mass media. Theater was, indeed, introduced into the country during that period, rapidly generating first attempts at composing pieces in the local language. However, into the nineteenth century, there was no middle class or bourgeoisie in Russia; there was only the nobility and the peasantry, the latter being divided into free farmers (*kulaki*) and serfs. Because of the immense distance between the small ruling elite and the common people, who did not even have a pretense to rights of their own, there was no need to develop instruments for directing the masses. Russia was—and may still be today—a particularly "belated" nation. Indirect instruments of exerting power were unnecessary because blunt physical force was a commonly practiced[315] and accepted means of ruling. Eighteenth-century Russian theater rather had the function of homogenizing the elites residing at court. It is a theater intended for *la cour* and not, as was the case with France, at the same time for *la ville*, the root of what was later to become, in the Age of

---

314 See Bernhart, *Volksschauspiele*; Drnovšek, *"Certa Mina Dant VICtorIas"*. I will come back to these plays in a later chapter (pp. 246–248); in order to elucidate what I am expressing above, I might say in anticipation that plots like the story of Phaethon or Griselda were frequently made use of.

315 It is the adverb that counts here; also in Western European kingdoms of that age, physical brutality was a means of deploying power; but, in contrast to Russia, it was already regularized and thus confined by emerging rules and procedures, by laws and courts of law. In Russia, the situation was different. Particularly with regard to the overwhelming majority of the population, the serfs, it was the direct and arbitrary decision of the respective feudal lord that decided on their fate in case their actions jarred with the prevalent and mostly non-codified norms. Into the nineteenth century, if not until the February Revolution, the political system remained similar to what it had been in Western Europe in medieval times.

Enlightenment, the "public sphere" in the sense of Jürgen Habermas's concept of "Öffentlichkeit".[316]

4.—If one provisionally accepts the hypothesis of early modern European drama as a variant of mass media, the issue to be discussed in this second part of the present study consists in the question of whether mass media structures can be described as maintaining a specific relation to the cultural net at large, and in particular whether the formal structures "extracted" from the net by mass media culture differ from comparable structures of elite culture on the one hand and (exclusively) popular culture on the other. The constitutive function of mass media is to produce social integration, whether from a liberal[317] or from an authoritarian perspective. Hypothetically, one could argue that mass media phenomena are in principle anti-traditional with regard to form. In order to foster cultural integration, they make use of patterns and of material available in the net that are traditionally linked to diverse social spheres and to their respective aesthetic standards. Many of the features of early modern theater which appear to be modern in the sense that they anticipate democratic ideas[318] may belong more to its overall societal function than to the actual message of the specific plays.

Mass media phenomena are a provocation for all theories of literature or the arts which link the label of "work of art" to a formally "pure" structure whose purpose is *not* the transfer of "pragmatic" cultural material.[319] It may be that twentieth- and twenty-first-century mass media products are relatively poor in artistic value. Yet with regard to at least some of the products of early modern mass media, e.g. the works of Shakespeare and Calderón, it would not be par-

---

316 See *The Structural Transformation of the Public Sphere: An Inquiry into a Category of Bourgeois Society*, Thomas Burger (tr.), Cambridge, MA 1991.
317 Throughout this book, the term "liberal" is used in the sense of a political orientation committed above all to individual freedom.
318 I am thinking of elements such as peasants claiming to be "honorable men" or "honorable women" in Spanish Golden Age drama; or the free interaction of noblemen and humble people to be observed widely in Elizabethan theater. As to the feature of peasants' honor, quite striking within a conservative estatist society, see my reading of Lope de Vega's drama *Fuente Ovejuna* ("Lope de Vega. *Fuente Ovejuna*", in: Harald Wentzlaff-Eggebert and Volker Roloff [eds.], *Das spanische Theater vom Mittelalter bis zur Gegenwart*, Düsseldorf 1988, pp. 105–122).
319 In that sense, I herein continue to historicize Immanuel Kant's theory of art (*The Critique of Judgment*), which is considered at least within the German tradition, but also in some of the anglophone debates, to represent the "truth" as such regarding the question of what art is (see my "Kants *Kritik der Urteilskraft* und die Philosophie der Aufklärung", *Zeitschrift für Ästhetik und Allgemeine Kunstwissenschaft* vol. 55,1/2010, pp. 9–23, and "Céline – Kant", *Poetica* vol. 44/2012, pp. 229–238).

ticularly convincing to dismiss them in terms of aesthetic refinement. Not as items circulating in a partly autonomous subnet—which may be an adequate metaphor for modernist art and literature—, but as part of the cultural net at large, they are outstanding vestiges of what we call culture. They thus raise a question which remains to be addressed by modern aesthetic theory.

Mediality

0.—"Intelligit [intellectus] [...] hoc complexum: 'quodlibet est vel non est', sine aliquo instrumento seu medio." // "The intellect grasps this formula: 'anything either is or is not [something]', [and it (the intellect) does so] without any further instrument or medium."[320]—This sentence summarizes a long-standing Western philosophical tradition which views the imperative to avoid contradictions as the most basic principle to be obeyed in all cases of cognitive activity that lay claim to being meaningful. In our context, it is of interest because of its implication: it demonstrates that the relevant tradition considers the mind's cognitive operations *stricto sensu* not to be mediated by something else. According to the principle mentioned, this means that all the other activities of human consciousness, primarily sensory perception followed by its cognitive processing, *are* considered to be mediated.

1.—Accordingly, the term "media" in the acceptation current in modern times always refers to a third-degree mediation. "Media", in a very broad definition of the term, are "instrumenti", that is, material items that may be *used* by humans in order to "understand something" (*intelligere*). All of the phenomena observable in the natural world are, from this perspective, media by way of which humans may grasp the principles and laws governing the physical world. Second-degree media could be defined as "instruments" *created* by humans in order to convey to other humans the findings they have made by recourse to first-degree mediations; symbolic practices of any kind, above all language, would be the paradigm of such second-degree mediation. Third-degree media would be, accordingly, *configurations* of second-degree media created with a view to conveying more complex "intellections" to specific recipi-

---

[320] The quote is from a thinker of the age at issue here (Nicolaus Cusanus, *Compendium*, cap. XI: 36), while the idea itself belongs to the core of the Aristotelian tradition; in the Middle Ages, the *intellectus* to which Nicolaus refers (i.e., the part of the human mind which is able to grasp certain "realities" without the mediation of sense perception) was commonly named *intellectus agens*. One of the major controversies between "pure" Aristotelians (Averroists) and Christianized Aristotelians (Thomists) concerned the question of whether this most dignified part of the mind is individual or not.

ents; world-models, partial or integral, of any kind (scientific, philosophical, religious, artistic) would be instances of such third-degree mediations. In this latter sense, drama is essentially a medium—theater would be a fourth-degree mediation—but not necessarily a mass medium.

At first sight, it might indeed seem somewhat problematic to subsume pieces belonging incontestably to canonical literature under the concept of mass media, all the more as this qualification is not meant to refer to evident characteristics captured by the Aristotelian distinction between *mimesis* (dialogue) and *diegesis* (narrative); and it also goes beyond the fact discussed in Part I, namely, that most early modern dramas are meant not to be read but to be received as staged action (*lexis/opsis*, in Aristotelian terminology). "Mediality" in the sense of mass media is meant to denote a specific characteristic of drama in the historical age concerned, that is, a trait that is not automatically concomitant with drama as genre.

Mediality in this sense means that there is a sender, a recipient, a channel of transmission, and, most importantly, an intention on the sender's part to communicate a specific message and to do so in a way that is appropriate for conveying this message and not another one. The possibly controversial implication of this book's guiding hypothesis—as far as this second part is concerned—is, consequently, that early modern drama is not adequately captured by conceptualizations of art from later times, meaning from the *Critique of Judgment* (1790) onward. From Kant's perspective, the transmission of a specific meaning renders a work, at least to some extent, into a pragmatic thing, an instance of didacticism, which automatically excludes it from the domain of art proper. As for modern instances of mass media "art", such a deprecation would remain uncontested, at least amongst so-called cultured recipients. Is there a completely or at least partially different compartmentalization of the cultural field in early modern times than in modernity proper, that is, starting roughly in 1800 CE? And if there is at least some difference, how could it be conceptualized within the broader methodological frame of the present study?

2.—There is an important reservation to be voiced before discussing the historical scenario: as we are dealing not with pragmatic, but mainly fictional, that is, not directly referential texts, there is the possibility of receiving the texts in question as instances of aesthetics in a Kantian sense. There is no obstacle to reading a seventeenth-century martyr play considering only its formal aspects. But this claim is, in a way, trivial. Such a reception is a potentiality opened up by any material items from former times, and very frequently the aesthetic or aestheticizing approach to cultural artifacts from previous periods of our own tradition, or of any artifacts from "foreign" civilizations, is indeed the dominant one, at least in the age of modernity. Medieval houses of worship—cathedrals, churches—are typically considered by modern people, including by believers, from a standpoint that valorizes formal organization above all else: the proportions of space, the relations between massive and ethereal parts of the building, the light effects produced by the alteration of day and night, etc. Further explanations regarding function within the original cultic contexts take on the shape of historical commentary. They tend to consider the conceptual edifice—symbolized by the material structure—as a signified in the Saussurean sense, that is, as a meaning arbitrarily conferred upon the material aspect of the "sign" by contemporary consensus, the arbitrary nature of which went unnoticed because the content of the signified held the status of transcendental truth.

3.—Are visualized third-degree mediations as briefly characterized above, that is, fourth-degree mediations, a universal structure? Arabists say that there is Arabic-language theater from the nineteenth century onward; but most of them, with the exceptions discussed below,[321] are ready to endorse what Jorge Luis Borges conveys in his short story *La busca de Averroes* (1949). In the mode of fiction, but with a totally justified claim to authenticity, the *Buenairense* writer hints to the fact that there is no drama or theater in traditional Arab culture; one might add that even today there is no word corresponding to our term "theater" in classical Arabic. As Western Japanologists who are not afraid of being anathematized as ethnocentrics say, this also holds true, *mutatis mutandis*, for traditional Japanese culture. In both cultures, there are, however, practices close to what we call theater in the West, practices that were assimilated after the spread of Western culture into a variant of what is considered theater in the West. In the case of the Arabic world, one might think of quasi-theatrical practices such as storytellers performing in public while "mimicking" in body language what they are telling; of Dervish dances; or of proto-farces performed in the streets by amateur groups. In the case of Japan, the most important such theater-like practice is Noh in its traditionalist variant, as it existed in the Edo period (1603–1868).[322] The question of how to separate drama and theater "proper" from such similar performative practices is all the more important as there seem to be in the Western performance tradition genres or quasi-genres which share this state of being "something close to theater" while not being theater in the strict sense. So, how should one define theater

---

[321] See pp. 281–283.
[322] See the detailed information to be found in Stanca Scholz-Cionca, "Nô within Walls and Beyond: Theatre as Cultural Capital in Edo Japan (1603–1868)", in: Gvozdeva et al. (eds.), *Dramatic Experience*, pp. 289–306.

and drama, and what does a possible definition imply for the problems here discussed, namely, the logics of cultural production?

4.—The first attempt at theoretically delimiting theater from performative practices which are not theatrical stems, to my knowledge, from Thomas Aquinas. Addressing the intricate question of whether or not what goes on at the altar during Mass is "theater"—one may infer from the fact that the question is discussed by Thomas that there were issues concerning this point—the *doctor angelicus* states in his clear-cut scholastic fashion: "Sed facere aliqua facta ad alia repraesentanda, videtur esse theatricum, sive poeticum; in theatris enim repraesentabantur olim per aliqua quae ibi gerebantur, quaedam aliorum facta. Ergo videtur quod huiusmodi non debeant fieri ad cultum Dei. Sed caeremonialia ordinantur ad cultum Dei, ut dictum est. Ergo caeremonialia non debent esse figuralia."[323] The delimitation is (merely) normative; for that same reason, it can be unrestrictedly dichotomous—there are no overlapping zones between ritual and theater.[324] Whether or not a performance is theater is bound to an assessment of it as a "real" practice or as an imitation of reality which is not reality itself. As soon as those involved believe that what is taking place is real, one is not dealing with theater, at least not according to Thomas' definition. As soon as they believe that the performance may hint at, imitate, or imply something real ("repraesentare"), while the actual interaction to be viewed is not a real-world situation, we call the performative practice taking place theater, and the textual basis, if there is any, drama. Since the delimitation is based on a consensual, but nevertheless subjective assessment, it is evident that it may vary. But in constrast to Aquinas' view, grounded in faith, the differentiation seems to be contingent on the attitude of spectators or listeners and not of those who produce the "show". A community of recipients or even an individual may come to assess a priest's action during Mass as a mere performance delivered by the religious official as a sort of theater in which he engages with the motive all actors have when exercising their profession: to earn his living; or they may assess it with regard to the more or less brilliant quality of the performance, that is, consider it aesthetically in the first place, as a work of

---

[323] "But doing something in order to represent something else is evidently a theatrical or poetical kind of procedure; the actions performed in theaters in former times represented things done by others. Therefore it is evident that this sort of thing should not be done for the worship of God. The ceremonial precepts have in view the worship of God, as we have seen. They must not, therefore, be seen as figurative." (*Summa theologiae* I^a II^{ae}, qu. 101, art. 2, arg. 2; my translation)

[324] —as there might be in the case of other imitative actions: a learner imitating a sentence first pronounced by a teacher may be mimicking under certain conditions; under different conditions, it may be that he is "really" speaking and wants others to react accordingly.

art and thus as something not real. Similarly, persons who were never taught what theater is may fall prey to "real" concerns when seeing that there are humans "killed" before their eyes, and may even fail to be cured from their "naïveté" when the same people suddenly return to life a little later in order to receive applause from the more enlightened part of the audience. In periods of human history when miracles were believed to belong to reality, such things may indeed have occurred. Avant-garde theater (Pirandello's *Sei personaggi in cerca d'autore* [1921], and even more so his *Questa sera si recita a soggetto* [1928/9]) made it an almost common device to playfully exploit the subjective character of the borderline described and to thus render explicit its subjective nature. And in older texts from the Western dramatic tradition, one may find numerous indications of the fact that the delimitation in question is nothing evident, but rather needs to be instituted, that is, taught to children as they grow up and to uncultured adults who do not know of its existence, as something that needs to be strictly respected.[325]

5.—There is another important feature which needs to be taken into consideration. Ritual performances such as religious services entail processes of "automatization"[326] because of their repetitive structures. Theater in general—as all art—has recourse to a variation of pre-existing patterns. Since it is based on variation, and not on replication, the potential level of attention on the recipients' part is much higher than in the case of ritual performances. And it is not by chance that variation is such a general characteristic of theater; as a non-ritual cultural practice, theater cannot rely on a pre-established audience who is obliged to attend,[327] as was the case with the religious service, at least in the age under scrutiny. Any attempt at attracting an audience thus had to be based on structures of enticement. Besides variation in general, specific visual effects ("magic", "marvel") and emotional effects (love and laughter, but also "fascinat-

---

325 In the Alsfeld passion play, version A, from 1511, one may read the following lines: "ich wyl uch vorkündigen eyn gebott, / das der her schultheys thut: / wer da betredden wirt in dissem kreyß, / [...] / der do nit gehoret in dit spil, / [...] /, der muß syn buße groiplich entphan." // "I wish to make known a proclamation from the mayor: whoever would enter into this circle who does not belong in this play, will be severely punished." (Quotes according to the bilingual edition by Larry E. West, Lewiston-Queenston, NY 1997, l. 109–129); for further details, see Bernhart, *Volksschauspiele*.
326 In the sense of the term as first introduced by the Russian formalists.
327 This feature may account for many of the differences to be found when comparing classical Greek drama and early modern European drama. In Athens, attending the theatrical performances was a norm, or even an obligation to be complied with by every adult free citizen; in terms of the pragmatic context as well as regarding form and content of the plays, there were remnants of the ritual predecessors from which, according to Aristotle, drama, specifically tragedy, emerged.

ing" horror) are the cultural resources typically extracted from the net in order to effect enticement. It is one salient trait of early modern drama that these resources are combined indiscriminately with "serious" material extracted from the net (religious, philosophical, moral discourses).[328] The impact-related potential based on de-familiarization and enticement is enhanced by poly-mediality: the reception situation is not individual, but collective. The actual artifact is mediated by language and vision. Sound and perhaps scent are additional channels of mediation. The shared experience of reception, the engagement of all the ("indirect") senses,[329] and the fusion of arbitrary (symbolic) and iconic sign systems result, for the recipient, in the state of being overwhelmed; or rather, it is the chief intention of the cultural practise called theatre, as well as of its modern variants, film and television, to bring about this effect.

6.–The relation between ritual re-enactment and theater is, however, not a two-term dichotomy. It seems that there is an intermediate zone between the two variants of performance which may be made use of or not in a given culture. Within the field considered here, there is one such intermediate practice to be observed, namely, the quasi-theatrical activities developed by the *Accademia degli intronati*.[330] Relying on Katja Gvozdeva's extended description of the work done by this *Accademia* and its emulators all over the early modern Latin world,[331] one could perhaps succinctly define the performances they delivered as a playful enactment of, and hence an adaptation to, certain behavioral standards to be fulfilled if the performers wanted to be accepted as full members of the community. Obviously, such in a way pedagogical performances were presented not by professionals, but by amateurs, namely those who educated themselves by performing within these activities. The performers were younger "men of honor"; they belonged to the stratum of contemporary society where there were indeed such specific behavioral standards to be respected, under the threat of social exclusion. The standards they had to learn were, according to Gvozdeva, the patterns of patriarchy and heterosexuality. The plays performed were full of risqué "gender trouble", but only to come to the result that men should desire women, and women men. The transgression of gender roles and even homoeroticism were presented onstage in order to playfully channel all possibly existing non-conformist desire into the "right" direction. In the

---

328 The boundaries of classical dramatic theory (Aristotle) are systematically transgressed; exceptions from this general rule (the French seventeenth-century stage) have to be carefully considered.
329 Meaning: with the exception of touch and taste.
330 The seat of the Academy was Siena. The activities started around 1520.
331 *Compagnie d'hommes joyeux*.

case of this and comparable phenomena, there is and was the consciousness that what is going on onstage is not reality, but rather a play, that is, a configuration described above as typical of theater; nevertheless, there was a gradual transition from play to real life. The device of play was used to implement norms by way of habitualization (*hexis*), that is, without the means of external discipline and coercion.

It seems that the classical variant of Noh, that is, the practice from the Edo period, can be described in a similar way.[332] Here, too, there is no strict differentiation between actors and audience. Every samurai was not only expected to attend Noh plays, but also obliged to perform in such plays. It seems that the didactic dimension was, however, more directed towards "exterior" behavioral patterns than in the case of the plays devised by the *Intronati*: samurais were meant to learn how to move, how to look, and how to speak in real life by performing as actors in Noh plays.

One might speculate that the process of learning is in both cases intensified by narcissistic gratification. As Aristotle argues in the first chapter of the *Poetics*, learning is always based on imitation. "Mimesis" is the shared ground of pedagogy and theater. In the case of Noh as well as of the *Intronati*, there is a fusion of the theatrical and the pedagogical variants of mimesis. The actors *learn* "by doing", and are at the same time gratified by applause and admiration if they *perform* well. One might consider linking playful agonistic practices such as sports to this tableau of performances which are neither ritual re-enactment nor theater in the strict sense and which primarily serve to implement behavioral patterns that are useful in a given place at a given time.[333]

7.—As a working hypothesis for all conceptual discussions in what follows, I should therefore like to suggest that theater, including drama as its textual basis,

---

[332] As to relevant details, see, once again, the article quoted in n. 322.

[333] A careful reader will notice that I have not come back to the quasi-theatrical practices to be observed in traditional Arab culture. Suffice it to say that Dervish dances certainly are ritual practices; they are theatrical only from an "orientalizing" Western perspective.—I would assign the quasi-pantomimical practices of story-tellers in order to' more effectively channel a verbal message to a feature common to all humans; the difference lies in the degree to which bodily expressions are considered appropriate or not; this degree varies according to places, times, behavioral patterns based on religiously inspired morals, and social class.—The point discussed shall remain an open question with regard to farcical representations by demi-professional amateur groups, which seem to exist in almost all premodern cultures about which I was able to gather some information. I would not exclude the possibility that such practices constitute the origin of theater as comedy (as ritual re-enactment is said to have been at the origin of the "birth of tragedy").

should be differentiated from ritual re-enactment, for the reason already mentioned: participants in ritual performances as well as observers who take neither an aestheticizing nor a "scientific"—that is, an anthropologist's—stance, subjectively believe that what is going on in the performance is real, and not just an imitation referring to reality, or a symbolic referencing.[334] Pedagogical performances, such as Noh plays or the plays staged by the *Intronati*, constitute, in ontological terms, an intermediate region between theater and ritual enactment, but they are, according to my intuition, to be seen as closer to theater proper than to ritual, not least because of the fact that there is a consciousness, on the audience's part, that the action presented on stage may be transferred to the level of "real" reality, but is not as yet such "real" reality. One might add that staged performances, on the "negative" ontological status of which the audience agrees (namely: that they are not real, but imitations), may pursue, in contrast to ritualistic performances, very diverse intentions. They may be created for mere entertainment, but also with a view to didactics, with a view to yielding frames for aesthetic, moral-philosophical, or even epistemological reflection, or with a view to "shaping", i.e. educating, those who are performing and submitting the quality of their performance to general scrutiny.

8.—There is one more characteristic that has to be mentioned: the fact that theater is dependent on *language* differentiates it from non-ritualistic performative cultural practices which could be sensibly subsumed under the heading of "performances as mass culture" as well, such as ancient gladiator fights, medieval and Renaissance festival culture (courtly and popular), or modern sports events. One could perhaps formulate the thesis that events and performances with a mass appeal have a general tendency to produce social cohesion, or are at least intended to do so. Theater as a specialized variant includes language, that is: specific meaning. Language-based performative practices which are presented in order to be consumed by a given public are thus apt to produce cohesion and then to steer, as it were, the social body in one specific direction.[335] It seems to be mainly the specificity of this steering capacity that

---

334 In that sense, the Catholic variant of referencing the Last Supper would be ritual re-enactment, the Protestant variant would be representation—without being theater. However, the latter shares with theater the consciousness, on the part of all participants, of a distance between referenced and actual action, and, in addition, the reflective mode implied in the symbolic relation: what is the *meaning* of what is going on during the representation? The answer to this question is delegated to the individual believer, and according to the extent to which her or his personal answer is in congruence with the arcane divine truth, she or he will later on be able to access paradise or not.

335 To come back to the already mentioned performative practice called "Mass": although Christianity is known to be one of the religions of the book, the status of language was a very reduced one in the ritual of Mass as practiced at that time; Luther's polemical engagement

differentiates theater from the other performative practices mentioned at the beginning of this paragraph.[336] And it is evident that this feature is the main enabling structure for making use of performative practices with a view to implementing norms, values, and behavioral rules. As paradoxical as such a claim may at first sight seem, it is meant very seriously: mass media fulfill their function by drawing primarily on the symbolic code of language. The mobilization of the full range of compact encodings (vision, sound, scent) and even the "sensationalist" hyperbolization of the effects to be gained by their privileging is a secondary device in order to better convey a specific message to a highly diverse audience.

The tentative parallel between the above-characterized activities of the *Intronati* and classical Noh allows for briefly addressing a question, not immediately pertinent to this chapter's line of argument, to which there will not be a definitive solution in this book, but which is highly relevant from the perspective of a theory of cultural exchange, namely, the problem of mono- or poly-genesis with regard to culture.[337] As to the biological world, modern science seems to have decided in favor of the former assumption. Genetic analysis suggests that all seven billion members of the species living at present on the globe descend from one "first couple", or, at most, from a very small tribe of (promiscuous) first parents. This may but need not hold true for cultural phenomena, too.

---

with the traditional variant of religious service targeted in particular this neglect of the *logos*. But another point also mentioned already is of even greater importance when it comes to assessing the effectiveness of the language-bound message in the case of theater on the one hand, the performance of the Mass on the other: at least for an adult recipient, nothing is new in the words she or he is hearing while attending a traditional (Catholic, Tridentine) religious service; the conveyance of the message is thus contravened by automatization. Dramas, however, have to present something "new", also in terms of the verbal message, in order to attract the audience.—Highly refined groups of recipients, "Kantians" so to speak, who do not care about the words, but only consider the relative formal characteristics of different stagings of identical pieces, are a restricted phenomenon and, anyway, a phenomenon of a later age than the one under scrutiny here; but even in this case, novelty is a primary criterion for assessing a performance. The requirement is, however, not to be fulfilled by the text, but by formal parameters concerning the relation between the text and the actual performance.

336 Sports events, e.g., could be conceived—beyond the integrative function which seems characteristic of all performative practices—as instruments of implementing a spirit of competition amongst those who attend and watch. Gladiator fights may have a "brutalizing" function, highly welcome within the social and cultural structure of an empire based on physical, military force. Court festivals might implement an attitude of admiration with reference to the one who enabled them to take place, that is, the prince or monarch (etc.).

337 There has already been some discussion regarding this question in the "Borderlines" chapter of Part I.

Given the immense efficiency of what is here called the cultural net to mediate between humans and regions which do not have any form of direct contact with each other, one cannot exclude that in case of practices such as those just mentioned, there is one specific "site of emergence", and a subsequent story of spreading, step by step, to other parts of the globe, where these patterns either became "extracted" from the net or not. But precisely because of the genetically proven biological monogenesis, humans from different cultural backgrounds may share numerous basic needs and also abilities to cater to these needs. Consequently, it cannot be excluded either that similar, but finally different practices like ritual, pedagogical performance, and theater were "invented" more than once in human history. The fact that they were not invented "everywhere", in other terms, that there are indeed—as mentioned—high civilizations without one or the other of these practices, does not testify to the contrary. Logics of control which remain stable for a very long period may lead to a veritable mental "blocking" of the individuals submitted to the control, up to the point that they are not able to imagine (even speculatively) what has been prohibited within their community for extended periods. In the case of the absence of theater in the classical Arab world, it might be the anti-representational attitude generally deriving from a rigidly conceived variant of monotheism that was the cause of the mental blocking.[338] This said, the massive and permanently reiterated anti-theatrical diatribes by Muslim theologians[339] from the very beginnings onward make clear that such mental barriers against the production of cultural patterns which cater to humans' basic needs are effective in the long run only with respect to secluded communities to whose territories the universal cultural net was able to ramify only under the conditions of technological modernity.

The only way to reasonably answer the intricate question of a mono- or polygenesis of culture would thus be to find out what level of cultural sophistication the primordial tribe had attained when its members decided or were forced to choose different ways. And did the various sub-tribes into which it split ever completely lose contact with each other, or was there, from time to time, a sort of exchange, be it a mediated one? At least as soon as the device of language had been invented, even one human being moving, willingly or under the pressure of external circumstances, from India to China could have been the "carrier" of enormous quantities of cultural material, not only Indic, but also Mediterranean or even Celtic and Germanic.

---

338 For a more detailed explanation, see below, pp. 281 f.
339 See the reference given below, n. 554.

The "Orientation Toward The Message"

0.—Didacticism,[340] the main distinctive feature of early modern European drama when compared to subsequent instantiations of the genre, is basically distinct from an unconscious encoding of meaning in the structures of certain objects which can be decrypted only from a specialist's standpoint. It is based on the intention to direct recipients' thoughts and actions in a specific way. It thus requires a certain level of explicitness. But didacticism—and this is the main feature separating the concept from various forms of coercion—can only be successful to the extent that its recipients are ready to accept these directions not as instruments of power (as devices of other people's interests), but as instruments intended to disclose to them that which is good for them but of which they may not be sufficiently aware. Didacticism is effective only when its recipients are ready to believe what they are being taught.—There is a second strand of didacticism which at first sight appears to be different from the one just characterized; but when it comes to concretion, that is, to creating actual didactic works, the two strategies of communication are in most cases hybridized. The second strategy is, obviously, persuasion, the attempt at luring people into accepting positions they might not be ready to accept willingly by offering them material to which they react positively without any further reflection; it consists in contents and devices that appeal to the recipients' basic needs, and in most cases to those they do not have the occasion to sufficiently accommodate in their "real" lives.

The instrumental aspects of such artworks, that is, the devices by which such texts or representations try to make people believe what they teach, will be expounded in more detail below. For the time being, I will limit my considerations with a view to illustrating the general questions to be discussed to the situation in two countries of quite distinct profile in that age, Spain and England.

1.—Early modern Spain was a stronghold of the Counter-Reformation, that is, of Catholicism's attempt to "roll back" the Protestant reform, which in fact constituted a revolution insofar as it destroyed the effective, material power of the traditional Church by postulating a "universal priesthood", that is, the equality of all baptized humans in matters of faith. The dogmatic essence of this reaction was conceived by the Council of Trent (1545–1563). Two sessions

---

[340] The formulation contained in the heading of this chapter is obviously borrowed from Roman Jakobson's famous article "Closing Statement: Linguistics and Poetics", in: Thomas A. Sebeok (ed.), *Style in Language*, Cambridge, MA 1960, pp. 350–377.

were in part dedicated to problems revolving around art.³⁴¹ These discussions were informed by the assumption that secular art is to be considered a medium in the sense roughly explained above, that is, as a channel through which sinful behavior and misguided thoughts may be represented to the populace. But it was also taken to serve as a channel for propagating morality, including religious orthodoxy. Succinctly put, the Council's attitude towards art was Thomistic as to content and Platonic as to function.³⁴² In order to prevent undesirable material from being diffused through this medium, the Inquisition was strengthened and further institutionalized by means of reinforcing its bureaucratic structure. The clerks working within this classic agency of cultural control were endowed with a compact set of rules to apply to the control process as well as with a set of procedures for dealing with problematic material and with its human producers or transmitters.³⁴³ This was the, so to speak, re-active component of the Counter-Reformation's instrumentalization of art. There was, however, also a pro-active component, which was less systematized for the obvious reason that the material in question did not exist as yet; it had to be "created". This pro-active component consisted in the appeal to make use of art's potential to impress and persuade its recipients with a view to propagating correct behavior and worldview both with regard to religion and beyond. It was left to the bishops and those under their guidance, that is, believers including persons who had the means to act as patrons, to develop concrete ideas of how to put this program of art-as-didactics into practice.³⁴⁴

2.—Spanish literature, above all drama, of the late sixteenth and early seventeenth centuries may be conceived as a paradigmatic instance of such didactic art. The first point worth mentioning in this regard is perhaps the fact that a "new" genre was created for that purpose, a genre which does not exist in countries where ideological homogenization was not as streamlined as in Spain and for which there are only very rare analogues in other European cultures of the time.³⁴⁵ From a historical standpoint, the *auto sacramental* was

---

341 *Sessio* XVIII and *sessio* XXV.
342 Regardless of his general reservation, based on the assumption of a second-degree distance from truth, Plato admits fictional texts apt to strengthen morals, especially those of the warriors (the "guardians" of his ideal republic).
343 See once again Summer-Schindler, *Zensur und Involution*.
344 See Werner Weisbach, *Der Barock als Kunst der Gegenreformation*, Berlin 1921 (mainly focusing on the graphic arts, but with a useful elucidation of the general ideological and confessional context); the introductory chapters of Henry W. Sullivan's book *Tirso de Molina and the Drama of the Counter Reformation*, Amsterdam 1976, continue to be, in my view, one of the most helpful publications concerning this point.
345 The Slovene Passion play mentioned above is one such non-Spanish analogue.

a sort of accommodation of the medieval European religious drama to the needs of the period in question.—In order to substantiate this claim, some brief points concerning the genre's prehistory shall be recalled: the practice of pilgrimages and processions is documented from the origins of Christianity onward, that is, starting in the first century CE. Processions have a more or less accentuated "mimetic" dimension; the scheme of the itinerary as well as the nature of its destination (an altar decorated with a crucifix erected somewhere in the countryside) illustrate that they derive from the idea of faith as an *imitatio Christi*. Processions emulate, in a way, the *via crucis*. Pilgrimages (which are not of particular importance in the context of this study) add the veneration of holy objects, relics, to the faith-grounded constellation employed by such performative practices.—Religious drama seems to have emerged in later times only. Most importantly, the mystery and morality plays we know about from the tenth to the twelfth centuries onward, depending on the vernaculars in question, seem not to have been linked to the practice of the procession.

The evolution of both performative practices, the "active" and the "receptive" variants, in the following centuries was characterized by a quantitative augmentation which led to the point of degeneration. Processions became longer and longer, frequently lasting for several days; as to the religious plays, it suffices to say that the oldest documented piece, the *Résurrection de Tours* (thirteenth century), consists of ca. 300 lines; the *Passion du Palatinus* (fourteenth century), of 1,900 lines; the *Passion d'Arras* (fifteenth century), of 25,000 lines; and the plays known as *Le Mystère de la Passion* and *La Passion Jhesuchrist*, dating from the end of the fifteenth century, contain, respectively, 35,000 and 55,000 lines. The factor of multiplication is roughly 175 within a period of 200 years. One should add that the performance of a standard early modern play comprising ca. 3,000–4,000 lines, e.g. by Shakespeare or Racine, lasts about three to four hours.

It is not astonishing to learn that the degenerative stage of these performative practices was one of the points chosen by the Reformers, in the first place by Luther, as a privileged target of the drastic polemics leveled against the traditional Church. And one may well imagine, even if there are no extant written testimonies, that such social practices, lasting over several days, indeed became the sites of parasitical bodily excess (*gula*, *luxuria*). In the period following the Council of Trent, there are still religious plays, but a disciplined variant conceived in the interest of countering the Protestant polemics as well as of reconverting the practices to restore their former purpose, namely, of shaping the masses' behavior by way of engaging them, actively and passively, in religiously connoted performances.—The form of these new plays was that of a short, one-act (Spanish: *auto*) play, the performance of which did not last longer than thirty to forty minutes. The spectacular formal revolution (or, rather, involution) was obviously based on the extraction from the net of material that had not been available for centuries,[346] namely, the concept of drama as the "mimicking" of something "particular" (*kat'hekaston*) that conveys something "more general" (*katholou*), that is, the integration of primary and secondary symbolization and the possibilities for semiotic concentration thus opened up. In Spain as well as in Slovenia, where the tradition is far less rich, these new, humanistically informed religious plays were incorporated into ostentatious, lavishly ornamented, and thus highly impressive processions.[347] The formerly separate active and passive variants of religious performance floating in the net became fused, presumably in order to enhance impact. The

---

346 For details, see pp. 190–193.

347 The author of this book, who was educated in the Protestant tradition, but in a primarily Catholic region of Germany, had in his youth the occasion to view, from the perspective of an unengaged spectator, a number of such Corpus Christi processions, which were at the time still customary in the Catholic parts of Germany and later on mostly shrunk to the dimension of a rather short walk around the cathedral of the city in question. What was to be seen in the streets on that day was, indeed, a sort of open-air "grand opera"; the priests as well as the believers taking part in the procession were dressed festively; the streets were decorated with freshly cut tree branches and banners; there were rich altars to be seen on street corners where the procession paused in order to sing, accompanied by instruments, etc.—The above descriptions of the situation in Spain and Slovenia are conceived for non-specialists. If one were to offer a more detailed characterization, one would have to take into account that the Slovene plays engaged all participants to a higher degree than their Spanish counterparts. In Spain, too, the Corpus Christi processions and the performances of the *autos* took place within one comprehensive (ritualistic) context. As to the plays in particular, however, the separation between performers and viewers was as strict as in the case of the (pre-avant-garde) secular stage. The believers took part in the procession; at certain points on the way, usually two, they stopped in order to view the performance of a religious play which took place on a mobile stage. The difference between stage and "real" space was thus clearly demarcated. The authors, the stage directors, the musicians, and the actors were the same as in the case of professional secular theater; this implies that the performances were highly stylized, to the point that they were open to a non-didactic, aestheticizing reception. In Slovenia, by contrast, the performers were amateurs who had rehearsed many times in the weeks before the festival day on which the procession took place. The play was enacted on the selfsame ground on which the procession took place; there was no topographical separation between the stage as secondary reality and the "normal" ground as primary reality. And in a manner that was reactivated in the last part of the twentieth century by stage directors such as Ariane Mnouchkine, the common believers were—to a certain extent at least—part of the performance; they were invited to enact the role of the populace of biblical times. To put the matter in a nutshell: the Spanish plays, which were mainly created for the metropolitan populations of Madrid and Toledo, represent a more intellectualized variant, whereas the Slovene plays manifest an impetus to "directly" (and corporeally) engage the targeted recipients.

content was either allegorical or "literal",[348] or, as in most cases, a mixture of both. The intention was, accordingly, either moralizing or ideological in a broader sense, or, as in most cases, both.

The stories presented by these *autos* display an amazing variety which goes far beyond what was known from medieval religious plays. There is still a category focusing on biblical history, of the Old as well as of the New Testament. As for the former, the re-narration always comprised a typological interpretation, as evidenced in many cases—e.g., Calderón's *Primero y segundo Isaac* (before 1674)[349]—by the plays' titles alone; what was implied in comparable medieval plays, the Christian version of salvation history,[350] is in a way laid bare in these early modern plays by way of a humanistically informed formal concentration. The additional interest of the entirety of these plays, including the ones drawing on New Testament material, was to acquaint believers with the manifold stories narrated in Holy Scripture, which Catholics were not allowed to read on their own, but in a way that freed the material from the cultic constraints of the Mass proper, where its status was reduced to such a degree that it remained opaque on the level of narrative. We are faced here with a sort of dramatized catechism, whose establishment, for the first time in the history of Catholicism, may have been an attempt at countering the Reformation's accusation of neglecting Scripture, while upholding the inderdict against individual reading.—Much more intriguing with regard to "drama as mass media" are the *autos* presenting mythological fables mainly drawn from the Ovidian collection, which was one of

---

348 In order to avoid any possible misunderstandings, I should like to explicitly stress that the following description of the new genre refers to its Spanish variant. The aforementioned Slovene play is much less sophisticated; it is, as to its content, a more or less traditional Passion play. It shares with the Spanish plays, however, a number of decisive features: the integration of active and passive religious performance (play and procession); the radical reduction of length; and, finally, the hybridization of the mimetic and the allegorical modes; as mentioned, allegories of the non-Western continents appear on stage in order to propagate the universalistic claim of Christian faith and of Western culture in general.

349 The first Isaac is the one to be found in the Old Testament. According to Christian figural hermeneutics, the "second" Isaac is Jesus Christ, who fulfills what the first Isaac announced or foreshadowed. By means of his consummated sacrifice, the covenant between Abraham and Yahweh is renewed, this time with respect not only to Abraham's progeny, but to humankind in its entirety.—The seminal publication on the hermeneutical practice of typology, including its repercussions in literary texts, is Auerbach's essay "Figura".

350 The conceptual frame of this and comparable constructs goes back to Romans 5: 14–17, where Paul establishes the relation between Adam and Christ. Adam is "forma futuri"; he caused death to reign amongst humans, a condition which was annihilated by Christ's salvific deed.

Renaissance readers' favorite books. In Calderón's *El divino Orfeo* (1663),[351] one of the most beautiful and intellectually fascinating instances of the genre, the reference is to the story of Orpheus' descent to the underworld and the liberation of his wife Eurydice from the bonds of death, which is interpreted as a piece of fiction ("fábula") under the surface of which is hidden the only true corresponding "historia", that is, Christ's Harrowing of Hell and his defeat of Death. Here, the intention is a more ambitious one, namely, to demonstrate that the stories and the wisdom of pagan times do not constitute an ideological cosmos of their own, or even an alternative to the spiritual world of Judeo-Christianity, but were rather drawn from biblical sources which were then distorted.[352] The purpose of the mythological *autos* was to present the mythical fables once again, but to reduce them at the same time to their "original" shape and meaning, the latter being contained in stories narrated in the Bible. The intention was, beyond plain catechizing, the "rolling back" of Renaissance pluralization: there is only one revelation, and all alternative systems pretending to the status of truth are based on nothing but "stolen" material, which is, consequently, to be restituted to its legitimate owner, Christianity.—This idea was not new, but stemmed from Justinus Martyr, who relies on corresponding concepts with regard to the relation between gentile and Jewish knowledge developed by Philo of Alexandria. As far as is possible to determine on the basis of the extant documentation, it was extracted from the cultural net and systematically merged with the Ovidean corpus for the first time in the *Ovide moralisé* at the end of the thirteenth or the beginning of the fourteenth century. In terms of basic interpretative practices, Calderón's play may be considered a renewed extraction of this medieval allegorization from the net. The playwright assembles it, however, in a new formal register, the post-medieval, humanistically inspired genre of a stage performance of short duration, thus dramatically shifting the targeted recipients: from the learned to the common people, from a restricted to a general audience.[353] In

---

[351] There is a first version from 1634 which is much less sophisticated. The fact that Calderón dramatized and allegorized this mythological fable twice (which he did in no other cases) testifies to the importance of this plot in particular for the endeavor of a Catholic restoration (see also my following remarks above).

[352] The ideological basis of these dramas was the aforementioned priority thesis; for all related questions, see the analysis of the piece in my *Discursive* Renovatio *in Lope de Vega and Calderón*, chap. 3.3.2.

[353] Language training in medieval colleges was different from what it became in the age of grammar books, that is, from roughly the sixteenth century onward. Pupils learned the language by a supervised reading of original texts, starting with simple texts such as *De bello gallico*. The *Metamorphoses* were an important part of this pedagogical compendium. Although the reading process was not directed at gathering information regarding the culture of antiquity, but mere language-learning, it seems that the ecclesiastical authorities who oversaw all sorts of instruction deemed it necessary to provide an authoritative take on the at times strik-

addition, Calderón draws on erudite material from Late Antiquity and from medieval and Counter-Reformation theological discourses thematizing the relation between Christian belief and pagan knowledge. The result of this mix of pre-existing features is astonishing; there seems to be not a single new element in Calderón's play; all of its features may be considered to derive from acts of extraction of items floating in the cultural net. Yet the composition as a whole provides one of the most fascinating comments on the relation between belief and myth available in the discursive history of Christianity.

The most startling section of the text corpus I am referring to, however, is comprised of the so-called "historical *autos*", that is, plays dealing with actual events from times posterior to those narrated in the New Testament. A particularly impressive example is entitled *La lepra de Constantino* (1647/1657);[354] it presents the world-historical watershed event of the fourth century CE, when the status of Christianity suddenly changed from that of a sect of violently persecuted public enemies to that of a legitimate cult and, shortly afterwards, the official religion of the Roman Empire. The intention here is obviously moralizing, and it is also anti-pagan, or, rather, it is directed against tendencies of re-paganization; but it is in the first place assimilative. The goal to be achieved was the demonstration of the fact that even post-biblical, secular history is governed in its entirety by the Christian God, that all worldly struggles are only a surface under which the basic structure of salvation history lies hidden as a recursive pattern, first revealed in Scripture, that will continue to structure secular time and history until the end of this world, which is initiated by the Parousia.

An embryonic achievement of this goal had already been accomplished in the age when the problem of how to conceptualize post-Incarnation history first emerged, i.e., in Late Antiquity. Lactantius and even more so Eusebius of Caesarea[355] had syncretized the Roman emperor's vita with the biblical pattern of Paul's miraculous conversion from a persecutor to a propagator of the "true" faith. Calderón reactivates this material in the *auto* mentioned above by extracting it from the net and connecting it to another pre-existing template, namely, the interpretation of every single believer's life as a repeti-

---

ing parallels between pagan mythology and the Christian narratives. Texts such as the *Ovide moralisé* were created in order to fulfill this task. By way of plays such as the one mentioned, what had been restricted to a minority of 1–5 % of the population in the Middle Ages became a "lesson" taught to the entire populace in the early modern age.

354 For an in-depth presentation of this play, see *Discursive* Renovatio *in Lope de Vega and Calderón*, chap. 3.3.3.

355 *De mortibus persecutorum* (ca. 315); *Bios tou megalou Konstantinou* (ca. 337).

tion of salvation history.[356] He thus succeeds in creating an effective device for divulging the concept of history-as-repetition, which had come under serious pressure since the discovery of the New World.[357]—The latter concept is an intentional feature of all *autos sacramentales*, and it is sedimented in their highly conventional ending: the reduction of all events, past, present, and future, to one foundational pattern is symbolized in a concentrated manner in the last scene of each play, when a tabernacle is exposed to the viewers while one of the characters comments on its contents. The Host as the "real presence" of Christ's body draws the audience's attention not only to the central tenet of Catholic dogma, but also, and even more powerfully, to the higher meaning underlying all worldly events: namely, God's firm intention to ensure human salvation.

One should add that the plays just outlined were performed as open-air spectacles on street corners. The stage was formed by carts so as to enable the theater to move from one part of the city to the next, engaging the largest possible audience. The plays were presented on a festival day, Corpus Christi, which was a general holiday, meaning that in principle everyone could attend. To further encourage attendance, the performances were open to the public without charge. Each year, those responsible saw to it that the plays would be different from the ones performed in previous years in order to arouse the curiosity of the public; the communal authorities sponsored an annual competition for two new plays. The promise of monetary reward and artistic prestige combined to ensure that the most talented playwrights would compete for the prize. The results are highly intriguing even today. Although the religious and secular authorities sought primarily to impress the people of Madrid, other parts of the population were not left out. After the Corpus Christi premiere in the capital, the actors would travel with their carts in the ensuing months from city to city, from town to town, and even from village to village throughout the rest of the country.

3.—It may seem obvious to refer to these early instances of mass media as blatantly didactic religious propaganda which made use of both visual and verbal instruments to demonstrate without ambiguity how believers were supposed to conceive of religious dogma, as well as to further its pragmatic application. The

---

[356] The Fall is equated with being stuck in the state of sinfulness before conversion; Christ's sacrificial death is equated with conversion and baptism; the state of the post-Incarnation world as redeemed but at the same time exposed to the dangers of sin is equated with the possibility of a relapse into sin on the part of the converted and baptized individual. The eschatological perspective is equated with the definitive renouncement of sin, preceding physical death, and with the ensuing access to paradise.

[357] See in more detail the explanations given above (pp. 89–92).

situation may be different, however, when one shifts one's attention from plays that did not try to conceal their didactic intentions to those which at first sight seem to be purely fictional, with no obvious message or purpose other than aesthetic and intellectual pleasure. Does it make sense to label the Spanish *comedias* of the era vehicles of prearranged ideological content? Or are they rather to be located in the tradition of ancient tragedy, as an artistic presentation of anthropological problems to which normative, conventional behavior does not apply, and which thus can only be empathetically exposed?

In order to be convincing in this respect, one has to avoid gross generalizations. As is well-known, Calderón's most famous *comedia*, *La vida es sueño* (1635), is so evidently didactic that the sophisticated and spellbinding action culminates in a formula repeated several times in near ritualistic fashion, a formula which expresses a sentiment regarding human behavior generally, independent of time or place: "[...] Mas sea verdad o sueño, / obrar bien es lo que importa."[358] Regardless of its philosophical sophistication,[359] Calderón's dream-play is a sort of extended *auto sacramental* as far as its intention and the precision of its message are concerned.[360] At first sight, the case may seem to be otherwise when it comes to the equally famous *dramas de honor* such as Lope de Vega's *El castigo sin venganza* (1631/1634) or Calderón's *El médico de su honra* (1637).[361] These dramas dealing with female marital infidelity—in the first case actual; in the second case either putative or imagined, but certainly not consummated—obviously do not contain a moral message articulated as explicitly as in *La vida es sueño*. But their implicit message is of that simplicity and easy accessibility which is typical of didactic literature, namely, that married women would do well to avoid adultery, or even situations which might raise concerns regarding their fidelity, if they wish to avoid being put to death.

Bearing in mind the above reservation that non-didactic readings of these dramas are distinctly possible, one could make a strong argument for the interpreta-

---

[358] "[...] Be it true or just / A dream, to do right is what matters most" (V. 2420 f.; William E. Colford [tr.], New York, NY, London, Toronto, and Sydney 1958).

[359] Let me stress for readers of this book who are not familiar with the corpus of *autos sacramentales* that very many of these plays, in particular the two plays (respectively mythological and historical) referred to above, are also intellectually highly sophisticated texts (see the above-cited chapters from my *Discursive* Renovatio *in Lope de Vega and Calderón*). For reasons of convenience, my above formulations refer to the stance vis-à-vis didactic literary texts that is current in modernity.

[360] See, once again, the essay of mine referred to in n. 64. For a more detailed analysis of the play, see Pawlita's book (*Skeptizismus im europäischen Drama der Frühen Neuzeit*).

[361] See the analysis of these plays in my *Discursive* Renovatio *in Lope de Vega and Calderón*, chaps. 2 and 6.

tion here proposed—i.e., that the *dramas de honor*, too, share the basic structure and function of the *autos*—based on the evidence of contemporary literary production in Spain. The most prominent Spanish author of the age in question was Cervantes. His attempts to gain access to the lucrative market of drama production were not crowned with success. However, his main novel, the *Quijote* (1605/ 1615), sold very well, as did his collection of short stories, the *Novelas ejemplares* (1613). The *Quijote*—by way of stories interpolated in the narrator's tale as the narrations of characters—and the novellas contain quite a few tales dealing with "honor", that is, with the question of female infidelity. But they treat the topic in a manner dramatically diverging from the *comedias* of the time. Whether one is dealing with *El celoso extremeño* or *El curioso impertinente*, even when adultery is physically consummated, as is the case in the latter story, there is never the slightest doubt that it is, morally considered, not a mistake on the part of the female which causes the imbroglio. The question around which these narrativized honor plays revolve is rather the problematic implications of normative patriarchy. It would be audacious to interpret them as anti-patriarchal texts, or even as instances of an emerging feminism. What these stories show is, rather, how difficult it is for females as well as males to master the contingent interactions between affects and societal (moral) norms. The endings of the stories—in one case, tragic, in the other, quasi-tragic—are based on so many heterogeneous factors, incapable of being systematized, that one hardly finds a possibility of equating them with real-life scenarios, which is a requisite for didactic tales. In contrast to the *dramas de honor* mentioned above, the Cervantine honor stories do not convey a message; Cervantes seems content to let them reflect the complexity of human life. Not only because these stories were available to a literate public only, but also because they have no discernible practical message, I am inclined to see them as playing a different role within the contemporary literary scenario from what I call an early form of literature as mass medium.

All of the texts mentioned above revolving around the theme of "honor" are based on related conceptual features, but also in part on ready-made stories dealing with honor cases which have been circulating in the cultural net since medieval times at the latest.[362] The difference between Cervantes and the play-

---

[362] Because of a lack of documentation, I shall not engage here in further discussions concerning possible antecedents to the relevant medieval texts, whether literary or pragmatic. It is plausible, indeed, to assume that the specific profile of the premodern European honor code derives from unwritten Germanic sources introduced to all of Europe via the raids of the Vikings. The common ground which these concepts share with the Greek concept of *arete* and the Roman concept of *virtus* or *pudor* are the universal, that is, abstract principles of patriarchy. When it comes to literary modelings of patriarchy, the fact that literary texts, though intended to convey the *katholou*, start from a *kat'hekaston*, may explain why most Spanish Golden Age honor narratives are not based on the extraction of floating material that we are

wrights is situated on the level of the respective abstract, evaluative, moral-philosophical discourses that the authors extract from the net in order to assimilate to the narratives they devised. In Cervantes's case, the extracted discourse is Aristotelian ethics, the ideal of *mesotes*, of using one's reason in order to behave in a way that avoids extremes of any kind. The playwrights, in contrast, assemble the theme of honor into a template whose basis is the (Christian) theological discourse, specifically the dogma of the Fall and its consequence, original sin, including the latter's most conspicuous symptom, *luxuria*. In some cases, it is possible to demonstrate even with regard to the details of formulation that they had recourse not only to the corresponding concepts, but also to relevant *texts* floating in the net, namely to Thomas Aquinas' description of the particular sin of *luxuria* and to a famous contemporary handbook, edited by Antonio de Escobar y Mendoza, instructing priests how to make believers tell the "real" (and frequently unconscious) truth about their sexual behavior.[363]

I will comment only briefly on the subgenre of *comedia* known as the *comedia de capa y espada* ("plays of cape and sword"). These include pieces such as Tirso de Molina's *Don Gil de las calzas verdes* (1615/1635) and Lope de Vega's *Dama boba* (1613), which are highly elaborate comedies of intrigue, well known for eliciting constant laughter. While one could readily take a more intellectualized approach to this type of play, this would inhibit studying its reception as performance. Comedy of any kind is for the most part a popular genre, a genre addressing the "masses", including intellectually sophisticated readers or viewers. In modern scholarship, one may detect the tendency to "Kantianize" or even to "Adornianize"[364] comedy, that is, to deny the presence of effects which in classical times were understood with reference to the saying *castigat ridendo mores* in order to focus either on formal parameters or on a supposed "subver-

---

able to trace back to classical times, but rather on material we are able to identify (as *written* material) in postclassical medieval texts.

363 *Liber theologiae moralis. Viginti quatuor Societatis Jesu doctoribus reseratus*, Monachii 1644; regarding this point, see my analysis of *El médico de su honra* in *Discursive* Renovatio *in Lope de Vega and Calderón*, chap. 6 (as indicated above, the play was written around 1637, that is, several years before the 1644 edition of Escobar's compendium, which is the oldest extant edition; the title page indicates that it is the 40th ["quadragesima"] print of the book; the first print is no longer extant); as to Thomas see below, n. 599.

364 Theodor W. Adorno's *Aesthetic Theory* (1970) famously posits that the central feature of non-trivial literature is its "negativity". What is completely justified within an argument focusing on high modernist literature might be questionable with respect to previous periods of literary history; in line with the present-day predilection for anachronisms of various kinds, the point made by Adorno has been applied to pre-twentieth-century comedy in many recent publications concerning the genre.

sive" sub-text contained in the plays. But these views seem to be based much more on a shift in literary theory, accentuating de-pragmatization and devaluing or even deprecating the traditional dimension of *docere*, than on the texts in question. As to formal parameters, comedy is highly standardized; as such, it might not be the best possible basis for initiating the "free play of the mind's capacities" which is, according to Kant, the dimension, not available in practical life, to be gained when receiving works of art. And as to a reading in line with the assumption of art as a counter-discourse, it is hard to deny that plays like the two mentioned above enact fantasies of female independence or emancipation; yet they systematically combine the obligatory happy ending with the female characters' willing return to the constraints of patriarchal law. Of course, these laws may well have been made to appear less onerous to contemporary female spectators due to the fact that their male executors have for their part been made to look somewhat foolish over the course of the play.

4.—It would be problematic to postulate that the situation of early modern English drama is roughly identical to the one just outlined for the case of Spain. This said, there are, in addition to the differences to be pointed out, striking similarities with respect to certain subgenres which can be explained on the theoretical basis suggested in this book, that is, without the problematic assertion of deeper similarities regarding the respective ideological or even political contexts. It is obvious that what I primarily have in mind is the last subgenre of the Spanish *comedia* discussed above, namely, comedy. Without going into the details, I would claim that the above characterization of the Spanish *comedia de capa y espada* holds true for Shakespeare's comedies as well. The materials extracted in both cases from the cultural net for the construction of plot are, to a large extent, the same. This material includes themes, formal elements, the (patriarchal) honor code, marvelous effects such as ghosts and metamorphoses derived from the medieval tradition, as well as farcical and obscene topoi which circulated in the cultural net as discursifications of a social practice described by Bakhtin as "carnival."[365]

As to the other subgenres, there seems to be much more difference than similarity. And there are good reasons for arguing that asserting this lack of similarity is not anachronistic, but grounded in solid historical evidence. The "source" cited above as the origin of theater as mass medium in Spain did not exist in early modern England. While there was religious controversy, there was no Counter-Reformation, nor was there an attempt to forge a homogeneous Protestant society—or, rather, these attempts were doomed to failure from the very

---

[365] See the reference in n. 60.

beginning. Rendering the thinking of the masses uniform as this was effectuated in Spain remained a mere dream of certain monarchs and religious dignitaries.[366] *Rebus sic stantibus*, social cohesion could only be produced by reducing the level of homogeneity aimed at. In a way, early modern England faced a problem well known from later, properly modern times: how to achieve a minimum of social consensus in an ideologically and religiously fragmented society, the various contingents of which at times even have recourse to physical violence in order to settle their disputes. In terms of function, modern mass media are an obviously effective answer to this question. Might there also be a mass media dimension of Elizabethan drama beyond the already mentioned domain of comedy?

As in most of Europe's countries affected by the early modern religious schism, there was no religious drama in contemporary England. The two medieval sub-genres of religious drama, which had in a way been revivified and fused in the Spanish *autos sacramentales*, continued to occupy the status of largely inactive, obsolete cultural material in Britain. The reasons behind this situation are not at all difficult to grasp: it is not feasible to stage such propaganda pieces—be they of Catholic or Protestant tenor—in the streets of a religiously divided country. In times of a religious effervescence difficult to understand from a modern perspective, such public stagings would have provoked uproar and violence.[367] As for the period I am dealing with, performances of religious

---

[366] One might speculate about the reasons for this difference. On the one hand, one may take into consideration that there was nothing in England that could have compared to the move towards ideological and confessional homogeneity triggered by the centuries-long *reconquista* of the Iberian Peninsula. And although there was much violence originating from difference of belief, there were no events that could be equated with such drastic "purging" measures as the Saint Bartholomew's Day massacre in France. The court itself and the ruling nobility were ideologically fragmented; a civil war or a coup as in France would most probably have had an uncertain outcome.

[367] Let me mention parenthetically that the practice of Corpus Christi processions provoked social tensions and incidental (if relatively harmless) violence in religiously divided cities of Germany during my own childhood, right up to the massive movement of secularization provoked by the cultural revolution of 1968. Such acts of violence, mainly perpetrated by male youths from Protestant families under the cover of night, consisted in the devastation of the temporary altars erected by Catholic youths on street corners on the day before Corpus Christi, altars that were mainly composed of arrangements of beautiful spring flowers and reeds exposed on wooden tables. There was no physical damage done to any human being; but one may imagine the fury felt by Catholic believers when they realized in the early morning hours of their festival day what had been done to the fruits of their endeavors. Since these temporary altars were consecrated only at the moment of the actual procession, when the tabernacle containing the host was placed on them, it was not a "real" sacrilege that was at stake, but

propaganda plays did exist in certain religiously divided countries, but only under the condition that they were not public. Jesuit school theater is one example of the constellation I am referring to.

This being said, there is a sort of secret life of the contents and devices of medieval religious drama in the secular theater of early modern England. Scenes of "mystery", and even more so structures evidently influenced by the pattern of personified allegories, are ubiquitous in the plays written by Shakespeare and his contemporaries. The presence of such structures even allows for the suggestion that certain plays of this sort be read in a manner that reduces them to morality plays.[368] I am, however, inclined to consider such interpretations of Elizabethan plays to be just as anachronistic as the current modern, "Kantian", aestheticizing readings of Spanish *comedias*. Such approaches are potentialities opened up by the non-conceptual character of all literary texts[369] and by the concomitant possibility to de- and re-contextualize them in a framework differing from the time and place of their origin and initial reception. The limits of such anachronistic readings of Elizabethan drama—which may, indeed, at times be fascinating—become apparent as soon as one attempts to compare Shakespeare's *Macbeth* (1606) with a medieval mystery or morality play.

What, then, is the didactic dimension of Shakespeare's "serious" (non-comical) drama, without the presence of which it would not make sense to consider these dramas as early instances of mass media? The mere fact that "everybody" was admitted to the performances is a necessary but not a sufficient condition for making such a claim. Does it suffice to concede that the didactic tenor is less pointed or less comprehensive than in Spanish dramas of the time in order to consider the question to be provisionally resolved?

---

rather a sort of preemptive one. Nevertheless, it typically took a number of days, and necessitated the official admonishment of the parish's youth by the Protestant minister in office, followed by several acts of apology, to reduce the tensions to the normal level of mostly peaceful cohabitation.

368 See Robert A. Potter, *The English Morality Play: Origins, History, and Influence of a Dramatic Tradition*, New York, NY 1975; see also Robert Weimann, *Shakespeare and the Popular Tradition in the Theater: Studies in the Social Dimension of Dramatic Form and Function*, Baltimore, MD 1978.

369 There are exceptions to such generalizations of which I am fully aware (and have dealt with; see my essay "Was ist Literatur?", *Zeitschrift für Ästhetik und Allgemeine Kunstwissenschaft* vol. 45,2/2001, pp. 187–215); one such exception is constituted by the corpus of moralistic literature (La Bruyère, Gracián, La Rochefoucauld, Joseph Hall). But these cases do not testify against the acceptability of the generalization in question if the latter still accounts for the vast majority of the instances to be taken into consideration.

I prefer to hypothesize that Elizabethan drama represents an entirely different kind of didacticism. The messages conveyed are meant to establish a social consensus and to enhance behavioral norms that do not require a common religious basis. The problems these dramas address are in principle problems we continue to face today—which is why the plays remain topical in our own time even though they deal with events and social constellations that are more than four hundred years old.[370] Their appeal lies in part in their "universal" approach. They do not deal with subtle psychological or emotional problems relevant only to certain strata of intellectuals; they do not deal with historical events which are so exceptional that it only makes sense to consider them as unique and unrepeatable; they are not experimental in form, a contingency that would limit their appeal to a certain, highly sophisticated segment of the public; they do not expound esoteric views; they are not self-referential. Or, to put it more positively: they deal with basic anthropological configurations— that is to say, with configurations we continue to consider anthropological[371]— and with the ethical questions provoked by them.

But do these dramas also answer the questions they raise? And if not, does it make sense to understand them as early instances of mass media when there is no instruction given to the audience should its members find themselves in situations similar to those presented on stage? Perhaps there is a middle way to ponder before opting for one of these two alternatives. The general argument expounded in this book is certainly linked, as is every scholarly argument, to the logical maxim first theorized by Aristotle which reads *tertium non datur*;[372] but the texts I am dealing with bear a moral dimension and are therefore phenomena with regard to which this maxim does not only *not* apply, but for which it would even be highly inadequate. According to the Stagirite, in all questions of ethics, *mesotes* is the correct choice—which does not simply mean the median between two extremes.[373] My suggestion is in essence to consider the hypothesis that serious Shakespearean drama "teaches" the audience to

---

[370] Let me say for readers not familiar with present-day German culture that, starting in the early seventies of the last century, it was and still is a widespread fashion to stage Shakespeare's serious plays as though they were set in Nazi Germany. Although the author of this book is less inclined to anachronisms than many currently working in the field of literary studies, I have to say that these "modernizing" interpretations are, at times, absolutely fascinating and enlightening.

[371] I have already mentioned that, *pace* Freud, the pattern of oedipal revolt is not a universal structure, at least according to my observations of the present-day globalized world.

[372] See *Metaphysics* 1005 b 19 f.

[373] See *Nicomachean Ethics* 1106 b–1107 a.

avoid extreme patterns of behavior by showing that such behavior leads to catastrophe.[374] Just as Aristotle's *Ethics* leaves the question unresolved of how to shape a viable middle ground of action, so the dramas similarly fail to propose a *via media* for their characters. The common norm they establish—or, rather, try to establish—is not a positive, but a negative one. They suggest avoiding certain patterns of behavior, namely patterns which may be particularly widespread in ideologically fragmented societies.—I shall conclude these remarks by drawing readers' attention to Shakespeare's most important play. It certainly does not teach its audience how to behave in the oedipal situation; but it does teach that excessive hesitancy is as devastating a pattern as an excessive, quasi-Nietzschean "will to power".[375]

5.—To return to the theoretical terminology outlined in the first part of this book: both the Spanish and the English plays seem to show that the most abstract principle governing the extraction or non-extraction of material circulating in the net, at least as far as this period is concerned, is the criterion of control, the concrete profile of which is defined by those who believe they have the right to govern the "masses". The striking feature shared by all the dramas mentioned[376] is their being composed of heterogeneous material circulating in the net; the ideal of homogeneity of internal structure seems in all cases to be outweighed by the intention to steer the masses.—Since mass media are a non-coercive instrument of directing subjects, all the plays mentioned manifest a second, subsidiary level of selection and extraction which is governed by the logic of enticement or appeal. When it comes to these "rhetorical" resources, the dramas of both countries exhibit a similarity that is as striking as their dissimilarity with regard to their respective ideological messages. I should like to add as a codicil to this chapter that in post-absolutist, so-called democratic societies, the hierarchy of these two different logics of selection has perhaps been inverted.

---

374 In anticipation of my polemics (see below, Part III) against the descriptive viability of such widely accepted basic parameters as "national literatures", let me point out that there is one very prominent Spanish author of the age in question, Cervantes, to whose writings one could ascribe the above-characterized message as well. What I say in generalizing terms in this chapter only applies to the great playwrights of each nation (Shakespeare on the one hand; Lope de Vega, Calderón, and Tirso de Molina on the other).
375 As to the necessary differentiations of this very brief characterization of *Hamlet*, see once again the references given in n. 54, n. 59, and n. 76.
376 I am aware of the fact that I have demonstrated this feature mainly with respect to the Spanish plays; but as far as I am able to gather from research concerning Elizabethan theater, a characterization of the plays as given above will not provoke the request for further demonstration.

The Predilection for Tragedy

0.—When it comes to the specific poetological features that characterize European drama in the early modern age, few specialists would contest that the reception of Aristotle's *Poetics* constitutes the most important factor. It makes sense to link the second striking commonality—besides the "orientation toward the message"—of the European drama of that age, namely, the predilection for tragedy, to this process. As is well known, the paragraphs of the treatise dedicated to comedy are lost. One may doubt whether this is a serious problem. In the rare passages of the extant text in which the Stagirite mentions comedy, he does not hesitate to clearly convey that tragedy stands at the top of the hierarchy of all "mimetic" literature; next comes epic, which he describes as a sort of narrativized tragedy whose cathartic effect is comparatively minor due to the more mediated mode of presenting the action. And one may conclude from many short remarks of a more or less derogatory tenor, articulated in passing, that Aristotle's esteem for comedy is rather limited.

1.—Before returning to the specific question of the early modern predilection for tragedy in subsequent paragraphs of this chapter, I would like to discuss the broader question of how the generally accepted view of the early modern literary era as an age of Aristotelianism might be described within the framework here proposed, and of how such a description might affect or even alter the standard assessment of the renewed reception of the *Poetics*.

A major consideration that turns out to be of particular interest from the vantage point of the approach here submitted is the frequently forgotten or even unknown fact that the text of the *Poetics* was actually circulating in the net during the period in which it was not received in Western Europe; it was available, but was not extracted from the material at hand. The short story by Borges briefly mentioned above, *La busca de Averroes*, is not one of the author's many stories which could be characterized as only seemingly factographical.[377] It is indeed partly fictional, but the basic motif around which it revolves is authentic, and there is documentary evidence for it. In his famous commentary on Aristotle's works, Averroes (1126–1198) deals in a most lucid fashion with all of the Stagirite's writings—that is, with the exception of the *Poetics*, a tract which he indeed comments on, but in an uncharacteristically confused manner. One may extrapolate from the extremely scarce remarks concerning this text that Averroes did not have any notion of what drama is; they attest to the

---

[377] —as, for example, the wonderful story about a French author named Pierre Menard who is supposed to have rewritten the *Quijote*.

tacit assumption that the various rules established by Aristotle in his tract are meant as directions for writing "good" narrative, including narrative poetry. His incomprehension notwithstanding, Averroes transmitted the text of the *Poetics*.—The status of the tract as material that was actually circulating but was not made use of did not change with Wilhelm von Moerbecke's rendering of Aristotle's works into Latin (1278), which included the *Poetics*. This translation of the complete works of a man who was largely referred to as *philosophus*, meaning, the most outstanding representative of the discipline in human history so far, marked the apogee of the age of scholasticism. The non-reception of the *Poetics* during the medieval heyday of Aristotelianism is all the more astonishing as there was during that age a flourishing drama and theater scene in the countries concerned.

But these dramas clashed with what Aristotle describes as a well-wrought play. The comic drama of the time (*farces, facéties*) was, as is evidenced by its name,[378] an extremely short genre, mainly consisting of brief scenes without the structure of a *mythos* in the Aristotelian sense,[379] whereas "serious" drama—the "mimetic" rendering of portions of biblical history, the Fall and the Crucifixion being the most important topics—was likewise incompatible with the basic description of tragedy provided by Aristotle. Within a Christian framework, there is hope even after the worst calamities; the catastrophes of the actual world are superseded by the prospect of an unlimited happiness in the world beyond. And however one interprets the genitive case in Aristotle's central definition of the genre (*pathematon katharsis*), from a Christian perspective, pity (*eleos*) is not something that needs to be discharged or purified, and the "purgation" of an affect like fear (*phobos*)—which might indeed be a useful thing within a society of warriors, as was Greece in those times—was not a desirable goal in a world governed by an omnipotent God who rules over the human part of His creation not least by establishing "commandments" and by instituting a netherworld called "hell" where those who fearlessly transgress these rules will be punished in eternity.—As to the third genre of medieval drama, the morality play, it may suffice to say that its basic allegorism is hardly compatible with Aristotle's praise of the imitation (*mimesis*) of "real" human action (*pragmata*) not only as an anthropological constant, but also as the basis of drama, a remark with which he begins his tract.

---

378 See above, n. 60.
379 A *mythos* being characterized as having a beginning, a middle, and an end; see, in addition, *Poetics*, chap. 7, for the Stagirite's disparagement of any items so small (in this case: brief according to the standards of classical tragedy or comedy) as to provoke ridicule or laughter by a form that is all too deviant from normalcy.

This scenario was radically altered when a part of the net that had been cut off from Latin Europe for centuries suddenly became reconnected. As early as during the first decades of the sixteenth century, many translations of Greek tragedies into Latin were produced; some decades later, such translations became unnecessary thanks to the systematic study of Greek among the educated classes, spurred by the flow of classical Greek texts from Constantinople into major European cities.[380] Every cultured person was immediately conscious of

---

[380] It would be problematic to hold that there had been absolutely no net-bound connectivity between Byzantium and the West in the preceding period. But the collapse of the Western Roman Empire in the fifth century CE and the definitive religious schism that occurred at around the beginning of the second millennium had created conditions unfavorable to the circulation of cultural material. There was contact, not least mediated by the commercial activities of the Venetians. As to the material allowed to float in the cultural net, it is symptomatic that there was a Greek translation of the works of Aquinas, but that the translator, Demetrios Kydones (1324–1398), was exiled to Crete for having tried to make such subversive material generally available. The circulation of literary texts is not submitted to such strict scrutiny as texts touching upon religious dogma. But in this regard, too, the quantity of material allowed to float and to be extracted from the net was remarkably reduced. Petrarchism, for example, made it to Cyprus, but not, as far as I know, to Byzantium. And as to the question of why the Greek tragedies were received in the West only after the Fall of Constantinople (even though it would have been possible, with a certain but not all too great effort, to access them previously), there is a point to be taken into consideration which I already referred to above (pp. 89–92): certain transformations occurring in Western Christian theology from the end of the thirteenth century onward, and massively present since the end of the fourteenth century, paved the way for the renewed extraction of the Greek tragedies from the net which occurred in Western literatures from the fifteenth century onward. This situation may also account for well-known anecdotal episodes of previous Western intellectual history, such as Petrarch's attempts at learning Greek from Barlaam di Seminara, a Byzantine scholar (although born in Italy), which the perhaps first early modern literary author discontinued after a while.—There is a highly instructive document from which one may extrapolate what the state of classical learning was in the generation immediately following Petrarch, but still before the fall of Byzantium. Leonardo Bruni's *Ad Petrum Paulum Histrum Dialogus* (written around 1400, staging a fictitious dialogue between leading Florentine intellectuals of the age, including Coluccio Salutati, which is said to have taken place around 1390) gives expression to the fact that these people, in contrast to Petrarch, had continued their studies and were able to read Greek; they say that they admire the famous Greek authors, philosophical as well as literary—a fact that leads many modern scholars of intellectual history to postulate that humanism and the Renaissance set in as early as in that age and that the Fall of Constantinople was without greater importance. However, Bruni's dialogue makes explicit that, while the generation in question knew the names of the great Greek authors as well as the titles of their works, the actual texts were not available to them, a state of affairs they lament in great detail. This situation also applies with regard to Aristotle's writings: they were well known, but only in translation, and the proto-humanists conducting the dialogue suspect these translations to have distorted the original, without having access to the textual documentation that would allow them to substantiate this suspicion. To put it succinctly: the Christian West was intellectually very well

the superiority of these dramas over their contemporary counterparts in the West, including highly sophisticated, but formally somewhat uneven ones such as *La Celestina* (1499/1504).

The rapid and enthusiastic reception of the original Greek dramatic works led to the nearly immediate elevation of Aristotle's *Poetics* from a quasi-unknown treatise to a canonical text. From an item merely floating in the net, it became once again an item that was actually extracted. The first humanist translation was produced by Giorgio Valla as early as in 1498. In the year 1536, another translation was produced by Alessandro de' Pazzi, and starting with Francesco Robertello's and Bernardo Segni's famous translations cum commentary (1548, 1549), a Europe-wide discussion of Aristotle's text took place which initiated a new era of European dramatic production.

The "fate" of Aristotle's tract seems to provide a good illustration of the hypothesis that the withdrawal of material from the net is mainly driven by demand. This demand may be direct or, as is the case here, indirect. Here, it is motivated by the impetus to "better" understand material that had been cut off from the "Western" part of the net for a very long period, but which was received anew as soon as it became available; the enthusiastic attitude with which it was received may be explained by the fact that the "Occident" was largely based on concepts stemming from the cultural tradition to which these dramas belonged. One would have to add that the second pillar on which European culture is based, the Christian dogma—with which, as has been noted, the concept of the tragic is hardly compatible—became substantially weakened exactly at that moment in time, on the one hand because of the religious schisms raging in the West, on the other hand on behalf of the discovery of the New World.

2.—There is an interesting detail to be mentioned with respect to this vogue of literary Aristotelianism. As noted above, the concept of *katharsis* (an intricate one, judging by the scholarly discussions having taken place up to the present[381]), and especially the notion of a total or partial "reduction", follow-

---

prepared when the ships from Constantinople came ashore some fifty years later; but without this event, the intellectual evolution of Europe might have looked different from what it actually looks like (*Ad Petrum Paulum Histrum Dialogus*, in: *Prosatori latini del Quattrocento*, Eugenio Garin [ed.], vol. 13, Milan and Naples 1952, pp. 44–99; see esp. pp. 54–56 ["Qui libri utinam nunc extarent [...]!"/ "if only those books (containing the writings of the Stoics, Academics, Peripatetics, Epicureans, etc.) still existed [...]!" (p. 54)]).

381 See my essay "Verschwiegene Illusion. Zum Tragödiensatz der Aristotelischen *Poetik*" (*Poetica* vol. 38/2006, pp. 1–30), in which I briefly summarize the scholarly discussion up to the current point in time.

ing upon arousal, of *eleos* and *phobos*, which is in Aristotle's view the main goal (*ergon*) of tragedy and the source from which spectators derive their pleasure (*hedone*), is an item that is difficult to harmonize—if possible at all—with basic tenets of the Christian dogma regarding behavior or moral philosophy.[382] The "solution" to the problem devised by the early theoreticians was a quite elementary one. At the same time, their approach seems to be representative of the way in which the "extraction" of cultural material from the net actually operates in many cases: the material (in this case: Aristotle's text) is decomposed into its different topical parts; parts considered useful were adopted, while parts considered "problematic" or "uninteresting" were *not* extracted from the net. In Gian Giorgio Trissino's famous preface (1514) to his *Sofonisba*, which may be considered the first tragedy ever written in the early modern West according to Aristotle's basic concepts, the entire complex of *katharsis* is not even mentioned. *Hedone*—literally, intense pleasure, bodily or otherwise—is rendered as *diletto* (delight); in addition, Trissino postulates that viewing the piece entails some *utilitate* for the spectators, in the sense of a moral lesson that can be drawn from it.[383] It need not be stressed that these two functions ascribed to the viewing of tragedies derive from descriptions of literary texts primarily by Horace, but also in part by Donatus and Diomedes, that is, from a corpus always widely available in the Christian West, in large part because it was readily adaptable to Christian doctrine, thanks to the emphasis on moralizing not present in Aristotle. Later stages of reception, up to Gotthold Ephraim Lessing's eighteenth-century discussion of the *Poetics*, foreground the *arousal* of pity (and of fear), that is, of emotions that have their place within Christian morality, while downplaying the emphasis on evacuating these affects by systematically reading the genitive in question as referring to a "cleansing" not *from*, but *of* pity, meaning: to a process of morally "refining" the emotion of pity. On this reading, it may even be asserted that the affects to be evacuated are other ones than pity and fear (e.g., envy, vanity, etc.), thus blurring the abyss which separates *eleos* from *agape* (*caritas*).

From my theoretical perspective, the most intriguing point to be observed in the entire scenario is the general attitude with which early modern theoreticians, starting with Trissino, make use of the *Poetics*. They treat the text in a way that allows it to be compared with a compound material in the literal sense, from which they take the parts considered useful or valuable while leaving all the "rest" without further consideration. The "reconstruction" of what the author,

---

[382] See above, p. 191.
[383] I am quoting from Gian Giorgio Trissino, *La Sofonisba*, Franco Paglierani (ed.), Bologna 1884, pp. 2 f.

Aristotle, might "really" have meant when giving his description of tragedy the shape that has come down to us is a very modern, a philological question, a problem that became widespread only with the rise of historical thinking in the late eighteenth century. Although all of us are familiar with the history of our discipline, philology, we frequently neglect this point, assuming the search for the historically "authentic" meaning of a text to be an uncontroversial goal. Meanwhile, the well-known fact that the text of the *Poetics* was most probably not written down by Aristotle himself, but rather by his pupils, and the constraints this fact imposes on attempts to reconstruct what the Stagirite "really" intended to convey, should serve as an invitation to look less condescendingly at the manner in which early modern theoreticians dealt with the *Poetics*.

Dismantling, disassembling texts or works floating in the net, appropriating parts of them, reassembling these parts, and combining them with different, "exogenous" material in order to construct a new text meeting the needs and demands of the contexts in which it is created—this seems to be the general logic of dealing with pre-existent material. Seen from this perspective, the "historical" approach—searching to reconstruct the text's "original" and "authentic" meaning—would be the exceptional case. Considered from a more abstract perspective, one may even say that there is no substantive specificity involved in such an approach; it is the expression of the wants and needs of the age in which it emerged, of Romanticism and its search for origins and "roots", for ordering paradigms to be found in history and tradition after the near suspension of the old paradigm of a God-given order which occurred in the Age of Enlightenment.

3.—I would now like to present some remarks on the more specific point at issue in this chapter, namely the predilection of the early modern age for tragedy, which in fact seems to have emerged independently from or at least parallel to the rediscovery of the Greek dramatic texts as well as the reception of the *Poetics*.[384] That tragedy should have captured the European imagination at this time is all the more astonishing since the concept of definitive failure seems squarely at odds with Christian doctrine, at least as far as Catholicism is con-

---

[384] My argument is linked to the above-discussed fact that Aristotle's text was accessible in the net before the age of humanism; it became extracted anew, however, only at a time when there emerged a "new" demand for tragedies. Had this demand not existed, the classical tragedies could well have been reconnected to the Western European part of the cultural net without having been reactivated, quite as this had happened to Aristotle's tract in the period from the rendering by Averroes to Giorgio Valla's translation. Need I mention that very many texts other than the classical tragedies brought by the Constantinopolitan scholars to Italy—texts from the period we nowadays call "Byzantine"—were *not* extracted in the age I am dealing with, but only in later times, namely in the age of historical thinking and modern philology?

cerned. Spain, and other Catholic countries, did in fact reject the tragic model. As already mentioned, Spaniards of the time characterized "mimetic" drama of any profile as *comedia*, meaning there is always the prospect of a happy ending, even if this ending takes place beyond the temporal bounds of the actual plot. To those whose sins are not too pernicious,[385] authors—and often fictional antagonists, too—accord a moment in which to repent and pray for forgiveness before receiving "just" earthly punishment, i.e., violent death. Thus, Spain too had "tragedy", though in a limited sense confined to the human world. In other words, tragedy existed on the Iberian peninsula as a literary genre, yet without endorsing the worldview on which the model was originally based.—As for contemporary Protestant cultures, the obstacles to assimilating the tragic model may have been less significant. One may even identify the assignment of a place amongst the *massa damnata* with what the ancients called negative fate, although this entails the conceptually problematic point that the mass of those who will go to hell is supposed to be huge while tragic fate is something quite exceptional according to the classical view.[386]—To summarize this first point: Europeans of the early modern age, be they Catholics or Protestants, were intelligent enough to manage the reconciliation of orthodox Christian views with the fascinating new genre of tragedy rediscovered after the Ottoman conquest of Constantinople. One may imagine how strange these reconciliations of Christian dogma and Greek tragedy might have appeared to those who first developed and theorized the genre (Aeschylus, Euripides, Sophocles, and Aristotle) had they had the chance to read them.

The truly astonishing factor in the flourishing of tragedy in early modern times thus concerns yet another point: how can one explain the prominence of tragedy in an age that developed the political model of absolutism? Absolutism is,

---

385 As, for instance, in the case of Tirso de Molina's Don Juan as presented in *El burlador de Sevilla* (1612/1625).

386 I allow myself the following speculation: Aristotle gives expression to the idea that a total lack of poetic justice (the "good" punished, the "evil" triumphant) is not suited for well-conceived literary texts because such plots are not, as he puts it, *philanthropon* (*Poetics*, chap. 13); they convey the view that this world is not a very pleasant place for humans. It would be congruent with this position to assume that Aristotle would have subscribed to the above statement (and there is, at any rate, the evidence of the texts; no classical tragedy is mimetic in the sense of nineteenth-century realism; they present exceptional constellations in all cases). My further speculation is that a radically pessimistic worldview—that of life as such as doomed to failure—solicits compensatory discourses; it solicits hope, which means in premodern times: religion, soteriology. The Stagirite, the first rationalist in documented intellectual history, did not like such features. He was an entirely worldly thinker.

as Carl Schmitt argued,[387] the first and perhaps most important instance of what the theoretician calls the "political", which he sees as characterized by a secularization of theological concepts. According to Schmitt's observations, the absolute monarch is a sort of worldly Mono-Theos. He does not depend on anyone. He is not bound by any rule or law. His position is defined by, or rather in need of assertion by means of acts of "sovereignty", i.e., acts which transgress all legal and moral norms and limits that subjects must respect. He is characterized by the fact that he is entitled to act on a merely voluntary basis. He is not responsible to anyone. As soon as he has been invested with royal dignity by God, he is no longer contingent upon anything but his own will.

How is one to harmonize such a political theory with tragedy, which is essentially about the misfortunes and fall of great men, and about how their fates are contingent upon the vagaries of fortune? Even within the pattern of tragedies with an irenic ending, there are in all cases many characters of high, aristocratic standing who die a violent death; the "happy" ending is restricted to the central personage(s). The entire scenario provokes the question of why it should have been precisely these conceptual and literary configurations that were selected for extraction from the cultural net under the political conditions of early modern Europe.

4.– One may consider some tragedies that might help to devise a possible answer to that very question. The most prominent amongst them would certainly be Pierre Corneille's *Le Cid* (1636). On behalf of the norms of honor, the eponymous hero is obliged to take revenge for an insult perpetrated against his father, who is too old to fight. The ensuing dilemma places the Cid—who is in love—between two irreconcilable demands: he cannot neglect to avenge his family's honor, for to do so would dishonor him, and as a dishonored knight he could never contract a marriage with an honorable woman; but unfortunately, the offender is the father of Chimène, the young woman whom the Cid loves and who reciprocates his feelings. The knight chooses vengeance. This, in turn, results in a dilemma for Chimène: she would dishonor herself by accepting the courtship of the man who killed her father; and as a dishonored maiden, she would not be a fit wife for a hero like the Cid. After a series of additional actions that are of no import here, the political theory of absolutism is "enacted" on stage, so to speak: the monarch suspends all moral rules and

---

[387] *Political Theology: Four Chapters on the Concept of Sovereignty*, George Schwab (tr.), Chicago, IL 1985.

societal norms, arranging a short supplementary episode[388] which will make it possible for Chimène to marry the man who killed her father—a possibility she is obliged to seize, since it was created by the sovereign himself, but which she also seizes independently of this obligation, on her own volition. The piece ends with the prospect of a future of fairytale-like happiness. In being based on the rationale that the monarch is entitled to transgress all rules, absolutism—that is the play's message—is an apt means to resolve all conflicts of social life which at first sight seem to be unresolvable.

There are several further plays which succeed in rendering the theory of absolutism and the pattern of tragedy compatible. The price these plays have to pay for this achievement is that they would be, according to Aristotle's categorization, "second-rate tragedy" (*deutera tragoedia*) only—this is the Stagirite's judgment of plays revolving around *pathos*, that is suffering, which conclude with a happy ending. Such plays, he remarks in a quite condescending manner, are popular amongst the uneducated because they match their wishful thinking concerning reality.[389]—It is well known that Corneille was aware of the problems attendant on a fairytale-like ending. He attempted to resolve them by refraining from displaying on stage the actual festive event, which would consist of a somewhat startling ceremony, uniting a woman in marriage with the man who killed her father. Instead, the Cid is called upon once again to take arms against the Moors. The marriage is thus postponed until his return. The device used to harmonize the political message with the norms of *bienséance* is ingeniously conceived. Since the play refers to a historical person whose biography, including his marriage to a woman named Ximena, is known to the spectators, there is no uncertainty implied as regards the happy ending—if not of the play, than of the story underlying it.

5.—But how to assess, in this context, a drama such as *Hamlet* or *Phèdre*?—that is, a piece about a king who is killed by his own brother, a murder in which his wife is involved at least as an accomplice, and the additional consequence of which is that his only son will die a premature death when he tries to take revenge? Or, in the case of the French drama: what is the "absolutist propaganda" contained in a play in which a king has his eldest son and heir

---

[388] By fighting the "Moors", the Cid has to prove that he is a most valiant warrior and, as such, indispensable for the future of the realm. In addition, it is conveyed that the imminent battle is to be seen as a divine ordeal.

[389] Because of its status as an esoterically intended text, the *Poetics* is not always free from internal contradictions; the most important one may be the gap between the argument summarized above (chap. 13) and the reference to the two *Iphigeneia* plays as paradigms of a well-conceived plot (chap. 17).

killed in a most cruel way because he blindly believes the false accusations brought forward by a servant named Œnone who is the governess of his actual wife, the son's stepmother, who in turn has fallen in love with the young man? And what about the numerous German *Trauerspiele* in which kings and queens lose their position from one moment to the next and are shown on stage subjected to cruel forms of torture before actually being killed? Why did the kings of that age take delight in seeing their dramatic analogues not as absolute at all, but rather as inescapably subject to blind fate and to the pitfalls of *hamartia*, that is, limited wrongdoing entailing terrible, devastating consequences?

The most prominent answer to this question was provided by Walter Benjamin in his book on the *Trauerspiel*, and his position has been reiterated again and again in the last decades, by outstanding scholars like Louis Marin[390] as well as by a huge number of junior specialists, to the extent that it may appear audacious to problematize what has become a nearly universal view. Benjamin's answer, which is, indeed, ingenious, considers tragedy as a setting in which self-reflection on the part of the absolute monarch is able to take place. By showing the kings as subject to fate, such plays would help, on the one hand, to strengthen the morale of the monarchs for the (inevitable) cases when "real" fate strikes them. And, as an additional feature, it would help them to evade the danger of falling prey to the ideology which is meant to subjugate the subjects: in order to perform successfully as an absolute monarch, a king must always be conscious of his being subject to Fortune. It is only under this condition that he will be able to counter her evil blows when she decides to strike, and to grasp the opportunity to enforce his will over hers when there is a propitious moment to do so.[391] This said, the exposition of the stark fact that all humans, including monarchs, are finally dependent on the whims of blind fate is supposed to create the overall atmosphere of *Trauer* (melancholy) characterizing the plays in question.

There is one problem, however, with this standard explanation of the interplay between absolutism and tragedy. Benjamin's argument would be entirely convincing were it the case that the tragedy of the period in question consisted in courtly theater only. Then one could legitimately interpret it along the lines familiar to modernity proper, i.e., as a device for self-reflection mediated by aesthetic distancing.

---

390 See, e.g., *Le Portrait du Roi*, Paris 1981.
391 The ideal royal spectator of a *Trauerspiel*, according to Benjamin, would thus be a monarch who views the performance on stage while bearing in mind the lesson conveyed by Machiavelli's *Príncipe* (1513/1532).

But even in the most hierarchical cultural community of that age, the situation was quite a different one. There is, of course, courtly theater, and it may be that the mental processes suggested by Benjamin and described in a more transparent fashion by Marin occurred when a play was staged at Versailles, at the Palace of Zarzuela in Madrid, or at St. James's Palace. But even in France, there were, in addition to the audience of *la cour*, the recipients labeled *la ville* in Erich Auerbach's seminal essay on French classical drama;[392] and in order to be successful, the authors had to meet the demands of both of their audiences. *La ville* refers, by metonymy, to the third estate, to those excluded from the sphere of power by absolutism, but only to its educated strata. In England and Spain, the theater audience comprised the lower strata of the population as well; these spectators, who were called "groundlings" because they could not afford a ticket entitling them to a seat, were in most cases illiterate.

6.—So, *rebus sic stantibus*, in early modern times, the view that mighty kings are subject to blind fate is conveyed not only to the kings themselves, or to potential kings, but to the "masses" also. At first sight, one might think of qualifying tragedy as subversive against such a backdrop—which would certainly provoke applause from the many for whom the link between literature and ideological subversion is a quasi-ontological one. However, I would like to propose another line of thinking which is in accordance with my assumption that early modern drama is the first historical instance of what we now call mass media.

Sigmund Freud argues in his essay "Der Dichter und das Phantasieren" ("The Relation of the Poet to Day-Dreaming")[393] that the main function of consuming fiction is fantasmatic compensation. Literature gives us what the real world will always deny us; the artistic or aesthetic sophistication of a piece of literature mainly has the function of helping cultured recipients repress the insight that it is such a trivial desire which makes them read books or view plays, a "help" the uncultured do not need because they do not consider their drives to be shameful—this is the reason why they can do without the "veil" of aestheticization.

Freud illustrates his theory of fictional texts as a device for the compensation of real-world frustration by referring mainly to love literature. But the Freudian concept of drives is all-encompassing. Accordingly, one might speculate that, within the frame of tragedy, it is primarily aggression[394] that is fantasmatically

---

[392] See, once again, the essay bearing this title ("*La cour et la ville*").
[393] See the reference above, n. 56.
[394] Need I mention that almost every tragedy also allows for a fantasmatic gratification of the recipients' libidinous desires? Extramarital and strictly forbidden, incestuous sexuality is in many cases (and in some in a hardly veiled fashion) at the center of the plot.

released for the duration of the performance. All those subject to the monarch's absolute power in real life—such as courtiers, the bourgeois, and humble people—were accorded the pleasure of witnessing, at least for the duration of the play, their oppressor, the king, at the mercy of the same fate as themselves. And they surely may have taken a subconscious delight in seeing how the high status of kings and princes did not only fail to protect them from the vagaries of fate, but caused even greater anguish than that faced by ordinary humans in proportion as the royal personages had more to lose.

Early modern tragedy as mass medium may have helped to channel and thus to tame the discontent experienced by the subjects of the political system of absolutism. From such a perspective, it might have served as a means of stabilizing the political and societal order. It may be considered as providing momentary relief from the dichotomization of monarch and subjects. Within tragedies, the monarch is presented on stage as nothing but a subject, too. All humans have to suffer on behalf of Fortune's caprices and, what is more, this suffering is all the more intense when the previous situation was a privileged one. After having viewed a tragedy, the "common man" was able to return home and even feel happy that his domestic misery was far less than what the king had to suffer in the last act of the play.[395]—The aesthetic fascination emanating from the literary treasures of classical tragedy committed to a renewed circulation in the net after the violent end of the isolation of the Byzantine sub-net was thus, according to me, supplemented by a strong demand originating in the contemporary political system. The interplay between renewed availability and new functionality may even explain the astonishing fact of the extraction of a genre from the net whose world-modeling parameters were incongruent with the still prevailing "official" world-model of early modern times, Christianity.

Since I refer to Freud's theory of the function of literary fiction at various times in this book, I should like to make a remark—not directly pertinent to my basic line of argument— regarding the critique of Freud's literary aesthetics which is the basis for the condescending attitude with which it is typically treated in literary scholarship, namely, Freud's "neglect", or rather his relative devaluing, of what makes a fiction a work of art proper, the formal dimension. Freud is, indeed, not a Kantian in matters of art. As has been said, he considers the formal sophistication of canonical texts as a sort of enticement ("Vor-Lust") for

---

[395] One might speculate that, at least in Europe, this former function of tragedy is nowadays served by the tabloid press, which presents, on a nearly daily basis, sensationalist stories dealing with the "fall of the mighty" of our days (in most cases, "celebrities").

the cultured reader, luring him into what he otherwise would never allow himself: indulgence in the fantasmatic gratification of his repressed aggressive and libidinous drives.

But I would not see it as a major problem to integrate a view valorizing the formal features of literary works as a primary rather than a subsidiary dimension into a theory in line with Freud's essay. The gratification emanating from a recipient's "penetration" of the formal rationale of a specific literary text would specifically consist in the gratification of his intellectual narcissism. It would nurture the recipient's illusion that, thanks to the capacities of his mind, he is able to "penetrate" the "world", to understand what keeps it going, and to grasp its formal principles of organization. This illusion would end as soon as the recipient in question leaves the fictional world and returns to the world proper, namely, reality, which will be hardly less impenetrable than before reading the text (or viewing the performance) in question. But for the duration of the reading or viewing, of the "immersion" in the world of fiction, he may have believed what he felt. In that sense, highly refined literary texts, even avant-garde texts, read from the perspective of recipients inclined to views derived from Kantian aesthetics, would also have a compensatory dimension: they are able to give us what all our intellectual endeavors directed at the "real" world will never be able to yield, the conviction that we fully "understand" it, that we see through its mechanisms and are perhaps capable of creating, on behalf of the capacities of our mind, another such world, maybe even a better one.

Devices of Enticement: Love, Horror, and Marvel

0.—It is a commonplace that literature as such—narrative, poetry, and drama—mainly revolves around the topic of love. This formula, when considered from a distance, does not give expression to anything other than the observation that literature is about what most preoccupies humans. Considered from a scientific perspective, our task is to spread our genes. In order to veil the consequences of the act—that is, the hard labor going along with the raising of one's offspring, as well as the possibility of quite poor results—nature has linked pleasurable feelings to the performance of that task, and human narcissism has added the concept of "love" and "emotions" in order to repress the consciousness that sexual activities are rather animalistic practices which might remind us of our proximity to the *fauna* at large.

1.—What is striking in early modern drama is thus not the fact that love is an important theme; it is rather its pervasive presence and, perhaps even more importantly, the recourse to explicit obscenity.[396] The striking character of this observation applies to serious drama only; comedy as a genre with strong historical affiliations to the practices of the carnival is a different case and can only be linked to my observations by taking this carnivalesque dimension into account.

I allow myself to immediately propose an answer to the question—that is: why was the register of love, sexuality, and obscenity so frequently extracted from the material circulating in the net, and why was it associated not only with comic, but also to a large extent with serious drama?—by examining what is perhaps the most obscene "serious" drama of the age, a text that had an enormous resonance and was, indeed, the most successful European drama of the sixteenth century.[397] It was the formal restrictions imposed on dramatic production by neo-Aristotelianism, to which it did not conform, that brought the reception history of *La Celestina* to an (undeserved) end. Contemporary readers willing to receive a drama no longer belonging to the canon will not have the slightest difficulty in understanding why educated Europeans admired this piece more than any other work of the period.

The plot deals with two youths of noble origin living in a city in southern Spain who come into contact with each other by chance; Calisto's falcon has escaped from him and come to rest in the garden of the home of Melibea's parents. Calisto falls in love with Melibea. After a short interval, she gives in to his desires. They spend a number of ecstatic nights together in Melibea's garden. On one occasion, however, Calisto hears a noise from outside the garden; he believes that his servants, who are waiting for him, are being attacked. Hastily, he climbs over the garden wall, takes a false step, falls to the ground, and is smashed to death. On the next day, Melibea commits suicide by jumping from the tower of her parents' house. The play ends with a long monologue pronounced by Pleberio, Melibea's father, who accuses the "world" (*mundo*) of being a site of permanent suffering without any compensation, not even that of a world beyond the grave, which he does not believe to exist.

As to its serious content, one could portray the text—leaving the plot as such aside for the time being[398]—as consisting of two components. On the one hand,

---

396 I insist on the epithet. From a Freudian standpoint, even the thematization of Platonic love is nothing but the slightly veiled invitation to have our desires or drives fantasmatically gratified. But here it is a matter of the degree of explicitness. In the case I will deal with in the following paragraph, as well as in many other cases one could mention, there is nearly no sublimation when it comes to thematizing bodily pleasures.
397 See, regarding this point, the study by Kilian (*"Escrituras andantes"*), as well as my essay on the *Celestina* (n. 43).
398 I will come back to the play in a subsequent chapter (pp. 293 f.).

it is a sort of compendium of proto-humanistic didactics. Large portions of the text are a sort of *cento* of quotes taken from crucial sentences to be found in prominent works of moral philosophy (Seneca, Augustine, Petrarch; in the latter case mainly from *De remediis utriusque fortunae* [1354–1367]). This component is not very entertaining; it is a matter of classical learning and philosophical reflection.—As to the complex of bad luck underlying the ending of the text, it may be considered as a radicalization of the classical tragic model.— The plot's abstract frame is based on three acts of disassembling material floating in the net: by separating the *phobos*- and *eleos*-provoking outcome from the mythical horizon to which it is linked in the original Greek and Roman tragedies, tragic failure is translated into the dimension of present-day, "common" life. By means of the explicit rejection of the idea of a spiritual life continuing beyond death, the conceptualization of the (physical) world as a *lacrimarum vallis*[399] is detached from the consolatory dimension linked to it within the (Christian) religious tradition. A third act of disassembly, evidenced in the play by way of Pleberio's final monologue, consists in the separation of the discourses of pagan moral philosophy from the palliative dimension which is, according to these discourses' claims, the "fruit" to be collected from reflecting on life's vanity. The daring step thus taken may legitimately be considered an unconscious anticipation of modern thinking: human life as such may be doomed to failure, and there may be neither an otherworldly compensation nor a means of mentally alleviating this fact. What is absent in this drama, which was written and received around the year 1500, is the compensatory horizon created by modernity proper in order to render such a gloomy conceptualization bearable: the discourse of endless "progress" which promises to provide for happiness on earth, if not in the present, then in a future to whose construction we are invited to contribute.

These discursive elements out of which the *Celestina* is assembled are enriched, or made palatable, by recourse to a discursive register of obscenity familiar from contemporary farces and narrative texts conveying patterns of the carnivalesque.[400] It is not possible here to provide examples; but the sentences emanating from the mouths of the two noble youths, the female as well as the male, are at times shocking even by present-day standards. The more or

---

399 This formula, a quote from Ps 84:7, is used in the Latin original in the final monologue pronounced by Pleberio when he gives expression to his conviction that there is no afterlife in the Christian sense.
400 Besides the undocumented popular oral tradition, one might mention the tradition of the Boccaccian novella and, with respect to Spanish texts in particular, the *Arcipreste de Hita* and the *Arcipreste de Talavera*.

less veiled appeal to the spectators' extreme sexual fantasies stands in somewhat sharp contrast to the internal plausibility of the plot configuration (where might a fifteenth-century Spanish noble girl of the age of fourteen or fifteen have acquired all these highly obscene words and concepts?) as well as to the significant dose of philosophical erudition and reflection to which the spectators are subjected. Given the enormous success of the play in all European countries referred to above, it seems that the anonymous author did find the right way to propagate his somewhat dire ideas on the futility of philosophical learning and on life as deprived of any sense whatsoever.

2.—Need I mention that horror was another device for effecting enticement in early modern drama and thus for rendering plays based on more serious ideas extracted from the net more palatable? With regard to the present-day critique of cruel practices as components of visual fiction, one should perhaps mention, without going into the details, that the representation of horrific cruelties on stage, or having them recounted in a most explicit and detailed manner, was a ubiquitous phenomenon in that age. In particular, Spanish, German, and Dutch theater of the time excelled in this regard. As an example, I should like to highlight the case of a Christian queen slowly torn to pieces and then, still alive, burnt on the pyre because she refuses to renounce her faith and become the wife of an "infidel" (Gryphius, *Catharina von Georgien* [1657]).[401] The primary context of such a motif in the play is evident, and it is telling with regard to many of the atrocities shown on the Spanish and the German stages of that age. The fascination with horror is exploited with a view to religious propaganda, or, to put it in terms of rhetoric, the "bitter pill" of religious didacticism is made easier to swallow by coating it with "sweet horror". In an age of religious division, the lesson of the moral depravity of the heretics (or, in the case mentioned, of non-Christians) was brought to the believers' consciousness by showing or telling of their evil deeds on stage, which, one must add, were not mere invention. Identification with the martyrs who were decapitated, boiled, torn to pieces, etc., as well as relief (*katharsis*) after the end of the performance, were major devices of religious propaganda. And the extremely drastic Protes-

---

[401] It is evident that the martyrdom of Queen Catherine of Georgia, who is an authentic figure (1565–1624) and who indeed died as a captive of the Persian Shah, could not be represented onstage; it is presented by way of a narration which indulges in all the details imaginable concerning the horrors of Catherine's torture.—As a footnote to the general theoretical frame of this book, I should perhaps mention that the story of the violent death of a Christian queen in Central Asia floated to the West almost immediately after Catherine's demise, became narrativized in France (Claude Malingre, *Histoires tragiques de nostre temps* [1641]), and then floated on to the remote eastern German province of Silesia, where Gryphius worked in the public service.

tant martyr plays—mostly, as in the case mentioned, school plays, that is, instruments of pedagogy for the education of grammar school boys—were probably meant to incline the audience to agree to the somewhat harsh dogma of predestination in its traditional variant:[402] only those prepared to undergo pains as described above may perhaps legitimately pretend to have deserved a seat in paradise. All others must resign themselves to accept what God has decided concerning their eternal fate.

Profane plays of the time also frequently have recourse to this variant of enticement, albeit with differing levels of explicitness. The last scene of Shakespeare's *Hamlet* is as paradigmatic of the contemporary English stage as the *récit de Théramène* from Racine's *Phèdre* is of the French theater of the time. A half dozen kings, queens, and princes killed on stage in the first case; in the other, the recounting, by an eyewitness, of the event of an innocent young prince torn to pieces by his horse, who is trying to escape from a sea monster—these two sequences are in a way indicative, in their similarities of plot and their differences of presentation, of a largely egalitarian popular theater culture in Britain and, on the other hand, of a theater linked to the refined taste and the ideal of sublimation practiced by *la cour* in France.—From the Freudian perspective presented above, there is little left to comment on in these and comparable pieces,[403] especially the explicitly religious ones.[404] They appeal, under the disguise of a dramatized catechism, to the audience's aggressive drives.[405]

3.—Present-day "enlightened" readers have a tendency to consider the device of marvel as a feature that is emblematic of the historical period in question, in the sense that it renders palpable the distance in time and mentality between the world of these plays and their own. Consequently, modern stagings of *Hamlet*, at least in Germany, refrain from having the ghost appear on stage; and neither Freud, who "forgot" how much the standard solution to the oedi-

---

[402] Present-day continental, especially German Lutheranism is, as regards the theology of grace, closer to Origen and his *theologoumenon*, in former times considered heretic, of an *apokatastasis panton* than it is to the teachings of the man still invoked by the denomination's name.

[403] I shall supplement my above remarks in a short sub-chapter of Part III dedicated to the Dutch drama of the time (pp. 223–226).

[404] As to my reading of the cruelties depicted in English and French plays like those mentioned above, see, once again, my discussion of Walter Benjamin's and Louis Marin's respective hypotheses (pp. 198 ff.)

[405] In the case of the explicitly religious plays, there is also always a dimension of explicit religious propaganda. In Gryphius's *Catharina von Georgien*, the soul of Catherine appears to her torturer after her death and announces that his evil deeds will not remain without punishment.

pal situation suggested by him owes to a reception of Calderón's *La vida es sueño* (stripped of its Christian implications, of course),[406] nor his disciples refrain from expressing their astonishment at one of Calderón's most "magical" plays, *La devoción de la cruz* (1628/1633).[407] Indeed, in this play, as well as in similar ones such as *El mágico prodigioso* (1637), spectators may watch the Devil appear in person on stage; they witness beautiful young ladies revealing themselves to be nothing but skeletons dressed up with flesh by the powers of evil in order to pervert decent young men; they see a sorcerer at work who is able to resurrect corpses (or, as is revealed later on, to make people, and not only naïve ones, believe that he is able to effect such miracles), etc.

Leaving aside the historical index of these marvelous incidents, one might admit that plays like the ones just mentioned do not do anything different from what present-day visual fantasy fiction does. Suggesting to viewers that there is something real or possibly real that transcends what regular, everyday sense perception conveys to us (e.g., that "the aliens are already amongst us") seems to be a transhistorically effective device for producing enticement. In both of the early modern cases mentioned above, it is evident that the device is mobilized in order to incline spectators to engage with problems that are neither exciting nor pleasant: the problematic character of so-called "bonds" of blood in the case of *Hamlet*; the problematic character of all this-worldly success and achievement in the case of the *Mágico* play.

The most convincing explanation for the extraction of such archaic fantasies from the net-bound material circulating in the early modern period, in order to then attach them—in a process of assembly—to serious material, may be provided by what Tzvetan Todorov proposed with respect to the Romantic gen-

---

406 —a negligence which might be related to a weak point of Freud's cultural theory. In Calderón, there is a transcendental compensation for the act of total sublimation (refraining from killing the father and waiting for power to be transmitted by the father to the son; refraining from physical appropriation of the mother-imago and transferring the sexual desire to another woman). In Freud, the only and rather shallow promise given to humans who are ready to repress their drives consists in that sublimation guarantees some decades of life under the imperative of constant self-control, that is, in a state of permanent frustration. Is the "prison" of society more comfortable than the prison one has to go to in case one does kill one's father and sleep with one's mother?
407 See Otto Rank, *Das Inzest-Motiv in Dichtung und Sage*. Grundzüge einer Psychologie des dichterischen Schaffens, 2nd ed., Leipzig and Vienna 1926, chap. 20, esp. pp. 550–554. In the years of the book's first print (1912), Rank was a close collaborator of Freud. Let me remind readers that Calderón was one of the most frequently staged playwrights in nineteenth-century German-language theaters, the most important of these being the Viennese *Burgtheater*.

re of the fantastic, known as the *conte fantastique*.[408] Todorov concerns himself with the question of how to explain the emergence of the genre and the re-emergence of a connected archaic conceptual pattern in an era that claimed to be thoroughly enlightened. It may be sensible to assume an analogous explanation for the period under scrutiny here as well.

The seventeenth century is, of course, not as yet an "enlightened" age. But starting in the epochal year of 1492, the rise of modern science had initiated the massive process of the "disenchantment" of the world. For an ever-growing part of the population, especially for those living in big cities—that is, for those targeted by early modern drama as mass media—daily realities, in the sense of real-life experiences, were not much more "miraculous" than for present-day inhabitants of Western cities. To return to Todorov's argument: the belief that there might be a "real" reality hidden behind the surface phenomena, an assumption rooted in our species' minds for hundreds of generations, still exists in the modern world, although it is more and more repressed and relegated to the unthematizable ("superstitions"). Literary fictions, as texts that refer to reality but are not bound to reproduce it, make use of this constellation. They have recourse to structures gratifying the desire for what got lost in the processes of modernization. The gratification of desires of the psyche that began to be less and less satisfied in early modern times might, as noted above, have made recipients ready to listen to the rather disillusioning messages of the texts in question.

4.—It is a symptom of a deep cultural change that serious literature of our time can no longer extract material like that mentioned in this chapter from the net in order to assemble plots, dramatic or narrative, that thematize persistent moral or epistemological problems which recipients experience in their own lives. In the present, such devices of attraction have become an index of the trivial status of the texts in question. The penetration of the results of scientific progress into the general consciousness has made "wonder" fall prey to rationalization, so that no enlightened person is willing to accept it as "real". The disappearance of "horror" from serious literature might be contingent on the generalization of previously exclusive humanitarian ethics to broader strands of the educated population. And in societies without erotic taboos, the appeal accompanying the staging of love and sex has become quite weak. This said, all these registers continue to play a prominent role in present-day fiction. As may be observed with regard to a variety of further phenomena, cultural trivial-

---

408 *The Fantastic: A Structural Approach to a Literary Genre*, Richard Howard (tr.), Ithaca, NY 1975.

ization always comes about by means of the appropriation of norms, patterns, and predilections first cherished amongst the elite by popular culture. If we infer from the scenario presented in this chapter that the distance in terms of taste and predilection to be observed between the elite and the "masses" was not as great in early modern times as it seems to be in our own, this is not a very reassuring diagnosis.

Mass Media, Early Modern and Present

0.—Talking about mass media today inevitably directs readers' attention to electronic media, particularly film, television, and the information conveyed by way of various other devices (computers, tablets, smartphones).[409] This technological "gap" notwithstanding, early modern and present-day mass media phenomena do have many features in common.

1.—There is, however, one important difference to be mentioned when it comes to applying the term to both early modern performance culture and present-day mass media; this concerns the question of degrees of mediation. It makes a difference whether we are witnessing a performance given by "real" humans, that is, actors on a stage in front of us—which is a fourth-degree mediation[410]— or whether there is an additional level of mediation involved as a result of the performance being electronically recorded and broadcast via television or streamed online. The "technical" aspect may even be a point of minor importance. The most relevant difference is that between the communal, collective profile of live performances in previous ages and the mainly private and remote viewing on electronic devices today. If, as is argued here, mass media performances fulfill their purpose mainly by activating or even unleashing emotions and by partially neutralizing reason, one may ask if it is sensible at all to hypothetically consider the reception of televised soap operas and of early modern theater performances as variants of the selfsame cultural prototype.

---

[409] Against the backdrop of my previous argument, it is evident that I will be dealing in this short chapter only with those sectors of present-day mass media production which are dedicated to divulging fiction, and not "news" in the strict sense. This said, one might think about the question of the extent to which this distinction has been in part leveled, at least as to those mass media catering to people whose self-image is not linked to the concept of the "intellectual". Most news of this kind is embedded in at least partly fictional stories, whose logic might be quite similar to the one described above with regard to early modern mass media.
[410] See above, pp. 164 f.

One might provide a quick and easy answer to the problem just raised by pointing to the fact that there are historically different stages of mass culture and that those mentioned above engage different levels of emotionality. Just as it was common practice—as one might infer from Aristotle's *Poetics*—to quake and weep in public during certain moments of a tragic performance, such uninhibited utterances of shared emotions were still possible in early modern theaters or theatrical courtyards. It may be the case that present-day recipients of trivialized tragic stories broadcast on TV weep at certain moments; but weeping in private or in the presence of one's nuclear family is quite different from sharing the expression of such affects with the entire ruling class of the community to which one belongs. One might end the discussion by pointing out that enhanced mediation dramatically increases the number of people reached by performances, but that the level of unifying affectivity decreases in the process. In sum, one could argue that the mere quantity of emotion unleashed (with a corresponding repression of reason), which can be channeled towards goals desired by the organizers of the performances (in most cases: state cultural agencies, religious authorities, private corporations dedicated to propagating the dominant ideology, or some combination of these agents), is probably much greater today than in previous periods, so that the price paid for the enhanced propagation—the relative reduction of shared and thus unifying emotionality—is well invested, seen from the investors' perspective. In that sense, the difference between early modern and present-day mass media phenomena is a real one, but the present-day mass media industry may be regarded as a continuation of the corresponding cultural constellation emerging in the early modern age.

2.—There is, in my view, yet another factor which might be taken into consideration when attempting to account for both the uncontestable differences and the overall similarities between early modern and present-day instances of mass media. I will try to introduce my corresponding reflections by referring to a performative practice[411] broadly disseminated by electronic media and especially popular in our time: top-tier club soccer matches,[412] in particular championships. As is familiar to everyone who from time to time watches such games on television, it is not only the game proper that is broadcast, but also

---

[411] I am conscious of the fact that my above deliberations (pp. 164–170) imply that it would be problematic to categorize soccer games as mediations; but as a widely known example of performance practices broadcast by the present-day mass media, they might be useful for producing a concrete idea of the historical evolution I will be characterizing in the following.
[412] Within North American contexts, baseball, football, or basketball games would be analogous phenomena.

a wide variety of ancillary material whose sole purpose is to convey the impression of intense emotion to individual viewers sitting in front of their TVs in the privacy of their homes. This is partly achieved by the notoriously hyperbolic commentary of sportscasters. More theatrical still are their cries of joy, disappointment, outrage, or affliction accompanying the fates of key players as they score goals, miss, receive a penalty flag, or writhe on the turf due to injury. In addition, there is the recording and subsequent display of the scenes taking place amongst the audience attending the match in the stadium. Over the years, these masses of direct spectators have literally been trained to display an extremely high, even exuberant degree of emotionality: shouting, weeping, standing up "spontaneously" from their seats, hugging each other, etc., etc. One could argue that the loss of direct involvement typical of electronic media is compensated by the fact that viewers at home are integrated into the on-screen spectacle, where the combination of the highly stylized, choreographed competition between opposing teams, the quasi-staged unruly behavior on the part of spectators in the stadium, and other visual and auditory effects of heightened emotionality stimulate a concomitant emotional reaction in the home viewers, thereby overcoming to a considerable extent the "distance effect" of the TV medium. In this way, the emotional participation of the home viewer in a championship football match today may be equated with—or at least compared to—that of an early modern playgoer.

As for soap operas, films shot for display in movie theaters, etc., there is no comparable means of enhancing affective identification. It would require a separate analysis to substantiate what I can only present as a personal impression here: it seems to me that popular film and TV today is constructed with an even greater attention to scenes of emotional tension than was the case in early modern or even modern plays (or films). Portraying in graphic detail the death of the beloved of the hero or heroine, complete with the latter's reaction to viewing the tragedy, was as uncommon in early modern performance culture as it is frequent in present-day Hollywood blockbusters.[413] Where this will lead—if my hypothesis is correct: heightened degrees of mediation and the subsequent loss of potential "direct" involvement are compensated for by increasing the intrinsic emotionality of the performances in question—remains to be seen.

---

[413] I am thinking of *Titanic*, but many similar examples might be named as well.

III. Historical Issues, Theoretical Perspectives

Some Case Studies

0.—This third part of the present study will highlight specific configurations that emerged in the course of the investigations of the DramaNet research team and which are relevant to the theoretical issues discussed in Part I. These configurations will be considered in a very concise fashion, leaving all more detailed discussions to the books or articles written by the junior scholars who worked with me.—As already announced in the introduction, there is one longer chapter of this third section that will polemically engage the concept of "national literatures", including its present-day derivatives: postcolonial and hybridity theories. But first, I should like to prepare the terrain by looking at a number of particularly interesting constellations of cultural material circulating in the net.

1.—One major difficulty for a theory of global literature as proposed here lies in finding a satisfactory way of generalizing observations derived from the analysis of European practices such that they apply beyond a European context. Is it possible to conceptualize the circulation of early modern European dramatic material to the East, to India and Japan, by means of configurations comparable to intra-Western processes of transculturation? At first blush, one may be inclined to answer the question affirmatively. Terms such as "within" or "outside" of Europe are concepts based on arbitrary delineations, not objective realities. Transculturation is as frequently linked to physical constraints (conquest, imperialism) or ideological subversion (missionary activities) within a continent as it is beyond. What is more, cultural distance is a relative phenomenon. It is contingent upon the level of abstraction involved. As Claude Levi-Strauss showed, it does not exist in the sphere of mythical patterns. Cultural material in the highly organized form of dramatic texts or performance practices is by no means abstract. But it is open to undergo processes of adoption and adaptation. Within such a potentially paradoxical context, the possibility that cultural difference informs different processes of appropriation should not be discarded at the outset.

Questions emerging with regard to non-Western cultures may specifically concern differing concepts of what "theater" consists of. "Occidental" theater is multi-medial, but it relies mainly on language in order to convey messages. This applies all the more to early modern European drama, in particular when compared to its medieval counterpart. What becomes of "occidental" drama when it is transferred to cultures whose performative practices rely much more on visual and auditory (musical) effects? What is the profile of appropriated and of rejected material, focusing on those cases in which processes of appropriation are relatively free, in the sense of not being imposed in an authoritarian way? Does the "import" of western cultural material change the local notion of theater (if there is any)? Is there any "reverse circulation" taking place? And if reverse processes are to be observed, are they part of larger floating processes, including additional cultural material, from the periphery to the European centers?[414]

Indian drama of the eighteenth and nineteenth centuries offers a great deal of insight into the questions outlined above.[415] The "transfer" of European drama, including translations, to colonial India took place as early as around the year 1800.[416] Some five decades later, the first (modern) plays written in Indian vernaculars emerge. I will concentrate my brief remarks on two early plays considered by specialists to be the most important ones and which, in addition, allow for the consideration of two different variants of working with "exogenous" material extracted from the net.

The play *Sermista* (1858/1859)[417] by Madhusudan Dutta—which, by coincidence, appeared in the very same year as the second play I will discuss, *Nil Darpan*—may be characterized as based on the "importation" of the formal structure of European, in particular Shakespearean drama (five acts, blank verse). However, the content associated with this new form is autochthonous; it consists of a mythological narrative derived from the tradition of the Sanskrit epics. The configuration of the narrative is not alien to Western literature; it is based on a love triangle. But the fact that the triangle involves one male and two females, as well as the fairytale-like ending "attached" to the conflict, are features which are rather uncommon in the Occident. Thus, what may be observed in the case of *Sermista* is the assembly of a dramatic work by means of the fusion of content and a formal pattern that had constituted distinct items in the universal cultural net up to that point in time. To understand the significance of the "extraction" of this formal pattern, it is crucial to keep in mind that there was no drama in the modern sense of the term within the Indian culture of historical, that is, post-mythical times.[418] There were small groups

---

414 All related questions are dealt with in detail by Gautam Chakrabarti in his book *Familiarising the Exotic: Introducing European Drama in Early Modern India*.
415 See Chakrabarti, *Familiarising the Exotic*.
416 I shall come back to this fascinating process in a later section of this chapter (pp. 217–220).
417 The Bengali version was written in 1858, while the date of 1859 refers to the translation into English.
418 This statement needs to be qualified, but the details are not pertinent to the above discussion (see n. 423).

of itinerant actors who presented a variant of performative practices one might call "street theater", performances close to what one would call farces in the West, that is, short scenes, mainly comic, partly obscene, and based upon personages derived from the fund of popular culture.

In the case of the second text I should like to highlight, *Nil Darpan* or *The Indigo Planting Mirror* (1858/1859) by Dinabandhu Mitra, it is, in addition to the formal pattern, the content, or rather the ideological narrative to which the content refers, that is imported from Europe.[419] Both features are then assimilated to an Indian setting. The story presented consists in a narrative well known from *The Communist Manifesto* (1848) and to be found later on in various fictionalized versions in Europe, for example in Zola's *Germinal* (1885): it deals with the shameless exploitation of the working poor by the bourgeoisie, the support of the exploiters by both the state and religious institutions, and finally the revolt of the exploited, which is thus presented as morally justified. The foundational parameters of a society committed to a rigid hierarchy, most pithily expressed in the caste system, were thus problematized from the standpoint of egalitarianism, which was indeed an exotic feature in nineteenth-century India, but which then became, no less than in the West, the dominant discourse on the organization of society.—It is essential to note that the above-characterized "import" of a formal structure, subsequently assimilated to a traditional story, opened Indian society up for the much more comprehensive import of a form-plus-content structure which was adapted to local social reality and thus able to produce, so to speak, an extra-dramatic social discourse which functioned as an instrument for propagating the concept of equality.[420]

With regard to the author of *Sermista* in particular, there are a few remarks to be made which are pertinent to the theoretical discussions undertaken in this book. Dutta was educated in British colonial institutions. As an adult, he converted to Christianity, took the additional first name of "Michael", and married an English woman. After divorcing her, he married a French woman. He wrote his works in Bengali as well as in English, translating the texts himself. He is the first great canonical author of modern Bengali literature. Because of his adoption of a British lifestyle, he had issues with his family, but the local ruling

---

419 The European form of drama had already been imported to India, as I shall explain in the following pages, by a Russian adventurer named Lebedev.
420 Taking the production dates of the two dramas into consideration, one must note that *Nil Darpan*, and even more so the ideology contained in it, began deploying its full impact only in the decades following the first performance.

class of nabobs and princes generously supported his work. He stands as a paradigmatic cultural mediator.

Dutta left behind an abundant correspondence in which he addresses the question of his self-image. There is practically no canonical author from the Western and Southern European literary traditions whom he does not mention as a model for his own works. It is striking, however, that two names appear more frequently than the rest: Virgil and Milton. If one keeps in mind that the *Aeneid* (29–19 BCE) is modeled on a Greek text, and that it is only in retrospect that the "classical pagan tradition" appears to be homogeneous—in fact, prior to the relevant processes of transculturation, Roman culture was as far away from Greek culture as the traditions of the Black Sea region—and if one keeps in mind that *Paradise Lost* (1667) is about a religious patrimony deeply anchored in England at that time, but which did not have its "roots" in that part of the world, Dutta's self-presentation as an Indian Virgil or Milton appears perfectly transparent. The concept underlying such a "self-fashioning" is apparently one of transculturation and its highly fruitful results. The idea is all but new. It is famously expressed, setting aside its implied presence in the *Aeneid*, as early as in the twelfth century, in Chrétien de Troyes's prologue to his romance *Cligès*.[421] If the *clergie*, that is, study and culture, has traveled from Jerusalem to Athens, then to Rome, and from there to Paris, it is in no way astonishing that it should continue to migrate—in this case, first to London, then to Calcutta; and it can be expected that it will probably not stop there. In terms of cultural theory, one may rightly conceive of Dutta as a new Chrétien de Troyes.[422]

It is not only the modern Indian drama proper, which emerges in the middle of the nineteenth century, but also its prehistory that is quite instructive with regard to the overall problems addressed in this study. At the time in question, the material substratum of circulatory movements within the cultural net is, as argued above, mainly constituted by traveling humans. In a later age, when printing becomes widespread, and even more so in the present-day era of electronic communication, the primary material substratum of circulation changes and the speed of circulation increases in a most spectacular way; but in the period under scrutiny, human agents are typically the media of transportation.

---

[421] "Ce nos ont nostre livre apris, / Que Grece ot de la chevalerie / Le premier los et de clergie. / Puis vint chevalerie a Rome / Et de la clergie la some, / Qui or est an France venue." // "Our books have informed us that the preeminence in chivalry and learning once belonged to Greece. Then chivalry passed to Rome, together with that highest learning which now has come to France" (vv. 30–35; W. W. Comfort [tr.], online edition, "heroofcamelot.com").

[422] In order to avoid misunderstanding, I would like to stress that I do not claim a similar rank for his literary works.

When it comes to specific forms of circulation, I have mainly considered in detail two different human modes of activity contributing to the circulatory processes. These two modes have in common that they are intentional and thus prearranged: the circulation does not just happen, but is planned, organized, and implemented. The first of these two patterns might be called "cultural exportation" and is based on cultural-ideological expansionism. One well-known example from the early modern age is the export of European Christian didactical drama to regions as different as Latin America and Japan, which occurred in the seventeenth century; the media of transportation in this case were mainly Jesuit missionaries. Another such example, from a period beginning about 150 years later, would be the exportation not only of drama, but of the entirety of French *civilisation*, orchestrated by the modern French state in the frame of nineteenth-century colonialism. The ideological basis shared by these mechanisms of export is typical of all such propagative circulatory activities within the net, including in the present: it is universalism, the (religious, secular, or hybrid) assumption that all members of the species are in essence the same and are thus capable of sharing, and in fact obliged to share, basic cultural patterns and features.

The second variant of such conscious and prearranged circulation may be labeled "cultural importation". The examples discussed above were the French importation of Italian culture in the Renaissance and the importation of French and German culture into Russia in the Age of Enlightenment. The vehicle of circulation is in most cases constituted by dynastic bonds—by princesses married off to monarchs of the "importing" countries—and the motivational basis might vary from quite down-to-earth and private aspects (making the new wife happy by allowing her to indulge in cultural events familiar to her) to political reasons: the recognition of the "receiving" monarchy that the spouse's culture is more developed than its own and that not only the dynasty, but the state and the society in their entirety might profit from the "transfusion" initiated by exogamy.

One should, however, not lose sight of the fact that a good deal of cultural circulation follows more fortuitous and contingent paths than the two conscious and prearranged patterns just summarized, even in cases where it is not a parasitic phenomenon, that is, a by-product of economic or military activities. Gautam Chakrabarti has studied the entire temporal range of the circulation of European drama to colonial India, its hybridization with the local production in its elite (Sanskrit) as well as in its popular forms,[423] and the return

---

[423] The plays in Sanskrit (a language accessible in modern times only to Brahmins) as theorized in the *Natyashastra* tract and still extant in modernity—the most famous being Kalidasa's play titled *Shakuntala*, translated into English by Sir William Jones in 1789 and later enthusiastically praised by Goethe—had no longer been performed on the Indian stage since times im-

flow of modern Indian theater to Europe, which mainly occurred in the second half of the twentieth century. From a nonspecialist's perspective, one of the most striking points highlighted in his book is the fact that, contrary to all possible expectations, the British colonizers were not the agents responsible for initiating this process. Chakrabarti argues that the British, at least up to the second half of the nineteenth century, when Queen Victoria adopted the title of Empress of India and started considering the subcontinent as an integral part of her realm, did not have the ambition to culturally colonize India. The reasons for this difference from Spanish, French, and, later on, American models may be multifarious and need not be discussed here in detail. One point to be taken into consideration is certainly the fact that the colonization of India was not a state activity at its outset. The East India Company was a private enterprise whose sole intention was to make a profit. For decades, if not centuries, the British considered India as a territory of exploitation, not of cultural propagation and ideological assimilation.

This said, one must account for the fact that European dramas, starting with pieces by Molière (*L'amour médecin* [1665]) and Richard P. Jodrell (*The Disguise* [1787]), were translated into Bengali with the intention of performing them on a stage in Calcutta, in India's first-ever modern theater, as early as at the end of the eighteenth century, that is, roughly half a century before the above-characterized emergence of "local" dramatic production.[424] The agent of this circulatory process was, astonishingly, not a British colonizer or cultural agent, but a Russian, Gerasim Stepanovich Lebedev (1749–1817). I will not go into the details of his remarkable biography, but will leave it at saying that he was born in a provincial town of his country of origin, became a musician, was taken to St. Petersburg as a young adult, came into contact with high-ranking aristocrats, traveled in their company to Vienna, Paris, and the rest of Western Eu-

---

memorial. Amongst the educated belonging to the highest caste, they continued to be read and thus were part of the cultural consciousness of those who, in some way, might be seen as the intellectual class of India.

424 As early as on November 27, 1795, Lebedev staged the first-ever "modern" play on the Indian subcontinent; it was written in the Bengali language and based on *The Disguise* (it seems that Lebedev forsook the project of staging the comedy by Molière). *The Disguise* in Bengali was more of an adaptation than a faithful translation, so this fact does not jar with the above remarks about the way in which Western theatrical culture entered modern India. In addition, it is controversial whether the translation was Lebedev's own or whether it was partly or even exclusively produced by Lebedev's teacher of Bengali, Goloknath Das. At any rate, the initiative was Lebedev's, and this is the only point that counts in the present context.

rope, and then, by chance, happened to travel to India,⁴²⁵ where he first sought to survive as a musician. He was not very successful in that line of business; in order to improve his economic situation, he shifted his focus to theatrical productions and established the above-mentioned stage.

Lebedev took an authentic interest in Indian culture. He learned Sanskrit and Bengali and discussed his translations of European plays with local scholars. In a way, he was one of the first Europeans to consider traditional Indian culture with respect and admiration. He was a precursor of those who, in the age of Romanticism, would cast India as the cradle of European culture (e.g., Friedrich Schlegel). What is less known, and has first been brought to light by Chakrabarti's book, which takes Lebedev's private correspondences into consideration, is the political motivation behind this attitude. Basically, Lebedev was a Russian nationalist. From his perspective, there is no question that it is Russia, not Britain, which is predestined to rule over India; let me recall that, up to the end of the Soviet Union, and possibly into the present, it has been a Russian ambition to control the Indian subcontinent, not least in order to become a maritime power of global dimensions, which was and is impossible as long as its influence is confined to its traditional territories, which contain no ice-free ports.⁴²⁶ In his letters, Lebedev gives expression to the idea that the superficial, materialistically oriented, capitalist colonial regime established by the British is not what India needs; what is required, according to him, is rather a cultural colonization, based, however, on the careful acquisition of India's cultural patrimony.

There is one minor and one major point to be derived from the astonishing scenario of a Russian acting as the agent of the circulation of Western European dramatic culture to British India. Had the British known about Lebedev's political convictions, they most probably would have flatly expelled him from their colony. Lebedev's interactions with the British authorities were not free from strife; but ultimately, the British let him do what he did. This constellation reconfirms a speculation already advanced above: literary items float more freely than explicitly ideological items do (political ideas, religions); and, as I should like to add, than material goods do, at least in the industrial age. With

---

425 There are some obscure points in Lebedev's biography. It may be that he traveled to India driven by exoticism, the longing for adventures, etc. But it may also be the case that he adopted from his aristocratic masters the habit of gambling and had to leave the Old World in order to avoid being imprisoned because of debts.

426 —or ports that are separated from the ocean by straits easily controllable by competing maritime forces (Crimea, the Dardanelles).

regard to ideology and industrial commodities, modern states have the tendency to make systematic use of their apparatuses of control in order to strictly contain the "intake" of exotic material. Culture in the narrower sense of literature and other forms of art is considered from Plato through Augustine, Aquinas, Kant, and Hegel as something that deserves a certain amount of attention, but does not count among the "truly important" things, such as religion, knowledge, or morals. It is the fact that culture in this narrower sense is ultimately considered as *adiaphora*[427] that allows for processes of circulation which at first sight no one would expect to be possible.

But the more important point to be drawn from the Indian scenario is this one: Lebedev is a maverick figure, an adventurer, not a scholar or someone who set out on his journey as a conscious cultural missionary. He is a somewhat eccentric figure. In this regard, he is not an isolated phenomenon when it comes to cultural transfer. As has been noted already, it was not intentionally, but by chance that he traveled to India—as it occurred by chance that another such eccentric figure, Christopher Columbus, traveled not to India, where he intended to go, but to a place which was later to become America. The consequences of this latter eccentric's activities in the field of culture were much more significant than Lebedev's. Columbus's voyage marks the inception of the more or less violent reconnection of the continents discovered by him to the universal cultural net, the ensuing westernization of South America, and, later on, of North America; and it is highly probable that it was the successful cultural colonization of these two subcontinents which paved the way for the westernization of the entire globe, a *longue durée* movement of human history which is still going on today.

How would India and the rest of the world look today had people like Lebedev and Columbus been a little bit more "cautious" and "reasonable" than they actually were? And what would the world look like had they fallen prey to a banal accident, say, a shipwreck, before they arrived, respectively, on the shores of America and of India? In the age of modernity proper, the circulation of cultural material seems to occur in most cases according to bureaucratized patterns, driven by state interests, ideologies, or the systematic search for profit on the part of private companies. Lebedev and Columbus seem to be representative of a pattern that may have been dominant in the entire premodern age, that is to say, during most of the species' history so far. Those of our first

---

[427] From the standpoint of all of the "official" philosophers named above, the truly dangerous discourses are the skeptical or cynical philosophies which deny the possibility of knowledge or the mandatory status of (specific) morals.

ancestors who dared to leave the East African savannah and migrate northward; the slaves leaving Egypt led by a fearless man later known as Moses; the Greeks travelling to Asia Minor; Alexander the Great conquering territories as distant as Northern India, etc., etc.—all these people were eccentrics, adventurers who might easily have failed. And many of them did fail, leaving no traces precisely for this reason. Processes of cultural exchange are subject, during the greater part of human history, to the non-existent laws of contingency. It is only interpretative frames like religions or philosophies of history which try to impose a logic upon what is basically a-systematic, erratic, and fortuitous.

2.—It may be that it is the case of the emergence of Russian drama that is best suited for the discussion of a point that has not yet been extensively addressed, namely, the interaction of multiple, highly diverse factors when it comes to the withdrawal of material circulating in the net and to its reconfiguration into novel entities, new ("original") works.

The (hi)story of Russian drama as expounded in Kirill Ospovat's book[428] may perhaps be systematized as follows: In keeping with the position of certain church fathers, all forms of theater were forbidden up to the late seventeenth century. It cannot be systematically ruled out that there were improvised sketches performed as street theater, that is, analogues to what are called farces in Western Europe. The vastness of the territory, its relative underpopulation, and the complete lack of written documentation pertaining to regions other than the urban centers (which were under the strict control of the ecclesiastical authorities, for which reason there was certainly no theater whatsoever in these places) make definitive statements regarding the point in question problematic. Religious theater in its Western forms—mystery and morality plays—was avoided as a consequence of the isolationist perspective adopted by the Russian Orthodox Church; any similarity with Catholicism raised the suspicion of heresy. But it may be that it was precisely this constellation that facilitated the emergence of a sort of liturgical drama in Russia starting in the sixteenth century. In Catholic territories, beginning in the twelfth century, drama as part of the liturgy had been abandoned in favor of a religious drama proper that was performed independently of the Mass. Consequently, the pattern of liturgical performance as such could be considered as no longer "contagious". Be that as it may, there is only one documented example extant of the Russian variant of liturgical drama; it is known as the "Act of the Furnace" (*Peshchnoe deistvo*). The play stages the Old Testa-

---

[428] *Terror and Pity.*

ment story of Daniel; it was regularly performed in cathedrals across the country before Christmas.[429]

Things began to change in the late seventeenth century, once Russia had reconquered Orthodox territories from Poland, where the Orthodox faith had been amalgamated with "Catholic" cultural practices such as public schools and school theater. But the main conditioning factor was the establishment of a courtly society, which occurred relatively late on Russian territory. Peter the Great (who ruled from 1682 to 1721) and the two empresses Elizabeth (1741–1762) and Catherine (1762–1796) were the monarchs who brought the Tsarist court to a level of cultivation comparable to the courts of Central and Western Europe. As for the latter of the two empresses, the reasons behind this development are rather obvious. When she "migrated" eastward from her country of origin, she made use of her rapidly attained position as absolute ruler to import, as it were, the cultural practices familiar to her. As French language and culture were dominant at contemporary courts located on German territories, it was mainly the model of French tragedy, but also of pastoral play, including the new genre of opera, which made their way into eighteenth-century Russia.

The first phase of this cultural westernization of Eastern Europe set in, however, as early as during the reign of Elizabeth.[430] Many of the first tragedies in Russian, written by Aleksandr P. Sumarokov, were not direct imitations of pieces by Racine or Voltaire. This said, the influence of the great French authors is evident; but in order to adequately describe Sumarokov's dramas, one must take another factor into consideration: in this book's terminology, the aspect of "local demand", which differed in profile, at least in part, from the case of France. French authors of the age carefully avoided writing pieces dealing with their own, that is, French history. If they thematized historical stories, they usually had recourse to Greece and Rome, in some cases to Spain (Corneille's *Le Cid* [1636]), and at times even to "exotic" material (Voltaire's *Zaïre* [1732]);[431] but they did not adapt the great tradition of classical Greek historical tragedy to their own national framework. The current explanation for this attitude of avoiding plots pertaining to French history seems to be convincing: in a coun-

---

[429] Sergei M. Eisenstein included one such performance in his famous film *Ivan the Terrible* (1944/58).
[430] Elizabeth was an illegitimate, then legitimized daughter of Peter the Great; that is, she was born and raised in the country. Some of her teachers did come from abroad, but her cultural background was of a different profile than that of her successor, Catherine II.
[431] Parts of this latter play were translated into Russian by Sumarokov.

try whose recent past had been characterized by factionalism—both political and religious—and where open civil war had only been avoided by events like the Saint Bartholomew's Day massacre, the regained peace, whether based on reconciliation or on repression, could well have been disturbed by bringing plots drawn from French history to the stage.

In Russia, things were different. There was no lack of internal conflict; several *coups d'état* had taken place, resulting in the permanent menace of civil war. However, there was also another factor to take into consideration: a demand that was even stronger than the one for stories fostering internal peace. This demand was for what is later known as "nation-building", in this case the constitution of something like a Russian identity with the Tsarist court at its center. Identity, however, is always based on historical narratives ("we are the ones whose ancestors fought this and that fight, who suffered this and that hardship, but who succeeded in recovering from the sufferings and are now heading towards a glorious future"). Consequently, some of Sumarokov's tragedies deal with the history of what became "Russia" only in the sixteenth and seventeenth centuries.

The legitimization of this at first sight quite bold reshaping of the French material drawn from the net made use of another "package" of cultural material available, namely, the text on which the entire post-fifth-century-BCE history of the genre is based: Aristotle's *Poetics*. As is well known, but was neglected in the French discussion, Aristotle differentiates between drama (tragedy) on the one hand and history on the other, but goes on to argue that plots for tragedies may be invented by the author, taken from the familiar fund of mythology, or drawn from history.[432] What might at first sight seem inconsistent is solidly anchored in the Aristotelian conception of the genre. If it is the task of tragedy to convey something "general" about the world, certain historical plots may be a very apt source; if history is largely the domain of the contingent and the fortuitous, this does not mean that every segment of it defies causal explanation. "Historical" drama is, to put it succinctly, one of the options an author is free to choose if he intends to conceive a well-wrought tragedy. This aspect of the Aristotelian argument was, as has been said, partially relegated to the background in the French discussion, at least as far as the country's own history was concerned; it was detached from the argument presented by the Stagirite.

---

432 *Poetics*, chap. 9.

However, the aspect was a prominent one in the German discussion on tragedy and serious drama.[433] The reasons for the revival and emphasis of what had been neglected by the French are evident: Germany, a not yet existent nation struggling for its cultural autonomy vis-à-vis its firmly established Western neighbor, was keen to demonstrate to the "world"—that is, to the educated classes of Europe—that it had a meaningful contribution to make to discussions of common European interest; or, to put it somewhat more bluntly: German theoreticians of the time had the ambition to prove the French wrong, to accuse them of having read Aristotle only superficially or even of having distorted him.—A strong "local" demand for cultural patterns of nation-building, the absorption of French tragic material (mainly Racine, but also Corneille and Voltaire), and the reception of the "anti-French" reading of the *Poetics* as developed in contemporary Germany seem to have formed the basis of pieces like *Khorev* (1747/1749), the first Russian neo-classical drama, or of *Dimitrii Samozvanets* (1771). Let me stress that I mean what I say: these items constituted the basis for what was then achieved by the author Sumarokov. One can legitimately doubt that any other author would have been able to create such masterpieces of tragedy[434] out of these diverse impulses taken from the net. But *creatio ex nihilo*, the godlike work allegedly performed by writers and artists according to the enthusiastic art theories emerging as simplifications of Kant's *Critique of Judgment* and which we subsume under the label of Romanticism—this seems to be an illusion when human affairs are concerned.

3.—Limitation is a feature of all human efforts. Sub-projects were conducted by the DramaNet research group treating what has been labeled in recent years *littératures mineures* (Slovenia, Tyrol); but for various reasons, it was not possible to undertake a more detailed analysis of the situation in medium-sized European cultures such as the Netherlands, Denmark, and Sweden. As an inevitably insufficient substitute for this missing part, which might be supplemented by further research in the future, I would like to improvise some remarks on the Netherlands and its theatrical culture in early modern times.

The most outstanding author in this regard is Joost van den Vondel (1587–1679). Born in Cologne of parents who had left Antwerp because of their adherence

---

433 See Johann Christoph Gottsched, *Noethiger Vorrath zur Geschichte der deutschen Dramatischen Dichtkunst* (1765); Gotthold Ephraim Lessing assigned the subtitle "Historiendrama aus der Zeit des Dritten Kreuzzugs" to his famous play *Nathan der Weise* (1779).
434 The literary quality of Sumarokov's plays is controversial. From my historicizing perspective, I read them with delight; but I will leave it to the specialists to assess them in terms of aesthetics.

to Protestantism,[435] he relocated to the Netherlands when he was an adult, later converting to Catholicism. Vondel is heavily influenced—in this specific case, directly and consciously—by the dramatic work of Shakespeare, as Dutch culture in general, both in its everyday as well as in its refined strata, has throughout the centuries mainly been modeled on English patterns.[436] Many of Vondel's plays are "emulations" of Shakespearean plays, in the sense of the term current in classical cultural and poetic theory: imitations with the intention of surpassing the model.

Reading Vondel's plays, one gets the impression that the author interpreted "better" mainly as "even more violent and bloody". Shakespeare's plays are already paradigmatically cruel. In the final scenes, there are frequently more corpses to be seen on stage than living people. But all of this is "nothing" when compared to Vondel's plays. Who would be able nowadays to conceive an episode consisting of several dozens of catholic nuns stabbed by the "heretics" and then lying on the ground quite like a "wreath of roses white and red", as the dramatist did in his most popular play, *Gijsbrecht van Amstel* (1637);[437] or who would indulge in the "pleasure" of having a decapitation recounted in detail twice, as in *Maria Stuart of gemartelde majesteit* (1646)?

Considering the scenario as a whole, one has to add that the contemporary dramatic production of the Netherlands' eastern neighbor, Germany, displays

---

435 Like many other Flemish-Dutch cities, Antwerp had embraced Protestantism; the Spaniards who ruled over this part of North-Western Europe at that time had more or less violently reestablished Catholicism as the only legitimate Christian cult. Cologne—not very far from Antwerp—, where many Flemish Protestants sought refuge, was mainly Catholic, but parts of the population had become Protestant. The period at stake is situated before the re-establishment of Catholicism as the exclusive denomination in that part of the Rhineland.

436 In addition, there is an important, but in comparison minor, influence of German as well as French models, the impact of the latter being limited to the upper strata of the population: the nobility, the wealthy bourgeoisie, and the intellectuals. The reason for the general preference of English over German patterns is obviously the territorial as well as linguistic affinity to Germany, the resulting fear of absorption, and the attempt of the nation to distance itself from the—perhaps all too—big neighbor by building close links with another big country which had stopped nurturing the wish to govern the continent or parts of it at the end of the Hundred Years' War.

437 See vv. 1435 ff.; the most recent publication characterizing Vondel's works is Nigel Smith's "The Politics of Tragedy in the Dutch Republic: Joachim Oudaen's Martyr Drama in Context", in: Gvozdeva et al. (eds.), *Dramatic Experience*, pp. 220–249.—I should add to the above remarks on the way atrocities were presented in plays by Vondel that there were prominent Dutch playwrights at the time, e.g. Jan Vos, who did not refrain from having events such as beheadings represented on stage.

quite similar tendencies. Within a traditional frame of stereotypes of national character, one would be tempted to explain the bloodiness of many of Gryphius's, Lohenstein's, and Vondel's plays by referring to a Germanic or Teutonic penchant for transgressing all moral boundaries when it comes to violent conflict. But even though the Netherlands were not always as peaceful and politically correct as they have been in recent decades, it would be quite problematic to explain the amount of atrocities in Vondel's plays by referring to a supposed propensity of "the Dutch"[438] to slaughter their enemies in a particularly cruel manner.

My tentative explanation would be quite another one. In contrast to Spain and France, but similarly to Britain, we are dealing in the cases of Germany and the Netherlands with religiously divided nations. The difference with regard to Britain and Germany consists in the fact that the Dutch religious divide is a rather open one. In Britain, political as well as cultural power was in the hands of the Anglicans. In Germany, there were kingdoms and principalities which were either (entirely) Protestant or (entirely) Catholic. In the Netherlands, the ruler was Protestant, since the country gained its independence in a guerilla revolt against a Catholic "oppressor", Spain. But the cultural, intellectual, and economic elite, as well as the populace, were more or less equally divided into the two major Christian denominations. The plays I mentioned originate from the post-Westphalian period, or from a period immediately preceding the peace treaty, that is, from a time when many European nations had decided, after thirty years of bloody war without a victor—half of the population had lost their lives—to no longer make questions of religious denomination a reason for killing each other. The emotional energies unleashed by thirty and more years of terrible atrocities, however, were still virulent. How to tame these aggressive affects?

As already partly suggested above, my speculative explanation would start from Freud's theory of literature as imaginary wish fulfillment, as a compensatory realm where we can get, thanks to our imagination, what reality is unable to give us.[439] The staged atrocities may have helped to catharticize the "real" aggression, still virulent, of spectators towards members of other denominations, and thus might have been a way to help establish inner peace. In this way, dramas such as Vondel's might be considered paradigms of what visual mass culture is, according to me: an instrument for producing social cohesion. The mimicked cruelties may have served as a palliative against the "suffering"

---

438 As said, Vondel was born in Cologne, Germany, while his parents were from Antwerp. But the point in question is not the author and his ethnic or cultural belonging; it is the audience who avidly received the above-characterized, at times incredibly bloody plays.
439 See, once again, the reference given in n. 56.

(the frustration) originating from the state-imposed reconversion of wild beasts on two feet into more or less civilized human beings.[440]

4.—There are extremely intricate questions implied when it comes to discussing the point, mentioned on various occasions, of the different degrees of organization of the material circulating in the net. There are elementary units ("functions" in the sense of Vladimir Propp); there are certain emblematic figures (like the *Hanswurst* in Austrian popular drama, both urban and "rural", whose Anglo-Saxon analogue would be figures like Pickelhering[441]); there are standardized assemblages of elementary units (certain joke-structures in comedies; *anagnorisis* and *peripeteia* in tragedies); there are genres; and finally there are entire stories which not only circulate in the net—according to my assumptions, all stories ever written or devised do this—but which are also extracted and then reworked as entire stories; the Griselda story is one such case of the highest level of organization of a given item floating in the net.

The study conducted by Pauline Beaucé as part of the DramaNet project[442] opens up interesting considerations pertaining to an intermediate level of rather high organization that is more strictly organized than a specific generic pattern, but nevertheless does not attain the level of detailed organization typical of a particular story and its variants. The difficulty of finding a correct term for such phenomena becomes evident in scholarship in which they tend to be labeled—unsatisfactorily—"traditions". In line with Beaucé's findings, I will be addressing the pastoral as one prominent example of such a tradition.[443]

When it comes to defining the (postclassical) pastoral, which seems to have originated as narrative, but is drawn upon in early modern times for drama as well—Guarini's *Pastor fido* (1580/1584) being the most prominent example—

---

440 From a Freudian standpoint, the dramas mentioned would achieve this compensatory function with regard both to Catholic and to Protestant audiences. The scene of the stabbing of the nuns would allow a Catholic spectator to fantasmatically unleash his aggressions against the heretics who are capable of perpetrating such unheard-of atrocities. A protestant spectator, on the contrary, would have indulged in his hatred against nuns and monks as the most powerful earthly agents of the Devil, who are being rightly punished for their evildoing.
441 See M. A. Katritzky, "Stefanelo Botarga and Pickelhering: Fishy Italian and English Stage Clowns in Spain and Germany", in: Küpper et al. (eds.), *Theatre Cultures within Globalising Empires*.
442 *Parodies d'opéra au siècle des Lumières* (chap. 5, "Parodie, ballet et pastorale: l'union des genres"); see also "Pour une réévaluation des formes mineures dans l'historiographie du théâtre des Lumières: le cas forain", *Horizons/Théâtre* vol. 5/2014, pp. 59–73.
443 Another example not discussed here directly, but which could likely be captured along similar lines as the following, would be the Hellenistic novel, of which Heliodorus' *Aethiopica* (third or fourth century CE) is the best-known extant textual instance.

the main features are easy to enumerate: the plots deal with shepherds and shepherdesses, but not "real" ones, not hard-working rural people whose bodies have become gnarled and buckled before their time as a result of back-breaking labor. Readers are presented, rather, with idealized shepherds who do not have to work in order to live, but who are eternally young, beautiful, and healthy. The setting is rustic, but without the inconveniences of an authentically rural environment; the scenery is pleasant, the weather serene. The plot revolves around love. There is no way to tell a story about love without dealing with the delicate problem of the instability of feelings and relationships, for if there is stability—as in fairytale endings—there is nothing more to narrate. But the pastoral invented what one could label a "non-traumatic" way of staging emotional instability. If, as frequently occurs, a certain Sylvestrus is forsaken by an unfaithful Phyllis who then continues her joyful life with a certain Corydon, Sylvestrus might sing a moderately sad song in which he laments the emotional instability of the female sex in general; but the beauty of his voice might then attract a certain Daphne who is immediately prepared to make him forget Phyllis forever.—It is evident that the scheme is episodic; it allows for a potentially endless concatenation of specific stories, and for easy variation just by changing the personages' names, or by slightly changing the features of the rustic setting (from riverbanks to mountains, etc.).

This pagan sort of paradise was devised in classical times. Theocritus, Virgil, and Ovid are the most important authors to thematize it. It was "reborn" in the age that bears precisely this name, then attained an amazing degree of popularity in all European literatures from the late sixteenth century onward. It ceased to be in such high demand in the nineteenth century, and in the twentieth became one of those items circulating in the net without being extracted; I should like to add that this is not the case for a comparable popular genre, the Hellenistic novel, which to this day constitutes the basic framework of most fantasy fiction. However, the pastoral tradition may be experiencing a powerful afterlife outside of Europe; very many Bollywood films could be considered "Indianized" variants of the pattern.

The questions provoked by the "tradition" mentioned within this book's framework concern two different points. Firstly, the (extremely) high stability of the pastoral's basic features contravenes the basic categories developed at the beginning of the twentieth century by the Russian formalists for the express purpose of differentiating the literature of high culture from popular fiction. According to the formalists—who are in the final analysis Kantians—innovation, originality is the main criterion for judging whether works are worthy of being called "literature." It seems that this is not always the case.—The second theoretically relevant point raised by the constellation outlined is the question of why the power of the pattern seems to have waned, why it has ceased (in the West) to be extracted from the net, at least for the time being.

The explanation proposed here as to the first question refers to a category made use of quite frequently above, namely, that of demand, which might be further specified by the following remark: when demand is high, the fact that there is not much innovation to be found in different instances of the genre or subgenre in question seems not to bother readers, not even sophisticated ones.[444] Regarding the second point to be discussed, one might speculate that certain demands are fulfilled by certain cultural or literary patterns in certain places and at certain times, but not everywhere and not permanently; the capability of cultural artifacts to satisfy a given demand may be liable to changing circumstances.

The concept of demand I am referring to is inspired, once again, by Freud's radically anti-Kantian short essay on the function of reading literary texts (or of viewing fiction) entitled *Der Dichter und das Phantasieren*. Based on his main insight that civilization is grounded on the repression of drives, Freud theorizes fiction as a compensatory register. Literary texts allow us to temporarily indulge in the illusion of living in a world where we are not subject to the manifold strictures regulating our "real" lives. They allow for imaginary wish fulfillment. Since our wishes are simple and constant, and since the apparatus of repression called civilization is stable as well, it is not astonishing, from a Freudian perspective, that there is much stability to be found in the history of fiction; and since the psychic apparatus is basically the same for all members of the species, it is no more astonishing that there is not much difference, as to

---

[444] I should like to add that this remark is also pertinent with respect to a problem I do not discuss in this book: why is it that even in post-Romantic times, that is, in periods of artistic production and reception obsessed with the criterion of "novelty" or "innovation", there is a very intense ongoing reception of works which are not novel at all to the audience? As to the performing arts (theater, music), every performance clearly introduces new accentuations; and even in the case of the arts which produce materially immutable works (texts, paintings), one can reasonably argue that every new reception on the part of a specific recipient will lead her or him to a "new" interpretation of the work in question. But even enthusiasts of reader-response theory (*Rezeptionsästhetik*) would hardly deny that there is a difference in terms of "novelty" between a renewed reading of, say, *Le Père Goriot* and a first reading of *L'Éducation sentimentale*. My speculation would be, succinctly put, that there is a (small) number of works for whose reception there is a sustained demand *although* they are already familiar to every cultured reader. As the above paragraph may elucidate, this statement does not mean that there is a (Platonic) timeless dignity of certain works. As we may observe in the present age, texts which were once believed to be beyond the vicissitudes of time, for example the *Iliad*, may lose their popularity. But, as I should like to say in order to distance my position, once again, from that of the Russian formalists (whom I otherwise highly esteem), "demand" may outweigh "automatization".

basic and abstract patterns, between the fictions devised by different cultures. In the case of the pastoral, this potential of imaginary wish fulfillment is not difficult to describe: pastoral novels, operas, and poems devise a world without the constraints of hard labor, without the strictures of civilized life, without the intemperate vicissitudes of "stepmother nature", without the bonds and burdens of family life, and without the traumas inflicted upon humans by lasting emotional and sexual frustration.

One possible answer to the question of why the pattern is no longer extracted from the net in twentieth-century Western literatures and of why it goes on being attractive in countries like India might not be very hard to imagine: the processes of industrialization and liberalization have freed Western people at least partly from those constraints their ancestors in early modernity experienced as so oppressive that they did not see any other way to cope with them than through compensatory fantasizing.—But there is another insight to be gained from a careful scrutiny of the history of the pastoral. In the age of the French Enlightenment, the tradition underwent a functional change or re-accentuation, whose best-known textual products are Rousseau's *Nouvelle Héloïse* (1761) and (perhaps even more) his *Du contrat social* (1762). I shall not go into details here; suffice it to say that the genre became mimeticized and underwent a functional transformation from fantasmatic to utopian, or rather uchronian.[445] The Rousseauian ideal of a rustic society whose members are free from hard labor, and where societal and emotional problems are tempered by benevolent circumstances as well as by the omnipresence of internalized *raison*, is nothing other than a rewriting of the pastoral with the aim of putting it into "real-world" practice.—It would not be misled to link Marx's praise of the future communist society as formulated in the *Manifesto* to this tradition of a mimeticized and "uchronized" pastoral.

Beginning at the end of the eighteenth century, the literary pastoral was recast as a political program. It may be that it was this re-functionalization alone which caused its rather complete loss of attractiveness as literary material from

---

445 This term, generated in analogy to the one created by Thomas More, was first introduced by Charles Renouvier in his novel *Uchronie (L'Utopie dans l'histoire), esquisse historique apocryphe du développement de la civilisation européenne tel qu'il n'a pas été, tel qu'il aurait pu être* (1857/1876); it designates literary models of an alternative "reality" that do not have recourse to a place (*topos*) unknown, but rather to a time or period (*chronos*) unknown, in most cases, to the future.—My above characterization of Rousseau's novel may not convince every reader of this book; it implies an interpretation of the heroine's premature death. According to my view, the end of the text does not convey that passion and reason are irreconcilable, but, rather, that it is necessary to "implement" even much more reason in the sphere of human relations than is the case in the novel.

the middle of the nineteenth century onward. But it may also be that the insight, fully realized only in the last third of the twentieth century, that the Rousseauian or Marxian conception of a pastoral put into practice will never be able to come true, compromised the pastoral pattern as a mode of fantasizing. Fantasies for which one must strictly exclude the possibility of their realization do not have a compensatory dimension.

5.—Finally, I would like to pick just one example in order to illustrate the astonishing degree to which processes of circulation of cultural material may lead to innovations completely unintended by those who first produced a constellation that was then extracted and reworked under different circumstances. The point to be discussed is apt to problematize all concepts of an (at least intra-literary) teleology, unless one is willing to make the assumption that human culture, including literature, is in the final analysis produced by a "higher" agency who carefully hides its activities by making their outcomes appear to be erratic and fortuitous.

When it comes to discussing the historical origins of the French realist novel as developed by Balzac, it is a nearly uncontested thesis that Diderot was the most important inspiration for nineteenth-century "realism".[446] By repudiating the model of classical tragedy as artificial and unconvincing, by calling for illusion instead of admiration, Diderot opened the way for a new literary paradigm whose adequate generic frame was prose fiction rather than the dramatic genre in which he himself still tried to excel. This role of precursor applies even in the case of specific devices. The technique of the *tableau* in particular as a means of producing illusion, which is suggested in the *Entretiens sur 'Le Fils naturel'* (1757),[447] is frequently referred to by twentieth-century scholars of the French realist novel who wish to point out the importance of Diderot.

The illusionary potential of *tableaux*—that is, of scenes on stage modeled after scenes of everyday life as depicted in genre paintings—has perhaps been best explained by the art historian Michael Fried, who is also a literary scholar. In his seminal book *Absorption and Theatricality*,[448] Fried argues that a major shift in the history of (representational) painting took place in the eighteenth century: persons depicted on canvases no longer look at the beholder in a quasi-theatrical fashion, that is, as actors on stage who speak to an audience;

---

446 See, once again, my *Ästhetik der Wirklichkeitsdarstellung* (as to Diderot's concept of *tableau*, see specifically pp. 22–24, including the notes).
447 In: *Œuvres esthétiques*, Paul Vernière (ed.), Paris 1965, pp. 77–175; as for the description of the device of *tableau*, see pp. 88–91.
448 Subtitle: *Painting and Beholder in the Age of Diderot*, Chicago, IL 1980.

rather, they are modeled in such a fashion as to convey the impression of being "absorbed" in what they are doing in the depicted scene and of not caring at all about who might be observing them. In the latter case, beholders have the impression of access to what the depicted figures "really" feel and to what preoccupies them; in the former case, they are left with the sense that the figures are just performing (for them), in other words, that what they display is not authentic, but staged. It is the "absorptive" variant of graphic art which is meant when Diderot talks about *tableau*-like techniques of representation as adequate means of producing illusion.

The fascinating constellation, referred to above, of the production of something new and completely unintended by the originator of the pattern it employs, is described in detail by Tatiana Korneeva: she found that the device of "*tableaux* on stage" was not of Diderot's invention.[449] He adopted (or should we say plagiarized?) it from Carlo Goldoni, who might rightly be considered the true father of the genre called *drame bourgeois* (a role typically ascribed to Diderot), which was later to become, transformed into narrative prose, the basis of novels like *Le père Goriot* (1834/1835). This fact is frequently neglected in literary history, but not totally ignored, since Diderot himself—while calling Goldoni, rather condescendingly, an "author of farces"[450]—admits it. The interesting connection revealed by Korneeva's study consists, however, in the fact that even Goldoni was not the first inventor of the device in question, that he was rather inspired by an obscure Neapolitan aristocrat and playwright named Domenico Luigi Barone (1685–1757). And one has to add another site of cultural activity in order to fully reveal the erratic character of literary production on display here. Barone's texts and techniques were largely inspired by the Spanish Baroque theater, which is in principle hardly astonishing; the Kingdom of Naples was in that age a colony ruled by a Spanish viceroy.

The paradox to be observed here is linked to the fact that the Spanish plays in question had little if anything in common with what was subsequently called literary realism. Without too much systematization, they may be labeled didactic dramas; they were either explicitly allegorical, or based on allegorical constellations which were superficially re-mimeticized by giving the personifications proper names. This "allegorical connection" can still be observed in Goldoni's work, for instance in plays like *Il genio buono e il genio cattivo* (1767), whose basic structure is more or less the same as in famous religious *comedias*

---

449 "Il pubblico teatrale nel *Genio buono e il genio cattivo* di Carlo Goldoni", *Italian Studies* vol. 70/2015, pp. 92–116.
450 *De la poésie dramatique*, in : D. D., *Œuvres esthétiques*, pp. 221–223.

by Calderón, in this case *El mágico prodigioso*, for instance. In the context of the Spanish didactic plays, *tableaux* on stage were "real" paintings (coulisses) exhibiting allegorical scenes interpreting or reconfirming the meaning of the action of the play proper. Goldoni's idea, adopted from Barone, to mix, so to speak, the devices of mobile (regular) performance with devices inspired by static (pictorial) performance as a way of producing impressive plays thus has its roots in the allegorical Christian drama of medieval provenance, which had been renewed and updated in the Spanish Counter-Reformation. As early as in Goldoni, the device was re-functionalized from didacticism to the production of illusion. Thus reshaped, it was presented by Diderot as his own invention and used as a centerpiece of his ideas on dramatic mimeticism. But it was only when Balzac transposed these ideas from the genre of *drame* to the novel—frequently termed, including by the author himself, (narrativized) *drame*—[451] that literary realism in the modern sense came into being.

The "extraction" of diverse materials and concepts from the floating processes taking place within the cultural net; the superimposition of different reshapings and re-functionalizations finally producing results which in the end have nothing in common with or are even in contradiction of the intentional dimensions of the works where one might first observe the techniques and devices in question—such processes may be paradigmatic of the productive dimensions of what I suggest calling the cultural net. Its main features are the universal availability of diverse material and the liberty of cultural producers to extract whatever they might need, to decompose it, and finally to reassemble it in a novel fashion. In some cases (Diderot), their "creations" may trigger long-lasting cultural effects; in other cases (Barone), their work may only serve subsequent cultural producers as material that calls for further dis- and re-assembly before attaining the level of general reception.

"Rootedness": Johann Gottfried Herder

0.—In terms of theoretical conceptualizing, the "antagonist" to my approach—that is, to the idea that works of art, including literature, as well as culture in general, may be conceived as products of a synthesis of items, content-related as well as formal, circulating in a universal virtual net—is, most obviously, the concept of "national literatures". Its first extensive theorization, which continues

---

[451] For more details, see the chap. on *Le colonel Chabert* in my *Balzac und der 'Effet de réel'. Eine Untersuchung anhand der Textstufen des Colonel Chabert und des Curé de village*, Amsterdam 1986.

to be influential up to the present, is the notion of popular culture in its acceptation as *Volkskultur* and *Volkspoesie*, developed by Johann Gottfried Herder (1744–1803). I shall link my theoretical remarks in this chapter to a specific text corpus which will allow for the assessment of the extent to which the notion of *Volkskultur* has a *fundamentum in re*, namely, popular theater culture[452] as documented in traditional, premodern Bavaria and Austria.—But before coming to the debates from the eighteenth century, I would like to formulate some remarks on how the situation might be assessed with regard to previous eras, limiting my scope to periods from which there is sufficient extant documentation to go beyond mere speculation.

1.—The Greeks of the classical period—as is the case with many or perhaps all ancient civilizations—did not concern themselves with the question of the extent to which their great texts were essentially "Greek", for the simple reason that they did not deem the literary production of other tribes or communities worth the effort of consideration. They were, to put it in current terms, communitarians. Universalism was a concept so far removed from their intellectual framework that they did not even compare their culture to that of the "others", the *barbaroi*.[453]—As a first point concerning the debate at issue, this observa-

---

452 For all necessary details, see Bernhart, *Volksschauspiele*.—There is a problem of translation involved in the topic of this chapter. *Volkspoesie*, *Volkstheater*, *Volkskultur*, *Volkslied*—these and similar terms are typically rendered in English by making use of the adjective "popular". The main difference, in my view, is that *Volkskultur* as well as all related terms primarily refer to the originating instances, whereas "popular" mainly refers to intended and real recipients. Pop music, for example, does not have to be created by the "common people"; the term is used to designate a genre of musical creation that appeals to everyone, in the first place to those who do not "know" anything about music (who are not able to read a score, who do not play an instrument, who are unfamiliar with musical traditions, etc.). Herder's concept of *Volkskultur*, by contrast, is based on the assumption that the works in question are created for, but also *by* the common people, in a sort of collective act that may span many generations during which an embryonic text is re-narrated again and again. The documents that have come down to us (the codices) are, according to him, not "creations", but mere recordings, that is, the result of the conversion of sound (orality) into letters (textuality).
453 Is it necessary to make explicit that this generalizing assessment is (as are all generalizing statements within the humanities) relative, that is, needs to be understood in relation to the modern Western situation? Since ancient Greeks maintained close economic relations with limitrophic tribes and empires, and also engaged in warfare with them as early as in archaic times, there was a certain knowledge of the barbarian cultures (in contrast to cases of absolute ignorance in this respect as conditioned by geological factors [communities living on islands far removed from other islands (Australia); small communities living scattered in vast territories difficult to traverse (Brazil)]). But as can be inferred from emblematic literary figures—Medea, for instance—there was nothing that could compare with the relations of exchange on an equal level and the ensuing combination of mutual esteem and agonistic competition that is characteristic of cultural relations in the West starting in the Middle Ages.

tion may produce the insight that the emergence of a concept like "national literatures" presupposes some sort of universalism, be it an emerging one, as its background. Only when humans consider other humans as in principle equal does the question of how to define one's "own" cultural products versus those of the "others" become relevant.[454]—It is precisely this feature which is absent in the system of a classical school of thought that has been very influential in Western modernity and is frequently seen as a precursor of modern universalism: skepticism. The skeptics' tolerance of the "views" (manners, social codes, artworks) of any imaginable tribe is not based on the assumption of equality; it rather emanates from a less aggressive interpretation of the concept of barbarism than that found in Aristotle, who deemed it legitimate to treat barbarians in the same way as wild beasts.[455] For the skeptics, the "others" and their cultures are without any importance. It is indifference that characterizes their attitude towards foreign cultures. As alien communities are committed to disinterest, there is no need to theorize what one's own culture might be in contrast to that of the "barbarians".—According to current clichés, Greek culture and self-conception underwent a radical change in the period during which the various tribes were violently unified and then bellicosely spread into regions hardly known to them before. Hellenism is a time of cultural imperialism which goes along with the partial integration of the cultural patterns of the subjugated into a "new" and more comprehensive Greek culture. Still, the processes occurring in this period did not provoke a reflection of what Greek (vs. non-Greek) culture is or was. The civilizational gap between the conquered territories and the Greek motherland was so significant that the encounter with the "others" did not irritate the pre-existing self-sufficiency of Greek reflection. Quite as was the case in later times, in the period of the Western penetration into sub-Saharan Africa for example, Greeks of Hellenistic times did not sense a need for self-reflection and self-problematization. The difference between "own"

---

[454] The above point may also be of a certain relevance with regard to the other early high civilization, China—a community that preserved its communitarian attitude much longer than Greece (which, as part of the Roman Empire, adopted universalism in the fourth century CE), in fact up to the period when it was opened up by military intervention on the part of the Western powers. Within traditional Chinese culture, there is no relevant interest in "foreign" artworks and, consequently, no need to reflect on what the dichotomously conceived "essence" of one's own, Chinese art is.

[455] See Plutarch's summary of Aristotle's advice in this respect to his pupil Alexander (*De Alexandri magni fortuna aut virtute* I 6). There is much controversy regarding the authenticity of the passage, but such discussions seem somewhat superfluous. Throughout his works, Aristotle equates *barbaroi* and *douloi* (slaves, who most frequently were of "barbarian" provenance); the juridical status of the latter was that of objects, instruments, without any human dignity or any rights (see *Politics* 1252a 30 ff., and 1253 b 30 ff.).

and "other" was cast as hierarchical and in addition as categorial; as long as they did not adopt Greek culture, the conquered remained *barbaroi* as theorized by Aristotle: intermediate beings between animals and "real" humans, meaning: Greeks.—In addition to the above-mentioned feature, tribal self-consciousness ("nationalism") seems to have a second prerequisite: the presence of various tribes of an approximately comparable civilizational level within a territory that is physically as well as conceptually manageable under a given standard of technological development.

At first sight, things appear to be different in the case of Rome; yet in essence, they seem ultimately to be the same. The Romans adopted Greek culture and literature as their own after having conquered the peninsula, partly translating or emulating the texts in Latin, partly preserving them in their original formulation. They chose the way of self-Hellenization. There was a "strong" concept of Rome as a power and regarding its mission; but there was no specific concept of an autochthonous cultural identity linked to it.[456] One might speculate about the reasons for this quasi-absence of a *cultural* "national" identity. As occurred in Late Antiquity, when the barbaric conquerors of the Roman Empire adopted Roman culture, the distance in terms of civilizational level may have appeared so immense that the idea of casting a Roman cultural identity in contrast to Greek culture might have seemed devoid of sense; and the inverse relation in terms of physical power might have facilitated accepting the narcissistic lesion going along with the adoption of a cultural model that was not the Romans' own.—This feature of an absence of "national" cultural identity was reinforced when Rome spread its rule over the entire Mediterranean world, integrating innumerable tribes and distinct traditions into its empire; it was given another strong impulse when the educated strata of the population received Stoicism and adopted its universalizing implications; it became definitive when, in the fourth century, the empire embraced the first religion ever with a claim to universality, Christianity, thus conferring an incontestable (since divinely revealed) ideological basis upon what had first emerged contingently.[457]

---

[456] The central text establishing the rising empire's self-conception with regard to its "origins", Virgil's *Aeneid*, does not present Rome as a product of autochthony, but rather as a product of transfer.

[457] I should like to stress that the "Roman case" is apt to elucidate an implication of my above claim that universalism is a *prerequisite* for the emergence of the concept of different national cultural identities: it does not *necessarily* provoke the feature of compartmentalized cultural identity.—Given the extremely scarce extant documentation of Rome's self-reflection in the early centuries (that is, before the conquest of Greece and the adoption of Greek culture), it would be audacious to present speculations aiming at causally explaining this feature of a quasi-absence of a cultural tribal identity. With a view to further discussions regarding this

2.—According to a widespread belief, the situation changed dramatically roughly one thousand years later, when Dante started theorizing the *volgare*—that is, the variant of classical Latin that had become the language of daily communication in Tuscany—as an instrument that is, at least on the level he calls *vulgare illustre*, no less dignified than Latin as a language for literary texts. As is well known, Dante even wrote a treatise, *De vulgari eloquentia* (1303/1305), concerning this postulate; but it is quite telling that he wrote it in Latin.[458] Ultimately, Dante's views have little in common with what we currently understand by the term "national literature".[459] The dichotomy underlying his argument is, indeed, the one of Latin vs. Italian, but not in the sense of "other" vs. "own"; what is meant is the dichotomy of *grammatica* vs. *sermo vulgaris*—that is, the standardized language of script[460] vs. the language of oral communication. The *grammatica* is not considered to be "foreign" or "other". It was not Dante, but another

---

question, I would like to offer the observation that a "low-level" cultural identity—in terms of an absence of a strict dichotomizing—may be characteristic of global empires, or even a prerequisite for spreading their (military, economic) power over the entire world. The Unites States of America may be, *mutatis mutandis*, such a parallel case. It adopted its basic cultural features from a nation it had defeated in a war; regardless of an extremely highly developed consciousness of its "imperial" status in terms of power and influence, the USA is remarkably open to exogenous cultural material of any kind (I should stress, once again, that this book is written from the perspective of an author who has spent almost all of his life in traditional European nation-states). In both cases, it may be the point given expression to at the end of the preceding paragraph which yields an additional explanation for this fact: if there is, finally, no competitor of an approximately comparable level, there is no need for a rigid cultural dichotomizing.

458 In anticipation of my argumentation above, I should stress that the treatise is written for people writing and discussing literary texts, that is, the educated only, whereas Dante's most important text, the *Commedia* (1307–1321), is a didactic text, that is, a text conceived for general divulgation.

459 Regarding this point, see Dante's explicit rejection of all sorts of "nationalism" and claims to supremacy of one tribe over another, as resulting from a lack of reason and from the state of being uncultured ("Nam quicunque tam obscene rationis est ut locum sue nationis delitiosissimum credat esse sub sole, hic etiam pre cunctis proprium vulgare licetur, idest maternam locutionem, et per consequens credit ipsum fuisse illud quod fuit Ade. Nos autem, cui mundus est patria velut piscibus equor, quanquam Sarnum biberimus ante dentes et Florentia adeo diligamus ut, quia dileximus, exilium patiamur iniuste, rationi magis quam sensui spatulas nostri iudicii podiamus". // "For whoever is so misguided as to think that the place of his birth is the most delightful spot under the sun may also believe that his own language, that is, his mother tongue, is preeminent among all others; and, as a result, he may believe that his language was also Adam's. To me, however, the whole world is a homeland, like the sea to fish; though I drank from the Arno before my teeth grew, and love Florence so much that, because I loved her, I suffer exile unjustly, I will weight the balance of my judgement more with reason than with sentiment." [*De vulgari eloquentia*, liber primus, VI, 2–3]).

460 Etymologically, *grammatica* derives from the Greek *gramma*, "letter". Grammars or grammar books, in the modern sense of the term, are a collection of rules applicable to the written

of the *tre corone*, namely Boccaccio, who made the reasons for the postulation of an equal linguistic dignity of the vernacular explicit: the knowledge of the *grammatica* was limited to a very restricted circle of educated people—less than 1% of the population—whereas the *volgare*, at least in oral form, was accessible to everyone.[461] There was no ambition involved to assert a separate Italian national identity which did not exist at the time;[462] the question at issue is that of an extremely limited vs. a general (potential) audience.

I am not sure that the situation changed substantively in the centuries called the Renaissance or the early modern age. The "grammaticalization" of the various vernaculars—meaning, their standardization, starting with Antonio de Nebrija's Grammar of Castilian Spanish (1492) and continued in the work done by the *Académie française*, established in 1635—did indeed have implications for a concept linking cultural products mediated by language to political units. Linguistic standardization was an important factor in the establishment of the modern state, that is, of political organizations governed by rules and norms universally applicable within a given territory. Yet it was not the assumption of "blood bonds" between inhabitants that formed the basis of these territories in case they emerged in this period, early modernity. As may be inferred from the history of Spain in the era of the *Reyes católicos* or from the history of the fragmented German principalities of the age, the logic of early modern state-building was that of dynastic constellations. The concept of the nation, of peo-

---

version of the language in question, which may be transgressed (and are, indeed, frequently transgressed) in oral communication.

461 I am referring to the proem of the *Decameron*, in which Boccaccio gives expression to the idea that his collection is written for a primarily female audience and, for this reason, makes use of the *volgare* instead of the *grammatica*.

462 I should like to recall that, as concerns politics, Dante was a partisan of the idea of the Holy Roman Empire and thus expected the "kaiser" to settle the situation of civil war in Italy, of which he had become a victim.—In order to avoid getting lost in details, I leave it to readers to extrapolate how I would answer to less important objections to my argument (I will indeed be addressing the more important ones). I will mention just one possible minor objection relevant to the above passage: there is, indeed, the example of Petrarch's famous *canzone* "Italia mia". It is not astonishing that this poem was read along Herderian lines when nineteenth-century Italians were fighting the Spanish, the French, and the Austrians in order to become a political nation, that is, as a testimony to the fact that "Italians" had been longing for national unity as early as in the Middle Ages; Dante's above-cited ideas had to be neglected, though, for this purpose. If one reads Petrarch's poem without any nationalistic emphasis, the text turns out to be a document not of "patriotism", but of nostalgia, of the longing for a period past and for the *topoi* where this period of the speaker's life took place. Nostalgia, however, is a universal feeling; it emanates from our incapacity to revivify the past in other ways than by remembering. Memory is always and by necessity impregnated with nostalgia, with the feeling of loss.

ple united not only politically, that is, by constraints of power, but also by bonds of birth, by natural bonds,[463] did not exist during the period in question. The link between soil, blood, and culture became a widely accepted, quasi-evident concept only in later times.[464]

3.—It might at first sight seem astonishing that the idea as such was not developed within the most extensively homogenized community of the time, that is, France. The concept of *Volkskultur* is rather linked to the name of Johann Gottfried Herder. Yet if one considers the hypothesis that it is not only fiction, but also the modeling of "realities" which may to a large extent obey the logic of compensation, it is not difficult to conceive of reasons why the concept of the nation as a homogeneous unitary culture—thus linking "natural" (biological, territorial) and cultural belonging—was first developed in the German-speaking territories, and particularly during the age in question. There was no political entity named "Germany" at the time, and there was no prospect of the creation of such an entity. The modern German state was not founded until 1871, roughly one century after Herder formulated the concept of *Volkskultur*. This concept may have been the only way to confer unity upon a fragmented territory that seemed belated in its development in comparison to other important European communities (England, France, Spain).—Herder's theorization of culture,[465] and

---

[463] The Latin noun *natio*, from which the modern term "nation" stems in terms of etymology, derives from the verb *nasci*, meaning: "to be born".

[464] There is, evidently, no story without a prehistory; as to one of the cases just mentioned, one could mention in this respect the politics of *limpieza de sangre* (meaning: being non-Jewish in terms of genealogy) implemented in Spain from the fifteenth century onward. But the decisive first element of the above-mentioned triad was missing in early modern Spain: the "right" blood bonds to be proved by anyone who wanted to avoid discrimination and, later on, persecution, were not linked, for their part, to a specific territory, but rather to the universal community of (Catholic) believers. An assimilated German or Italian whose denomination was Roman Catholic would not have had any problems being accepted as a full member of the polity in early modern Spain.

[465] Specialists of Herder's work will not be satisfied by the following portrait of his positions; but, as expressed at various occasions, this is not a book written for specialists. The concession I would be ready to make is that Herder's argumentation is self-contradictory with regard to many problems, as I shall point out in the course of this chapter. But the "racial" component I will be foregrounding is undeniably a very prominent element of his entire thinking. In addition, I should stress that it is not my intention to provide an adequate and balanced précis of Herder's theorizing in its entirety or to offer speculations regarding the question of what he "really" might have thought. When it comes to the *reception* of Herder's ideas, that is, to their influence, the point emphasized here seems indeed to be by far the most relevant one.—At this point in the present study, readers might have realized that my approach differs from standard present-day cultural theory not least by trying to avoid any moral judgments concerning the positions discussed. As to Herder in particular, and notwithstanding the devastations some of his concepts may have triggered in twentieth-century European political history (including

in particular of culture as language, that is, literature, formed the basis of the Romantic concept of "national culture" throughout Europe. Although such an approach to culture was relegated to the background in the age of avant-gardism, the emergence of "new" nations that went along with the collapse of colonialism revitalized it in a most remarkable way. As was the case in Europe at the beginning of the nineteenth century, the process of postcolonial nation building was accompanied by a discourse aiming at the delimitation of what is essentially one's own from that which belongs to others; or, to put it in current terminology, it was accompanied by an identity discourse.

Vernaculars indeed differ from one another; that is a fact. They are, however, hardly sufficient for substantiating the postulate of identity. The long-standing practice of vernacular multilingualism, widespread amongst the nobility and the educated parts of the middle class in Herder's day, might have resulted in the impression that language alone was an all too frail basis for postulating a cultural "identity" in a substantive fashion. The concept of *Volkspoesie*[466] (national literature) seemed appropriate for neutralizing this lack. According to the Herderian conceptualization, popular culture and literature in particular are not the creation of individual geniuses, but rather the collective creation of the common people amongst whom they first emerged. By means of the repeated narration and re-narration of stories or "songs" over thousands of years, and before the emergence of the fixed textual products known to us, these stories or "songs" became—according to Herder—the direct expression of a *Volksseele* (literally: national soul, in the sense of national character), that is, of the entire set of mental parameters of the people concerned. The texts were thus conceived of as no less "rooted" than the people, that is, the common people, who may, indeed, seem to have been "rooted" quite like trees and plants in the times before the liberation of the third estate.

Nazi cultural theory), he can hardly be held responsible for the consequences some of his ideas may have produced. The issue is a different one if considered from a posterior perspective. In my view, twenty-first-century cultural theory has to take into consideration the question of why the concept of "national cultures" turned out to be as highly polemogenous as it did in twentieth-century political history; my suggestion would be to consider the hypothesis that the attempt at "proving" a conceptualization which was highly ideological (as opposed to real) might have been one of the reasons for the general radicalization of political life observable in Europe from the middle of the nineteenth through the middle of the twentieth century.

466 In eighteenth- and nineteenth-century usage, the German term "Poesie" designates not only poetry, but also narrative and drama; its equivalent in present-day standard German is "Literatur". "Poesie" as well as "Literatur" exclude all variants of low-level trivial fiction, but not valuable "popular literature" in the sense hinted at by Herder's conceptualization.

Such a conceptualization might at first sight appear plausible due to the fact that there are certain features of human culture which are, indeed, directly contingent upon the conditions reigning in specific habitats. The architecture of houses, as well as clothing and styles of dress, nutrition, etc., are dependent upon climate and geological factors. Since literary texts are clearly different in different regions, the indicator being the difference of language, it seemed convincing to transpose this concept of the rootedness of more pragmatic cultural practices and products to literary texts, above all to popular texts, and to thus arrive at the well-known and still prevalent notion of *Volkspoesie* as an expression of *Volksseele*.[467]

One might add a detail regarding German cultural history which has been touched upon in passing at various occasions above: Herder's theory had an aim which is transparent on almost every page of his tracts. The culture of eighteenth-century Germany was under the sway of a strong influence from France. Noblemen as well as intellectuals mainly communicated in French. German seventeenth-century, that is, Baroque literature was considered "barbaric"—it is indeed somewhat odd, linguistically as well as conceptually—and the treasures of Middle High German literature were largely unknown at the time. Herder was one of those thinkers—they exist in all tribes and at all times, including the present—who, for whatever reason, were opposed to this early vogue of "globalization", that is, the absorption of less well-performing cultural entities by those that perform better. He was a communitarian. In order to make the claim that German culture is valuable, he could not do otherwise than to postulate that there is an "essential" difference between French *civilisation* on the one hand and German *Kultur* on the other.

---

[467] As I shall mention in the following, the influence of Herder's ideas in the Latin world was less significant than among the Germanic and Slavic nations; but they were influential, in particular in the first half of the nineteenth century, with its cult of *couleur locale*. On the level of theory, Herder's ideas were an inspiration for the concepts of a theoretician as important as Hippolyte Taine, who propagated the parameters of *race, milieu et moment* as determinant factors of all cultural production. And even in the twentieth century, the influence of Herderian concepts may be detected in French culture. As an example, I shall quote a specifically pointed and polemical passage from Guillaume Apollinaire: "Furthermore, poets must always express a milieu, a nation; and artists, just as poets, just as philosophers, form a social estate which belongs doubtless to all humanity, but as the expression of a race, of one given environment. Art will only cease being national the day that the whole universe, living in the same climate, in houses built in the same style, speaks the same language with the same accent, that is to say never" ("The New Spirit and the Poets" [1918], in: G. A., *Selected Writings*, Roger Shattuck [tr.], New York, NY 1971, p. 229).

It is striking to see the innumerable logical twists this highly learned man is obliged to make in order to invest his rather bizarre but influential conceptualization with the semblance of argumentative coherence. The most illustrative example of these logical leaps and breaches may be his portrait of English literature.[468] The English tradition is presented as Germanic, and thus as the expression of a *Geist* that is parallel if not identical to that of the Germans residing on the continent. This assumption is "substantiated" by way of a brief recapitulation of the political history of the British Isles that gives prominence to the numerous invasions by Scandinavian tribes. There is not much room for the Celtic component of the English tradition in this narrative. Yet above all, there is no room for an event as major as the conquest of 1066. It is not mentioned at all. And yet, from that date onward, English language and culture have been a mix of Celtic, Germanic, and French elements, the latter feature linking all posterior English culture to the entirety of the Greco-Roman heritage and its Mesopotamian, Egyptian (etc.) antecedents.

Herder's blindness in this respect also informs his eulogy of Shakespeare as a Teutonic genius who supposedly gave expression to the *Volksgeist* of all Germanic tribes. Yet Shakespeare's use of Latin, Italian, Spanish, and Greek sources receives little, if any mention. Herder's readers are given the impression that Shakespeare's dramas mainly consist of the appearance of ghosts, witches, and other related strands appropriate for a refutation of the superficiality of rational French *civilisation*, represented by Racinean tragedy, in the name of a comprehensive Germanic *Kultur* whose attributes are linked to dimensions of a "higher" or "deeper" truth not accessible by mere reason.

4.–On a more general level, the argumentative frailty of Herder's tracts becomes apparent in a recurrent and rather amazing feature. On the one hand, the author relentlessly stresses that "authentic" culture is bound to its location and to the "tribe" (*Volksstamm*) inhabiting the location in question; he claims that cultures are autochthonous in the very literal sense. If that were the case, there would be "national cultures" as diverse as the planet's climate and geology (moderate climates, cold climates, hot climates; coastal, maritime spaces, plains, deserts, mountains, etc., etc.). But Herder himself again and again detects with great joy and enthusiasm that all these different cultures bear far-reaching commonalities as long as one goes back in time sufficiently. The pris-

---

[468] See the essays "Shakespear" (1773) and "Von der Ähnlichkeit der mittleren englischen und deutschen Dichtkunst" (1777); one should also read "Auszug aus einem Briefwechsel über Ossian und die Lieder alter Völker" (1773); quotes are from the standard edition (*Sämmtliche Werke*, Bernhard Suphan [ed.], 32 vols., Berlin 1877–1909, vol. 5, pp. 159–257 and vol. 9, pp. 522–535); translations are mine.

tine products of the different national cultures are analogous, if not identical; in congruence with the findings of emerging evolutionary biology, Herder advocates the thesis of the species' monogenesis.[469] Starting from this assumption, and in formulations to be found some decades later in myriad texts by Romantic writers, he praises the "patriarch's tent" as the first and best model of human congregation. The "values", cultural as well as societal, that developed on this "ground" are "wisdom instead of science, piety instead of knowledge, love of parents, spouses, and children instead of courteousness and debauchery. Life well-ordered, the rule by divine right of a dynasty—the model of all civil order and its institutions—, in all this mankind takes the simplest, but also the most profound delight.[470] [...] The human spirit received the first forms of wisdom and virtue with a simplicity, strength, and majesty that [...] has no equal, no equal at all in our philosophical, cold, European world. And just because we are so incapable of understanding this anymore, of feeling it, let alone of taking delight in it, we mock, we deny, and we misconstrue!"[471] And he ends his diatribe, directly addressing his contemporary educated readers, by devaluing "your philosophical deism, your aesthetic virtue [...] your universal love of all peoples" as symptoms of either ignorance or hypocrisy.[472]—Herder does not discuss explicitly what factors might have vitiated this early culture, including its literature, which was an "immediate" expression of humankind's *Seele*. But from the above formulations it is evident what he had in mind: it is rationality, refinement, progress, in brief, civilization that brought about the detrimental move away from literature as an expression of the *Volksseele*.

Herder is a (pre-)Romantic, but a naïve Romantic. He posits as "true" and "essential" what more enlightened thinkers of the age, such as Schiller, would apostrophize as a legitimate longing for a past that is past, which may be recreated by way of works of art, though under the condition that these works preserve and manifest the artificial character of the recreation. This is the essence of Schiller's concept of *das Sentimentalische* as opposed to *das Naive*;[473] the latter concept designates the "authentic" vestiges of pristine human culture which exist in modernity as fragments only.—It remains an open question, however, whether such a "naïve" approach to the world ever truly existed. It may be that mediation, in other words, the introduction of language and reflection, put an

---

469 The following arguments are most clearly expressed in *Auch eine Philosophie der Geschichte zur Bildung der Menschheit* (1774), in: *Sämmtliche Werke*, vol. 5, pp. 475–593.
470 P. 479.
471 P. 484.
472 P. 486.
473 See *On Naïve and Sentimental Poetry* (1795).

end to all such "naïveté" grounded in "immediacy" (*Unvermittelheit*), which thus would be an attribute not of the human, but of the animal world.

5.—Before I start discussing the text corpus to which I shall link my critical remarks concerning *Volkspoesie*, I should like to make one additional point with regard to Herder's conceptualizations and to the innumerable theories, up to and including postcolonialism, that are more or less direct continuations of these ideas. As already mentioned in passing, it is not without reason that concepts of national culture and rootedness first arose in a German context, nor is it astonishing that they were enthusiastically received in Northern and Eastern Europe and later on in Latin America,[474] in fact in the entire (former) Third World, including amongst its intellectuals. The influence of such ideas in the strongholds of occidental culture (France, Italy, Spain, England, in later times also the USA) has always been relatively limited. The explanation seems obvious: it would be devoid of sense to claim that French (or Italian, Spanish, etc.) literary culture is the expression of a *Geist* or *Seele* of tribes residing in these territories since times immemorial, for two different but intertwined reasons. It is not possible for the people living in these countries to be unaware of the fact that their ancestors have not been "rooted" in the soil for thousands and thousands of years, that they are rather the descendants of a somewhat wild mix of locals (Celts), Roman conquerors or immigrants (meaning: people from the Mediterranean in a very broad sense of the term), and Scandinavian conquerors of the Roman Empire (Goths, Vikings, Normans). Secondly, they cannot be unaware of the fact that their languages as well as their entire cultures, including their literary texts, are to a very large extent the result not of "rootedness",[475] but rather of transfer, of a *translatio studii* accompanying the

---

[474] It is perhaps no surprise that it was Jorge Luis Borges—amongst others, including the most famous Brazilian novelist to date, Machado de Assis—who polemicized, in his typical way impregnated with irony, against the widespread notions, arising in the age of Latin American "nation-building", of a peculiar Latin American (or even Argentine, Mexican, or Brazilian) literature: "The idea that Argentine literature must abound in differential traits and in Argentine color seems to me to be a mistake. [...] Furthermore, I don't know if it needs to be said that the idea that a literature must define itself by the differential traits of the country that produces it is a relatively new one, and the idea that writers must seek out subjects local to their country is also new and arbitrary. [...] The Argentine cult of local color is a recent European cult that nationalists should reject as a foreign import." ("The Argentine Writer and Tradition", in: J. L. B., *Selected Non-Fictions*, Eliot Weinberger [ed.], Esther Allen [tr.], New York, NY 1999, pp. 421–427).

[475] Let me say in passing that the most important French precursor of Romanticism, Rousseau, bases his description of the early sedentary communities, no less tainted by nostalgia than Herder's, not on the assumption of family ("blood") bonds between members, but on the concept of contract (*contrat social*). This said, one may detect—as I shall briefly explain in the following— a strong influence of Herder's ideas in the two or three decades of "acute" Romanticism in

translatio imperii. In the Latin parts of Europe, including England, culture evidently emanates from network-like structures and their constant and finally uncontrollable ramifications.[476]

France, namely in authors like Chateaubriand and Lamartine (see my "Sentimental Revivals: Gérard de Nerval's *Voyage en Orient*", in: Stephen G. Nichols, Joachim Küpper, and Andreas Kablitz [eds.], *Spectral Sea: Mediterranean Palimpsests in European Culture*, New York, NY and Bern 2017, pp. 157–202; Nerval's text contains massive ironizations of the basic concepts of Romanticism as displayed in his predecessors' "oriental" travelogues; it was published in 1851, that is before Flaubert's *Madame Bovary* and Baudelaire's *Fleurs du mal*, which both appeared in 1857).

[476] The history of literary studies is an example of the paradoxical impact generated by Herder's ideas all over Europe. Vernacular literary studies as a discipline taught in universities is, all over Europe, an "invention" of the early nineteenth century. It did not exist previously; traditional humanistic literary studies treated the classical texts (Greek and Latin) only. The following fact might be hard to believe: French literary studies were first established in Germany, in the newly founded, Humboldtian University of Bonn, by Friedrich Diez, the first professor ever appointed to the study of Romance languages and literatures (1830). It is not very difficult to imagine that literary studies at early nineteenth-century German universities were practiced along Herderian lines. And there is, indeed, one segment of postclassical European literature (texts to which I shall come back later) that ideally fits the Herderian parameters, namely, medieval texts. Consequently, modern (nineteenth-century) literary studies were originally almost exclusively medievalist. As Middle High German texts are to a large extent based on French models, the first modern literary scholars in Germany had to study not only their "own", but the medieval French texts as well—which were largely unknown in their country of origin at that time, with the exception of the lyrics of the troubadours. This latter portion of the French literary patrimony had been rediscovered already by François-Juste-Marie Raynouard (*Choix de poésies originales des troubadours* [1816–1821]), who was deeply influenced by Herderian concepts; his endeavors were carried on by Claude Fauriel, the first-ever professor at the Sorbonne to hold a chair for "littératures étrangères" (1830). Fauriel had absorbed the basic concepts of German Romanticism as a close acquaintance of Mme de Staël, author of the famous book titled *De l'Allemagne* (1810), which is generally regarded as the first manifestation of Romantic ideas in the French language. Scholars like Gaston Paris, who had studied with Diez, began to systematically establish French literary studies, emulating the "German" style, that is, the emphasis on medievalism. In 1835, Francisque Michel, a young scholar inspired by these new ideas, traveled to England. In the Bodleian Library, he found the manuscript of the *Song of Roland* and thus "created" what has since been regarded as the French national epic. Paris and his followers adopted the Herderian notions of "rootedness", although, as I express above, these do not make much sense in a French cultural context (this is, by the way, the reason why the very first "Herderian" medievalist in France, Jean-Charles-Léonard Simonde de Sismondi—an amateur scholar, much better known as an economist—had excluded French literature from his *De la littérature du midi de l'Europe* [1813]: it is all too obviously influenced by classical [Latin] models and thus does not fit the Herderian parameters). It constituted another decisive step, leading directly to what literary studies has been in French universities up to the present, when pupils of these medievalists transposed the concept of "national literature" to more recent periods. Herderian concepts thus became highly influential into the twen-

The difference, I would argue, between the case of these parts of Europe and that of regions such as the Germanic lands, Eastern Europe, and those parts of the former Third World which were not totally absorbed into Western culture during the process of colonization[477] does not even consist in a fundamental dissimilarity between their respective situations; it is the consciousness of the situation that differs. The fact that "tribes" as well as "tribal cultures" are nothing stable and "rooted", but rather the result of constant processes of exchange of genes and memes, cannot remain hidden in ages when the documentation of the past has become a routine practice. The French (and the Italians, Spanish, etc.) *know* from written evidence what their history has been from roughly the first centuries before the Common Era onward; and they are not able to deny what they and everyone else knows, however strong their longing for "rootedness" may be. In these countries, Romanticism—with the exception of brief periods—has always remained a mindset of the uncultured, the peripheral and non-intellectual parts of the population. In the Germanic territories, the past is known only from the age of Charlemagne onward; as to Eastern Europe, the threshold of documentation is situated even later in time. Since substantial written records are lacking, Central and Eastern European nations have a tendency to *construct* a past, building their construals on the basis of their longing for certainty and stability in a world where these do not exist, where "substance" is nothing but a phantasm. The political and ideological instability of many of the Central and Eastern European nations (as well as nations of the Third World[478])

---

tieth century, and they continue to be so in present-day literary studies not only in France and Germany, but all over Europe (for details, see Hans Ulrich Gumbrecht, "*Un souffle d'Allemagne ayant passé*: Friedrich Diez, Gaston Paris, and the Genesis of National Philologies", *Romance Philology* vol. 40 / 1986/87, pp. 1–37).

477 As for Latin America, where this total absorption did occur, the enthusiastic reception of Herderian ideas is linked to a massive re-valorization of the pre-Columbian heritage. Similar to what happened in eighteenth-century Germany, but on a frailer basis (since there is not much left from pre-Columbian times), the rediscovery of the "autochthonous" tradition is part of the attempt at emancipating the Latin-American nations from the culture of the colonial "oppressors".

478 The great nation and culture of India first became westernized by physical force, but later on adopted Western ideals (equality, democracy) on its own volition; with certain qualifications ("people's democracy" instead of Westminster-style democracy), this description also applies to another of the great nations and cultures of global history, China. When present-day Chinese party officials make it their task to reassert a "Chinese identity" by fending off detrimental "western influences", they are not aware of the extent to which they are unconsciously reproducing and thus falling prey to a basic concept of western Romanticism. One can only pray to the gods that Chinese leaders will become conscious of this constellation before they give in to the temptation of instigating nineteenth-century-European-style tribal wars.—Why does India seem to perform better on the stage of global politics? In contrast to China, India never knew the situation of the numerical predominance of one ethnic community

is, at least in part, closely linked to the fact that their historical belatedness favors attitudes of self-reflection that come close to a loss of touch with reality.

6.—In order to demonstrate *in concreto* the extent to which current clichés about "authentic" popular culture are biased by a combination of wishful thinking and ignorance, I shall address a text corpus which seems particularly well suited to a further scrutiny of the Herderian conceptions.

Popular theatrical culture flourished in the southern regions of the German-speaking territories in the period in question. In the northern Germanic world, even in territories with a population mixed in terms of religious denomination, the culture of popular performance never recovered from the blows inflicted upon all performances apt to stimulate the passions by the Protestant Reformation, which followed Augustine's and Plato's denunciation of *spectacula*. In southern Germany and in Austria, by contrast, there was an early modern theatrical culture which at first sight seems to be a quasi-ideal realization of Herder's concept of *Volkskultur*: the performances were arranged without professional organization (such as that of theater companies or wandering troupes), being orchestrated instead by amateurs, that is, the common people. They took place all over the region, even in villages of no more than 100 or 200 inhabitants. The seasonal period of the performances comprised the weeks following the harvest (the second half of August, the first half of September), when the village population was temporarily free from otherwise permanent agricultural labors and the meteorological conditions were still clement—which was a necessity, since the performances were held out of doors. The initiative to organize and stage the pieces lay in the hands of groups organized according to the "democratic" principles of brotherhoods.[479]

All of these factors, as well as others that could be listed, would at first sight seem to yield a perfect basis for producing plays that might teach us, two hundred years later, interesting facts about the nature of the *Volksseele* of the Germanic population of the Alpine valleys. But when one goes to the archives and studies the historical records—as yet unprinted manuscripts of the performances which were most probably written down by village priests or administrative

---

(in China: the Han); religiously, linguistically, and in terms of mores, India is a culture of myriad facets. To claim an Indian or Indic identity in terms of dichotomies ("us" vs. "the others") is much less favored by the realities than in other parts of the world, including the European nation states.

479 For details, see Bernhart, *Volksschauspiele*; see also Toni Bernhart, "Imagining the Audience in Eighteenth-Century Folk Theatre in Tyrol", in: Gvozdeva et al. (eds.), *Dramatic Experience*, pp. 269–288.

officials—one discovers a very different picture than that suggested by "Herderian" conceptions. The plots of these plays, which were "popular" not only in terms of the spectators, but also in terms of the performers—who, in turn, were the initiators and organizers (the "creators") of the performances—were in most cases drawn from biblical history or from the classical mythological tradition; for example, a figure as "exotic" as Phaethon is frequently included in these works.[480] Well-known vernacular texts which had attained a Europe-wide standing, such as the story of Griselda, were often made use of. There were also historical plots, dramas dealing with the Scottish Queen Mary Stuart presented as a martyr, or with Martin Luther exposed as an incarnation of the Devil. Finally, the entire hagiographical tradition is made use of in order to produce attractive plots. As a comic figure, the *Hanswurst* (created in Vienna) almost always appears. The texts as such are composed of spoken as well as sung passages; the latter follow the alternation of arias and recitatives as known from the elite genre of opera. In cases where the scores are still extant, it is obvious that they were modeled on the works of the famous metropolitan composers of the age, Bach, Händel, Mozart.[481] The only local feature to be detected in the manuscripts is, indeed, language. The texts are not written in standard German, but in the various dialects in use at that time in the respective locations of the performances.

To put it succinctly: there is close to nothing in these instances of "authentic" popular or folk culture[482] that is "chthonic", rooted, in the literal sense.[483]

---

480 The reasons for this latter predilection seem evident: the story of Phaethon perfectly fits the didactic needs of patriarchy. I leave it to readers to add the corresponding speculations with regard to the other privileged plots mentioned above.
481 Regarding this point, see Franz Gratl, "The Role of Music in Folk Drama: An Investigation based on Tyrolean Sources", in: Bernhart et al. (eds.), *Poetics and Politics*.
482 That is, in contrast to the centers and their "sentimentalizing" appropriations of the strands of popular culture that may appeal to evasive desires.
483 There is a plethora of similar phenomena one could adduce in order to further substantiate my point. The best-known may be the Ossian scandal: the "translation" produced by James Macpherson, allegedly based on authentic Gaelic oral material, turned out to be a fabrication. Another example of a quite different order might be the folk dress (the German word is *Tracht*) allegedly worn in the Alpine parts of Bavaria since times immemorial; as Oktoberfest has become a popular item of global event culture over the last decades, this garb, supposedly "authentic" and "ethnic", has become familiar worldwide. It is not even necessary to refer to learned books produced by historians specializing in Bavarian history in order to grasp the constructed character of the supposed authenticity and rootedness of this garb. The economic basis of the Alpine regions was agricultural up to the age of industrial production and mass tourism. As in all mountainous regions, the productivity of the soil was low, meaning people were very poor. Before the introduction of industrial textile production, fabric, and all the more multicolored fabric,

Excluding language, there are no such autochthonous elements. Consequently, the idea of a specific "identity" of the people in question that is given expression by way of these folk plays is somewhat problematic. Every item in the plays is the result of acts of extracting material floating in the cultural net and of reconfiguring it according to local demand. And there is not much speculation required when it comes to discussing the question of the material process of transmission. The infrastructure of this part of the net, spreading out to valleys which are in some cases difficult to reach even in our times, was constituted by traveling humans, mainly priests, but also state officials who carried all the items mentioned above in their mental baggage, as it were, without being conscious of this fact.

What is known about cultural life in medieval Europe in general allows for the postulate that performance practices existed in these remote regions from the earliest times, if only at an elementary level—as in the case of other cultures analyzed here which did not develop an elaborate theatrical tradition of their own. Does it make sense, then, to maintain—in accordance with classical Marxism—that the "authentic" local culture of the Middle Ages was later suppressed by the itinerant officials of the ruling class and replaced with the plots and stories mentioned? In the age we are dealing with, the places concerned presented no danger of a regionalist revolt that could have put the central power in Vienna at risk; it thus would have been highly probable that the government or ecclesiastical agents under whose patronage the performances took place would have integrated local plays or at least local features into the repertoire, had there been any. But it seems that for various reasons discussed in other parts of this book, the imported stories mentioned above were attractive from the perspective of the "creators" as well as the target audiences; they may have appealed to the needs recipients try to satisfy by attending performances. And, considered from a Lévi-Straussian or Maussian perspective, these stories and plots taken from "higher" strands of culture were, perhaps, nothing but particularly well-wrought variants of universal narratives which, as such, might have existed in the minds and practices of those inhabitants of remote alpine villages before they became connected systematically to the cultural net, in a first step by the process of Christianization, and in a second step by the introduction of the modern, absolutist State.

---

was a luxury good which only the wealthy parts of the European population could afford. In short: this garb is not at all based on a long-standing ("identitarian") cultural tradition; it was literally invented in the age of Romanticism, mainly by elementary school teachers, that is, people who had acquired a certain level of education and had absorbed primitivized variants of Herderian-Romantic thinking during the period of their studies in Munich.

The text corpus to which I have linked my critique of Herder's concept dates from the eighteenth century;[484] going further back in time, I should first like to refer to my above remarks on Herder's somewhat striking portrait of Shakespearean drama. But it has to be mentioned that there is, of course, strong evidence for a conceptualization along Herderian lines if one considers periods predating humanism, namely with regard to classical as well as medieval epic literature.[485] It is quite plausible to assume that, after Charlemagne's military campaign in northern Spain, there emerged idealizing oral narratives created by those who were part of the enterprise. It may well be that these elementary stories were re-narrated again and again, including by illiterate people, that they became subsequently enriched with more "learned" material, that their idealizing tendencies became stronger and stronger—until one day a scribe sat down in his study and fixed on parchment what is nowadays known as the "Oxford Roland".

So, in the final analysis, the issue is not whether or not there are collective (popular, or rather folk-based) processes of cultural creation. The critical point is quite another one, namely, whether, when we are dealing with "pristine" collective textual products, different tribes (*Völker*) indeed produce works of art that are so different as to warrant ascribing to them a specific *Geist* expressing the mentality of the specific tribe in question and no other. Finally, the controversy is about whether there are indeed tribal mentalities that diverge to such an extent as to make dichotomous claims appear sensible (a German *Volksgeist* that is basically different from, or even opposed to, a French *esprit*; an "Aryan" *Geist* that drastically differs from a "Semitic" mentality, etc.). Is there a substantive difference between the radical deconstruction of a concept as widespread and as cherished by all humans—for evident reasons—as "blood bonds" or "family bonds" to be found in classical Greek mythology on the one hand and Teutonic mythology (the *Nibelungenlied*) on the other? And what differentiates, in the final analysis, the one-dimensional heroism of Roland from the attitude of those valiant warriors in the *Iliad* who finally fall prey to their heroism? Finally, are the differences between a Greek fighter tried by fortune and fate who is in the end restored to his riches and his loved ones (Odys-

---

[484] I would like to highlight that the stress is on "texts"; it is highly probable that there were earlier written outlines of the plots or even rudimentary manuscripts going back to the seventeenth or sixteenth centuries which were not preserved.

[485] As to classical epic literature, the explanation offered above with regard to the *Song of Roland* might apply as well. Before it was written down by a man called Homer, the story contained in the *Iliad* might well have circulated as an oral material based on "authentic" reports of the events delivered by the warriors involved in the fights.

seus) and a Spanish warrior (the Cid) who has to suffer a similar period in his life significant enough to substantiate the postulate of diverse "national" spirits? I could go on by referring to non-"Western" narratives and their basic features, to the *Epic of Gilgamesh* as well as to the already mentioned mythical narratives of the ancient Mayas. There are many more factors in cultural and literary history which point to basic commonalities between cultural traditions of all kinds— be they grounded in anthropological constants or in permanent processes of exchange—than there are factors that evidence essential differences.

"National Literatures": Topoi and Languages

0.—There may be objections to the conceptualization of literary traditions developed in this study which take as their starting point a text corpus that is beyond its temporal frame, but of particular importance for all (Western) literature of the more recent past, namely the nineteenth-century European novel, especially those texts commonly subsumed under the heading of realism, that is, texts by Dickens, Balzac, Flaubert, Tolstoy, and Fontane, to mention just a few well-known authors. Perusing these novels and studying them[486] may, indeed, give readers the impression of experiencing the essence of "Frenchness" or of "Prussianness", that is, of the specificity of life in Paris or in the remote *province* at the time of Charles X or of Louis Philippe, or in Prussia during the era of Bismarck. Taking this mighty strand of literary realism into consideration—a tradition which has been declared obsolete many times, yet continues to flourish, in particular in North America, but also in Europe, where it experiences most impressive renaissances or even "resurrections" again and again, usually right after having been declared definitively "dead" a couple of years before—is it sensible to hold that a category like "national literatures" is misconceived right from the start?

---

486 Starting with my doctoral dissertation, I have published a good deal (and continuously) on the nineteenth-century European novel and on the theoretical issues involved in the notion of realism (*Balzac und der 'Effet de réel'*; *Ästhetik der Wirklichkeitsdarstellung*; *Zum italienischen Roman des 19. Jahrhunderts*. Foscolo, Manzoni, Verga, D'Annunzio, Stuttgart 2002; "Das Ende von Emma Bovary", in: Hans Otto Dill [ed.], *Geschichte und Text in der Literatur Frankreichs, der Romania und der Literaturwissenschaft*. Festschrift Rita Schober zum 80. Geburtstag, Berlin 2000, pp. 71–93; "Mimesis und Botschaft bei Flaubert", *Romanistisches Jahrbuch* vol. 54 / 2003, pp. 180–212; "Considérations sur *Salammbô*", *MLN* vol. 125 / 2010, pp. 731–782; "Fiacre et grenier. Quelques remarques sur *Madame Bovary* et *Effi Briest*", in: Christoph König and Heinz Wismann [eds.], *La lecture insistante: autour de Jean Bollack*, Paris 2011, pp. 255–284).

1.—The question is evidently linked to the device of description, especially the description of places, that is, to literary topography. Balzac's famous portrayal of the *quartier latin*, which culminates in a description of the *pension Vauquer*, where the young Rastignac will spend his first two years in the capital, and where he will decide to do everything he can in order to leave such petty-bourgeois misery behind for the rest of his life; Flaubert's description of the city of Rouen when Emma Bovary first sees it and is fascinated by this modern "Babylon", hence ready to behave as people in such cities do;[487] or Fontane's description of the winter landscape on the shores of the Baltic Sea, which, by conveying an atmosphere of oppressive provinciality and the sense that "nothing will ever happen here", makes it all the more plausible that Effi Briest succumbs to the sophisticated seduction techniques of Crampas[488]—all these, and a number of other famous sequences from famous novels, seem to be inextricably linked to specific places which we are used to taking as emblematic, that is, as places in which the "essence" of specific national cultures of specific periods is concentrated.

First of all, I should like to make the trivial point that there are no such descriptions in dramas (or in poetry). In the case of drama, recipients are typically given some information concerning time and place, but these indications almost always remain on a very elementary level. At the beginning of *Hamlet*, we are told that the castle where the action takes place is located in Denmark, but there is nothing particularly Danish about the place or the people living there.[489] The same holds true in the case of the Polish setting of Calderón's *La vida es sueño* or the Spanish setting of Corneille's *Cid*, and even more of the "Trézène" or the "Athènes" of Racine's *Phèdre* (1677). And even if the action is set in the same broader period as the composition of the play and in a region where the language of the play is the official vernacular, as is the case with Shakespeare's histories and, in a later period, the dramas of Ibsen and Strind-

---

487 "Cela se fait à Paris" is Léon's argument convincing Emma to get in the coach in which their first sexual encounter takes place (quotes are from the first chapter of the third part of the novel).

488 The first adulterous encounter takes place inside a sleigh, when the Briest couple and a number of other people are riding home after a most boring New Year's reception in a nearby village (see chap. 19).

489 It is well known that the drama does discuss (albeit not very frequently) the question of what it means to be Danish. The most detailed answer provided in Shakespeare's text is that Danes are heavy drinkers (l. 4. 16–18); given the present-day statistics on alcohol consumption in European countries in general, which seem to describe deeply rooted habits, one is inclined to say that if national character is based on nothing else, there is no such national character, at least not in Shakespeare's play.

berg, one does not tend to see these plays as instances of a specific Britishness or a specific Scandinavianness.[490]—The only relevant difference between such plays and narrative texts written in the same languages consists in the fact that in the one case there is topographical description whereas in the other there is none or close to none. From a theoretical perspective, this might at first sight lead to the assumption that there are "national literatures" on the one hand comprising the genre of the novel, particularly the realist novel, and more or less transnational or non-national genres on the other (drama, poetry). Put in a nutshell in this manner, the extent to which such a view is misconceived becomes apparent. Yet it must be said that what I have just formulated is, by implication, the tacit basis of current studies in the field of literary history. The propagation of Herder's concepts was fueled by the "rise of the novel" to the status of dominant genre, a process which began at the start of the nineteenth century.

It seems that the concept of "national literature" is generated by the non-problematized (over-)interpretation of the bonds literary texts of any kind necessarily maintain with the extra-literary reality from which they originate. The most important of these bonds is language, which is a given for any literary text. Leaving aside such experiments as Ludwig Lejzer Zamenhof's strictly non-national language, Esperanto, there is no denial that every literary text is written in a specific language that originates from a specific community, a point I shall discuss separately below. The second feature which links fictional texts to factual realities, nurturing the illusion described above, is indeed topography. Since places (cities, mountains, lakes[491]) and landscapes are "realities", a literary text which marks its fictional topography by giving it the name of an existing place is more or less inevitably conceived of by recipients as "organically"

---

490 Regarding this point, see once again the aforementioned polemics of Machado de Assis and Borges against the Herderian, Romantic conception of literature: "I shall [...] ask if *Hamlet*, *Othello*, *Julius Caesar*, and *Romeo and Juliet* have anything to do with the history of England or the British territory, and if, nevertheless, Shakespeare is not, as well as a universal genius, an essentially English poet" ("Notícia da atual literatura brasileira. Instinto de nacionalidade" [1873], in: Joaquim Maria Machado de Assis, *Obra completa*, Rio de Janeiro 1962, vol. 3, pp. 801–809; my translation); "I think that Racine would not have begun to understand anyone who would deny him his right to the title of French poet for having sought out Greek and Latin subjects. I think Shakespeare would have been astonished if anyone had tried to limit him to English subjects, and if anyone had told him that, as an Englishman, he had no right to write *Hamlet*, with its Scandinavian subject matter, or *Macbeth*, on a Scottish theme" ("The Argentine Writer and Tradition", p. 423).
491 One might think of the wonderful description of Lake Como at the beginning of Manzoni's *I promessi sposi* (1827/1840–42).

linked to this specific place. The more detailed the descriptions are and the more "real" items they contain (famous churches, well-known streets, topographical characteristics of any kind in the case of landscape), the more recipients are inclined to see the entire story as linked to this specific place and thus as emblematic of its specificity, that is, as *substantially* different from stories that could have happened in other places during the same time.

I would like to come back to two famous novels mentioned above: what is, in essence, the difference between *Madame Bovary* and *Effi Briest*? There is indeed a huge difference; Fontane's most famous novel is not a simple rewriting of Flaubert's text. One might formulate the primary difference as one of atmosphere (*Stimmung*). The somewhat "overheated" and hyperactive temperament of Flaubert's heroine, culminating in her dramatically staged suicide, is countered by the reserved and subdued mode of talking and acting of Fontane's most prominent female figure. Even so, the plot line—a young and naïve woman lured into a marriage of convenience to an older man she hardly knows; the incongruence of the couple's characters, needs, and desires; the relative stupidity of the (benevolent) husband, who does not realize that his wife is unhappy; the frustrated wife's falling prey to an experienced seducer; the gloomy ending with the heroine's premature death; the lasting incomprehension of the entire constellation on the part of the mourning widower—all this is basically parallel. Differences in detail are mainly linked to the difference in social class of the central characters. But the classes as such—the petty bourgeoisie on the one hand, the nobility serving as high-ranking state officials on the other—are not at all specific to the "national cultures" in question. It would be possible to identify all those features of Fontane's text, including the psychic profile of the heroine, for which there is no direct equivalent in Flaubert's text, in other realist novels from the French tradition which are set in a social sphere comparable to that of *Effi Briest*; in particular, one might think of Balzac's *Le Lys dans la vallée* (1836).

With respect to topography—where there is, indeed, a substantial difference—I would argue that the integration of "real" extra-textual material into a literary text gives recipients the illusion that the link between the story and the "real world" to which it refers is not unidirectional, but rather operates in both directions. Since the action of *Madame Bovary* is set in nineteenth-century Normandy, recipients tend to believe that this action is typical of the provincial France of that age. Logically seen, the operation just described reverses the proposition. In the narrative sequence mentioned above, it is not the city of Rouen as such that is of any importance; it is Rouen as a paradigm of the "big city" that is made use of to render Emma's actions plausible, which are not at all specifically French; unhappy marriages seem to be a rather universal phenomenon. *Mutatis mutandis*, the same holds true with respect to Fontane's description of the desolate Pomeranian coast. And in Balzac's *Père Goriot*, the portraits of miserable Paris on the one hand and splendid Paris on the other have the function of motivating what the entire text is about: ambition ("parvenir! Parvenir à tout prix")[492]—an impulse that is, at least according to the Hebrew Bible, the most fundamental and universal characteristic of human beings.

2.—Still, doesn't the argument here expounded reduce literary texts to a collection of motifs? Or to a collection of pre-existing elements, including motifs, formal structures, profiles of personages, and pragmatic (non-literary) discourses of many kinds? The main difference between my approach and existing framings of the nature of literary texts and cultural products in general consists in my rejection of the view that there are *substantive* intermediate levels between what I call the material circulating in the net and actual, individual works. The individual work is specific; otherwise it is nothing but an instance of trivial literature whose mark is pervasive standardization. As mentioned above, Fontane's text is indeed different from Flaubert's. What is questioned by me is the assumption that this difference consists in the one novel being a typically "French" version of the story of a woman in an unhappy marriage and in the other being a typically "German" or "Prussian" version. The fundamental difference is rather one of individual ingenuity. The differences regarding "real" extra-textual material (the reference to Catholic cultic practices and officials in Flaubert, to Protestant ones in Fontane; the reference to *sous-préfets* in Flaubert, to *Landräte* in Fontane; the reference to endlessly stretching meadows in Flaubert, to the endless sea in Fontane, etc.) are necessary components of texts of this genre from the century in question; the specificity of these components is irrelevant to the problem of what makes the texts in question great works of art, even if we reject, for the time being, an orthodox "Kantian" reading of them. This irrelevance is underpinned by the fact that readers totally unfamiliar with the "real material" integrated into the respective texts—people who have never traveled to Normandy or who have never had the occasion to experience the Prussian territories known as *ostelbisch*[493]—read them with

---

492 I quote from the edition of the text to be found in vol. 2 of the *Comédie humaine*, Marcel Bouteron (ed.), Paris 1963 (Bibliothèque de la Pléiade), pp. 847–1085, quote: p. 935.
493 Do I have to stress that for a West German of my generation (I was born in 1952), this latter constellation did indeed apply to all of my readings of Fontane's novels which occurred before the reunification of Germany (1990)? Although I never experienced the regions "described" in these texts before the age of maturity, my impression as a young person (a very naïve view, as I would now say) was that the rendering of the landscape in Fontane was in perfect accordance with "reality", and that the personages and their interactions were "typically" Bismarckian-Prussian.

great delight, indeed with no less delight, it seems, than people from the "national cultures" from which the texts respectively originate.

3.—The intricate questions discussed in this chapter have not only a production-oriented, but also a reception-oriented dimension—which, for reasons of the homogeneity of the theoretical approach, has for the most part been passed over in my overall argument so far. Yet this dimension cannot be entirely discarded, as it is, indeed, essential for a comprehensive theory of literary texts—which, however, is not the ambition of this book. I shall thus offer no more than some remarks in this respect.[494]

In the ninth chapter of the *Poetics*,[495] Aristotle situates the literary text, drama and narrative, by relating it to both historical and philosophical texts, coming to the conclusion that it shares certain features with these pragmatic textual categories. History, according to Aristotle, deals with "particulars" ("a 'particular' means, say, what Alcibiades did or experienced");[496] as such, it is relevant only to readers who take an interest in the specific events recounted. Philosophical texts, by contrast, convey messages that are non-specific and abstract, that is, "general" or "universal" (*katholou*). Literary texts—fictional ones, but also those with an authentic substratum—are conceptually a sort of hybrid; they present "particulars", while they are "more philosophical" (*philosophoteron*) than historical texts. They narrate "events", that is, items clearly situated in space and time and related to individual people. Yet their message, Aristotle argues, is located on the level of the *katholou*: they convey something more general.

In the course of the rather succinct presentation governing this chapter of the tract,[497] there is no specification of this postulate.[498] But my goal is not to

---

[494] Readers might wish to consult my essay "Das Denken, das Unterscheiden und die Literatur", where the following argument is developed in detail.
[495] *Poetics* 1451b.
[496] Astonishingly, if considered from a modern perspective and thus from the perspective of the way in which history is written in modern times, Aristotle seems to consider historiography to be bound to do exactly that, and nothing more—which would mean that at least in this passage (perhaps for the sake of argumentative coherence), it is chronicle-style texts which he is referring to, rather than, say, Thucydides' works.
[497] The *Poetics* belongs to the so-called esoteric part of the Aristotelian corpus, meaning, to the texts written for the internal purposes of the academy where Aristotle taught, and not for a broader public. This context explains the at times rather uneven course of the argumentation. There are numerous passages indulging in details of minor importance and others where exoteric, specifically modern readers might wish to receive additional information in order to fully grasp the argument.
[498] One may infer from other passages of the tract that the "more general" concepts which, according to Aristotle, need to be contained in literary texts are meant to refer to the causal chain linking the events recounted; literary texts are to be more consistent in terms of logic

produce a "correct" exegesis of the *Poetics*. Rather, I shall take the liberty to consider Aristotle's brief remarks as the first theoretical articulation of the way recipients consider literary texts in contrast to documentary texts. And I should like to add just one thought to this argument, which might even be my own contribution to the debate:[499] In the case of many literary texts, this "general" or "universal" level is not just "there"; it is not something made explicit by the author. Rather, it is a dimension whose existence is assumed by the readers. For what, after all, should the meaning of an invented story about people who never actually existed be, if not the allegorical encoding of something more abstract, which becomes evident when one takes these fictional lives into consideration? Such narratives may be disregarded as meaningless or as idiotic in the etymological sense, as having a meaning only to the author who produced them. If, however, we agree to consider them as meaningful, this dimension cannot be found on the level of the specific action narrated, since we know it to be fictional; it can only be extrapolated by assuming that the individual events are instances of a "more general", a more abstract, a conceptual level of meaning.

It was the twentieth-century semiotician Yuri M. Lotman who continued the discussion regarding the "ontological" status of literary texts initiated by Aristotle, while going beyond the somewhat restricted or vague understanding of the *katholou* as it can be derived from the *Poetics*. Taking a famous novel by Tolstoy as an example, he arrives at the following conclusion, which deserves to be quoted in its entirety; thanks to its rigorous argumentation, it does not require commentary:

> Thus the plot of *Anna Karenina* reflects, on the one hand, a certain narrow object—the life of the heroine, which we are fully capable of comparing with the lives of individuals who surround us in everyday life. This object, which has a proper name and all the other trappings of individuality, constitutes only a part of the universe reflected in art. [...] [T]his same subject [plot] [...] is a reflection of another object which tends to expand without limit. We can regard the life of the heroine as a reflection of the life of *any* woman belonging to a certain epoch and a certain social milieu, [or as a reflection of the life of] *any* woman, [or of] *any* person [of any human being]. Otherwise the tragic vicissitudes of her life would only be of historical interest, and would simply be boring for a reader far removed from the special task of studying the life and manners of past epochs.[500]

---

than enumerations of random events. There is an interminable discussion amongst specialists on the question of whether the causality Aristotle has in mind is restricted to the relation of a given character to her or his concrete actions or whether what is at stake are the more general rules governing the human or rather the social world.
499 Or perhaps I read it somewhere and forgot that the idea is not my own.
500 *The Structure of the Artistic Text*, p. 211. Additions in brackets are mine.

To this quote—which is of capital importance for the semiotics of fiction—I should like to add one further remark concerning writers such as Kafka and Borges: The particulars some of their texts deal with are obviously not "real"; even the option of tentatively casting them as possibly real is excluded; they are fantastical, that is, they are evidently inventions of an ingenious mind. In such cases, readers proceed immediately to an allegorical level in order to confer sense upon what cannot be taken to be in any respect documentary. It may be that the absence of a literal level assignable to "real" places and "real" periods is, to a significant extent, at the basis of the continued global popularity and enthusiastic reception of the above-mentioned texts. They clearly transcend cultural boundaries of all kinds.

4.—Still, there might be some reluctance to accept the above reasoning with regard to an important subgenre of the realist novel, namely, the historical novel as first created by Walter Scott and continued in famous texts by Stendhal, Balzac, Tolstoy, Flaubert, as well as by a host of writers of the twentieth century, one of the most recent masterpieces being Gabriel García Márquez's novel on Simón Bolívar, *El general en su laberinto* (1989).[501] These texts link the narrated plot not only to specific places, but also to specific periods, particularly to periods that are highly individualized—that is, to events we consider turning points of history, or rather of the specific history of a specific community, a feature that would make such novels, at least at first sight, rather uninteresting for readers whose "belonging" ties them to spatiotemporal parameters far removed from those thematized in the respective texts.

The most lucid writer and theoretician of the genre, Alessandro Manzoni, reflected on its conceptual basis again and again, finally coming to the conclusion that the historical novel is indeed a "componimento [...] intrinsecamente contradittorio"[502]—by which he refers to the fact that historical events are always and by necessity particular, whereas fictional events and plots only make sense when readers are willing to attribute to them a "more general", that is, an abstract meaning in the sense already theorized by Aristotle. In logical terms, the argument is hardly refutable.

---

[501] See my "Re-Historisierung, De-Historisierung. García Márquez' Bolívar-Roman als Musealisierung eines geschichtsphilosophischen Mythos (*El general en su laberinto*)", in: Ulrich Schulz-Buschhaus and Karlheinz Stierle (eds.), *Projekte des Romans nach der Moderne*, München 1997, pp. 195–236.

[502] For a detailed analysis of *I promessi sposi*, as well as of the tract *Del romanzo storico*, see my "Ironisierung der Fiktion und De-Auratisierung der Historie. Manzonis Antwort auf den historischen Roman (*I Promessi Sposi*)", in: J. K., *Zum italienischen Roman des 19. Jahrhunderts*, pp. 52–84; quote: *Del romanzo storico*, in: *Opere varie* (= *Opere*, Michele Barbi and Fausto Ghisalberti [eds.], Milano 1943, vol. 2), pp. 623–674; here: p. 632.

From the perspective of the literary texts in question, Manzoni's own contribution to the genre, *I promessi sposi*, may be highly suitable for elucidating the reasons behind the subgenre's eminent success, the problem of its categorially hybrid basis notwithstanding. When Manzoni describes in his text—deriving his depiction from authentic historical sources from the period in question— the beginnings of the terrible plague which hit Northern Italy during the Thirty Years War and deprived it of one third of its inhabitants, he begins by stating that the population of Lombardy was physically weakened at the moment when some soldier of the imperial army brought the bacterium to Italy. The prehistory of this condition was the failure of crops the previous year and the resultant food shortages, but above all the measures the government of the largest city in the region, Milan, had taken in order to handle the problem: the imposition of a maximum price on bread, with the—at first sight laudable— intention to make bread available to everyone. The factual consequence of the decree, however, was that farmers and bakers hoarded grain instead of selling it at the price imposed by the government, because this was not sufficient to cover the costs of production. The ensuing famine then created optimal conditions for the rapid spread of the pathogen amongst the population.

The amazingly lucid analysis of the economic mechanisms at play in the city of Milan in the year 1628 reaches its decisive point when the narrator equates the situation to what happened in another place and at another time, namely in Paris during the period of *la terreur*: "Ci si permetta d'osservar qui di passaggio una combinazione singolare. In un paese e in un'epoca vicina, [...] si ricorse, in circostanze simili, a simili espedienti [...]" / "I allow myself here to consider in passing a remarkable constellation. In a nearby country and an epoch close to ours, [the authorities] had, in similar circumstances, recourse to similar expedients".[503] Since the period the narrator is referring to is still "vicina", he does not need to explain the extent to which the two situations are parallel: as Lombardy's history was influenced for many decades by the indirect consequences of the government's mismanagement of the situation, so was France's. The discontent provoked amongst the *tiers état* supporters of the Revolution by the bread shortage paved the way for the *thermidoriens* to take over and, finally, for the "first consul", who would then become the Emperor Napoleon, to end the period of Revolution, but to start at the same time the devastating period of the Napoleonic Wars.

---

503 *I promessi sposi*, in: *Tutte le opere*, Alberto Chiari and Fausto Ghisalberti (eds.), Milano 1954–1974, vol. 2,1, pp. 1–673; quote: p. 477.

The above-cited comment by the narrator of Manzoni's text lays bare a more abstract characteristic: at least in part, the subgenre of the historical novel indeed deals with particulars that actually occurred; but the way it deals with real-world, historical events—or rather, the way readers deal with such events[504]—is similar to the way readers deal with obviously fictional events presented in narratives. The interest is not only or not even primarily directed at the events in their concrete particularity.[505] Readers are searching for the "more general", for the possibly transferable meaning of the narrated events, or, as Manzoni has it, for events "che [...] hanno fatto un simil corso"[506] / "that have followed a similar course". I should stress that Manzoni's conceptualization of this "more general" level implied in the particulars of the plot targets the question of cause and effect. It is thus directly linked to the meaning of the *katholou* contained in Aristotle's text.

And it indeed seems to be such a process of abstraction which governs the reception of historical novels beyond the confines of the communities who would be inclined to read them, in part at least, as quasi-documentary, that is, as about "their" past. Non-British readers of the *Waverley Novels* (1814–1831) may take the historical background of the particular plots as a possible contribution to the "more general" question—applying almost everywhere and at various times—of how to overcome internal strife after a more or less violent merging of previously distinct political entities; readers of Flaubert's *Éducation sentimentale* (1869) might read the famous chapters on the events of 1848 as a "more general" claim that the historical period of revolutions is a thing of the past, and that all such current and future events are but poor, if not ridiculous imitations of 1789 (etc., etc.). In a nutshell: their being bound to specific places and times, and, thereby, to specific communities notwithstanding, historical novels may be received in the same manner as entirely fictional novels—that is, by way of abstracting from the vestiges of their "roots".[507] There is nothing

---

504 It must be stated that not every author gives such explicit hints at a "more generalizing" way of interpreting the historical events narrated as Manzoni does in the above-quoted passages.
505 The alternative implied in this statement may characterize the attitude of "national" readers on the one hand and that of "international" readers on the other.
506 *I promessi sposi*, p. 542.
507 It would by far exceed the limits established for this book were I to continue this line of reasoning and begin discussing how we are used to receiving authentic historiographical works. I shall leave it at saying that, at least as far as narrative (in contrast to chronicle-style) historiography is concerned, we mostly read it in a manner comparable to the way we read historical novels, and also (entirely) fictional novels. In the case of historiographical works proper, however, we usually pay far more attention to the literal level—that is, to the portrayal of the "real" events narrated—before we proceed to a symbolic or allegorical interpretation; in

contained in them that would *in principle* resist their being absorbed by the universal cultural net and thus becoming productive beyond the confines of the communities whose crucial "national" events they respectively thematize.

As expressed at the beginning of this section, hermeneutical problems of this kind do not stand at the center of this book; but it should be evident that the specific way readers deal with texts they know to be "literary" is representative of the boundary-transcending tendencies that derive from the specific "ontology" that may be ascribed to cultural artifacts in general. As has been theorized by Jan Mukařovský, the de-pragmatizing approach readers automatically adopt when reading literary texts is a potentiality for other cultural products as well.[508] Mukařovský, who is a neo-Kantian, labels this attitude "aestheticizing"; he emphasizes that such an approach to architecture, or even to products of daily life (pottery, clothes), privileges the internal formal organization of the specific object under scrutiny. It is particularly in this respect that I should like to point out a major difference between the aestheticizing re-functionalization of pragmatic artifacts and the way we are used to receiving literary texts: in the latter case, it need not only be the level of formal features to which we dedicate our attention at the moment when we decide to discard the reference to any specific "real" context; it may also be—or rather: in most cases it is primarily—the level of "general" meaning in the sense of abstract and thus transferable concepts to which we pay attention.

5.—As a conclusion to these deliberations concerning the status of literary topography, I should like to present some remarks on how to conceptualize the concrete phenomenon I took as a starting point, the nineteenth-century realist novel, in terms of a network theory of cultural production, by adding some lines of thought to my above explanations.[509] Why is it that we find, beginning in the first decades of that century, a "new" narrative genre which is distinguished not least by a propensity for topographical description unknown in all of previous literary history, Western as well as non-Western?

As Karlheinz Stierle has shown in a seminal article on the section of Baudelaire's *Fleurs du mal* entitled "Tableaux parisiens", the techniques of topogra-

---

that sense, the reading differs from the *modus legendi* in the case of fiction. Yet I would guess that no reader receives a historical account dealing with, say, the history of WWII exclusively with regard to the specific events narrated. More or less inevitably, he or she will ponder the question of how such large-scale disasters can be prevented in our times, or (on an even more abstract level) of what they might impart as regards the invariable nature of human beings.
508 See *Aesthetic Function, Norm and Value as Social Facts*, Mark E. Suino (tr.), Ann Arbor, MI 1979.
509 See pp. 230–232.

phical description which are to be found in nineteenth-century literary texts were extracted, according to the terminology I have introduced here, from a pragmatic genre circulating in the net, namely the genre known as *Tableau de Paris* (1781) established by Louis-Sébastien Mercier.[510] Mercier's text is a mixture of what one could call a "travel-guide description" with a "*flaneur* description", the latter component being focused on unusual but noteworthy details of everyday Parisian life. Balzac's description of the *quartier latin* in the first pages of his *Père Goriot* (1835), for instance, is clearly an imitation of descriptive techniques to be found in Mercier's manual[511]—which was a great success on the literary market at the time. This, of course, raises the question of why there was suddenly a demand for a description of Parisian sceneries that was modeled in principle on the genre of city-*epideixis*, existing since antiquity,[512] but much more detailed and much less laudatory in nature, instead foregrounding "interesting" places, objects, and people.

This shift in demand may be linked to another factor of importance with respect to the emergence of literary realism which, in principle, has already been investigated by scholarly specialists for a long time:[513] when Balzac calls his novels *drames* (as he frequently does),[514] he is referring to a generic label introduced by Denis Diderot in his reflections concerning the problem of how a tragedy adapted to modern times might best be conceived. In the *Entretiens*

---

510 "Baudelaire and the Tradition of the *Tableau de Paris*", *New Literary History* vol. 11/1980, pp. 345–361. The basic assumption underlying my argument is, of course, that France was first in creating literary realism. This will go uncontested as to Italian, Spanish, German, Scandinavian, Russian (etc.) literature. Is it too daring to advance the thesis that Dickens might have been inspired by texts created immediately beforehand by Balzac? If this is not the case, one might consider a sort of direct line from Richardson to Dickens in the English tradition. Be that as it may, it needs to be stressed once again that the Brits' insistence on their "insularity" is, at least as far as high culture and its products are concerned, one of the many myths created primarily for political purposes. Cultural transfer between Britain and continental Europe, especially France and Germany, has always been extremely intense.
511 Regarding this point, including remarks on topographical descriptions in *Le Colonel Chabert* (1832) and *Eugénie Grandet* (1833), see my *Balzac und der 'Effet de reel'*, pp. 109–115.
512 For a convenient overview of the genre's history from Greco-Roman times onward, see the first chap. of Jeffrey S. Ruth, *Urban Honor in Spain: The* Laus Urbis *from Antiquity Through Humanism*, Lewiston, NY 2011.
513 See H. R. Jauss, "Diderots Paradox über das Schauspiel (*Entretiens sur 'Le Fils naturel'*)", *Germanisch-Romanische Monatsschrift* vol. 42 / 1961, pp. 380–413; see also my *Ästhetik der Wirklichkeitsdarstellung*, chaps. I–IV (pp. 6–100).
514 Most famously, perhaps, in the narrator's characterization of the plot of *Le Père Goriot*: "Ah! sachez-le: ce drame n'est ni une fiction, ni un roman. *All is true*, il est si véritable que chacun peut en reconnaître les éléments chez soi [...]" (p. 848).

sur 'Le Fils naturel' (1757) and in the *Discours sur la poésie dramatique* (1758), Diderot adopts the Aristotelian argument that the purpose of drama is to arouse emotions in the audience. His concept of "emotions" is, however, much broader than in the case of the Aristotelian reduction to *phobos* and *eleos*; it also comprises less intense affects such as sympathy and empathy. But Diderot's most important argument for the creation of a substitute for the, according to him, obsolete genre of tragedy is linked to the specific recipients he has in mind: why should the emotions of late eighteenth-century middle-class Parisians be aroused by scenes from a world so different from their own, a world of princes and kings which the Enlightenment had taught them to regard skeptically, if not with downright hostility? Some decades later, it was François-René de Chateaubriand—a political reactionary—who produced the most impressive characterization of this shift in literary demand linked to a shift in the nature of the audience itself, which in turn reflected a political evolution, the abolition of the feudal system: "Avant la Révolution, on n'interrogeait les manuscrits que relativement aux prêtres, aux nobles et aux rois. Nous ne nous enquérons que de ce qui regarde les peuples et les transformations sociales".[515]

Diderot, for his part, invested his energy in speculating as to what might be the best way to arouse emotions in the new kind of audience when presenting dramatic plots based no longer on the fates of royalty and aristocrats, but instead on the life of the bourgeoisie.[516] Is it possible to feel as deeply shocked

---

515 "Préface" to the *Études historiques* (1831), in: Chateaubriand, *Œuvres complètes*, Paris 1861, vol. 9, pp. 5–99; quote: p. 29.
516 I would like to stress that I am here referring to another strand of Diderot's reflections concerning a "new" drama than the one already discussed above (pp. 230–232). It might be confusing that in the previously discussed argument by the philosopher, the term and concept of *tableau* plays a major role, as is the case in the context here expounded, where the term as such is not Diderot's, but is rather linked to the "new" genre created by Mercier. When Diderot talks about the *tableau* as a means of enhancing emotionalization, he has in mind scenes on stage—as I tried to put it by recourse to the dichotomy introduced by Fried—that are no longer theatrical, but "self-absorbed". Balzac obviously received this argument and adapted it to the frame of narrative text, where instances of spectators "seeing" something can only be intra-fictional. In one of his earliest masterpieces, *Le Colonel Chabert*, the "widow" of a Napoleonic general who has since married a man of the old high aristocracy has to figure out how to deal with a somewhat problematic situation when her supposedly dead first husband suddenly appears in Restoration Paris. She finally succeeds in making him renounce his real identity and thus stay "dead" by arranging a scene in which she exchanges motherly caresses with her two young children and complains that the innocent kids' happiness will soon come to a cruel end, while feigning that the entire scene has not been prearranged by her. She thus creates a "self-absorbed", emotionally convincing situation—with her former husband as the targeted spectator—which is explicitly labeled by the narrator as a *tableau* ("Les mains [des deux en-

by the vicissitudes of the fortune of a humble "père de famille"[517] as in the case of a king whose horrible, but unconscious past mistakes lead the entire polis into destabilization and disaster? Diderot's answer, once again, draws on basic arguments found in the *Poetics*, while, once again, changing the emphases of the argument in question. Aristotle holds—though somewhat in passing—that there is a prerequisite for empathy, namely, the possibility on the recipients' part to consider themselves as *homoion*,[518] that is, equal or similar to the tragic hero. It seems that in Aristotle this clause is mainly meant to refer to the psychic and intellectual profile of the hero, and not primarily to his social status. This said, the "democratic" Athens of the fifth century BCE was structured in a way which differs dramatically from eighteenth-century Europe. The audience attending performances of plays like *Oedipus Rex* consisted mainly of adult full citizens, who represented not more than roughly 10% of the population. According to a terminology familiar from early modern and modern times, the audience of the classical Greek tragedy performances was aristocratic.[519] There was indeed a certain distance between their real-world situations and the settings represented on stage, but it was not unbridgeable, at least not in terms of imaginary identification.

Things were dramatically different in Europe in the Age of Absolutism. The lifeworld of bourgeois (*tiers état*) people was so far removed from that of the court that emotional identification might have been a difficult thing; and the closer one comes to the actual Revolution of 1789, the more there might have been a conscious unwillingness, on the part of the *tiers état*, to identify with the stage analogues of people whom they considered to be oppressors and decadent profligates. Consequently, Diderot proposes that the genre of *drame*— that is, modern-style tragedy—should present "dramatic" scenes of bourgeois life. Still, there is the question of how to reach a level of identification that is sufficient to provoke empathy. Is everyday misery (looming bankruptcy; the

---

fants] étaient étendues vers la mère, et les deux voix enfantines se mêlaient. Ce fut un tableau soudain et délicieux ! [...]"; *Le Colonel Chabert*, Pierre Citron [ed.], Paris 1961, p. 123). In the case of the argument discussed above, it is rather Mercier's concept of *tableau* which is at stake, that is, detailed topographic description. With regard to this acceptation of the term, Diderot did not produce the concept as such, but rather theorized the reasons for its integration into the repertoire of the emerging realist novel: *tableau*-style description may yield a "reality effect", albeit one that has a profile different from the device of onstage *tableau*.
517 This being the title of one of Diderot's *drames*, created in 1758.
518 *Poetics*, chap. 13, 1453a 4–6 (see also chap. 15, 1454a 24).
519 See also the more differentiated assessment of the Athenian audience of classical times above, pp. 158 f.

pregnancy of an unmarried daughter)[520] apt to provoke emotions in the audience, especially if they are aware of the fact that the concrete configuration is fictional? Diderot's answer to the question is inspired by a device he extracts from the net, namely, from the novels of Samuel Richardson.[521] Without disclosing to his readers the rationale behind this technique, Richardson endows his novels—particularly *Pamela* (1740) and *Clarissa* (1748)—with what is, according to Diderot, a distinctive feature: "une multitude de petites choses [auxquelles] tient l'illusion; il y a bien de la difficulté à les imaginer".[522] The effect of all these—at first sight contingent, that is, meaningless—details is, according to Diderot, the impression on the recipients' part that the entire action is not something invented, something fictional, but rather something real.[523] It is no longer the immensity of catastrophe that provides the basis for the recipients' emotional arousal, but the "reality effect", the conviction that "all [this] is true" (to quote from Balzac's *Le Père Goriot*),[524] that provides the emotional engagement which is a prerequisite for the readers' positive response to the text.

To summarize: it seems that literary realism's most conspicuous device, the accentuation of topography, owes its "origins" to a shift in the recipients of literary products that occurred in the eighteenth century, especially in the prerevolutionary second half. The bourgeois class—whose members had achieved a high degree of literacy—constituted the principal consumers of books in the emerging literary market. These new readers did not find the traditional genre of classical tragedy relevant to their middle-class lives, so different from the milieu of the classics, and thus impossible for them to empathize with. The "new" genre of *drame*, proposed by Diderot as an adequate substitute, is, according to him, a combination of tragedy and comedy;[525] from comedy, it takes the setting of everyday bourgeois life; from tragedy, it takes the element of calamity befalling the principal personages. The question of identification on the recipients' part—provided for within the reception process of classical tragedies by the narcissistically fueled imaginary "bridging" of the gap between kings and an aristocratic audience—is resolved by "lowering" the impression

---

[520] I am referring not only to Diderot's, but also to Mercier's contributions to the new genre.
[521] As to his *Éloge de Richardson* (1762), see *Ästhetik der Wirklichkeitsdarstellung*, pp. 13–55.
[522] *Éloge de Richardson*, in: *Œuvres esthétiques*, pp. 29–48; quote: p. 35.
[523] Let me add in parenthesis that Roland Barthes built his theory of literary realism as developed in his famous essay "L'Effet de réel" on this argument first advanced by Diderot (first print in *Communications* vol. 11/1968, pp. 84–89).
[524] See the reference given in n. 514.
[525] See *Entretiens sur 'Le Fils naturel'*; as to the description of the genre of *drame*, see specifically pp. 137–140.

of fictionality and by increasing the level of alleged "reality"; this (amongst other devices[526]) should be achieved, according to Diderot, by way of creating reality effects based on an accumulation of descriptive details without an obvious function in the narrative as a whole. This "new" technique, to be found in a somewhat embryonic stage in Richardson, only became systematically implemented starting with Balzac, who extracted the specific descriptive techniques from a pragmatic genre already circulating in the net, the Mercier-style *Tableau de Paris*, which, while being based on the classical genre of "praise of one's city (of birth)", distinguishes itself from its model by focusing on the "interesting", that is, the "curious" features of present-day city life, thus catering to the needs of a new readership who, on behalf of its social position, is no longer interested in questions of origin and provenance, but rather looking for a presentation of the "real" world as a scene or a stage, a mentality that later on became the basis of middle-class tourism.—As a result of these processes of extraction from the net, recombination, and refunctionalization, there emerges, finally, the new genre of the realist novel with its accent on literary topography.

6.—A second major objection to the views expressed in my polemics against Herderian-Romantic theories might emanate from the fact, mentioned in passing on various occasions but not yet discussed in detail, that *literary* artifacts are by necessity bound to one specific language—meaning, to an arbitrary code that only "works" within certain ethno-geographic and historical contexts. This factor needs to be addressed at some length, all the more as literary texts are, insofar as they are not referential, bound to what is undeniably their own, namely: the way they make use of language. Isn't the particular message conveyed by a (literary) text inextricably linked to the particular language in which it was first conceived? This is the Herderian claim, maintained and developed further in Wilhelm v. Humboldt's famous essay "Über die Verschiedenheiten des menschlichen Sprachbaues" (1827–1829).[527] The latter even postulates that specific worldviews ("Weltansichten") are linked to specific languages. The point at issue is of a more intricate nature than the question of "topoi"; for there is no *standard* process of abstracting from the language in which a text

---

526 I refer to my above discussion of another device recommended by Diderot, the onstage *tableau*, whose functional dimension consists, in the final analysis, in providing emotionalization, mediated by the recipients' impression that what they are viewing is a "real" (and not an arranged) scene (pp. 230–232).
527 *On Language: On the Diversity of Human Language Construction and Its Influence on the Mental Development of the Human Species*, Michael Losonsky (ed.), Peter Heath (tr.), Cambridge, MA 1999.

is written during the process of reception; or, to put it more adequately, perhaps: even if one abstracts from the specific acoustic or graphic units by which concepts are conveyed in the process of listening or reading, these—including their "musical" and above all their associative potential—remain present in the recipient's mind.

Yet, as evidenced by the practice of translation not only of pragmatic, but also of literary texts, including poetry, there seems to be the *possibility* of such a process of abstraction in the case of language, too. The price to be paid for the "loss" of the original acoustic and associative dimensions needs to be discussed; but dismissing translations of literary artifacts as "poor" in principle, or as makeshift solutions only for the uncultured who have not mastered several foreign languages, seems to be a position which neglects many prominent cases testifying to the fact that translations, as "inadequate" as they might be, may attain a high relevance in terms of literary evolution and dynamics. One might think of the influence of the "German Shakespeare" from the age of Romanticism onward, of the extensive reception of English and German translations of Baudelaire's *Fleurs du mal* (1857), of various Western European translations of works originally written in Scandinavian or Slavic languages, etc.

Before I come to deal with the question of the "quality" of translations, I should like to stress that my general theoretical postulate—that culture evolves in virtual circuits and networks that are in principle not restricted by linguistic, political, or mores-bound frontiers—would not even be affected by the finding that translation is always "inadequate", since my framework rejects the assumption that a literary text is reducible to the "intentional formation"[528] it might have expressed when it was conceived by its author. And it also rejects the assumption that a literary text's "essence" consists in its "identitarian" reduction within the (ethno-linguistic) community from which it emerged.[529] The floating-in-the-virtual-net of a given work is a process that is factual without regard for the intentions of those who give "birth" to the works in question. In very many cases—the most prominent one in cultural history might be the circulation of the text commonly known as the Bible beyond linguistic and cultural borders—processes of floating-in-the-net involve distortions if considered from the standpoint of the "original" document.[530] But culture is primarily

---

528 The term was coined by Roman Ingarden, *The Literary Work of Art: An Investigation of the Borderlines of Ontology, Logic, and Theory of Language*, George G. Grabowicz (tr.), Evanston, IL 1974, p. 366.
529 I am thinking, e.g., of *I promessi sposi* as a first manifestation of an Italian "national" identity—this is to date the current reading of the text in Italy.
530 I should like to emphasize that I have consciously avoided having recourse to the perhaps most expedient device for fending off possible objections to my conceptualization of the status

an enterprise consisting in re-appropriations of pre-existing material. The main question is not the one of "loyalty" to a supposed original, it is the one of intellectual and artistic productivity.[531] This applies all the more if we move, once again, from the perspective of production to that of reception. Recipients who are not able to compare the translation with the original (as is the case with me when I read, for example, Henrik Ibsen) are not able to register the "loss" that goes along, almost inevitably, with translation. And even if there are dimensions which elude translation, processes of circulation beyond linguistic borders may produce "new" and interesting constellations completely alien to the original. Within the virtual network of culture, there is no dichotomy of right vs. wrong reception; it is superseded by the dichotomy of productive vs. non-productive reception.

This said, there are many more adequate renderings of texts beyond linguistic borders than the assumptions prevalent in an academic world that continues to be bound to basic concepts of Romanticism allow scholars to concede. On the other hand, there is no denying that *Madame Bovary* in French is different

---

of the original language in which a literary work of art is written, namely, the reference to Walter Benjamin's well-known essay "The Task of the Translator". Benjamin, here as elsewhere in his writings, is indebted to the speculative philosophy of German Idealism and to the aesthetic theory of the early Romantics: if there is one "true" language which is no longer accessible to us on behalf of the process of rationalization, (good) translations might add further fragments to the fragment of truth that is contained in the original text and thus help readers gain a sort of pre-linguistic intuition ("eine Ahnung") of the truth as such. From such a perspective, translations are in principle a "good" thing (quite as they are in principle a "bad" thing from the standpoint of a Herderian approach). My suggestions are equidistant from both of these, in my view similarly exaggerated, positions. Of course, a work of art "loses" something when it is translated into another language; but it may be an all too enthusiastic speculation that the work at stake should also automatically "gain" something by way of the same process. The essential point is whether translations impede or enlarge a given text's cultural impact beyond the confines of its original tongue. From such a perspective, it is less the question of translation as such that seems crucial than the question of the quality of a given translation. It is, of course, conceivable to reduce *Madame Bovary*, by way of a negligent and hasty translation, to the level of one of the trivial love stories Emma indulges in reading when she is a pupil in a convent. But in the case of translation as practiced in Europe and beyond for centuries now, such primitivizations are absolute exceptions. If translations are done carefully, they succeed in preserving, if certainly not the original, its level of sophistication (once again, lyrical poetry may be a separate case), even if there is partial "misunderstanding" or a reduction of complexity involved. It belongs to the paradoxes of what we call "culture" that such relative primitivizations may have productive effects with regard not to the singular work in question and its understanding, but to cultural production in general (see, once again, my remarks on Petrarch's "reductive" translation of Boccaccio's story of Griselda, pp. 142 f.).

531 —which also means that not all reworkings of a pre-existing text are valuable.

from *Madame Bovary* translated into English, German, or Russian. As already said with regard to the respective heroines of Flaubert's and Fontane's most famous novels, there is, *mutatis mutandis*, a difference in atmosphere also with respect to language. Almost automatically, a reader links a text written in French to other texts written in that language that are known to her or him—that is, to "French culture"—whereas the systematic character of arbitrary codes makes it almost impossible not to link a text that has been translated from French into German to other texts written in German—and thus to "German culture". Since the references to "real" places are typically not altered in translation,[532] there are, conversely, certain barriers that prevent the total absorption of a translated text into the culture of the language into which it has been translated. Still, and as may be extrapolated from my above remarks on drama and topographical description, the scarcity of such barriers in the case of theater might be conducive to a total absorption. Perchance it is not entirely contingent that it was an English dramatist rather than an English novelist who was adopted by German culture to such an extent that he became part of the imaginary German cultural heritage.

In the following, I should like to make two points of different levels of abstraction in order to illustrate my position: the fact that literary texts are (initially) bound to one specific language does not yield a sufficient basis for rejecting the view that the concept of "national literatures" is mainly an ideological one whose functional context is above all political.

7.—The first point I should like to adduce in this respect concerns the historical nature of natural languages. Highly cultured present-day speakers of French may be able to read the *Chanson de Roland* (ca. 1100) without much additional aid or instruction; average readers would capitulate before this task. Things are even more difficult in the case of a text like the *Nibelungenlied* (ca. 1200). Apart from professional medievalists, even educated present-day speakers of German would not be able to grasp more than the bare outline of the text. As to the British "national" epic, *Beowulf* (ca. 700),[533] no one who has not been previously trained will be able to understand much of anything from the text if confronted with the original version. To restate this on an abstract level: the supposedly "natural" link between texts from a specific "national" tradition and readers from that same nation is subverted by the continuous historical

---

[532] An English (or any other) translation of *Madame Bovary* also stages the action in Normandy, that is, in France.
[533] As to the dates in brackets, I ask possible readers who are medievalists for their benign indulgence (while stressing that this book does not belong to the *Medievalia*).

evolution of natural languages. This may (and frequently does) cause such a degree of difference between the current language and its earlier stages as will render older texts incomprehensible to present-day readers even though they may originate from "their" ancestors—and this to an extent that does not systematically differ from the incomprehensibility of "foreign" texts. For a present-day speaker of English, it does not matter whether she or he is asked to summarize a text written in Old English or in contemporary Norwegian; she or he will not be able to perform the task.[534] The assumption that readers have a "natural" (non-mediated) access to any texts composed in the same region where they were born is a perspectival illusion produced by the fact that, in the case of contemporary texts and readers, the mediatedness of the semiotic process is not apparent, due to automatization. Since verbal communication of any kind is bound to arbitrary systems of encoding, there is in principle no obstacle to an in-depth decoding of the texts in question by recipients who started mastering the respective linguistic code at a later age than those who acquired it as children.

8.—Different languages open up, however, diverse possibilities of encoding, of modeling the world. Even within so-called "language families" such as that of the Indo-European vernaculars, there are certain terms that seem to be linked to specific linguistic contexts to the extent that speakers who are able to make use of a variety of such contexts preserve these terms in their original formulation, integrating them as they are into their primary language.[535] The dichotomy of *eros* and *agape*—whose blurring in the vernacular terms of *love*, *amour*, *Liebe*, etc. is of crucial relevance to Western literary and art history—is difficult to reproduce in modern European languages; the feeling of *ennui*—widespread amongst modern artists and intellectuals—seems to be untranslatable; for very good reasons, Freud rejected the vernacular term *Seele* ("soul") when theorizing his ideas on the human mind, instead having recourse to the Greek term *psyche*, which, indeed, has a conceptual profile and an associative potential differing considerably from that of the standard vernacular renderings. It need not be stressed that, quantitatively as well as qualitatively, such problems of "untranslatability" are much more significant if one proceeds to a comparison of linguistic codes that are systematically very different from one another, such as English and Arabic or French and Chinese. (Literary) texts may be translated

---

534 —unless, of course, she or he is a specialist of medieval English language and literature, or a scholar of Scandinavian languages and literatures.
535 I set aside the question of further functional dimensions of a limited macaronism, such as the potential for social distinction or the effect of "dignification" as described by Aristotle in the *lexis* chapters of the *Poetics*.

from one such language into another, as is evidenced by a long-standing practice; but in order to grasp what the original text is intended to convey, a reader not familiar with its language needs more than just a translation. In addition, she or he will require an erudite commentary on the specific conceptual profile and associative potential of this or that term in the original version.

In principle, my main argument for the refutation of the necessity of concepts such as "national literatures", supposedly emanating from the diversity of the conceptual profiles of various vernaculars, has already been articulated. A "national" or "ethnic" (tribal) belonging—having been raised within one specific cultural community—does not preclude the acquisition of foreign linguistic codes and of the cultural systems linked to them. The mastery of a consciously acquired language may indeed reach a level that is judged by its regular (native) speakers as outstanding. Samuel Beckett's texts in French as well as Vladimir Nabokov's and Joseph Conrad's texts in English may be among the most illustrative examples from recent literary history. In the contemporary globalized world, there are a great number of even more "exotic" examples of the same phenomenon: well-known writers whose mother tongue is Turkish writing in German; Iranians and Americans writing in Chinese; Chinese or Japanese authors writing in English; a Japanese-American writing a fantastical historical novel about a twentieth-century world not governed by Western people, but rather by descendants of the Aztecs, etc., etc. And there are also more modest stages of such a "xenology", as I would perhaps name it: that is, people like this book's presumed readers, cultured Westerners born in the second half of the twentieth century who do not have difficulties reading sophisticated texts written in languages such as French, Spanish, Italian, English, German, or Russian—for the simple reason that, in the course of their adult lives, they have acquired a passive mastery of several of these linguistic systems, in addition to the knowledge of a quantitatively considerable text corpus in the languages in question, which allows them to acquire a sense of the associative potentials of certain terms and formulations, and also a certain familiarity with the cultures—the social codes, the history, the traditions—of these specific linguistic communities.

It will remain an unanswerable question, however, whether the reading of *Madame Bovary* by a person whose mother tongue is English or German has the potential to become indistinguishable from a reading by an "autochthonous" speaker of French; or, to rephrase this as a more sophisticated question, whether the differences in reading that emerge amongst readers from different linguistic backgrounds are any more significant than differences emerging amongst readers from a homogeneous linguistic background who differ with respect to other parameters governing semiotic processes (gender, social class, generation, educational background, temperament, etc., etc.).

9.–Yet what about an item as important as sound–what about the "musical" qualities of literature within such a framework? Even if the texts in question are not actually performed or read aloud, recipients are conscious of the acoustic dimension of language as such–and in the case of artistically functionalized language, of literary texts, they are even trained to pay attention to this level. A novel by Flaubert does, indeed, "sound" different in the original language, French, than in English or German, let alone in Arabic or Mandarin. Still, if French has a reputation as a particularly harmonious and acoustically elegant language, would a native speaker of, say, German or Dutch who is familiar with the French original judge a well-executed translation into his native vernacular to be a repugnant demonstration of his mother tongue's acoustic ugliness? In every language, there are registers prone to produce the impression of harmony and others prone to produce the opposite effect; regarding euphony, the transposition of a literary work of art into another language is acceptable without any restrictions in case the acoustic *registers* of the original[536] are preserved in the translation.

I am even inclined to extend this postulate to the entire level of what we are used to calling style. As to wording, it is not the fact that Flaubert's text is written in French that makes it unique; it is rather the way Flaubert makes use of French. And if "style" is characterized by the systematic choice a text makes from all the choices possible within a given linguistic system, this relation as such is transferable from one vernacular to another. Current characterizations of style such as the classical triad of *humilis*, *mediocris*, and *sublimis*, as well as more concrete features such as "concision", "verbosity", "transparency", "obscurity", "metaphoricalness", "plainness", etc., are always meant to describe not essences, but rather relations between a standard usage of the linguistic patterns of a specific language and various deviations from this standard. This even applies to the "social" styles (sociolects) which frequently seem to be linked to literary texts from specific linguistic communities. The fundamental linguistic difference between Racinean and Shakespearean tragedy does not lie in the alleged fact that the former plays are "typically French" whereas the latter are "typically British". The linguistic code is, indeed, French in the first case and English in the second. But the difference of style can only

---

[536] Meaning: not necessarily the original sounds and their composition.

be captured by the opposition courtly/refined vs. popular/mixed,[537] that is, by relational terms describing configurations which might exist in either linguistic community.—A certain question raised by this argument—namely, whether there may be distinctions between "national" literary cultures resulting from the respective privileging of specific stylistic constellations—will be discussed in detail below.

10.—Yet there is an additional point to be taken into consideration which is located on a level of linguistic specificity even more basic than style: it would be problematic to deny that there is an associative potential of language linked to the level of sound. Only a person capable of reading French, or another language deriving from Latin, will be able to grasp the allusion to cattle (*bovis* in Latin, *boeuf* in French, with the adjective *bovin*) encoded in the name of "Bovary", along with the ensuing subtext: namely, that Emma's husband is more of a dull animal than a full human being—meaning, a person without any refinement and subtlety and, consequently, someone who is not suited to the task of fulfilling the young wife's vaguely romantic aspirations. One could argue that the entire plot is, in a way, foreshadowed as soon as the recipient learns that young Emma will be married to a man named "Bovary"; this effect will materialize, however, only in the case of the text's reception in its original language, not in translation.[538] Since "internal (over-)structuring" seems to be a distinctive feature of literary texts in contrast to pragmatic texts, is it tenable, given constellations such as the one briefly characterized here, to regard the link between (literary) text and (original) wording as not being of primary importance?

It is evident that this problem is particularly relevant when it comes to that genre for which the level of plot, if there is any at all, is characterized by an extremely high degree of standardization, whereas the important, original level is the one of formulation, including sound—that is to say, for the genre of poetry. It is for this reason that rendering poetry in translation is believed to be difficult or even impossible. Even so, it can hardly be denied that there is a reception history of poetry in translation. It is far from an exaggeration to say that the only poem by Sappho that has come down to us in its entirety, the so-called Fragment 1—or rather its circulation in the net for more than two and a

---

[537] In the sense of Erich Auerbach's famous thesis that literary realism is characterized by a free mixing of the three (distinct) levels of style as theorized in ancient rhetoric (*Mimesis: The Representation of Reality in Western Literature*, Willard R. Trask [tr.], Princeton, NJ 2013).

[538] —or only with respect to readers who are in principle able to read the original as well and may thus realize what the "untranslatable" proper name implies.

half millenia by now—is the origin of and main inspiration for the vast and multifaceted corpus of (Western) love lyrics, and this despite the fact that most readers and poets have been, and continue to be, unable to read it in its original form.

To put my point in more abstract terms: The level of sound is not negligible. But if one provisionally sets aside high modernist attempts to reduce poetry to sound and bring it close to music,[539] one might hypothesize that sound is one among a (literary) work of art's many parameters, the workings of which cannot be theorized in a generalized way with regard to processes of reception. The extent to which a recipient makes use of the level of sound and allows this dimension to influence the direction of his or her inspirations is highly idiosyncratic. It is not primarily based on the question of whether the text at issue is written in the recipient's mother tongue or not. Differences between the associations perceived by two different French readers of *Madame Bovary* (different with regard to age, social class, individual life experience, degree of aesthetic sensibility, etc.) may be greater than those between a French and a German reader who share such or similar traits. The same applies to all non-standardized items accompanying processes of communication: to the "calligraphic" dimension of print, the "tactile" qualities of paper, the "acoustic" qualities of the voice of a performer, the "olfactory" dimension of the setting, the degree of focused attention a given recipient is able or willing to invest in a concrete act of reception, the recipient's level of cultivation, his or her immediately preceding artistic or real-world experiences—all of these are *individual* dimensions of the reception of a work of art. They are legitimate dimensions, especially for the reason that the work in question is received as art, that is, without referring immediately to any pragmatic context. Even so, these dimensions elude systematization. They are essential within any particular act of reception. Yet the concrete shape they assume is not bound to one specific language. It is rather bound to a specific act of reception in its fundamental singularity and non-iterability. The multiplicity of such factors is mainly an indicator of the limits of systematization that go along with all receptions of works of art.

---

539 Even texts which are untranslatable in the literal sense since they systematically transgress the rules governing the language-system they are based on are not, for that reason, excluded from floating beyond linguistic borders. The attempt at "translating" such texts will consider the logic underlying the specific acts of linguistic transgression (fragmentations of words and subsequent reassemblies of elementary units that are distinct in standard usage; systematic avoidance or replacement of certain letters, etc., etc.) and try to apply it to another language; even if the language of origin and the language of translation are very diverse in terms of basic grammatical concepts (Indo-European; Mandarin), a skilled translator will succeed in conveying to foreign readers the principles of wording of the original text.

11.—If one engages in a discussion of the question of which generalizing categories one might reasonably conceive in order to describe the immense quantities of literary texts the entire species has produced to date,[540] concepts like that of "national literatures" seem to be problematic in that they tacitly reduce literary texts to the functional dimension that might have been at the basis of their creation while neglecting their exogenous components as well as their potential appeal to exogenous recipients. The impression of "adequacy" which such concepts may produce at first sight is tailored to spheres which are not identical with, or even far removed from, literature and art: political discourses, identity discourses, nationalistic dichotomization, and the subsequent essentialization of entities that are highly fluid with regard to space and time.

The overall argument presented in this chapter may be put in a nutshell by recalling the basic insight of modern linguistics: languages are arbitrary systems—nothing "natural" inheres in them. Like all arbitrary or artificial things, they may be appropriated by any member of the species, and their configuration as systems—which is the enabling structure of their semiotic potential—allows for the transfer of any specific constellation from one such system to another.

"National" Styles? "Hybridity"? "Third Spaces"?

0.—Apart from the spatio-topographical specificity assignable to many literary works on behalf of the referential components they contain, apart from the linguistic specificity assignable to them on behalf of the vernacular they make use of in order to express "themselves", there is a third, in a way intermediate component typically ascribed to works of art by means of which the advocates of a Herderian approach try to substantiate the claim that there are essential differences between artworks of diverse "national" provenance, namely, the assumption of different "national styles". I shall address this point by taking a look at the (literary) culture of Europe which most insists on its "exceptional" status, namely, that of France.

1.—What does "style" mean in this context? It is certainly a category much broader than the one indicated by the proper acceptation of the term, that is, broader than actual wording, formulation, and phrasing; however, as literary artifacts consist of nothing but words, "style" in the broader sense, too, is inextricably linked to the level of actual formulation. Yet in particular when we try

---

540 —and we are only talking here about the fraction that has been preserved until our times.

to describe so-called "great works", we almost always take such works to be characterized by a high degree of internal coherence not only on the level of choice of words and their concatenation, but also on that of a more general impression of compelling unity. The level of abstraction on which we locate this unity varies historically. In high modernist art in particular, it is frequently not to be found on the level of the formal organization of the artifact itself, but rather on that of an abstract concept that informs the at times quite erratic actual structure of the work. But it seems hardly convincing to talk about a given artifact as a "great" work if one is not able to ascribe to it a superior degree of internal cohesion. Works of art are not measured by their capacity to convey an adequate image of reality—this being a standard of quality that applies to many pragmatic texts—but are rather assessed according to their capacity to impress even though their recipients know that the works are devoid of any direct practical use-value. What else could lastingly impress recipients if not the work's subtlety of internal organization? There may be further factors (for instance, the potential to connect to other great works, artistic or non-artistic, of the period and thus to contribute to constituting a more comprehensive internally coherent unity we tend to call an "age" or "epoch"), but the item mentioned seems indispensable.[541]

2.—I would like to link my speculations concerning the question at issue to my above deliberations on early modern drama: many of the differences observable between various "national" traditions of drama may be contingent on different principles of establishing internal unity; but it remains to be discussed to what extent such differing principles of coherence can be convincingly linked to particular national communities.[542]

---

[541] In order to avoid misunderstandings: the argumentation in the above passage is not contrary to my frequently quoted point of reference with regard to the function of receiving literary texts, namely Freud's essay "The Relation of the Poet to Day-Dreaming". Here, I am dealing not with questions of function, but rather with the problem of relative preference for one work over others, that is, with the dimension that provokes, according to Freud, what he calls "Vorlust": the *conscious* pleasure a reader takes in reading a text (or a beholder takes in viewing a painting). This "Vorlust" is linked to the formal sophistication recipients are able to detect when receiving a work of art. Although it may be an instrument of self-deception with the aim of precluding consciousness of the "real" motives behind reading fiction, the recipient's preoccupation with formal sophistication is a factual dimension of dealing with art.

[542] It is perhaps at this point in my argument that I should refer to a case study published by Stephen Greenblatt in the volume *Cultural Mobility* (n. 5). Greenblatt narrates an intriguing story about his idea to rewrite, with the help of a present-day American playwright, one of Shakespeare's lost dramas, namely *The History of Cardenio* ("Theatrical Mobility", pp. 75–95). Like many of Shakespeare's plays, this one, too, was based on a written source of non-English provenance, namely on one of the stories interpolated in Cervantes's *Quijote*, the English translation of whose first part (1612) had been a great success on the literary market. The Cardenio

If one is prepared to sufficiently narrow down the temporal scope, it is striking to observe that serious French drama of the early modern age is characterized by only one verse pattern, the twelve-syllable alexandrine, whereas English drama is much more open to varying verse patterns; there is prose, there is blank verse, and there is rhymed verse. But the most "open" variant of early modern drama, at least in terms of versification, is to be found in Spain. Spanish dramas of the late sixteenth and seventeenth centuries display passages in *endecasílabo* (verses of eleven syllables), *décimas* (ten syllables), *silvas* (a combination of verses of eleven and seven syllables), *romances* (verses of sixteen syllables), and *redondillas* (verses of six to eight syllables), just to name the most important patterns. The uniformity of the French standard verse is echoed by a relatively restricted vocabulary, whereas English and Spanish dra-

---

story deals with two couples who first become separated from each other, partly due to unfavorable circumstances (that is the "Hellenistic" strand of the story), partly due to the egocentric misbehavior of one of the male protagonists. As befits the Hellenistic scheme, the ending is happy: the couples are reunited and the egotist marries the young lady to whom he once proposed, leaving the other, whom he courted in the middle section of the tale, to the man she is in love with, that is, the second male protagonist.—Since nothing is preserved of Shakespeare's play except the title, Greenblatt and his collaborator were free to reassemble the pieces they extracted from the cultural net in a way they thought productive. They boldly decided that another of Cervantes's interpolated stories, the famous *El curioso impertinente* (which is linked to the Cardenio story in that it is being read from a manuscript when Cardenio interrupts for a while with the account of his own past adventures), is much more suited for dramatization. The *Curioso impertinente* is also a story about the intricacies of love, but it reduces the scheme of four personages to a triangle consisting of a jealous husband, his best friend, and his wife. Its basic pattern is the motif of the "love test", by which the husband intends to find out, with his friend's help, whether his wife is unconditionally loyal or not; the outcome is tragic, as the wife and the friend finally do engage in an adulterous relationship; when the husband becomes aware of it, he dies, while the two adulterers fall prey to vicissitudes in which they become entangled because of bad conscience.—In the context of the present study, it is worth mentioning that, in addition to the recombination just referred to, the authors decided to substitute the original ending of the *Curioso impertinente* with the happy ending of the Cardenio story, that is, to cast the play as comedy (which it was, supposedly at least, in Shakespeare). Greenblatt ends his account of his career as a playwright by referring to some stage productions based on his play; the one which astonished him most took place in Japan and seems to have been a *Regietheater*-like alienation (in the sense of Brechtian *Verfremdung*) of the original play; rendered in English, the title of the Japanese production was *Motorcycle Quijote*. According to Greenblatt's account, it consisted of a sort of hybridization of his rewriting of Shakespeare/Cervantes with popular clichés about twentieth-century American youth culture as presented in films such as *Easy Rider* (1969).—The entire constellation is a sort of quasi-ideal paradigm of the primacy of what I here call the reassembly of pre-existent material when it comes to the processes of cultural production, and it also illustrates how ideas of "unity" and "coherence" shift when we consider different periods or different communities.

mas of the time make use of the whole range of linguistic registers available, including popular and even vulgar strata. The figures acting on stage are likewise diverse when compared to the mostly homogeneous characters of French tragedy;[543] and one could even regard the frequent feature of "gender trouble" (females disguised as males and vice versa) in English and Spanish serious plays of the time—I am not referring here to comedy proper—as a further reflection of a formal as well as content-related "openness", entirely absent in the case of the French classical tragedy.

Perhaps paradoxically, the examples briefly characterized above yield a strong counterargument to an all too complete relapse into the concepts of idealist aesthetics:[544] the remarkable formal "openness" of the Spanish drama of the time is neutralized if not annihilated by its overall ideological illiberality. The texts, praised by none other than Goethe as the apogee of world literature,[545] are in terms of their message most rigid instances of Tridentine Counter-Reformation propaganda. Was it the mix of ideological "closedness" and formal openness which led to the great success of these dramas throughout Europe, but only during a brief period stretching from the beginning to the middle of the nineteenth century? Shakespearean drama, which was no less successful in that age, but which continues to be enormously popular in our own times, is characterized by the rejection of closedness on *all* levels of the text. French tragedy, still popular in its country of origin, but no longer outside, is a paradigm of formal closedness and of maximum semantic coherence. Even if this closedness does not include, as in the case of the Spanish drama, the level of general worldview (including the afterlife), the French classicist tragedy with its specific variant of internal coherence may have lost some of its former transcultural fascination when Romanticism—which was a pan-European attitude— and its somewhat enthusiastic ideas of generalized freedom, including artistic freedom, gained the upper hand.

---

543 I am referring to the level of important characters only; of course, there are servants in French tragedies; but compared to their analogues in Shakespearean or in Spanish Golden Age (serious) dramas, their role is a very marginal one.
544 I am referring to the Hegelian conviction, expounded in the latter's *Lectures on Aesthetics*, that art is characterized by a correspondence, albeit to varying degrees, between "content" and "form".
545 It is in particular Calderón's drama on the first attempts at discovering unknown worlds, *El príncipe constante* (1628/1629)—which deals with the Portuguese expansion into Morocco— that was hailed by Goethe as a work from which one would be able to rebuild the entire system of poetry and fiction ("Poesie") if one day all literary works were lost (Letter to Schiller, January 28, 1804; in: *Gedenkausgabe der Werke, Briefe und Gespräche*, Ernst Beutler [ed.], Zürich 1948–1954, vol. 20, p. 964 f.).

As to the varying logic of internal organization, there seems to be no more to be said than that a certain degree of cohesiveness is mandatory if a newly assembled artwork is to become popular instead of remaining inactive in the net. If the shaping does not attain a level sufficient to individualize the work in question—to make it distinguishable from other individualized works floating in the net—it will sooner or later be absorbed by other, similarly structured works, and go on hovering as a mere instance of a pattern or paradigm, e.g., that of the "trivial love story". But whether the principle of this individualizing formal coherence needs to be a "positive" or a "negative" one, whether it is total or rather non-total coherence which tends to pave the way towards a worldwide reception—this question shall remain unanswered here and left to my readers' own reflection. For the time being, the only means I see of grasping these historically shifting conceptualizations of coherence would be Ernst Robert Curtius's model of alternation between phases of what he calls "classicism" (a strict and pervasive concept of coherence) and "mannerism" (a much more flexible way of building coherence, in many cases just by opposing classical features).[546] In addition, one should take into consideration an aspect of historical conceptualization which Karl Mannheim has called the "non-contemporaneity of the contemporaneous",[547] meaning that in every epoch there are both dominant and non-dominant features, the latter being previously dominant (that is, obsolete) or precursory items. In the above, I have merely given one concrete hint at what I mean by referring to the reception of French classical tragedy since the age of Romanticism.[548] But as to the questions of "why" and "why exactly at this moment" schemas of preference for this or that way of establishing unity change, I am afraid I have to leave it at the unsatisfactory reference to the contingency of historical processes.

3.—The partaking of the formal features in question in the transnational patrimony floating in the net explains the constant and at times rapid changes to which these secondary constellations are subjected, and it is in particular this incontestable feature which seems to destabilize the expediency of the category of "national style", which does seem to suggest itself when one only takes short-term scenarios of literary production into consideration. French texts from the eighteenth century are very different from those written in the seventeenth century, as are nineteenth-century texts from eighteenth-century texts.

---

546 See *European Literature and the Middle Ages*, chap. 15.
547 Regarding this point, see Mannheim's "Das Problem der Generationen", *Kölner Vierteljahreshefte für Soziologie* vol. 7 / 1928, pp. 157–185 and pp. 309–330.
548 See the end of the preceding paragraph.

It is an illusion produced by the (roughly) identical language in which all of these texts are written which may make an observer believe them to constitute a homogeneous fund. The complete transformation of the "pacific" and "provincial" orientation of the German culture of early-nineteenth-century *Biedermeier* into the aggressive attitude, also manifest in culture, which characterizes Germany from 1871 through 1945, as well as the reconversion to a relative provinciality from 1945 onwards, would be another example of the extremely high flexibility of these secondary determinant constellations. There is not much in the domain of culture which could be called the legitimate "property" of one specific community.[549]

4.—In order to round off the complex of questions discussed in the above pages, I should like to invite readers to take a brief glance at the drama that seems to represent the essence of French literature, that is, Racine's *Phèdre*, as well as the drama that seems to represent the essence of English literature, that is, Shakespeare's *Hamlet*. Measured by many of the parameters here discussed, these two texts are indeed distinct. But, as stressed by Jan Mosch in his comparative analysis of the two pieces,[550] there is a strong tendency, due to our Herderian view of literary history, to overlook their commonalities. The latter begin with the fact that both dramas do not base their plots on autochthonous narratives, but rather on exogenous source material (Sophocles/Seneca; Saxo Grammaticus). Consequently, the action is not located on "home ground". These "external" commonalities comprise the fact that both texts have been as intensely received beyond the borders of their respective cultures of origin as they have been at home.[551] And there are a few points with respect to the works themselves that need to be mentioned: They share the characteristic of being difficult to

---

[549] The most striking phenomenon with regard to the entire constellation discussed in this chapter is the fact that reception processes in modern times, that is, in a period deeply marked by the concept of "national cultures", operate right from the beginning beyond the boundaries of the national cultures involved; one might think of the German reception of Shakespearean and of Spanish Golden Age drama, or of the French reception of Shakespearean drama. The remarkable fact that a foreign country's dramatic and theatrical culture may be "adopted" almost officially contests the nationalistic assumptions regarding culture that were discursively prevalent during the same period in the countries involved. The question one could raise starting from this observation is whether there is anything "national" at all about dramatic or literary texts in general, that is, of course, apart from language. Is literary culture an instrument of cultural imperialism, or is it a genuinely universal structure which combines cultural material in a form that engages basic (psychic) needs of humans as a species?
[550] *Moral Agency and Heteronomy in Shakespearean and Racinian Tragedy.*
[551] I have already addressed the problem of the differences between the two dramas as to these international reception processes (pp. 277 f.).

assign to one of the two parties in the religious controversies so important for their age; it is not at all clear whether Shakespeare's Denmark is meant to be pre- or post-Reformation; Racine's plays, and *Phèdre* in particular, which were created in a "Catholic" country, are frequently associated with a Jansenist background, that is, an Augustinian or crypto-Protestant theology of grace. The action is in both cases marked by the political context of absolutism; in both plays, the concept of the theatricality of power, essential for the political formation we call absolutism, plays an eminent role. There is a multitude of shared motifs and metaphors, which one may attribute to the common ground of knowledge and to the transnational profile of pedagogy in the early modern age. Both dramas, in contrast to earlier stages of European drama, attest to the reception of Aristotle's *Poetics*, though with varying degrees of emphasis. Both manifest the interactional codes of courtly societies. And I shall not address here in detail the many commonalities that one might attribute to anthropological constants, e.g., the basic motif of incest; the struggle for power; the propensity for cruel violence in order to settle problematic situations (etc., etc.).—Considering all these points, I am tempted to no longer qualify *Hamlet* as "the most important English drama" or *Phèdre* as "the most eminent French drama"; I would rather suggest regarding the two pieces as the most impressive dramas from post-classical times which have come down to us, respectively, in English and in French.

5.—In view of further nuancing this argument, I would like to come back to the general concept of national culture as discussed above, while trying to differentiate my polemics from the postmodernist and postcolonial discourses that have become the mainstream in recent times. One very instructive example of these latter conceptualizations which is linked to this book's specific literary field is Friederike Pannewick's essay in the volume *Cultural Mobility: A Manifesto*.[552] It deals with the question of an Arab theatrical culture, which, as Pannewick concedes, only emerges in proper terms during the first half of the nineteenth century, that is, concomitant to the process of Western penetration into the countries of Muslim culture. As I am no expert in the field, the claim that there has been a burgeoning "autochthonous" theater scene in the Arab world during the subsequent period shall remain uncontested here; if this is, indeed, the case, it would constitute yet another confirmation of my hypothesis regarding the mechanisms of cultural dynamics. The point to be discussed rather concerns the period before the (to put it in a neutral fashion) "transfer" of occidental theatrical culture to the Muslim world.—Everyone reading this book will be familiar with

---

552 "Performativity and Mobility: Middle Eastern Traditions on the Move", in: Greenblatt et al. (eds.), *Cultural Mobility*, pp. 215–249.

Jorge Luis Borges's aforementioned short story dealing with the problem at stake, which is entitled *La busca de Averroes*. In a fictional manner, it tells of the famous Aristotelian's incomprehension regarding the argument of one of Aristotle's texts, namely, his tract on theater, the *Poetics*, although the rest of the philosopher's oeuvre is fully accessible to him. The reason for this incapability consists in the fact that it is impossible to "understand" concepts which do not already exist in one's own intellectual horizon. Since there was no theatrical culture in the traditional Muslim world, Averroes was not able to grasp what Aristotle wanted to convey.[553]

Pannewick's approach—paradigmatic of present-day scholarly discourses—contests what Borges conveys in his short story regarding theater in precolonial Muslim cultures. Her argumentation is characterized by what I have come to call the "me too" or the "we too" attitude. By referring to performative practices like the one of storytelling in front of an audience, and, in addition, to a (quantitatively) extremely limited tradition of martyr plays in Persia, Pannewick does not explicitly postulate, but rather insinuates that the assumption of the non-existence of theatrical culture in the traditional Muslim world is based on Eurocentrism, that is, the at the same time ignorant and arrogant attitude of the West towards non-Western cultures, which are thereby conceived of in terms of deficits, as less "inventive" and less productive.—In the following, I would like to make one point with respect to the argument proper and another with regard to the intention at its basis.

Pannewick is intellectually honest enough to go no further than a conceptual blurring of the boundaries between performative practices at large and theater proper; she does not explicitly deny the difference. And she provides valuable source material that is apt for explaining—from her perspective as well as from mine—the reasons why there was no theatrical culture proper in the traditional Muslim world. These reasons did not consist in a lack of cultural or intellectual inventiveness; they consisted in the fierce opposition to theatrical practices on the part of Islamic theologians. Reading the "Arab" polemics against staged performances quoted by Pannewick,[554] one is instantaneously reminded of Plato's as well as of Augustine's diatribes against such cultural practices as prone to stimulate the less dignified parts of the soul—the emotions or affects—and thus to induce the spectators to act in an inappropriate way in their subsequent "real" lives. Given the fact that these Islamic tracts were written in regions not

---

553 This is the (according to me, highly convincing) line of argument suggested by the serene *Buenairense* skeptic.
554 "Performativity and Mobility", p. 223.

very far from or even identical to the ones where Plato and Augustine professed their views, one might be inclined to see these texts as perhaps not specifically Islamic at all. They may rather belong to a broader strand of texts inspired by the worldviews of Mediterranean monotheisms.

To summarize the first point I should like to make on a more abstract level: It would be pointless to deny that there are differences between different cultures. The question at stake is how to conceive of these differences. It is only an essentializing or, to put it in more explicit terms, a racial approach that is problematic from my perspective. But in order to evade the traps of thinking in terms of racial concepts, it is neither necessary nor sensible to level or to implicitly refute the fact of cultural difference. In the case in question, one would have to discuss in detail the reasons why the theological diatribes referred to above remained dominant in the Muslim world until the dawn of westernization while they lost the discursive battle in the Occident as early as the sixteenth century, albeit without ever disappearing—there is no blockbuster movie whose reception is not accompanied by cultural critics' voices incriminating it as "dangerous for the populace", especially for the younger generation. I cannot go into details in this respect, but will leave it at two points which should be taken into consideration: The motives behind the proclamation of the founder of the Christian religion, Jesus, that his kingdom is not of this world (John 18:36) might have been quite profane or even opportunistic. Had he articulated the opposite view, he would have been executed by the Romans even before he was able to gather a number of disciples who would carry on the divulgation of his ideas. The consequences of the utterance in question, however, were enormous as soon as Christianity was adopted by the Roman Empire and its successor states. As in the Islamic world, Christian theologians nurtured the ambition of totally controlling society, of becoming the "real" rulers. But pluralism and the ensuing reduction of religion to one functional sphere (Niklas Luhmann) amongst others is inherent in Christianity's basic doctrine. Within the dominant religion of the West, there is a (biblical) basis for rejecting the theologians' pretense to totalitarianism. In Islam, there is no such basis. Pluralization thus requires a previous secularization.

The second point I should like to suggest for a more penetrating discussion is the fact that, for whatever reason, Christianity is not a "pure" monotheism; from the standpoint of other monotheistic religions, it even appears to be a poorly veiled polytheism. When it comes to artistic production, this conceptual "impurity" might, however, bring advantages. The idea of God having become incarnate and having lived and died amongst humans makes it impossible to anathematize—as other monotheisms do—that he be imagined in the very literal sense, that is: represented. Since the Dark Ages, religious paintings and their "kinetic" variant, religious dramas (mystery plays), belonged to the cultural practices accepted or even propagated by the religious authorities. Comic interludes, that is, short profane plays (farces), were admitted, with the intention not to bore the audience with too much doctrine. As a consequence, it would have been a somewhat difficult undertaking in the Christian West to "protect" society against what was leaking out of the net when the ships bearing the manuscripts of classical dramas arrived after the Ottoman conquest of Constantinople.

6.–The example just outlined would appear in the final analysis to mean that it is religion, or worldview at large, that constitutes the basic determinant factor when it comes to the observable differences between the works assembled within different cultural communities by making use of a common fund of cultural material floating in the net. As may be evident from all I have said so far in this book, I am indeed much more inclined to emphasize the role of religion in cultural dynamics in general than most present-day research in the field, at least in Europe, typically does. But my entire approach implies that there are no such one-way determinant factors, no strict causal chains, when it comes to systematizing cultural dynamics. As important as several specific features of Christian dogma may have been for the specific formation of works of art (mainly literary texts, but also performative practices, and not least all variants of graphic art) we usually call "occidental", the rapid spread of this religion—in its origins an unorthodox and persecuted sectarian movement within a small community under foreign rule—can only be explained by referring to contingency, a label that any reader is free to replace by that of "God", as long as she or he is conscious of leaving the section of the discursive field (*champ discursif*) assigned to scholarship and of entering the section assigned to faith. It was not an item of necessity that the Mediterranean world was politically organized as one massive unit, as an empire, when this sect started its attempts at propagating its somewhat unheard-of views. Without this enabling structure, a religious movement based on the ideals of "peace" and "love" (thus contrasting with another sectarian religious movement which would emerge in the same region some six hundred years later) would hardly have had the chance to extend its influence beyond the borders of the small kingdom where it originated. And it is an instance of even greater contingency (if contingencies can be quantified at all) that after three centuries of bloody persecution, the head of the state, the Roman emperor, suddenly decided to embrace this somewhat strange oriental cult and to oblige all his subjects to comply with this step.

But from that time onward—that is, for a period of at least one and a half millennia—certain parameters regarding the "assembly" of cultural material into single works were, indeed, more or less fixed for the region in question. Representational art (painting, theater) is in principle legitimate; the representation of "everything", including the ugly parts of reality, is legitimate, since God himself became incarnate, that is, part of this world;[555] narrative, the basic formal pattern of this religion's holy text,[556] is legitimate; narrative clearly recognizable as fiction, that is, a strand of narrative that Plato would have liked to prohibit, is legitimate, since the religion's founder made use of the device when proselytizing, the reason for the choice of this register being evident: those he wanted to convince were primarily humble, uneducated people.—I could go on enumerating basic formal principles that distinguish, partly or totally, Western art from the artworks of other communities, but I think the examples expounded so far suffice to illustrate what I wish to express on a more abstract level: Conceiving of culture as originating from a decentralized and de-territorialized net does not imply that there are not specific features of works of art that one can legitimately link to certain regions and to certain periods. And it does not imply that it would be pointless to ponder external (that is: non-artistic) factors responsible for the evolution of art, in a specific area and period, in one particular direction rather than another equally conceivable one. But these determinant factors seem not to constitute an "ultimate ground". The factors themselves are various (political, ideological, and, as one must certainly add, economic—there may be a few more as well); but more importantly, they are linked to such a multifarious variety of possible "causes" that we finally are unable to say more than that they are contingent; nevertheless—and this is the decisive point—they are factual.

Referring to contingency as the "black hole" of causal discourses—the site we conceptually assign to all those items which are, for the time being, inexplicable—may, however, be somewhat unsatisfactory. From the 1980s onward, the word has evolved into a catch-all term for all sorts of complex items which cultural theoreticians do not deem worth the effort of further reflection. This inclines me to hazard another metaphor—apart from the basic image of the "net" which informs this entire study—in order to overcome at least partly the state of a complete *nescio* (William Occam),[557] which one frequently tries to

---

555 I am referring to Auerbach's theorization of "Christian" realism in his famous book titled *Mimesis* (which is indebted to Hegel's remarks on "die romantische Kunstform" [part III of his *Vorlesungen über die Ästhetik* (1835–38)] and to Victor Hugo's "Préface de *Cromwell*" [1827]).
556 Let me stress that this feature is specific; the formal organization of the *Quran* is different.
557 As to this basic nominalist *confessio*, see William Occam, *Super quattuor libros sententiarum subtilissimae quaestiones earumque decisiones* (1317–1318), I, dist. 38, q. I ("Potest tamen dici quod ipse Deus, vel divina essentia, est una cognitio intuitiva, tam sui ipsius quam omnium aliorum factibilium et infactibilium, tam perfecta et tam clara quod ipsa etiam est notitia evidens omnium praeteritorum, futurorum et praesentium. [...] tenendum est quod Deus evi-

veil by applying the learned term of "contingency": One might consider the various determinant factors described above according to planetary constellations such as the solar system. This system consists of more and of less important (large) stars. There is one star which seems to be the center (the sun). But this is only an apparent "fact". Considered in a more penetrating way, this "fixed star" reveals itself to be nothing but a mobile object, albeit in constellations that transcend the limits of our solar system. But the most important point which makes me suggest this metaphor in more than just a frivolous manner is the fact that the stability of the system is guaranteed by nothing other than the mutual physical attraction existing between all of its components. If one eliminated only one of the smaller components, the entire system would collapse. It is thus senseless to argue that the sun is the "truly" decisive player within this system; if a seemingly dependent celestial body such as the moon were destroyed, the Earth would be destabilized, all living organisms would disappear, and our globe would be decomposed into fragments or absorbed by larger bodies, which would then be absorbed by the sun, which would in turn be absorbed by larger stars (etc.).

In culture as well, there are quite a few separable determinant factors which constitute the system as a whole, as in the case of planetary systems; and there are factors which at first sight seem to be more important than others. But finally, it turns out that all these factors are able to play their conditioning roles only because the system exists as a whole.[558] And it seems to be in particular this latter feature—the dependency of these various factors on their being items of a structure, their relational "essence"—which accounts for the fact that they might change their concrete places in the structure in question,[559] leading to a constant reconfiguration of apparently "fixed" systems.

7.—The date of 1453, mentioned at various occasions in the course of my argument, brings me to a corollary point regarding ideology which I would like to

---

denter cognoscit omnia futura contingentia. Sed modum exprimere nescio." / "It could nevertheless be said that God himself, or the divine essence, is one single intuitive cognition both of himself and of every other thing, feasible or infeasible, so perfect and so clear that it is itself an evident notion of everything past, future, and present. [...] It is to be held indubitably that God knows all future contingencies certainly, but in a way which I am not able to express.").
558 In order to avoid misunderstandings: this latter metaphor must not be mixed with the metaphor of the net, which is here applied to explain the internal logic of processes of exchange occurring within the system of culture. The planetary system metaphor is meant to (partly) elucidate the relationship between the diverse "fields" (*champs discursifs*, in Foucault's terminology) by which we usually compartmentalize the undifferentiated unit of "culture".
559 —which, within cosmic time frames, applies to planetary systems as well.

make with respect to the "me too" or "we too" attitude—a point which starts from the observation that this attitude, along with the discourses linked to it, is mainly professed by Western intellectuals who work on the "subaltern" cultures in question, or by scholars from these countries who have become completely assimilated and integrated into Western academia, to the extent that it would be devoid of sense to conceive of these people as non-Westerners, as "other".

I am inclined to say that it is, in the final analysis, nothing other than unconscious racial thinking which constitutes the basis of the discourses targeted by me. The somewhat "generous", but in essence condescending basic gesture with which these discourses postulate that "they too", the "subaltern" cultures, developed cultural practices similar to the ones existing in the West, implies that these Western practices "belong" to us, that is, to present-day Western people, that they are "our" intellectual property, quite like the blueprints for our industrial products. But who wrote *Oidipous tyrannos* (fifth century BCE)? Who wrote *Iphigeneia he en Aulidi* (fifth century BCE)? Who wrote *Hamlet*; who wrote *Phèdre*; who wrote the *Wallenstein* trilogy (1799), or *Faust* (1808)? At least as far as I am concerned, I have to say that it was neither me nor any one of "my" ancestors. But, a Herderian may object, my ancestors may perhaps have contributed to the production of these works, in particular in the case of *Wallenstein* and *Faust*, by partaking in the process of narrating and re-narrating, stretching over several millennia, that finally led to the written texts that have come down to us. The somewhat vague information I am able to gather from the extant records, however, makes it extremely improbable, at least as far as this part of the world, Northern Central Europe, is concerned, that there ever was a stable relation between spaces and tribes residing in these spaces lasting for more than a century.

Traditions are a mix of heterogeneous materials; homogeneity is a projection *a posteriori*. Consequently, there is nothing I (or the overwhelming majority of present-day Western people) am entitled to be proud of when reading the plays mentioned or seeing them on stage, all the more as the fact that we are able to receive them is linked to historical contingency, as is best evidenced by the erratic transmission history of some of them. I can legitimately admire them, but that is it. It is by chance that I and my occidental contemporaries were born in this part of the world. There is no personal "merit" at all implied in the fact that our cradles were located in Western Europe or in North America. It is a more difficult question whether or not we are entitled to be proud of our own, personal contribution to the tradition we inherited. But as to the tradition itself, it was bestowed on us; there was no activity on our part involved. Conceding to "other" cultures that they are equal in "value" to our "own" culture always implies the pretense that there is a substantive link between us as individuals and "our" culture.—Racial thinking is far from having disappeared from our intellectual discourses; under the disguise of multiculturalism and identity politics, it is more virulent than it ever was, except perhaps in the 30s and 40s of the last century.

8.—Finally, I will not refrain from making explicit the extent to which the theorization of processes of cultural exchange suggested in this book is at odds with the central metaphorical concept of postcolonialism, which has become most influential even beyond its field of origin: "hybridization". Like all metaphors derived from biology, the concept is in my view *in principle* problematic when applied to cultural phenomena, because these are fundamentally different from natural ones—which is a truism, since, if it were otherwise, there would be no necessity to distinguish between *natura* and *nutritura*, or, in the field of academic disciplines, between the natural sciences and the humanities.[560] But the main problem concerning the hybridization concept is a more specific one. Its internal logic implies that there are pre-existing "pure" items, which then become "hybridized" in the course of processes of cultural interaction.[561] It would be contrary to the basic principles of reason to talk about the

---

[560] For a critical view of present-day attempts to overcome this dividing line, see my "Einige Bemerkungen zum Verhältnis von Geisteswissenschaften und Theorie", in: Joachim Küpper, Markus Rautzenberg, Miriam Schaub, and Regine Strätling (eds.), *The Beauty of Theory. Zur Ästhetik und Affektökonomie von Theorien*, München 2013, pp. 19–33.

[561] It is amazing to see that postcolonial theory is at least to a certain extent conscious of the problem mentioned above, while at the same time it holds on to the concept of hybridity. In his "Adagio" dedicated to the memory of Edward Said, Homi K. Bhabha quotes Said's resistance to "'essentializations' of natural or cultural ideal-types—*the* Jew, *the* Indian, *the* French—because such 'universals' represent the imperial legacy 'by which a dominant culture eliminated *the impurities and hybrids that make up all culture.*'" (*Critical Inquiry* vol. 31, 2 / 2005, pp. 371–380; here: p. 376; the quote from Said is drawn from *Musical Elaborations*, New York, NY 1991, p. 52; my italics). In the following sentences, however, referring once again to quotes from Said himself, Bhabha underpins Said's enthusiastic reaction to writers such as Rushdie for the achievement of having introduced "'a particular kind of hybrid experience into English.'" ("Adagio", p. 376; Said, "The Road Less Traveled", in: Gauri Viswanathan [ed.], *Power, Politics, and Culture. Interviews with Edward W. Said*, New York, NY 2001, pp. 409–418, quote: p. 416). The only explanation for this paradox of insight and blindness may be implied in what Bhabha says about Said's reasons for rejecting essentialism. They are not primarily descriptive or logical, but political. This applies to postcolonial theory in general. It inscribes itself in the broader trend of Western Marxism in the post-'68 period, when the conviction that either the Soviet Union or Maoist China could yield a model for universal "liberation" waned rapidly. In this moment, it was no longer Marx, Stalin, and Mao who were the idols of Western Marxists. Antonio Gramsci took their place. With his emphasis on the "super-structure", and his claim that it is this part of the entire societal structure, namely: all of culture, that needs to be revolutionized first before

hybridity of certain ("postcolonial") cultural phenomena without making the claim that there are art forms that are, for example, essentially British, while there are others that are essentially Indian.

In the final analysis, postcolonial theory is bound to the Herderian concept of culture as an instance of "rootedness", which is then supposed to be superseded by the "truly" valuable hybrid works. Rootedness, however, is by necessity nothing but a metaphor; the literal soil, or rather ground, from which artifacts or cultural phenomena originate are people, human beings. If the cultures in question are posited as homogeneous—and if not, it would not make any sense to postulate that their products are "pure"[562]—there are no barriers left that would prevent a racial subtext from making its way into such a theory of culture. And it does not matter whether this is racial thinking "from above" (the racism of the dominant) or "from below" (the racism of the subaltern), because it is part of the entire political project behind the façade of postcolonialism to invert such hierarchies. As in all revolutionary movements from the French Revolution onward, equality is a postulate for a remote future. In order to secure the revolutionary movement's success, it is necessary to establish a (as it has turned out in the past: never-ending) dictatorial regime of the formerly suppressed immediately after the victory.

---

the "real" taking over by the revolutionaries can take place, the left started in on its huge attempt at changing the thinking of Western societies, of "constructing" new (conceptual) realities which would then produce new factual realities. As a result of this idealistic turn of leftist thinking and activities, theories inscribing themselves into this "grand project", such as postcolonialism, are not primarily descriptive, but rather, according to their self-conceptualization, performative. They want to bring about the structures they describe. It is not a matter of introducing the concept of hybridity as a descriptively adequate scholarly category, but rather of making use of certain variants of the hybridity concept in the interest of "subversion", of "empowering" the "marginalized", the "subaltern", etc. For these reasons, postcolonial theory has to hold on to the postulate that there is a difference between "regular" hybridity, applying to cultural phenomena of any kind, and "real" hybridity as the dialectics characterizing the cultural situation of the (mainly ethnically defined) subjugated and subaltern, who are to become the rulers after the revolution. Hybridity as a characteristic of cultural artifacts produced in situations of balanced power relations and without any "racial" implications that could be ascribed to the configuration in question (France and Italy in the Renaissance; present-day Western Europe and the US, etc.) is of no interest to postcolonial theory. And the fact that, finally, all of culture is hybrid has to be more or less silenced in order to postulate the political dichotomy of dominators and dominated in the sphere of culture as well.

562 The extent to which postcolonial theory is bound to the assumption of essential divergences becomes apparent in many of Bhabha's famous and ubiquitous formulas, for example in his definition of "third space" as a place of "negotiation of *incommensurable differences*" (*The Location of Culture*, London and New York, NY 1994, p. 218; my italics).

For the reasons mentioned above, culture and cultural artifacts are here theorized as resulting from extremely flexible and varying interactions between a "free" floating and various mechanisms of control that try to "regulate" this free floating and which may produce certain forms of stability assignable to certain periods and certain places, if one only takes the aspect of statistical frequency into consideration. The products resulting from this interplay between free exchange and the attempt to direct cultural production are, however, finally all too diverse for it to be possible to sensibly hold that there are typically British or typically Chinese art forms. All such ideas are, as argued above, to a large extent the results of reverse conclusions of a particularly naïve profile:[563] a work of art is written in English and portrays "traditional" British culture; for that reason, "Englishness" is taken to be its primary feature when it comes to describing the specificity of the work in question.

Stability, essentiality, and purity are but momentary impressions based on the consideration of certain phenomena at a certain time and place which are then projected on entire spaces and epochs for which, in most cases, they do not apply, at least not in their entirety. It is from such illusionary constructions of substances or essentialities that all theories revolving around the concept of hybridity take their point of departure. Talking about "essential" constellations or, as postcolonial theory does, basing one's own, non-essentialist categories on the assumption that there are previous essentialist categories is ideological. The entire attitude derives from the world of power, its interest is political, and its means are purely rhetorical.

9.—It must be stressed, however, that the dichotomous differences which are the logically necessary prerequisite for the concept of hybridity *do* exist in the field of power. It makes a difference, indeed, whether a given person is the decapitated or the executioner, the conquered or the conqueror, the dominated or the oppressor. In the sphere of culture, things might be much more complicated. The above remarks on the situation in colonial India[564] may illustrate the extent to which the assumption—finally based on classical Marxist claims— that culture is nothing other than a structure reflecting "real" power relations is oversimplified. If one did not know anything about the colonial history of

---

[563] For a more detailed discussion of the problems produced by such (very current) reverse conclusions, see above, pp. 104 f. and pp. 253–255.

[564] I would like to stress once again that more detailed information may be found in the book by Gautam Chakrabarti; what I here expound in terms of a mere description of the historical phenomena is based on this study (*Familiarising the Exotic: Introducing European Drama in Early Modern India*).

the subcontinent and was simply told that the East India Company established its first strongholds in the second half of the seventeenth century, that the British state took control over large parts of the territories in the decades following the mid-nineteenth century, and that the British effectively ruled the country until 1947, one would assume, from such a Marxist perspective, that the latter also tried to colonize the minds of the subjugated by imposing on them the English language and British culture. But this was not the case. For whatever reason, the British benignly neglected the entire field of culture during the largest part of their rule over the subcontinent. In the field of literary culture, it was the above-mentioned, somewhat obscure Russian adventurer Lebedev who first brought its Western variant to India. Later developments in this sphere were not primarily instances of imposition, but derived from the local "demand" for more "Western" literary culture, which originated from the first encounters of the Indian audience with Western-style theater.—The same applies to other instances of culture. The English language was not imposed. No one ever forbade the use of the myriad autochthonous languages. The efforts made by large parts of the Indian population to learn English were motivated by their wish to partake in economic, cultural, and scientific negotiations and developments from which they had been excluded for centuries or even millennia. "European" culture indeed made its way into colonial India, but not by way of a process that emulated the political situation.

I should like to stress that such an irenic or idealizing picture of processes of colonization is certainly not paradigmatic in the sense that it would apply to all comparable situations—quite to the contrary. I have already expressed above that processes of conquest originating from communities with universalistic convictions (my examples were Christianity, Islam, and the secular West of the post-Enlightenment era) typically go along with at times quite brutal processes of transculturation, of implementing one's own culture—the only "right" culture—in the conquered territories. On the other hand, I should like to emphasize that the above-characterized model of the early British in India is not the one and only exception to a general rule. It follows patterns recognizable in developments that are of primary importance in world history. The most prominent of these developments may be the story of our own, Western origins, parts of which were already mentioned: In order to get rid of the danger emanating from incidental barbarian incursions on their territory, the Romans conquered, step by step, Western and parts of Central and Northern Europe. They did not at all harbor the ambition of "romanizing" the locals. They wished to end the unrest at their frontiers. In addition, they wanted, as all conquerors do, some economic return for their military endeavors, so they exploited their colonies. The historically crucial development—neglected to date by the innumerable politicized books on colonization and globalization—occurred when the empire collapsed, for whatever reasons, in the fifth century CE. Not only did the colonized locals preserve the Roman culture and language they had adopted during the centuries of foreign rule instead of throwing off the yoke of an "alien" culture; the "Teutonic" conquerors who had made the *imperium* collapse also adopted the Roman mode of living. It was not that the Roman conquerors imposed their cultural patterns; it was, in a first step, the conquered who adopted them and, in a second step, the (second-degree) conquerors who adopted the culture of the defeated.—I will not indulge in further speculations regarding the point in question and will leave it at the remark that cultural theory informed by Marxian concepts, that is, the overwhelming quantity of cultural theory extant, is hardly compatible with the history of the culture from which Marxism originated. In many cases, the transfer of culture follows the deployment of power. But in many other cases, including several of world-historical import, it does not. Greece and Rome in classical times would be another example; Christianity and pagan Rome would be a third constellation in which the culture of the subjugated becomes the prevalent pattern. I do not have, for the time being, to suggest a viable alternative to the cultural theory of Marxist provenance; suffice it to say that, from my perspective, the historical ignorance accompanying the never-ending repetition of this pattern in mainstream cultural studies is quite astonishing.

In the sphere of culture, all seemingly essential "differences" are based on merely conceptual accumulations of the endless chain of gradual differences which make up "reality". Metaphors such as "circulation" or movements within "networks" seem to be more adequate for making sense of the specificity of cultural phenomena and processes than metaphors based on the assumption of dichotomies. If there are dichotomies at all in the cultural sphere, they are in almost all cases superimpositions resulting from the intentional instrumentalization of culture for political purposes. Political activities are legitimate; no reasonable person would contest that. But talking about culture while pursuing not descriptive, but rather ideological goals is a strategy that convinces only those who do not need to be convinced, because they are already part of the political project. It is a ritual repetition, that is, a public demonstration of belonging—in this case: to the congregation of the ideologically "correct"—which informs most present-day "scholarship".

IV. Concluding Remarks

Culture as Network: Subversive and Innovative Potentialities

0.—My concluding remarks will be brief. The first chapter of this section will address constellations touched upon in passing above while trying to demonstrate the extent to which a "technical" approach to literary and artistic creation as described in this book is able to integrate dimensions of the creative process which are typically considered not to be accounted for by the concept of art as *techne*. A second chapter will formulate some ideas concerning the limits of the approach here submitted.

1.—I should like to resume a point already discussed briefly, namely, that works of art typically convey the impression of "unity", of coherence. As mentioned previously, it shall remain an open question whether the impression of such internal coherence is the consequence of an effective structuring that is more consistent than in the case of pragmatic texts (or images), or whether this impression is rather the result of an attitude recipients automatically adopt as soon as a text or image is presented to them as a "work of art". Classical literary theory, for example Aristotle's *Poetics*, would argue for the former alternative, while many modernist artworks, literary as well as visual, make it even their primary message that there is no "material" difference between pragmatic objects and art objects;[565] from such a perspective, the difference consists, rather, in the attitude towards the object on the recipients' part, triggered by decontextualization. The point, however, is that even in the case of such high modernist, seemingly "un-structured" works, the assumptions concerning a sort of "over-structuring"[566] as a distinctive feature of artworks persist in the process of reception. The difference with regard to the reception of pre-high-modernist works consists in the fact that the assumption is directed at a different level of the work: in the case of high modernism, the over-structuring is supposed to be operative on the level of the conceptual framework underlying the actual work. A random collection of extremely banal objects from everyday life is differentiated from an equally banal collection of objects from everyday life exhibited as a "work of art" in a museum by the fact that the viewers, in the

---

[565] One might think of the works of such influential visual artists as Andy Warhol or Joseph Beuys.
[566] See Jürgen Link, "Das lyrische Gedicht als Paradigma des überstrukturierten Textes", in: *Funk-Kolleg Literatur*, vol. 1, Helmut Brackert and Eberhard Lämmert (eds.), Frankfurt/Main 1977, pp. 234–255.

latter case, are ready to assume that there is a "concept" governing the ensemble, which is thus no longer considered a random group of objects, but rather a carefully chosen arrangement whose logic is to be deciphered. In most cases, this logic is very abstract; it is constituted by basic aesthetic categories, for example the position that art is not necessarily linked to beauty or harmony, but rather to the parameters of defamiliarization and subsequent reflection.

In general terms, this discussion, as interesting as it may be, is not a point of particular relevance to the theoretical approach developed in this book. What is pertinent to my theorizing is the fact that the above-mentioned assumption recipients are ready to make in case they are dealing with objects that are generally accepted as artworks enables the synthesis of extremely diverse material extracted from the net. If one takes the entire history of art into consideration, including high modernism, one is tempted to say that it is art's privilege to mix materials of such diverse provenance that it would hardly be possible to merge them in non-artistic objects.[567] In the process of art production, the artist is free to assemble previous material that, at first sight, does not seem to fit together at all, and he may be able to derive effects from such a "wild mix"—aesthetic, semiotic, but also pragmatic—that would otherwise not be attainable. This applies not only to the modern period, but also to more classical times.

The highly sophisticated text known under the name of *Celestina* provides a good opportunity to consider such a particularly complicated, or, to put it in more down-to-earth terms, "wild" manner of dealing with the material circulating in the net. Without exaggeration, one can conceive of the drama as an "intertextuality" in the sense of Julia Kristeva's theorem. Similar to works of high modernism or even postmodernism, it does not try to feign "originality"; on the contrary, from the perspective of an educated reader, the intertextual character is laid bare in a most obvious fashion. This applies to all textual levels. The deep structure of its "core", the love story, is taken from medieval (more "realistic") variations of the pastoral tradition (*Pamphilus de amore* [twelfth century], *Arcipreste de Hita* [fourteenth century], *Arcipreste de Talavera* [1438], etc.), while the maxims that almost all the personages constantly cite are taken from Petrarch's *De remediis utriusque fortunae* (1354–1367) and its classical, mainly Stoic sources, to mention only the two most important pre-existent elements assembled by the text's author. As already explained, there is also a prominent component deriving from popular discourses, specifically

---

567 Think, for example, of techniques of *collage* in modernist graphic art, as well as in high modernist literary texts.—As to literary texts in particular, see my essay "Was ist Literatur?".

those belonging to the tradition known as the carnivalesque. One could thus say that the *Celestina* is systematically assembled out of extremely diverse units extracted from the net and re-synthesized into an entirely "new" and—as evidenced by the reception history—fascinating work. The important point to be highlighted, however, is that there seems to be no ideological homogenization to which this highly diverse material is submitted; or, to express it in more simple terms: the text merely presents diverse and contradictory interpretations of the story, without suggesting which might be the most satisfactory one. In addition, it does not show any obvious formal unity that might serve as a compensation for what at first sight appears to be a lack of consistency as to message; the text comprises twenty-one acts of most unequal length—a characteristic that is representative of its overall erratic organization.

Before concluding from such an observation that the *Celestina* is a precursor of high modernist or even postmodernist ways of making use of the cultural net, one should perhaps consider a more historicist alternative and concede that there may be quite diverse functions fulfilled by similar "techniques" of interacting with the net. Taking the text of the *Celestina* as a whole into account, one might discuss the hypothesis that it conveys the following message: the entire fund of moral philosophical knowledge, as well as of knowledge about the world "embodied" in all sorts of previous literary texts, is *not* able to consistently explain or render transparent what takes place in the drama, namely, that two frivolous but not at all immoral youths suffer a violent death as a rather oblique consequence of a banal extramarital love story. The world is incomprehensible. The text makes this message explicit in Pleberio's lament at the end of the play. Life is impenetrable to the tools we have at our disposal; and there is no "aesthetic" compensation for this absence of order—that seems to be the (in that age subversive) "message" of the extremely extravagant way this text deals with the material it extracts from the net.

2.—A second such example of an audacious, at first sight quasi-modernist use of the highly diverse material floating in the net is Cervantes's *Entremés del retablo de las maravillas* (1615), briefly addressed above.[568] As to the underlying processes of circulation, I should stress that the basic motif of the play (the deceived are tricked by prior information that makes them assume it is better for them to assert that they see something than to bluntly say that they do not see anything) is not unique in European literary history. It cannot be excluded that Hans Christian Andersen based his fairytale *The Emperor's New Clothes*

---

[568] See pp. 24–26; for a detailed analysis, see once again Pawlita's book (*Skeptizismus im europäischen Drama der Frühen Neuzeit*).

(1837) on a reading of Cervantes's *entremés*; but it may as well be the case that the two authors drew independently from corresponding material already available prior to Cervantes. The motif as such can be found in the *ejemplo 32* of the *Conde Lucanor* (1330–1335), a collection, written in Spanish, of entertaining as well as instructive short narratives that derive from the medieval oral tradition and may go back to autochthonous or to exogenous sources (Arab, Oriental). There is, however, a unique feature of Cervantes's extraction of this motif. In the instances preceding and following it, the audience acquiesces to the veracity of what they have been told in order to avoid censure by the authorities. In Cervantes, by contrast, the bloody ending shows that many of them really believe to see what, according to the deceivers, is "represented" onstage. What might be considered, with respect to the other texts that make use of the motif, an incrimination of conformism by way of ridicule, assumes in Cervantes the rank of a quasi-epistemological speculation: conformism might block cognition to the point of leading to disaster.

There is another point of divergence to be addressed: of the two prerequisites for seeing what is allegedly happening onstage according to the tricksters of Cervantes's play, one finds only the first one in the *Conde Lucanor*, namely, the imperative of legitimate birth. The motif belongs to the traditional repertoire of the comic, since it refers to the body and its permanent resistance to the superimposition of those restrictive norms and laws we call civilizational, societal, or religious. As to what is known about the realities in premodern rural Europe, legitimate birth (as opposed to birth out of wedlock) was more the exception than the rule—which is not astonishing, since legitimacy of birth is of relevance only in case there is something to inherit. For the lower class, it is without any functionality. It is one of those many patterns of behavior that are constantly reasserted verbally while being more or less ignored practically.—Cervantes adds to this traditional comic motif an item he draws from a completely different discursive strand, the contemporary controversies revolving around the "right" religion and the "right" way to practice it. Highly intricate questions of orthodoxy in the literal sense are introduced into comedy[569]

---

[569] As I have argued in an article dedicated to the subgenre of Spanish Baroque *comedia* known as the "peasant drama", the question of right conduct in terms of sexual practices was of great importance in post-Tridentine times also with respect to the common people (see the reference in n. 318). The Cervantian *entremés*, however, is not about the question of marital or extramarital sexuality, but rather about the question of legitimacy of birth. As strict as the Church's regulation of believers' sexual practices may have been, there was never an official discrimination against those who owed their life to illegitimate intercourse. In that sense, one part of the mix presented by Cervantes is, indeed, comic only in the most conventional sense, while the other is highly explosive ideologically.

and thematized in a way that would have been inconceivable in pragmatic and non-comic texts at that time. The concept of *limpieza de sangre* (purity of blood) refers to the first stages of racism in European history. Pressured by the increasingly successful Christian re-conquerors of the peninsula, many Spanish Jews had converted to Christianity in the fourteenth century. As delighted as the Iberian Christians might have been at first that so many Jews gave up their "stubborn"[570] resistance to acknowledging that Jesus was the Messiah announced in Scripture, they soon had to face the fact that the "new Christians" (*cristianos nuevos*) were not only sisters and brothers in Christ, but also became, on the grounds of the act of conversion, serious competitors in the worldlier sphere. As Jews, they had been excluded from all of military and civil service, including the clergy and higher education. After baptism, these social spheres became accessible to them on equal grounds. With the skills and the adaptability their ancestors had to acquire during a long history of persecution, the *cristianos nuevos* performed well in these sections formerly reserved for the "old Christians". The reaction to this evolution was a series of pogroms which exceeded in their violence what was known from previous European history. In order to cool the overheated atmosphere, the authorities promulgated the first statutes of *limpieza de sangre* in 1449, that is, rules that made all the aforementioned professions accessible only to those who were able to produce evidence that they were so-called *cristianos viejos*, that is, of non-Jewish lineage. Even without going into the details,[571] one might be able to imagine what the (perhaps unintentional) consequences of these statutes were, namely, the general atmosphere of a witch-hunt that degenerated into a sort of proto-totalitarian racism in the year 1492, when all non-converted Jews and Muslims were exiled from Spain, and even more so in the course of and after the Counter-Reformation and the reinforcement of the Inquisition going along with the Catholic Church's attempt at regaining ideological control in the West. Being accused of illegitimate birth was nothing that would have had serious real-world consequences in the rural Spain of that time. Being suspected of not being a *cristiano viejo*, in contrast, would lead sooner or later to a trial by the Inquisition under the charge of being a "judaizer".[572] In case of a first trial,

---

[570] "Stubbornness" (*obstinatio*), the willful rejection of what one is able to recognize as true but not ready to acknowledge, is the main "vice" ascribed by medieval Christian polemics to the "Synagogue" (the common metonymy for all people of Jewish faith).

[571] The seminal publication on the scenario briefly characterized above is David Nirenberg's *Communities of Violence: Persecution of Minorities in the Middle Ages*, Princeton, NJ 1996.

[572] Spanish: *judaizante*. The term, to be found as early as in the New Testament (where it is made use of in order to criticize those Christians who do not entirely "cleanse" their lives, including their daily practices, of the ritualistic behavioral patterns of Judaism), refers in the

acquittal was the statistically prevalent outcome; in case of a second trial, the inverse was the case. Being accused twice of not being *limpio de sangre* meant in those days in almost all cases being submitted to torture and then burnt at the stake following upon an extorted confession.

It is thus an extremely sensitive material that Cervantes touches upon in his *entremés*. By combining, in a process of assembly, comic material with highly intricate material revolving around the question of orthodoxy and, ultimately, of life and (violent) death, he re-functionalizes a genre whose task had been nothing more than to provide comic relief into an instrument of anti-totalitarian reflection. The pressure exerted by the *limpieza de sangre* statutes and the ensuing atmosphere of all-encompassing conformism is leading Spain into "seeing what is not there and not seeing what is there", into a complete loss of touch with reality—that is the message conveyed by this at first sight so harmless interlude.

An additional, albeit minor aspect which should be mentioned is that Cervantes extracted another ideologically relevant discursive material from the net when he produced the play in question. The first noun of the title, *retablo*, has two different semantic dimensions. Its primary meaning referred to in this specific context is: "a stage for puppet (or else dumb) shows". Its well-known secondary meaning—well-known because it is the standard meaning—is "decorative altarpiece". And there is a second word in the title referring to religion, namely, *maravillas*. The primary reference of the term is the content of the play within the play, the "miraculous" onstage appearance of wild beasts from other continents. The secondary meaning—which in this case as well is the standard meaning—refers to supernatural phenomena that are not only staged, but supposed to be "real".

The discussion revolving around the question of whether there are indeed miracles or whether these are delusions produced by the will to see them, or by deceivers who profit from making the populace believe that they are real (in this case: by God's ministers), belongs to the fiercest ideological controversies of early modern Europe. Protestantism as well as the more "enlightened" strands of Catholicism (Erasmianism) held that the Resurrection and the Ascension (etc.) were the last miracles before the end times, when there may be further ones. However, traditional Catholic dogma, and even more so the Church's ritual practices, were firmly linked to the idea that miracles were an

---

period of the Counter-Reformation to people of Jewish descent who were said to continue adhering to their former ritual practices after having "hypocritically" embraced Christianity; "evidence" was drawn from practices such as the avoidance of pork or taking a bath on Fridays instead of Saturdays (etc.).

integral part of contemporary reality. Pilgrimages, devotion to saints, miracles happening in such contexts, and the system of money collection linked to such practices were vital for Catholicism. During the deliberations at Trent, these practices had been vigorously reasserted. Neither certain texts by Erasmus of Rotterdam (*Colloquia familiaria* [1518]) nor a literary text like the *Lazarillo de Tormes*, with its famous *buldero* chapter, would have been conceivable after the Council. But Cervantes ingeniously synthesizes this anti-Tridentine material with comic material of—as it seems—completely harmless profile.

Let me recall in this context that Erasmus' critique of miracles, as well as that of the anonymous author of the *Lazarillo*, also took recourse to comic devices (parody, satire) in order to treat a question which would not have been treatable on the peninsula in a "serious" way in those days. In his play, Cervantes reactivates this technique of "re-functionalization through assembly of the diverse" and thus succeeds at producing a decidedly anti-Tridentine text despite his status as an "official" and honored author of contemporary Spain.[573] But his text is not an imitation of the precursors mentioned. What Cervantes introduces in order to secure this discursive and ideological margin in more difficult times than those of Erasmus and the *Lazarillo* is a change of register and an ensuing discursive diversity that is hardly conceivable for non-literary texts. It is not satire or parody—comic genres that have always been linked with more serious forms of ideological critique—but the, generically speaking, "lowest" variant of comedy, farce, that is here chosen in order to veil the ideological subversion conveyed by the text.

3. —It is perhaps not necessary to stress that the concept of cultural evolution as presented here stands at a certain distance from teleological models. I prefer to take an agnostic stance vis-à-vis the question of whether or not the historical process as such follows a pattern one could call "progress". It can hardly be denied that our lives are different from those of humans living on the banks of the Euphrates 5,000 years ago, and even more different from those of our common ancestors living in the East African savannah 150,000 years ago. But it

---

[573] Cervantes was as successful as a writer of novels as he was unsuccessful as a playwright. The *entremés* was never performed during his lifetime; but it was printed, wherefore I would doubt that this fact is contingent upon the play's ideological non-conformism. All of Cervantes's plays remained without success during their author's lifetime. Compared to the pieces by the three great dramatists of that age—Lope de Vega, Calderón, and Tirso de Molina—one would be inclined to concede that, notwithstanding Cervantes's exceptional qualities in general, there were more well-wrought plays at hand for stage directors to choose from with a view to actual performances than those by Cervantes.

shall remain an open question whether or not such differences may be adequately modeled by the concept of progress; the assertion of such a claim, as well as its refutation, relies upon ideological choices, which are legitimate but not necessary ingredients of scholarly discourses as I understand them.

When it comes to culture in a narrower sense, e.g. to literature, the theoretical view here developed also stands in a rather clear-cut opposition to (intra-cultural) models of consistent "evolution". If the "extraction" of cultural material mainly follows, as I have argued, external needs and demands, or conscious processes of active transculturation, cultural evolution may follow a variety of diverse logics which are not immanent ones. This implies that my skepticism vis-à-vis a possible theory of literary dynamics also applies to non-teleological theories like those developed by the Russian formalists. From the perspective of a cultural theory inspired by the metaphor of the net, most artistic development is caused by the random, or at least non-systematizable combination of pre-existent material.

This said, it seems reasonable to consider factors of a limited intrinsic logic of literary evolution, in particular when it comes to answering the question of why there are, albeit not very frequently, literary modes and elements one might legitimately call new, in the sense that it would be counterintuitive to conceive of them as nothing but reconfigurations of material which was already there. One such "novel" mode, which is the basis of the third of the three strands of narrative in modernity proper postulated above, is the meta-fictional, autoreferential narrative text, that is, a text which articulates the poetological assumptions on which it is based not by way of a preface or separate theoretical texts, not (only) by way of explicit theoretical discussions inserted into the text, but by way of illustration on the level of the configuration of the narrative itself.

This strand seems to emerge with Romanticism; it then becomes what is perhaps the most important component of literary modernism, of avant-garde narrative, in the novel as well as in drama. The idea that Romanticism suddenly "appeared" and has no links with previous literary history is a rather naïve assumption which belongs to the rhetorical repertoire of all cultural revolutions, but which should be qualified within scholarly discourses. Literary Romanticism makes, as I have argued elsewhere, ample use of cultural material of medieval and Baroque provenance, and the lyrical poetry of the age is to a significant extent based on the extraction of mystical material from the net, which is then subjected to re-functionalization.[574] The turn towards autorefer-

---

574 See my "Zum romantischen Mythos der Subjektivität. Lamartines *Invocation* und Nervals *El Desdichado*", *Zeitschrift für französische Sprache und Literatur* vol. 98 / 1988, pp. 137–165;

entiality, however, seems difficult to explain.[575] Is it an authentic "creation", inspired by the philosophical speculations revolving around art that emerge after Kant's positing of art as "autonomous"?

Tatiana Korneeva claims that the first autoreferential texts of the European tradition are to be found in the corpus of a widely neglected author of the Italian Enlightenment, Carlo Gozzi,[576] whose reputation in modern times suffers from the fact that he was politically conservative and poetologically a fierce enemy of the "progressive" Goldoni, who introduced mimeticism to the Italian stage, including on the level of language, by having his characters converse in their local dialects. Gozzi's *Fiabe teatrali* (1761–1765), whose close links to what would later on be called Romanticism have been brilliantly demonstrated in a recent book by Tiziana Corda,[577] are wrought according to a pre-existent and indeed archaic pattern, that of the fairytale. They are emancipated right from the start from any claims to verisimilitude, literally understood. Gozzi makes use of this traditional pattern in order to have his characters discuss onstage how a "good" play should be conceived and then to act accordingly. Goldoni's poetological positions are incriminated as trivial and banal, while Gozzi's own positions conceive of literature as a device whose pleasurable dimension derives from its capacity to emancipate the mind from the strictures of the given, leaving it free to indulge in its fantasies; according to Gozzi, literature is primarily a means of providing relief from the tediousness of "real" life ("l'unico desiderio di giovare, e di divertire").[578] As to the aims to be pursued by literary texts, Gozzi is a mind who belongs to the same school as Freud (of which, to a certain extent, Cervantes is also

---

see also the chapters on Mme de Staël, Chateaubriand, and Hugo in *Ästhetik der Wirklichkeitsdarstellung* (pp. 59–82).

575 Let me stress that I mean what I say: autoreferential structures are something different from reflexive structures to be found in literary texts; in scholarship, the two concepts are in many cases not distinguished in the way they should be. Of course, certain premodern literary texts do contain passages that reflect upon the structure, the devices, and the style of the text they are part of. The most prominent example may be the conversation between the *Quijote*'s eponymous hero and the canónigo de Toledo about the way a "good" novel should be conceived (I, chap. 47–52). But in all of premodern literature, such reflections are explicitly articulated; they are re-mimeticized tracts. Autoreferential structures are a different thing. The category refers to texts whose narrative level constitutes an illustration of the formal principle according to which they are conceived.

576 See Korneeva, "Entertainment for Melancholics".

577 Tiziana Corda, *E. T. A. Hoffmann und Carlo Gozzi. Der Einfluß der commedia dell'arte und der Fiabe Teatrali in Hoffmanns Werk*, Würzburg 2013.

578 Gozzi, "Prefazione al *Fajel*" (1772), in: C. G., *Scritti di teoria teatrale*, Anna Scannapieco (ed.), Venice 2013, pp. 186 f.

a member⁵⁷⁹). As to particular devices, in some contrast to Freud's argument, anti-illusionism and the laying bare of fictionality informs the logic of his plays.⁵⁸⁰

As has already been stated, there are many features of Gozzi's texts which can easily be explained as reactivations of pre-existent material: the fairytale elements and the entire complex of the *maraviglioso* are nothing but structures taken from popular strands of the net, where they had been circulating for a long time as primitivized versions of autochthonous, Celtic-Germanic myth. The allegorical mode (for example in *L'amore delle tre melarance* [1761], which stages a love story between three oranges)⁵⁸¹ is also nothing new; its prehistory goes back to medieval literature, and it had experienced a significant revival in the more recent period of the Baroque. But making use of such devices in order to stage poetological questions within the frame of fiction seems to be something authentically novel—is there any way to explain such emergences within the theoretical frame presented above?

The hypothesis I should like to advance focuses on the possibility that net-bound cultural production, while following the logic of extraction and remodeling, might be characterized, as far as the component of remodeling is concerned, by additional factors admitting some degree of systematization. In the case at issue here, one might provisionally call the specific logic at work one of "reaction".

The seventeenth and the eighteenth centuries are marked in all (Western) European countries by an unusually dense discussion of poetological problems revolving around the genre of drama. These discussions, however, are conducted within treatises, prefaces, manifestos, verdicts pronounced by academies, etc. There are—albeit few—implicit references to poetological problems in the plays proper,⁵⁸² but throughout the ample dramatic production of the centuries in

---

579 —whose close to unique canonical status may be due to the fact that he succeeded in hybridizing in a most compelling way the mimetic and the fantastical modes.
580 In a passage above, I offered some thoughts on how one might integrate anti-illusionist texts into the functional description of fiction as developed by Freud (p. 202).
581 One might mention that the text became, after having been translated into Russian by Vsevolod Mejerchol'd, the basis of a modernist opera of the same title, created by Sergei Prokofiev and first performed in Chicago in 1921.
582 To give just one example, I quote the concluding lines from Lope de Vega's most famous piece, *El castigo sin venganza*: "[...] Aquí acaba, / senado, aquella tragedia / del castigo sin venganza / que, siendo en Italia asombro / hoy es ejemplo en España." // "And with it [the scene in question] ends / This tragedy, a timely lesson for / All Spain, a wondrous sight for all/ Of Italy." (Lope de Vega, *Three Major Plays*, Gwynne Edwards [tr.], New York, NY 1999,

question, there is no self-referential mode to be found, in the sense of a thematization of poetological problems within the plays by way of actual mimesis.[583] The idea to make use of drama proper in order to propagate one's own ideas regarding the correct way of writing drama was not far-fetched, however, since the stage reached a much greater number of recipients than written discussions or the polemics conducted in the somewhat boring and specialized genre of the treatise. The "modal" transposition of such questions from the theoretical to the fictional-representational level encountered, however, one specific obstacle difficult to overcome. This obstacle was the commitment of late seventeenth-century and, even more so, of eighteenth-century drama to the concept of *imitatio naturae* as encapsulated in the central value of *vraisemblance*. It was a minority position held only by "reactionaries" like Gozzi to discard this "bourgeois" ideal and to propagate instead the right of fictional discourse to make use of whatever fantasy may devise in order to produce pleasure and entertainment. As a playwright who, on behalf of his general convictions, was free from the contemporary commitment to "realism", Gozzi had occasion to make use of the stage for the treatment of poetological problems, for literary polemics, and for the propagation of his ideas by way of emplotment. Ultimately, his own contribution to questions of poetology might be considered marginal or retrograde, but he "created" a new mode of narrative, the autoreferential mode, whose subsequent career would prove to be spectacular.

On a more theoretical level, the instance of an emergence of something "novel" that I have tried to highlight in the above example comes down to a point that is not at all out of reach for a net-bound theory of cultural production as theorized in this book. The new mode created by Gozzi was made possible by the author's freedom from contemporary mainstream poetological commitments, a freedom he used in order to reactivate devices on the level of the plot itself which his competitors were not able to make use of because of their commitment to mimeticism.—It is a point of another order that the mode first created by Gozzi was then re-functionalized to serve purposes unconceivable from the standpoint of this conservative aristocrat. The mode as such, however, persists, and from the historically uninformed perspective of later times, it might be conceived as something new, or even as an instance of cultural revolution. For

---

p. 266, v. 3017–3021). The lines refer to the fact that the plot was taken from an Italian source, Matteo Bandello's *Novelle* (1554/1573). The poetological relevance of the passage is implied in the dichotomy of "asombro" (marvel, wonder, astonishment) and "ejemplo". Indeed, Lope converted one of the many *strani casi* (strange events) presented by Bandello into an exemplary, that is, didactic narrative.

583 —to be understood in this context according to the dichotomy of *mimesis* vs. *diegesis*.

Gozzi's somewhat strange texts are not the end of the story. Gozzi was received enthusiastically in the period of German Romanticism, including by minds that one would not call "romantic" without qualification, such as Goethe and Friedrich Schlegel. And Gozzi was not the only somewhat "strange" author—considered from a post-Enlightenment perspective—from previous times who was avidly read ("extracted from the net") in the early nineteenth century; Calderón and his dramas became, as mentioned on several occasions in this book, immensely popular during that period of German cultural history. Or, to put it differently: after a hundred years of thoroughgoing rationalization and subsequent disenchantment of the world, the "obscurantism" of the Baroque acquired a renewed attractiveness. Traditional Catholicism; marvel; wonder; miracle; fantasy—all this was drawn from the net once again. The consequence of this renewed withdrawal was, however, not a restoration, it was something "new", namely, the substitution of aesthetics for religion, of the ritualized reception of works of art for cultic practices.

Limits of the Basic Metaphor

0.—Limitation is the basic principle of any serious research; for that reason, it is not necessarily a default of a theoretical model if there are phenomena pertinent to the overall question discussed that to a certain extent remain unaccounted for by the suggested modeling. But it is necessary to be conscious of the limits of the theoretical frame chosen.

1.—I shall therefore briefly discuss, in this very last chapter of the present study, a discursive constellation which is apt to elucidate what other factors should, in principle, be taken into consideration if one were dealing with a comprehensive theory of cultural production; there might be more such factors than the ones outlined in the following, but I believe that these are of particular import.

I should like to come back to a subgenre that has already been addressed in the above chapters, namely, the religious drama.[584] I wish to emphasize, once again, that my basic metaphor and its detailed description as given in that context is highly useful for explaining the presence of the genre—which is first documented in France—in all European "national" cultures, including colonial cultures. The point that remains to be discussed is the *emergence* of this genre, which dates from a period preceding the one which constitutes the proper tem-

---

584 See pp. 175–178.

poral scope of this book. Medieval religious dramas (morality plays and biblical plays, mainly Nativity and Passion plays) are certainly not "dramas" in the sense in which the term has been understood since the inception of humanism and the generalization of the Aristotelian descriptive categories concerning that genre. But it can hardly be contested that medieval plays consist of dialogue, that they have plots with a beginning and an end, and that they were performed on stage—in this sense, the pieces are indeed dramas, and any other designation would entail falling prey to a normative conception.

However, it would be problematic to unqualifiedly explain their emergence with reference to the metaphor of drawing on a pre-existing cultural material floating in a virtual network. The dramas of classical pagan times were mostly unknown in the West until the Renaissance, and totally unknown in the period under consideration here, that is, in and prior to the tenth century CE. It would be questionable to posit that there was a secret, as it were subterranean cultural network, or, in proper terms, an extremely long and ramified chain of oral transmission by way of which Europeans from the tenth century gained some more or less vague knowledge of what had been performed in the arenas and amphitheaters whose ruins they were still able to admire. The tremendous quantitative disproportion between the pieces actually mentioned in Aristotle's tract and those that have been handed down to us constitutes impressive evidence for the fact that the "Dark Ages" (*tenebrae*) bear their name not without reason: when the Western Roman Empire collapsed and large parts of the Eastern Empire were conquered partly by Scandinavian, partly by Arab or Turkish troops and tribes, many written documents were definitively destroyed. One might furthermore adduce the hostility of the Church fathers towards all kinds of *spectacula* as prone to stimulate the affects—that is, the less dignified, if not outright sinful motions of the soul—in order to explain why there was either a cessation of classical dramatic material floating in the net or a consistent interdict to extract it until the Fall of Constantinople and the subsequently renewed circulation of the preserved material.—How, then, can one account for the presence, documented from the tenth century onward, of proto-dramatic genres in Western Europe, first, as it seems, in France and Italy,[585] and later also in other Western and Central European vernacular communities?

---

[585] My cautious formulations are intended to hint at the fact that, for obvious reasons, there is no full transparency to be gained as to the question of the actual point in time when these proto-dramatic genres first emerged. It is more or less probable that not all of the manuscripts have been preserved and that the written texts we know of were preceded by improvised first sketches. Keeping the entire cultural scenario of the age in mind, I do not find it all too audacious to speculate that these new forms were devised no sooner than in the period when rela-

2.—The deficient documentation does not allow for any reliable remarks concerning the question of what came first, morality plays, which were entirely allegorical, or mystery plays, which dramatized sequences taken from biblical history. In the case of both variants, the oldest (fragmentary) manuscripts preserved date from the tenth century. If I first address the morality plays, this does not imply a claim regarding chronology.[586]

Morality plays, with their plethora of personified virtues and vices, the allegorical representative of humankind (*l'homme* in the French texts), and their quite elaborate allegorically encoded action (the *bivium*, the sea voyage, the *procès de paradis*, the *psychomachia*,[587] to name the most important motifs underlying the plots[588]), seem to have been preceded by more elementary structures that are proto-dramatic in the proper sense and whose being written in view of performance can only be extrapolated from the content and the general cultural context. These latter pieces, commonly named *altercatio* in Latin, *desputaison* in Old French, or *contrasto* in Italian, consist of elementary moral didacticism; they were not conceived for the educated, but for the illiterate populace. Consequently, the channel of mediation was most probably a public performance. In these early, proto-dramatic morality plays, the debate hinted at by the subgenre's name is conducted between the personifications of body and soul. The body typically accuses the soul of denying it any sensual gratification and consistently restricting its spontaneous actions; the soul accuses the body of being disrespectful of the ethical rules preached by Christianity, of longing only for corporeal pleasures, and of being oblivious to death and, more importantly, the afterlife, that is, the alternative scenarios of eternal beatitude and everlasting pain. The scheme as such is elementary; but over the centuries,[589] the dialogues became longer and longer and began to include detailed discus-

---

tive pacification set in, that is, during or after the reign of Charlemagne; but this is, indeed, speculation. As I shall argue in the following, the ideological structures enabling medieval proto-drama did already exist prior to Charlemagne.

586 As to the concrete examples I will present, I am indebted to an article by Gaia Gubbini ("Body and Soul: Medieval Dramatizations"); for details and for the secondary literature, see Gubbini's article.

587 Without going into the details regarding this point, it should be more or less evident that the later, more elaborate form of the morality play is inspired, as far as many of its features are concerned, by a (narrative) text of Prudentius which bears exactly this title and dates from the end of the fourth century CE.

588 The best overview of the allegorical medieval drama I know of is included in the first chapters of Werner Helmich's *Die Allegorie im französischen Theater des 15. und 16. Jahrhunderts*, Tübingen 1976.

589 The body and soul *altercationes* flourished particularly in the twelfth and thirteenth centuries.

sions of the entire didactic complex addressed, comprising extensive and impressive metaphorical characterizations of death, heaven, and hell, as well as doctrinally elaborate deliberations concerning the intricate question of the extent to which not only the body, but also the soul, even in its redeemed state, has been lastingly damaged by the Fall.[590]

The dichotomy of body and soul is crucial to Christian dogma,[591] which relies on the belief that the soul is godlike, the terms in the Vulgate being *imago* and *similitudo*.[592] Christian theology specified the rather summary remarks to be found in this respect in the Hebrew Bible by positing that each human soul is created by God Himself and then implanted, as it were, into a body whose structure was also initially created by God, but whose historical instances are produced by *generatio*, that is, a physical act carried out by humans.[593] The second

---

590 Without being an expert on this text corpus, I allow myself to suggest that the theologically exact allegorical presentation of the point in question was achieved no earlier than in the age of the Counter-Reformation; Lope de Vega's *El viaje del alma* (1604) might be considered a good example. In these later plays, there are, in addition to the personification of the soul as such, personifications of its parts, according to the Platonically inspired Augustinian model: Reason, Memory, and Volition. Only Reason is godlike; Memory is weak and vacillating; Volition is impetuous and has a "natural" tendency to will the wrong. In the final analysis, it is only the *pars rationalis* (strengthened by baptism and the regular ritualistic practices of confession, penance, and communion, and occasionally but not systematically supported by memory) that is able to subdue the rebellious Volition, while the latter, after having been tamed, is able to control the "naturally" sinful tendencies of the body. I would speculate that it was the pressure exerted by the emergence of Protestantism, in particular the *theologoumenon* of *servum arbitrium*, which in a way forced the Catholic Church to introduce this differentiation into popular didactic drama. Without assuming that there is at least one "part" of the (baptized) human being which has not been lastingly damaged by the Fall, the assumption that ethical behavior (*mereri*) is possible on behalf of the individual's own choice would hardly have been tenable any longer. Even so, further intricacies of the theological debates, for example Luther's drastic thesis that reason is, after the Fall, nothing but a "whore" willfully subservient to sinful volition (meaning that it speciously justifies the gratification of *ira* and *concupiscentia*), were not thematized in popular didactic drama (as to Lope's play and its context, see my *Discursive Renovatio in Lope de Vega and Calderón*, chap. 3.2.).
591 With respect to the epoch I am addressing, it is evident that I do not include in my above précis the reformed churches' position (which is, to a certain extent, characterized in the preceding footnote).
592 See Gen I: 26 and 27.
593 I should like to add that all of "our" political and ethical concepts (which most Westerners have a tendency to consider "reasonable" or self-evident), namely the equality principle in general, including political, racial, and gender equality, the principle of individual responsibility, as well as "human rights", are contingent upon this myth of humans having an individual soul created by and similar to God. As bodies (as a variant of higher mammals, as present-day natural sciences would have it), humans are very diverse, and, in the final analysis, not that different from certain other higher mammals. Consequently, the "universal" ethical principles Westerners

basic assumption that has to be taken into consideration when discussing the Christian variant of the dichotomy of body and soul is the dogma of original sin, that is, the belief that the sin committed by Adam and Eve was punished by Yahweh in a manner bound to an archaic, basically pre-Christian principle: in traditional human societies,[594] it is not only the individual perpetrator who is punished, but rather his entire clan or tribe; in particular, his offspring is held responsible for the crime in question.[595] Accordingly, Yahweh did not only curse Adam and Eve, but also all of their descendants, by imposing death,[596] that is, the decay of the body, as part of the general human condition.

It was not Judaism, but Christianity that added the idea that this punishment is justified even from the perspective of individual responsibility. Early Christian theology, in particular Paul, who was followed in this regard by Augustine, claimed that every single human being is a sinner, and it defined sin, in general terms, as the rebellion of the body against the action-oriented impulses originating from the (for its part, godlike) soul.[597] This new anthropology—humans as composites of godlike souls and of bodies which do not tend to do what the soul tells them to do—is essential to Christianity. The main dogma of the new religion, by which it distanced itself from its mother religion, Judaism, consists in postulating that Jesus was physically resurrected after his death and that he performed this resurrection by virtue of his own power (a constellation that provides the basis for a great portion of the second variant of medieval plays to be dis-

---

believe in are not always easy to grasp for people who do not have a Judaeo-Christian background. The much more significant point is, however, the fact that the basis of Western political ethics consists in a narrative that most present-day Europeans no longer accept as true, at least in its literal understanding. Is there a utilitarian basis for these principles? All existing suggestions (in the first place: the reciprocity principle) appear to be rather poor in substance.

594 As far as ethnology teaches us, this feature applies to all cultural communities on the globe.

595 Subconsciously, this archaic principle continues to be present in more "enlightened" times. Most people who consciously share the principle of individual responsibility would approach an individual of whom they know that his or her father or mother was a murderer in a way that differs from the way in which they would approach someone about whose ancestry they know nothing.

596 As is well known, the Hebrew Bible explicitly mentions birth pangs and hard labor as the punishment imposed by God; there is only implicit mention of death (Gen 2: 17 and 3: 19). It was Christian theology which, while preserving the two punishments referred to, claimed that human life before the Fall had been eternal. The main reason for this alternative accentuation of the account given in Genesis is the possibility thus opened up to construct a typological relation between the loss of eternal life and its restoration after Christ's resurrection.

597 Crucial passages include Galatians 5: 17, Romans, passim, and 1 Corinthians, passim, as well as *De civitate Dei*, XIV.

cussed in this chapter). If this is true, one has to assume that he was and is (a) God, as humans are not capable of resurrecting themselves. But, why must God sacrifice Himself?—the emergence of this question is a necessary consequence of the postulate of resurrection. If humans, or at least some humans, had the capacity to redeem themselves, that is, to live in accordance with the Decalogue, it would suffice to extrapolate from their behavior certain ethical rules which the others should imitate. Only if such a possibility is to be systematically excluded does it become plausible that God had to sacrifice Himself in order to save humankind. So, by internal dogmatic constraints, Christianity could not do otherwise than to cast all humans as sinners; and since the godlike soul is capable, by virtue of this essential quality, of distinguishing between right and wrong,[598] deviation from the "right way" can only be ascribed to the, as it were, second component of the human being, the body.

As a consequence, one encounters the topic of the controversy between body and soul in all of medieval Western European vernacular literature. It should be emphasized that there is no such feature in classical pagan literature or thought. The metaphor of body and soul as horse and rider can indeed already be found in Plato; its Christian reinterpretation was perhaps best formulated by Thomas Aquinas.[599] The preservation of the metaphor notwithstanding, the meanings of the pagan and the Christian variants differ dramatically: in Plato, the soul of a reasonable human being has no difficulties in taming the horse (or, in Plato, the two horses), and the less reasonable human beings will not even be able to grasp the necessity of self-control; they live according to their bodily desires without any inhibition.[600] In Aquinas, the soul (*anima rationalis*, that is, the rational part) is incapable of taming the bodily desires unless the rider has received baptism and regularly complies with the ritualistic practices prescribed by the Church: confession, penance, and communion.—It seems to be for this reason, namely, that the relation between body and soul is cast as a permanent and inescapable antagonism within Christianity and that the related issues are constitutive of the dogma's core, that there emerges, in medieval popular didacticism, a proto-dramatic genre commonly called *altercatio*, a controversy staged as a dialogue between personifications, that is, a variant of the genre in its broad sense which is not inspired by classical models.

---

598 —with the differentiations explained in n. 590.
599 See *Phaedrus* 246a – 254a and *Quaestiones disputatae de malo*, qu. quarta ("De peccato originali"), spec. art. 2.I, sol. 4.
600 —and within a world-model without a hell, they are not even punished for their "animalistic" attitude towards life; they are, however, excluded from any higher office in the ideal republic.

Put in theoretical terms: if there is a similarity as to content and/or form between artworks originating from different places and different times, one need not assume by necessity that there has been a previous exchange of a corresponding material by way of network structures. In addition to a monogenesis of genres, motifs, etc., there may as well be polygenesis, that is, cases of similar forms emerging independently from each other in different places and at different times. In the case discussed above, the reason for this second emergence in the Mediterranean West of the generic form called drama is ideological—the new, Christian religion has a propensity for dichotomous conceptualizing which is translated to the level of dissemination by way of proto-dramatic performances, by a staged *agon*. But, as I have tried to convey in my above remarks, this "second" emergence of the genre of drama in Western literary history may also be modeled according to the basic metaphor expounded in this book; the theoretical difficulty which persists and shall remain unresolved consists in finding an adequate answer to the question of whether or not it makes sense to differentiate between phenomena of parallel but independent emergence based on re-assembly and phenomena that may be described as the re-utilization of a precise pattern already circulating in the net.

3.—The following remarks concern the genre of the mystery play, in particular the Passion play, a variant whose insular "survival" into present-day times has been indicated above.[601] It seems that the emergence of this generic pattern, which also occurred in the tenth century, is due to a different background than in the case of the morality play.

Even if common people of pre-Reformation times had been allowed to read Scripture, they would not have been capable of actually doing so. Reading extended passages to believers—a channel of dissemination which was in principle possible—entailed the risk that they would cease to pay attention after some minutes of listening. Staging central events of biblical history, e.g. the Passion, on the contrary, was a most attractive and therefore effective way to communicate the message to an illiterate public. It is not primarily doctrinal content, or the specific structuring of doctrinal content, but rather a medial condition that seems to be at the origin of the emergence of biblical plays in medieval Europe. This postulate is corroborated by the genre's history: over the three or four centuries during which they flourished, mystery plays, as explained above, underwent a quantitative expansion unparalleled in all of Western literary history, from approximately 300 lines in plays dating from the

---

601 See n. 256.

twelfth century to approximately 55,000 lines in plays from the fifteenth century. The weakening of the targeted audience's attention, caused by an effect later called "automatization", was counteracted by adding more material to the core scene (the representation of the Crucifixion) every year. The prehistory of this core element, that is, the story of the Creation and the Fall; the eschatological accomplishment of the entire story, that is, the Last Judgment; intercalated scenes dealing with further "ontological" levels of the story (e.g., devils and angels fighting for supremacy during Christ's nightly stay in the Garden of Gethsemane)—these and similar sequences were added in order to complement the basic action and thus rekindle the audience's curiosity.

It is quite fascinating to observe that the religious authorities, by allowing or even propagating the new genre of religious play—in particular the "mimetic" variant, that is, the mystery play—made use of an instrument they considered sinful in principle. What motivated the audience to attend the performances was probably not the burning interest to learn more about Christ's self-sacrifice—the story as such, including its doctrinal dimension, was known to everyone. It was, as I should like to speculate, the sensational interest in viewing cruelties, even atrocities—that is, to put it in theological terms, the gratification of *concupiscentia oculi*, of a sinful desire—which attracted the recipients to the temporary open-air stages on which the plays were performed. Sinful drives were thus made use of in the interest of working towards a repression of sinful drives—a paradoxical situation which might have laid the grounds for the rather smooth penetration into the Christian West of secular, classical pagan drama in the period after the Fall of Constantinople, the subsisting theological reservations regarding *spectacula* notwithstanding.

4.—I should like to conclude by highlighting an aspect of the Passion plays that is apt to elucidate another important dimension of literary and cultural evolution which might be difficult to capture with the metaphor of a cultural network as here discussed. There is a long-standing controversy regarding the emergence of secular love literature, beginning with *troubadour* poetry, within a culture that considers physical pleasure as sinful for the cogent doctrinal reasons just explained.[602] One main strand of argumentation which, if not "true", is in any case worth the effort of consideration, is based on the observation of rather close links, as to wording, between texts thematizing the Passion in the literal sense—Christ's self-sacrifice—and texts thematizing what has be-

---

[602] —a controversy to which I recently made a contribution pointing in a direction that differs from the view referred to above ("Leone Ebreo's *Dialoghi d'amore* as Provocative Text: Revelation as Elliptic, Physical Love as Legitimate" [forthcoming]).

come, over the centuries, the standard acceptation of the term, that is, intense and painful erotic desire.[603]

The phenomenon in question might be described as a multilayered metonymical shift which ultimately provoked far-reaching and long-lasting consequences. The concept of *passio* (which means nothing other than "suffering") is, in a first step, "positivized", that is, turned against its primary meaning as found in the mental lexicon, by making Christ's suffering on the Cross the center of attention: the physical pain is superseded by the effects of this pain, in this case, general salvation. In addition, it is alleviated by giving expression to the voluntary character of the suffering and, most importantly, by indicating the "fact" that it will be counteracted by a final annihilation, by resurrection. In a next step, still occurring within the discursive field of religion, Christ's pain is metonymically transferred to the pains suffered by those who imitate him, the martyrs. Accordingly, the "positivization" of the suffering is preserved as well. The pains are, in the final analysis, "sweet" pains, because their ultimate effect is the martyr's immediate eternal beatitude.[604] The next metonymical shift, which occurs within mystical discourse, transfers the concept of "sweet pain" to a merely spiritual level: the pains, as well as the wounds, are subjectively real, but not objectively so. The mystic may have the impression of being crucified, but the suffering takes place only in his or her imagination. What is entirely preserved, however, is the effect of the suffering, namely, the impression of sweetness linked to it, as well as its supposed redemptive power. The decisive metonymical shift is, of course, the last one, by which wounds and bodily pains which are subjectively real but objectively non-existent are transferred to a broader semantic field called *amor* in Latin and in all Romance languages—whereas in Greek there had been a differentiation between *eros* and

---

603 I have dedicated an article to the description of these links, dealing with Petrarch's *Canzone alla Vergine* (*Canz.* CCCLXVI): "Palinodia e polisemia nella *Canzone alla Vergine* del *Canzoniere* (con alcune brevi considerazioni sulle condizioni della differenza tra arte classica ed arte moderna)", in: Klaus W. Hempfer and Gerhard Regn (eds.), *Letture petrarchesche*, Florence 2007, pp. 147–190.

604 To put it more precisely: since the pains voluntarily suffered by the martyr surpass, as to the implied "quantity" of *mereri*, what is necessary for the individual martyr's salvation, part of this spiritual "capital" is saved by assigning it to a "treasury" which is administrated by the Church (*thesaurus Ecclesiae*). The Church and its dignitaries are free to make use of this "capital" in cases of particularly grave sins (murder, etc.) which cannot be compensated by regular practices of penance; the prerequisites for being granted parts of this *thesaurus* are confession and contrition. The martyr's consciousness of not only saving his or her own soul, but also contributing to saving the souls of individuals who are not strong enough to resist sin—grave ones in particular—adds another portion of "sweetness" to the suffering.

agape—while privileging those parts of the field which refer not to religious and spiritual, but rather to secular and physical love.[605]

As a consequence of this chain of metonymical shifts there emerges a strand of literary discourse, namely love poetry,[606] which makes ample use of discursive configurations first developed within (Christian) religious texts, such as the praising of the suffering resulting from love as a finally pleasurable and gratifying emotion.[607] At the same time, these emerging secular texts dealing with erotic love propagate an attitude towards life that is considered sinful from the standpoint of Christian orthodoxy—a discursive margin that might have succeeded in establishing itself because it was, to a certain extent, legitimized as to its formulaic dimension by the pre-existing, religiously functionalized pattern.

Radical re-functionalizations constitute an important resource of literary and cultural dynamics. But it seems that they can hardly be captured with the metaphor of an extraction and recombination of cultural material floating in a virtual network—a resource which, consequently, needs to be addressed separately and as a complement to a network-based framework if one has the ambition to devise a comprehensive theory of cultural dynamics.[608]

---

605 This last metonymical shift in particular has been masterfully described in Erich Auerbach's "Passio als Leidenschaft", *PMLA* vol. 56 / 1941, pp. 1179–1196.

606 While diverging in my above-quoted article (n. 602) from this standard explanation of the emergence of love poetry in the Middle Ages, I agree with it insofar as I assume that medieval European love poetry can hardly be explained as an immediate product of the extraction of the classical pagan material floating in the net (Sappho, Ovid, Catullus, Propertius). As I explain in my forthcoming publication, the modeling schemata are all too different to make such a *translatio* hypothesis acceptable. This said, starting in the Renaissance, there is an impact of classical love poetry on the European love poetry of subsequent times. The works of the French *Pléiade* poets could be adequately described within this book's framework: they are based on the extraction of the classical texts from the material floating in the net, a process which was favored by the political events I have referred to in the corresponding context.

607 With respect to the current alternative explanation for the emergence of secular love poetry in medieval Europe, assuming a direct inspiration by Greek and Latin poetry, one might mention that this feature in particular is not to be found in classical love poetry.

608 I should like to remind readers that important work has already been done concerning the description of the eminent role of re-functionalization in the evolution of art; I am thinking in particular of the groundbreaking essays concerning this question by Mukařovský (see above, n. 508).

References

(Titles cited in passing are not listed)

Auerbach, Erich, *Scenes from the Drama of European Literature*, Manheim, Ralph (tr.), Manchester 1984.
Auerbach, Erich, "Figura", in: Auerbach, *Scenes from the Drama of European Literature*, pp. 11–76.
Auerbach, Erich, "*La cour et la ville*", in: Auerbach, *Scenes from the Drama of European Literature*, pp. 133–182.
Auerbach, Erich, *Mimesis: The Representation of Reality in Western Literature*, Trask, Willard R. (tr.), Princeton, NJ 2013.
Auerbach, Erich, "Passio als Leidenschaft", *PMLA* vol. 56/1941, pp. 1179 – 1196.
Bakhtin, Mikhail M., *Rabelais and His World*, Iswolsky, Hélène (tr.), Bloomington, IN 1984.
Barthes, Roland, "L'Effet de réel", *Communications* vol. 11/1968, pp. 84–89.
Beaucé, Pauline, "Pour une réévaluation des formes mineures dans l'historiographie du théâtre des Lumières: le cas forain", *Horizons/Théâtre* vol. 5/2014, pp. 59–73.
Beaucé, Pauline, *Parodies d'opéra au siècle des Lumières*. Evolution d'un genre comique, Rennes 2013.
Benjamin, Walter, *The Origin of the German Tragic Drama*, Osborne, John (tr.), London 1998.
Bernhart, Toni, "Imagining the Audience in Eighteenth-Century Folk Theatre in Tyrol", in: Gvozdeva et al. (eds.), *Dramatic Experience*, pp. 269–288.
Bernhart, Toni, *Volksschauspiele*. Dimensionen einer Gattung (forthcoming).
Bernhart, Toni, Drnovšek, Jaša, Kilian, Sven Thorsten, Küpper, Joachim, and Mosch, Jan (eds.) *Poetics and Politics: Net Structures and Agencies in Early Modern Europe*, Berlin and Boston, MA 2018 (forthcoming).
Bèze, Théodore de, *Abraham sacrifiant*. Tragédie françoise, Soulié, Marguérite and Beaudin, Jean-Dominique (eds.), Paris 2006.
Bhabha, Homi, *The Location of Culture*, London and New York, NY 1994.
Bhabha, Homi, "Adagio", *Critical Inquiry* vol. 31, 2/2005, pp. 371–380.
Blocker, Déborah, "The Accademia degli Alterati and the Invention of a New Form of Dramatic Experience: Myth, Allegory, and Theory in Jacopo Peri's and Ottavio Rinuccini's *Euridice* (1600)", in: Gvozdeva et al. (eds.), *Dramatic Experience*, pp. 77–117.
Bloemendal, Jan, "Rhetoric and Early Modern Latin Drama: The Two Tragedies by the "Polish Pindar" Simon Simonides [1558–1629]: *Castus Ioseph* and *Pentesilea*", in: Mayfield (ed.), *Rhetoric and Drama*, pp. 115–134.
Blumenberg, Hans, *Beschreibung des Menschen*, Berlin 2014.
Blumenberg, Hans, *The Legitimacy of the Modern Age*, Wallace, Robert M. (tr.), Cambridge, MA 1983.
Bung, Stephanie, "Playful Institutions. Social and Textual Practices in Early Spanish Academies", in: Bernhart et al. (eds.), *Poetics and Politics*.
Burke, Peter, *The European Renaissance: Centers and Peripheries*, Oxford 1998.
Casanova, Pascale, *The World Republic of Letters*, DeBevoise, M. B. (tr.), Cambridge, MA and London 2004.
Chakrabarti, Gautam, *Familiarising the Exotic: Introducing European Drama in Early Modern India*, Berlin 2016.
Chakravorty Spivak, Gayatri, *Death of a Discipline*, New York, NY 2003.

Clubb, Louise George, *Italian Drama in Shakespeare's Time*, New Haven, CN 1989.
Connors, Logan J., "Pierre Nicole, Jean-Baptiste Dubos, and the Psychological Experience of Theatrical Performance in Early Modern France", in: Gvozdeva et al. (eds.), *Dramatic Experience*, pp. 172–188.
Cooppan, Vilashini, "Codes for World Literature: Network Theory and the Imaginary Field", in: Küpper (ed.), *Approaches to World Literature*, pp. 103–119.
Corda, Tiziana, *E. T. A. Hoffmann und Carlo Gozzi. Der Einfluß der commedia dell'arte und der Fiabe Teatrali in Hoffmanns Werk*, Würzburg 2013.
Curtius, Ernst Robert, *European Literature and the Latin Middle Ages*, Trask, Willard R. (tr.), Princeton, NJ 2013.
De Landa, Manuel, *A Thousand Years of Nonlinear History*, New York, NY 1997.
Deleuze, Gilles and Guattari, Félix, *A Thousand Plateaus*, Massumi, Brian (tr.), Minneapolis, MN 1987.
Denifle, Henri, O. P. (ed.), "Opiniones ducentae undeviginti Sigeri de Brabantia, Boetii de Dacia aliorumque, a Stephano espiscopo Parisiensi de consilio doctorum sacrae scripturae condemnatae", in: *Chartularium universitatis parisiensis*, Paris 1891–1899, vol. 1, pp. 543–588.
Diderot, Denis, *De la poésie dramatique*, in: Diderot, *Œuvres esthétiques*, pp. 221–223.
Diderot, Denis, *Éloge de Richardson*, in: Diderot, *Œuvres esthétiques*, pp. 29–48.
Diderot, Denis, *Entretiens sur 'Le Fils naturel'*, in: Diderot, *Œuvres esthétiques*, pp. 77–175.
Diderot, Denis, *Œuvres esthétiques*, Vernière, Paul (ed.), Paris 1965.
Dijk, Jan A. G. M. van, *The Network Society: Social Aspects of New Media*, London 2006.
Dimock, Wai-Chee, *Through other Continents: American Literature Across Deep Time*, Princeton, NJ 2006.
Dreyer, Edward L., *Zheng He: China and the Oceans in the Early Ming Dynasty, 1405–1433*, New York, NY 2007.
Drnovšek, Jaša, "Early Modern Religious Processions: The Rise and Fall of a Political Genre", in: Bernhart et al. (eds.), *Poetics and Politics*.
Drnovšek, Jaša, "Frühneuzeitliche Passionsprozessionsspiele als Projekt der katholischen Erneuerung", in: Zavarský, Svorad et al. (eds.), *Themes of Polemical Theology Across Early Modern Literary Genres"*, Newcastle upon Tyne 2016, pp. 321–333.
Drnovšek, Jaša, *"Certa Mina Dant VICtorlas"*. Die Prozessionsspiele der Gegenreformation zwischen Politik und Poetik (forthcoming).
Du Bos, Jean-Baptiste, *Réflexions critiques sur la poésie et sur la peinture*, 2 vols., Paris 1770 (17th print), reprint Geneva 1967.
Erken, Günther, "Die Rezeption Shakespeares in Literatur und Kultur. Deutschland", in: *Shakespeare-Handbuch*, Schabert, Ina (ed.), Stuttgart 2009 (5th print), pp. 627–651.
Freud, Sigmund, "Civilisation and its Discontents", in: Freud, *Complete Psychological Works*, Strachey, James (ed.), vol. 21, London 1961, pp. 64–145.
Freud, Sigmund, "The Relation of the Poet to Day-Dreaming" in: *Art and Interpretation: An Anthology of Readings in Aesthetics and the Philosophy of Art*, Dayton, Eric (ed.), Orchard Park, NY 1998, pp. 300–304.
Fried, Michael, "Orientation in Painting: Caspar David Friedrich", in: Fried, *Another Light: Jacques-Louis David to Thomas Demand*, New Haven, CN and London 2014, pp. 111–149.
Fried, Michael, *Absorption and Theatricality: Painting and Beholder in the Age of Diderot*, Chicago, IL 1980.
Goldmann, Lucien, *Le Dieu caché*. Etudes sur la vision tragique dans les *Pensées* de Pascal et dans le théâtre de Racine, Paris 1955.

Goodman, Nelson, *Languages of Art: An Approach to a Theory of Symbols*, Indianapolis, IN 1968.
Gottsched, Johann Christoph, *Noethiger Vorrath zur Geschichte der deutschen Dramatischen Dichtkunst*, Leipzig 1757/1765.
Gratl, Franz, "The Role of Music in Folk Drama: An Investigation based on Tyrolean Sources", in: Bernhart et al. (eds.), *Poetics and Politics*.
Greenblatt, Stephen, "Culture", in: Lentricchia, Frank and McLaughlin, Thomas (eds.), *Critical Terms for Literary Study*, Chicago, IL and London 1995 (2nd print), pp. 225–229.
Greenblatt, Stephen, "Theatrical Mobility", in: Greenblatt et al. (eds.), *Cultural Mobility*, pp. 75–95.
Greenblatt, Stephen, *Shakespearean Negotiations: The Circulation of Social Energy in Renaissance England*, Berkeley and Los Angeles, CA 1988.
Greenblatt, Stephen, "A Mobility Studies Manifesto", in: Greenblatt et al. (eds.), *Cultural Mobility*, pp. 250–253.
Greenblatt, Stephen, Zupanov, Ines G., Meyer-Kalkus, Reinhard, Paul, Heike, Nyíri, Pál, and Pannewick, Friederike (eds.), *Cultural Mobility: A Manifesto*, Cambridge, MA 2010.
Gubbini, Gaia, "Body and Soul: Medieval Dramatizations" (forthcoming).
Gumbrecht, Hans Ulrich, *"Un souffle d'Allemagne ayant passé*: Friedrich Diez, Gaston Paris, and the Genesis of National Philologies", *Romance Philology* vol. 40/1986/87, pp. 1–37.
Gungwu, Wang, *China and the Chinese Overseas*, Singapore 1992.
Gvozdeva, Katja, *Compagnie d'hommes joyeux*. Performances carnavalesques (rite, jeu, théâtre) et culture académique en Italie et en France au seizième siècle (forthcoming).
Gvozdeva, Katja, "Why Do Men Go Blind in the Theatre? Gender Riddles and Fools' Play in the Italian Renaissance Comedy *Gl'Ingannati* (1532)", in: Gvozdeva et al. (eds.), *Dramatic Experience*, pp. 35–76.
Gvozdeva, Katja, Korneeva, Tatiana, and Ospovat, Kirill (eds.) *Dramatic Experience: The Poetics of Drama and the Early Modern Public Sphere(s)*, Leiden and Boston, MA 2017.
Habermas, Jürgen, *The Structural Transformation of the Public Sphere: An Inquiry into a Category of Bourgeois Society*, Burger, Thomas (tr.), Cambridge, MA 1991.
Hardy, Swana L., *Goethe, Calderón und die romantische Theorie des Dramas*, Heidelberg 1965.
Hayles, N. Katherine, *How We Became Posthuman: Virtual Bodies in Cybernetics. Literature and Information*, Chicago, IL 1999.
Henke, Robert and Nicholson, Eric (eds.), *Transnational Exchange in Early Modern Theater*, Burlington, VT 2008.
Henke, Robert and Nicholson, Eric (eds.), *Transnational Mobilities in Early Modern Theater*, Burlington, VT 2014.
Herder, Johann Gottfried, "Von der Ähnlichkeit der mittleren englischen und deutschen Dichtkunst", in: Herder, *Sämmtliche Werke*, vol. 9, pp. 522–535.
Herder, Johann Gottfried, "Auszug aus einem Briefwechsel über Ossian und die Lieder alter Völker", in: Herder, *Sämmtliche Werke*, vol. 5, pp. 159–207.
Herder, Johann Gottfried, *Auch eine Philosophie der Geschichte zur Bildung der Menschheit*, in: Herder, Sämmtliche Werke, vol. 5, pp. 475–593.
Herder, Johann Gottfried, *Sämmtliche Werke*, Suphan, Bernhard (ed.), 32 vols., Berlin 1877–1909.
Herder, Johann Gottfried, "Shakespear", in: Herder, *Sämmtliche Werke*, vol. 5, pp. 159–257.
Humboldt, Wilhelm v., *On Language: On the Diversity of Human Language Construction and Its Influence on the Mental Development of the Human Species*, Losonsky, Michael (ed.), Heath, Peter (tr.), Cambridge, MA 1999.

Ingarden, Roman, *The Literary Work of Art: An Investigation of the Borderlines of Ontology, Logic, and Theory of Language*, Grabowicz, George G. (tr.), Evanston, IL 1974.
Iser, Wolfgang, *The Implied Reader: Patterns of Communication in Prose Fiction from Bunyan to Beckett*, Baltimore, MD 1974.
Jakobson, Roman, "On Realism in Art" ["O chudožestvennom realizme"], in: Jakobson, *Language in Literature*, Pomorska, Krystyna and Rudy, Stephen (eds.), Cambridge, MA and London 1987, pp. 19–27.
Jauss, Hans R., "Diderots Paradox über das Schauspiel (*Entretiens sur 'Le Fils naturel')*", *Germanisch-Romanische Monatsschrift* vol. 42/1961, pp. 380–413.
Kalff, Sabine, "Sterne auf der Bühne. Astronomie und Astrologie im Drama des 17. und 18. Jahrhunderts", *Comparatio* vol. 8/2016, pp. 35–58.
Katritzky, M. A., "Stefanelo Botarga and Pickelhering: Fishy Italian and English Stage Clowns in Spain and Germany", in: Küpper et al. (eds.), *Theatre Cultures within Globalising Empires*.
Kilian, Sven Thorsten, "Opening Spaces for the Reading Audience: Fernando de Roja's *Celestina* (1499/1502) and Niccolò Machiavelli's *Mandragola* (1518)", in: Gvozdeva et al. (eds.), *Dramatic Experience*, pp. 13–34.
Kilian, Sven Thorsten, *"Escrituras andantes"*: *Concepts of Text and Scripture in Early Modern Drama* (forthcoming).
Korneeva, Tatiana, "Il pubblico teatrale nel *Genio buono e il genio cattivo* di Carlo Goldoni", *Italian Studies* vol. 70/2015, pp. 92–116.
Korneeva, Tatiana, "Entertainment for Melancholics: The Public and the Public Stage in Carlo Gozzi's *L'amore delle tre melarance*", in: Gvozdeva et al. (eds.), *Dramatic Experience*, pp. 140–171.
Korneeva, Tatiana, *The Dramaturgy of the Spectator: Theatre, Audience, and the Public Sphere in Late Seventeenth- and Eighteenth-Century Italy* (forthcoming).
Küpper, Joachim (ed.), *Approaches to World Literature*, Berlin 2013.
Küpper, Joachim, "Lope de Vega. *Fuente Ovejuna*", in: Wentzlaff-Eggebert, Harald and Roloff, Volker (eds.), *Das spanische Theater vom Mittelalter bis zur Gegenwart*, Düsseldorf 1988, pp. 105–122.
Küpper, Joachim, "The Traditional Cosmos and the New World", *MLN* vol. 118/2003, pp. 363–392.
Küpper, Joachim, "Das Denken, das Unterscheiden und die Literatur", *Poetica* vol. 45/2013, pp. 249–269.
Küpper, Joachim, "*Hamlet*, by Shakespeare, and *La vida es sueño*, by Calderón, or the Problem of Scepticism", *Germanisch-Romanische Monatsschrift* vol. 58/2008, pp. 367–399.
Küpper, Joachim, "*La vida es sueño*. 'Aufhebung' des Skeptizismus, Recusatio der Moderne", in: Wolfzettel, Friedrich and Küpper, Joachim (eds.), *Diskurse des Barock: Dezentrierte oder rezentrierte Welt?*, München 2000, pp. 383–428.
Küpper, Joachim, "Mittelalterlich kosmische Ordnung und rinascimentales Bewußtsein von Kontingenz. Fernando de Rojas' *Celestina* als Inszenierung sinnfremder Faktizität (mit Bemerkungen zu Boccaccio, Petrarca, Machiavelli und Montaigne)", in: Graevenitz, Gerhart v. and Marquard, Odo (eds.), *Kontingenz*, München 1998, pp. 173–223.
Küpper, Joachim, "Sentimental Revivals: Gérard de Nerval's *Voyage en Orient*", in: Nichols, Stephen G., Küpper, Joachim, and Kablitz, Andreas (eds.), *Spectral Sea: Mediterranean Palimpsests in European Culture*, New York, NY and Bern 2017, pp. 157–202.

Küpper, Joachim, "Was ist Literatur?", *Zeitschrift für Ästhetik und Allgemeine Kunstwissenschaft* vol. 45,2/2001, pp. 187–215.
Küpper, Joachim, *Petrarca. Das Schweigen der Veritas und die Worte des Dichters*, Berlin and New York, NY 2002.
Küpper, Joachim, "Fiacre et grenier. Quelques remarques sur *Madame Bovary* et *Effi Briest*", in: König, Christoph and Wismann, Heinz (eds.), *La lecture insistante: autour de Jean Bollack*, Paris 2011, pp. 255–284.
Küpper, Joachim, "Perception, Cognition, and Volition in the *Arcipreste de Talavera*", in: Nichols, Stephen G., Kablitz, Andreas, and Calhoun, Alison (eds.), *Rethinking the Medieval Senses: Heritage, Fascinations, Frames*, Baltimore, MD 2008, pp. 119–153.
Küpper, Joachim, "Some Remarks on World Literature", in: Küpper (ed.), *Approaches to World Literature*, pp. 167–175.
Küpper, Joachim, *Ästhetik der Wirklichkeitsdarstellung und Evolution des Romans von der französischen Spätaufklärung bis zu Robbe-Grillet*, Stuttgart 1987.
Küpper, Joachim, *Balzac und der 'Effet de réel'. Eine Untersuchung anhand der Textstufen des Colonel Chabert und des Curé de village*, Amsterdam 1986.
Küpper, Joachim, *Discursive Renovatio in Lope de Vega and Calderón. Studies on Spanish Baroque Drama. With an Excursus on the Evolution of Discourse in the Middle Ages, the Renaissance, and Mannerism*, Berlin and Boston, MA 2017.
Küpper, Joachim, *Zum italienischen Roman des 19. Jahrhunderts. Foscolo, Manzoni, Verga, D'Annunzio*, Stuttgart 2002.
Küpper, Joachim, "Considérations sur *Salammbô*", *MLN* vol. 125/2010, pp. 731–782.
Küpper, Joachim and Pawlita, Leonie (eds.), *Theatre Cultures within Globalising Empires: Looking at Early Modern England and Spain*, Berlin and Boston MA, 2018 (forthcoming).
Latour, Bruno, "On Recalling ANT", in: Law, John and Hassard, John (eds.), *Actor Network Theory and After*, Oxford 1999, pp. 15–25.
Latour, Bruno, *Reassembling the Social: An Introduction to Actor-Network-Theory*, Oxford 2005.
Lévi-Strauss, Claude, *L'autre face de la lune. Ecrits sur le Japon*, Paris 2011.
Liber theologiae moralis. Viginti quatuor Societatis Jesu doctoribus reseratus, Monachii 1644.
Link, Jürgen, "Das lyrische Gedicht als Paradigma des überstrukturierten Textes", in: *Funk-Kolleg Literatur*, vol. 1, Brackert, Helmut and Lämmert, Eberhard (eds.), Frankfurt/Main 1977, pp. 234–255.
Lotman, Yuri M., *The Structure of the Artistic Text*, Matejka, Ladislav and Suino, Mark E. (eds.), Lenhoff, Gail and Vroon, Ronald (tr.), Ann Arbor, MI 1977.
Luhmann, Niklas, *Social Systems*, Bednarz, John and Baecker, Dirk (tr.), Stanford, CA 1995.
Mannheim, Karl, "Das Problem der Generationen", *Kölner Vierteljahreshefte für Soziologie* vol. 7/1928, pp. 157–185 and pp. 309–330.
Maravall, Antonio, *Culture of the Baroque: Analysis of a Historical Structure*, Cochran, Terry (tr.), Manchester 1986.
Marin, Louis, *Le Portrait du Roi*, Paris 1981.
Marx, Karl, *Die Deutsche Ideologie* (1845), in: *Marx-Engels Werke*, 43 vols., Berlin [GDR] 1956–1990, vol. 3, pp. 5–530.
Mattelart, Armand, *Networking the World, 1794–1900*, Carey-Libbrecht, Liz and Cohen, James A. (tr.), Minneapolis, MN 2000.
Mayfield, D. S. (ed.), *Rhetoric and Drama*, Berlin and Boston, MA 2017.

Mayfield, D. S., *The Vicarious: Variants in Blumenberg. Delegation in Early Modern Drama (Rojas, Machiavelli, Shakespeare)* (forthcoming).
Mosch, Jan, *Moral Agency and Heteronomy in Shakespearean and Racinian Tragedy* (forthcoming).
Mukařovský, Jan, *Aesthetic Function, Norm and Value as Social Facts*, Suino, Mark E. (tr.), Ann Arbor, MI 1979.
Nirenberg, David, *Communities of Violence: Persecution of Minorities in the Middle Ages*, Princeton, NJ 1996.
Ospovat, Kirill, "The Catharsis of Prosecution: Royal Violence, Poetic Justice, and Public Emotion in the Russian *Hamlet* (1748)", in: Gvozdeva et al. (eds.), *Dramatic Experience*, pp. 189–219.
Ospovat, Kirill, *Terror and Pity: Aleksandr Sumarokov and the Theater of Power in Elizabethan Russia*, Boston, MA 2016.
Pannewick, Friederike, "Performativity and Mobility: Middle Eastern Traditions on the Move", in: Greenblatt et al. (eds.), *Cultural Mobility*, pp. 215–249.
Pawlita, Leonie, *Skeptizismus im europäischen Drama der Frühen Neuzeit. Untersuchungen zu Dramentexten von Shakespeare, Calderón, Lope de Vega, Rotrou und Cervantes*, Berlin 2015.
Potter, Robert A., *The English Morality Play: Origins, History, and Influence of a Dramatic Tradition*, New York, NY 1975.
Pratt, Mary Louise, *Imperial Eyes: Travel Writing and Transculturation*, London 1992.
Preston, Carrie J., "Trouble with Titles and Directors: Benjamin Britten and William Plomer's *Curlew River* and Samuel Beckett's *Footfalls/Pas*", in: Preston, *Learning to Kneel: Noh, Modernism, and Journeys in Teaching*, New York, NY 2016, pp. 203–242.
Rank, Otto, *Das Inzest-Motiv in Dichtung und Sage. Grundzüge einer Psychologie des dichterischen Schaffens* (2nd print), Leipzig and Vienna 1926.
Ruderman, David B., *Early Modern Jewry: A New Cultural History*, Princeton, NJ 2010.
Rüegg, Madeline, *The 'Patient Griselda' Myth in Late Medieval and Early Modern Literature* (forthcoming).
Ruth, Jeffrey S., *Urban Honor in Spain: The* Laus Urbis *from Antiquity Through Humanism*, Lewiston, NY 2011.
Said, Edward, "The Road Less Traveled", in: Viswanathan, Gauri (ed.), *Power, Politics, and Culture. Interviews with Edward W. Said*, New York, NY 2001, pp. 409–418.
Schmitt, Carl, *Political Theology: Four chapters on the Concept of Sovereignty*, Schwab, George (tr.), Chicago, IL 1985.
Scholz-Cionca, Stanca, "Nô within Walls and Beyond: Theatre as Cultural Capital in Edo Japan (1603–1868)", in: Gvozdeva et al. (eds.), *Dramatic Experience*, pp. 289–306.
Schöne, Albrecht, *Emblematik und Drama im Zeitalter des Barock*, München 1964.
Smith, Nigel, "The Politics of Tragedy in the Dutch Republic: Joachim Oudaen's Martyr Drama in Context", in: Gvozdeva et al. (eds.), *Dramatic Experience*, pp. 220–249.
Stierle, Karlheinz, "Baudelaire and the Tradition of the *Tableau de Paris*", *New Literary History* vol. 11/1980, pp. 345–361.
Sullivan, Henry W., *Tirso de Molina and the Drama of the Counter Reformation*, Amsterdam 1976.
Summer-Schindler, Waltraud, *Zensur und Involution. Aspekte gegenreformatorischer Überformung der italienischen Renaissance-Novelle*, Maastricht and Herzogenrath 1996.
Todorov, Tzvetan, *The Fantastic: A Structural Approach to a Literary Genre*, Howard, Richard (tr.), Ithaca, NY 1975.

Wade, Geoff, "The Zheng He Voyages: A Reassessment", *Asia Research Institute, National University of Singapore, Working Papers Series* vol. 31/2004, pp. 1–33.
Weimann, Robert, *Shakespeare and the Popular Tradition in the Theater: Studies in the Social Dimension of Dramatic Form and Function*, Baltimore, MD 1978.
Weisbach, Werner, *Der Barock als Kunst der Gegenreformation*, Berlin 1921.
Zürcher, Erik, *The Buddhist Conquest of China: The Spread and Adaptation of Buddhism in Early Medieval China* (3rd print), Leiden 2007.

www.ingramcontent.com/pod-product-compliance
Lightning Source LLC
Chambersburg PA
CBHW070300240426
43661CB00057B/2598